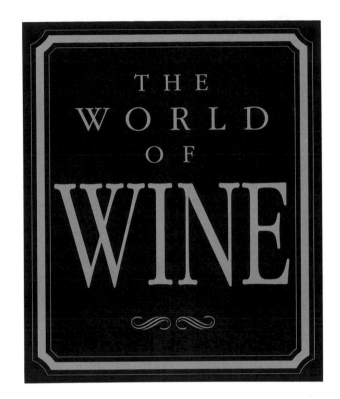

THE WORLD OF WINE

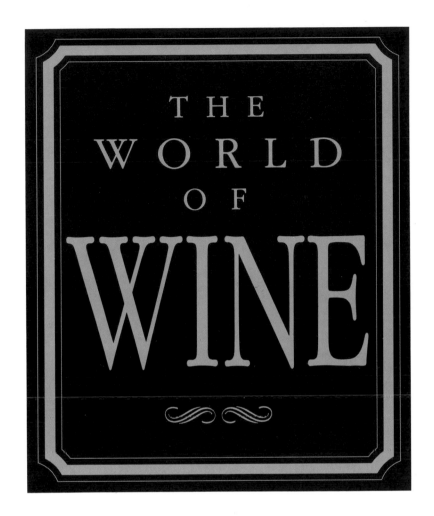

THE WORLD OF WINE

Caroline Camarra
Jean-Paul Paireault
Foreword by Robert Mondavi

**MALLARD
PRESS**

MALLARD PRESS

An imprint of BDD Promotional Book Company, Inc.,
666 Fifth Avenue, New York, New York 10003.

Mallard Press and its accompanying design and logo
are trademarks of BDD Promotional Book Company, Inc.

CLB 2434
Copyright © 1990 Colour Library Books Ltd., Godalming, Surrey, England.
Reprinted 1991.
First published in the United States of America
in 1990 by The Mallard Press.
Printed and bound in Italy by New Interlitho.
All rights reserved.
ISBN 0 7924 5231 3

Produced by:
Copyright Studio, Paris France
Editor; Jean-Paul Paireault
assisted by François Collombet
Designer; Jacques Hennaux
assisted by Mireille Palicot, Patrick Lainé
Picture Editor; Véronique Cardineau
assisted by François-Joseph Guillier
Contributors; Nathalie Antonin, Lynn Jennings

Translation by Pholiota-Translations, London
(Josephine Bacon, Fergus McGrath, Beryl Stockman)

Pictures: Jean-Paul Paireault, Hubert Josse, Pix and Gamma

CONTENTS

FOREWORD

I am extremely honoured to be asked to introduce The World of Wine. As the interest in wine grows, we find ever more interesting facets concerning this temperate, civilized, romantic beverage.

A product of many cultures, wine is itself a cultural product, praised for centuries by statesmen, philosophers, poets, physicians and scholars. It is enjoyed by many as the primary beverage at mealtimes, as well as simply for the pleasure and diversion that it brings.

It is produced for its taste pleasures, not to alter anyone's mood. Wine can stand the scrutiny of any responsible cultural or scientific critic, because its benefits have been recognized since civilization began.

Wine is the natural beverage for every celebration: the birth of a child, graduation, engagement, weddings, anniversaries, promotions, family gatherings, toasts between governments and many other cultural occasions. These uses exist in the cultures where wine is made, and also in other civilized countries around the world.

The World of Wine is an exciting view of this wonderful beverage, which adds so much to our lives and human existence. Common sense tells us that wine will be with us forever as an integral part of our culture, heritage and the gracious way of life.

ROBERT MONDAVI

FROM THE
ORIGINS OF THE
VINE TO THE
FIRST FINE WINES

Like wheat, the vine is one of the oldest cultivated plants known to mankind, and it is undoubtedly the most prestigious. In both ancient Greece and Rome, wine was associated with the gods, with Dionysos or Bacchus. It was the sacred right of the Olympian gods to drink nectar and ambrosia, and although milk and water were the most common beverages of antiquity, people only sought pleasure and consolation in wine.

Long before it was celebrated as the "blood of Christ", wine was considered to be a divine drink. But it was the rise of Christianity that really determined its future.

Bacchus with grape,
Graeco-Roman Art,
Paris, Louvre Museum.

Saint Emilion,
Chateau La Gaffelière
Detail of a Roman
Era Mosaic.

"The Last Supper",
by Van Cleve Joos,
16th Century,
Paris, Louvre Museum.

THE FIRST ROADS LED TO ROME

We have proof that there were vines, plants of the genus Vitis vinifera, and a primitive form of viticulture in Asia, as long ago as the third millennium B.C. Originally, vines were woody creepers that grew in forests. Once cultivation had begun, they became progressively more widespread as the populations of the east migrated westwards. The first Italian vineyards were probably planted by the Etruscans in about 1000 B.C.

From the choice of vines and the mastery of propagation through making cuttings, there was still a long way to go before real wine-growing techniques came into being. The fact is that viticulture developed simultaneously with the wine trade. Methods of producing and transporting wines evolved in ancient times solely in order to meet the demands of a wealthy clientele. As a result, there was also a great demand for pottery, because amphoras soon became far more popular than goatskin bottles.

So we know for sure, from archaeological findings, which Greek and Phoenician roads led to the west, thus increasing the extent of the wine trade. Rome eventually became a huge centre for the importation and consumption of wine. During the latter part of the Republic and throughout the era of the Empire, thousands of gallons were sold every week. At the time, Campania was the region responsible for the production and transportation of wines, having the same kind of pre-eminence in the wine trade that Bordeaux was to have in the Middle Ages.

A HAZY NOTION OF QUALITY

Was abundance matched by quality? Probably not. The Greeks always watered down their wine considerably unless they were drinking it for medicinal purposes, and the widespread practice of *poissage* prevented aromas from developing. As for the wines the Romans loved so much, no doubt they were far removed from what we would call *vins fins*, even though the poets of the time attributed many virtues to them. There is no evidence to suggest that the Greeks and Romans possessed more than the haziest notions of quality.

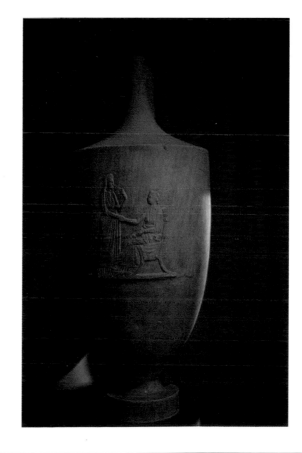

For a start, the way in which wine was stored was largely a matter of chance. If it was for consumption on the spot, it was simply kept in open earthenware jars. But if it had to be able to withstand transportation, it was "forced" by adding honey. Another method was to heat it up so that at least a third of the liquid evaporated, leaving a sort of condensed wine that probably tasted as if it had been cooked. We know that the Romans did not keep their wine in cellars away from the heat. Instead, they stored it over the kitchens, where the heat caused even more of the liquid to evaporate. So it was probably necessary in any case to add water to wine before drinking it.

Later on, aromatic wines became the fashion. Myrtle, incense, aniseed, pepper and vanilla were used to enhance the flavour. Locally, this practice stood the test of time. Nevertheless, it shows a highly suspect notion of quality and so we can be sure that no great wines were ever produced in ancient times. The vineyards of Italy, Spain, Gaul and the Rhine valley certainly existed then, but it was not until centuries later that the idea of taste took shape and quality began to improve.

Greek Amphora.

FROM THE MONASTERIES TO THE FIRST FINE WINES

The early Middle Ages marked the beginnings of a decline in the vineyards which coincided with the decline of the Mediterranean countries and the Saracen invasions. Since the Moslem religion forbade the consumption of wine, the vineyards were gradually abandoned because there were no outlets for the wine. Those that survived were few and far between, and the produce stayed within narrow confines. The situation was little better in the non- Mediterranean countries because, there, food was in such short supply that the inhabitants could not permit themselves the luxury of drinking wine. So, given the conditions that prevailed during the early Middle Ages, we can attribute the survival of viticulture to the church alone. Not only did the monks continue to grow vines, they also ensured the spread of viticulture by adapting vines for use in northern countries such as Holland, Germany and England. So, as Christianity spread, the wine trade found new openings in the north. At the same time, the fact that vines had to be adapted to more

rigorous climatic conditions meant that far more care had to be taken in choosing good quality stock. It was at this point that *cépages nobles* first made their appearance. So from the 11th century onwards, viticulture really flourished in the north, under the strict regime of the medieval monasteries.

For all that, the wine map was not yet complete. It was to undergo new and extensive developments during the course of the 17th century. These changes were largely due to the emergence of Holland, and later England, as major naval powers. The wine trade was extremely active by the beginning of the 17th century, but it had yet to reach international proportions. Wines would not keep, therefore they did not stand up well to transportation.

Furthermore, the Dutch, who then ruled the seas, started to buy large quantities of brandy, a drink which was able to withstand even the longest sea voyages without deteriorating. They preferred to purchase their brandy in France, mainly from the Charentes region. The heavy demand encouraged the growth of vineyards all over south-western France. The region also supplied robust wines, which were despatched from Bordeaux. From that time onwards, the port benefitted from the decline of viticulture in Germany, establishing a position for itself that was strong enough to survive even the Franco-Dutch war, which broke out at the end of the century. During the war, the Dutch turned to Spain and Portugal for their supplies, and the English vied with them ferociously over the sherry and port which were to supersede the clarets of Bordeaux during the Continental Blockade. Thus, when trade between France and England resumed at the beginning of the 18th century, the wine growers of Bordeaux had no weapon other than quality with which to combat the invasion of Spanish and Portuguese wines.

The aristocracy of the time had extremely refined tastes, so this was just the right moment for such a development. With the co-operation of British merchants, Girondist notables established the first true range of fine wines (*vins fins*) from restricted regions (*terroirs délimités*).

These wines were produced in barrels and stored in bottles. It was also at this time that sterilisation using sulphur was first used, as well as the process of fining with egg-whites. Thus the tradition of quality was born, and the active participation of British merchants enabled it to develop.

Grape Harvest scene in Saumur, illumination by Pol de Limbourg, 15th Century.

Transporting the Grapes, illumination from the book,"The Hours of the Duchess of Burgundy", 15th Century, Chantilly Museum.

Overleaf:
The Grape Harvest, Burgundian studio, Paris, Cluny Museum.

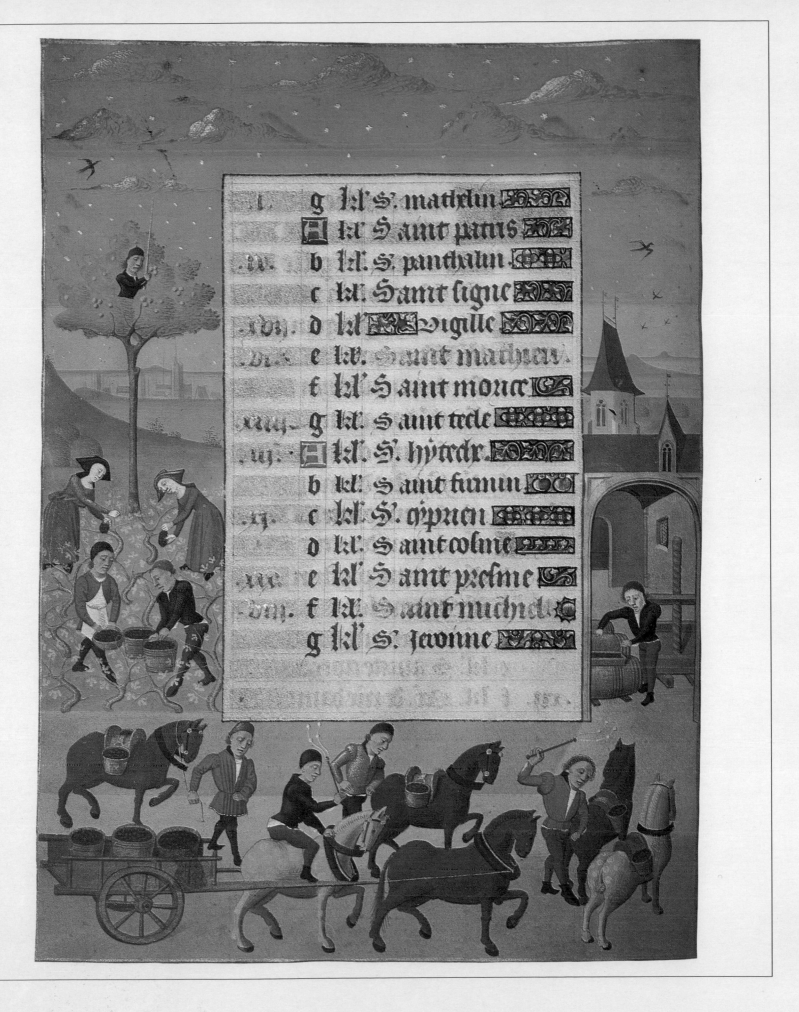

FRUGALITY FIRST
AND FOREMOST

Soil and climate are two essential and equally important factors in determining the quality of wines and other products of the grape.

Napa Valley, Sterling Vineyards, palm trees in the vineyards

Graves, Bordeaux, the characteristic soil of one of the best wines in the world.

POOR SOILS

Which soils suit vines the best? The answer is that almost any kind of soil is suitable provided it is poor. In other words, humus is absolutely out and rock is best of all. The arable soil stratum may vary in composition provided that poverty is a principal characteristic. A rich soil means a high yield, and therefore poorer quality.

Pebbles are also suitable, as are sand and stones. Taken collectively, the regions that produce great wines offer a wide range of soil types, and this in turn leads to a wide range of characteristics in the wine. Thus, siliceous soil produces light fresh wines, limestone makes for a high alcohol content and a delicate bouquet. Clay, on the other hand, is liable to produce rich-coloured, full-bodied tannic wines. But apart from all this, a basic characteristic of all vine-growing soils is their capacity to retain heat and water, and the extent to which they do this varies. Stony soils are particularly suitable because the heat they absorb during the day is diffused again at night. In the same way, dark-coloured soils absorb the sun's rays more easily. The fact that vines need as much sunlight as possible explains the choice of hillsides. Sloping ground heats up more easily and has less of a tendency to retain cool air than flat terrain.

THE VITAL ROLE OF THE SUBSOIL

The importance of poor soil can be further explained by looking at the nature of the vine itself. It has very deep roots, capable of reaching down to depth of 15 to 21 feet provided they do not encounter some obstacle such as a layer of dense soil or a water-table. So the soil must be quite poor in order to allow access to the subsoil. Futhermore, if the roots do not plunge downwards they will creep along the ground instead, thus exposing the vine to the dangers of drought or excessive humidity. In the case of drought, the pores (stomata) in the leaves tend to close up, thus inhibiting the process of photosynthesis and preventing the grapes from ripening. If it rains heavily, the plant gorges itself with water to such an

Napa Valley, fan used to protect vines from frost.

Saint Emilion,
Fields dating from
the Roman Era.

extent that the grapes burst their skins. If, on the other hand, the roots have to take their fill of water from the subsoil, they will find enough there but not too much. If a vine is to produce good grapes it must not produce too abundantly. Furthermore, a good grape is one that ripens slowly, without rotting or withering. So, although water is necessary, it should be administered in moderate doses. There are three more physical qualities of soil essential to vine-growing. It must be porous, well-drained and deep. These characteristics prevent the roots from becoming clogged with water and ensure relatively frugal conditions.

SUN IS NECESSARY, BUT TOO MUCH IS DESTRUCTIVE

Weather conditions have a greater influence on grapes than on any other fruit. The ripening period lasts for six weeks, and once the fruit is ripe, bad weather is its worst enemy.

Vines need sunshine, and sunny conditions suit them very well. Too much sun deprives the wine of the acidity necessary to guarantee finesse, but sun is necessary all the same, for in order to grow well, vines require three things - heat, light and moisture. For a start, light is the only thing that ensures the assimilation of chlorophyll. It has been calculated that vines require a minimum of 20,000 lux, and a spring or summer sky will provide this, even if it is cloudy. So there is no need for the sun to be beaming down all the time, threatening to wither the plants, as it inevitably does. Ideally, the temperature should not rise much above 28°C to 30°C or much below 10°C.

That does not prevent vines from surviving extremely harsh winters, because they can actually withstand temperatures of -25°C, or even -30°C. The only real danger is spring frost, particularly on level terrain, where the air can sometimes be very still. A remedy does exist, however, and it is a paradoxical one. If the vines are watered before the frost arrives, the water freezes and forms an insulating shell over them. If vines are to develop properly, they must have plenty of moisture. In addition to the water contained in the soil and subsoil, dew, seasonal mists and fogs help to maintain the ideal level of 70% humidity. Vines are perfectly well able to cope with rain, even very heavy rain, provided it falls at the appropriate stages of the growth cycle. It then proves considerably less harmful than excessive sunshine.

Napa Valley, Vines after pruning.

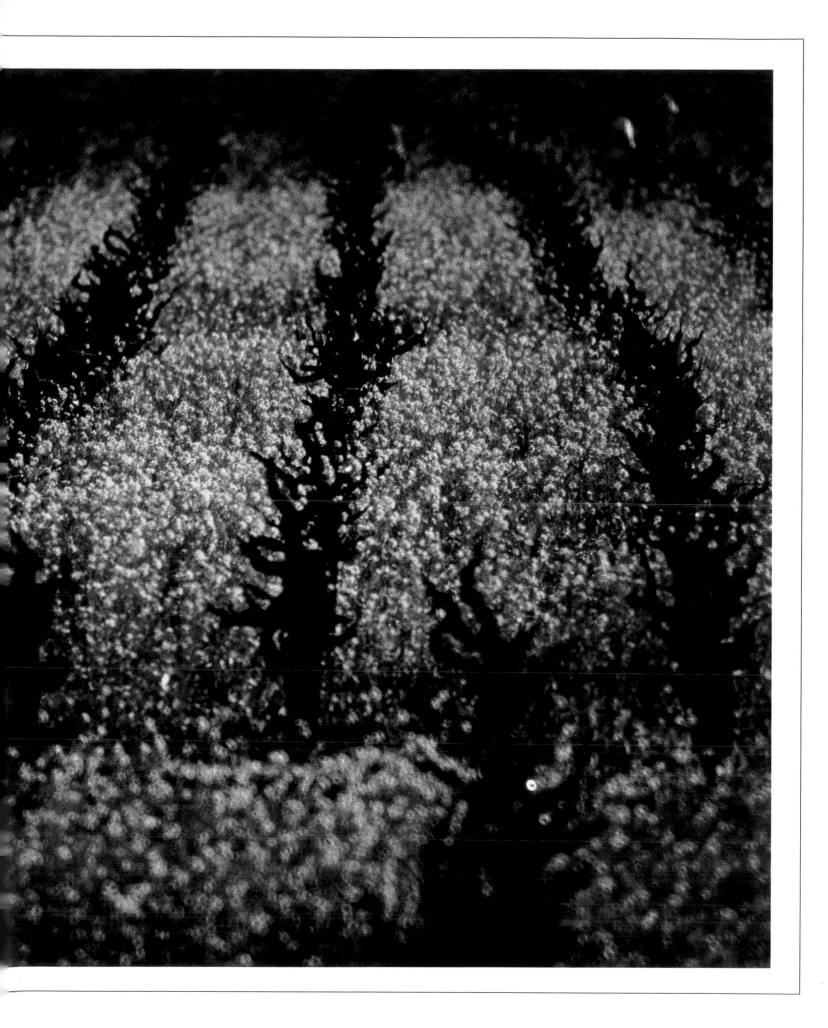

No Good Wine Without Water?

Even though vines need water, irrigation is prohibited by law in many appellation controlée areas. However, irrigation is essential in the hottest wine-growing regions of the world, such as Chile and parts of California, where there is no summer rainfall. In these cases, the effects of watering are entirely beneficial, provided that the vines are only watered in spring, in other words, well before harvest-time. Too much watering, or watering too late tends to dilute the grape-juice. It is therefore important to limit the amount the irrigation to the minimum.

Climatic Conditions and Vintage

The vintage is the date of birth of a wine. It is principally a reference to the prevailing weather conditions of the year in question because, although these are constant to some extent, they can still vary considerably from one year to the next. No two vintages are ever exactly alike. Furthermore, it is impossible to predict the quality of future vintages because current methods of weather forecasting are incapable of doing this. It is also still impossible, to detect any obvious pattern. The relative quality of each vintage is entirely subject to the whims of the

What is a terrain (terroir)?

The concept of terrain is often wrongly included in the wider concept of climate. However, the latter involves an entire region whereas the terrain (terroir) is a purely local element. Nor is the terrain purely a definition of the soil type. The effect of the terrain is more complex than that. It is the effect of the soil and sub-soil, topography and water supply. There are enough variables in this equation for each terrain to have its own very individual personality, and one which is strictly confined within its borders.

On the island of Santorin, the vine struggles to survive in the volcanic soil.

Sauternes vines, Bordeaux.

THE HALLMARK
AND IDENTITY OF
THE WINE

Some experts say that the variety of grape-vine (*cépages*) constitutes 90% of the factors which determine the character of a wine. This may be attributing too much importance to it. However, it is a readily acceptable fact that, when it comes to the three determining factors - air, soil and grapes - the grapes are the most important element, so much so that increasing numbers of wines are named after the grapes from which they are produced.

Medoc, Bordeaux, Cabernet Franc variety.

Thus, the wine-grower has a difficult decision on his hands when it comes to the choice of vine stock, because his choice is the determining factor. Although there are classic combinations of soil and grape, such as limestone and Chardonnay, scientific research has not yet managed to establish a consistent link between such combinations and the ultimate goal of quality. Furthermore, vines have a lifespan of between 40 and 50 years, and the quality of the wine they produce improves so much as they grow older that they cannot be used to make appellation contrôlée wines until they are four years old. All the vine stock in the world may have originated from one Indo-European species called Vitis vinifera, but that does not alter the fact that there are now over 4,000 varieties. However, it is also true to say that of this huge number, only 40 are really well-known to wine lovers, and there exists only a handful of classic, internationally famous vine stocks. Grapes, whether red or white, can be distinguished from one another, mainly by their flavour and how pleasant they taste.

There are *cépages nobles or cépages fins*, which are notable for their strength and the unusual nature of their bouquet.

Then there are *cépages demi-fins*, and in many cases, these only reveal their prowess when grown on particular terrains. Finally, there are the so-

THE TEN "CLASSIC" VINES

These include five red vines, namely: Cabernet Sauvignon, Pinot Noir, Merlot, Cabernet Franc and Syrah;

and five white vines, namely : Riesling, Chardonnay, Gewürztraminer, Sauvignon Blanc and Muscat.

called *cépages communs* which are known more for their fertility than for their flavour. Vines can also be distinguished from one another by their hardiness and resistance to disease, their yield and, finally, by their growth cycles.

In the latter case, the vine used for standard reference purposes is the Chasselas. Vines may be described as *tardifs* (late), *hatifs* (early) or *précoces* (precocious) in relation to the Chasselas. So, there is a vast choice, and by means of the process of *assemblage* (blending), it is possible to produce an infinite variety of flavours and nuances. So the fact that the international trend is moving towards the use of a handful of *cépages champions* (prize varieties) is not really a cause for rejoicing. For although the classic grapes are endowed with unsurpassable qualities, many of the so-called *cépages secondaires* (secondary varieties) have sufficiently rich and pleasing characteristics to merit careful preservation.

It is impossible to mention all the varieties of vine stock within the scope of this book. It is not even possible to examine every single one of the classic grapes. So the four descriptions which follow only serve as examples to illustrate the great variety of behaviour and characteristics of the various strains.

THE SIGNATURE OF THE VINE

It is becoming increasingly common for a bottle of wine to bear an extra label indicating the grape-stock from which it was made. This practice is particularly common in new wine-growing areas, such as California, where nearly all the wines are named after the stock used. On the other hand, in countries where the wine-growing tradition goes back further, the relationship between certain types of grape and certain geographical areas is so well established that it is only necessary mention the name of the wine. Thus, the mere mention of the name "Barolo" means that it was produced from Nebbiolo grapes.

CABERNET SAUVIGNON

This is the red vine stock par excellence. It is reputed to be the best in the world. The fact that it is used to make the most prestigious châteaux wines of the Médoc region of France immediately confirms its aristocratic pedigree.

Cabernet Sauvignon is easy to cultivate because it stands up well to stress, and even to spring frosts. The blue-black grapes with their dusty bloom are thick-skinned and the bunches are sufficiently tight to protect them from rain and insects. The only drawback with Cabernet Sauvignon is that it ripens late but, at the same time, the somewhat low yield adds still further to its nobility, enhancing the rich range of aromas. The predominant aroma is that of blackcurrant, but there are also hints of resin, spices and even smoke, or sometimes a touch of liquorice or seaweed.

Cabernet Sauvignon produces a tannic wine that needs to mature slowly, preferably in oak casks. It is ideal for blending with more supple varieties such as Cabernet Franc or Merlot. It enjoys great prestige the world over and travels extremely well. Although still rare in vine-growing countries like New Zealand, South Africa and Spain, it is widely used in California, Italy and Bulgaria. It is even found in Romania and Yugoslavia, and is beginning to make an appearance in China and Japan, where it produces wine worthy of its aristocratic status.

PINOT NOIR

The Pinot Noir grape has little in common with Cabernet Sauvignon except for its nobility. It is no globe-trotter and refuses to allow itself to be tamed. Although it prefers cool climates, it does not stand up well to excessively rigorous conditions. It has one major advantage in that it ripens early, and the black grapes produce a fruity wine with predominant aromas of strawberry and blackcurrant. The wine is low in tannin, and therefore does not need to age for very long.

Although mainly found in France - it is the sole variety in Burgundy and is well-established in Champagne - it is also grown in Germany, north-eastern Italy and in the Neuchâtel region of Switzerland. It is even grown as far away as California, though the results it has produced there are not as spectacular as might have been expected.

CHARDONNAY

Chardonnay is now the most sought-after white grape in the world. No doubt that is partly because it produces the great white wines of Burgundy. There is also the fact that it is the most adaptable variety on account of its hardiness, resistance to the cold, early ripening and generous yield. In addition to all these virtues, it is easy to vinify, to turn into wine. It will adapt to a wide range of treatments, from the Champagne method to maturation in oak vats. Thus it engenders a number of quality wines with markedly different characteristics.

Chardonnay produces matchless Burgundies and is also one of the great aristocrats of Champagne. It has now made a considerable mark in California too, where it shows great prowess, even outshining the excellent results obtained in Australia and Italy where the heat does not seem to affect it adversely.

RIESLING

A white grape of German origin, the Riesling is well-equipped to compete with Chardonnay for supremacy. Firmly established in Germany, it is even more widely used in the USSR, where more than 50,000 acres in the Ukraine are devoted to its cultivation. The yield varies according to the location. It is extremely high in Germany, only middling in California and low in South Africa. However, the Riesling is equally hardy wherever it grows, and will withstand low temperatures with unusual vigour. But that is not its main characteristic. The Riesling holds its own on account of its exceptionally rich bouquet. The predominant aroma depends on the nature of the soil, as does the degree of mellowness or acidity.

Cabernet Sauvignon

FROM THE VINE
TO THE FINISHED
PRODUCT

It is a long way from the judicious choice of vine-stock to the careful uncorking of the bottle, and the various stages of this journey are determined as much by nature as by human expertise.

Medoc, Bordeaux, the harvest.

FROM THE VINE-STOCK TO THE GRAPE

How are grapes formed? Quite simply, they are part of the life cycle of the vine and all the plant's vital organs combine to produce them. The vital organs are, basically:

The ROOTS, which are responsible for respiration, nutrition and sap distribution.
The ROOT-STOCK or trunk from which the vine-shoots grow.
The VINE-SHOOTS or branches, on which there are swellings called nodes.
The NODES, upon which buds, leaves and bunches of grapes grow.
The BUDS, some of which produce new vine-shoots.
The LEAVES, which are responsible for respiration and the conversion of sap.
The fruit, or GRAPES, which grow in BUNCHES.

Each of these vital organs comes into play during the different phases that make up the life-cycle of the vine. It all starts at the onset of spring, when the temperature starts to rise and the vine comes out of its dormant winter state. This happens somewhere around the end of March or the beginning of April. At this stage, the buds burst open, shed their downy protective covering, and leaves start to appear.

This process continues until early June when the vine flowers. That moment marks the beginning of a 100-day period, during which several crucial stages occur.

About half-way through June, bunches of tiny

"Débourrement", or budding.

green grapes appear. These absorb nourishment and start to grow. The sugars form extremely slowly, and so at this stage acids are accumulating all the time. Around mid-August, the grapes reach their full size and change colour. The colour varies from one type of vine to another. They may turn yellow, with varying degrees of translucency, or they may turn to red verging on black.

We are now into the ripening period, which lasts from 35 to 45 days. The colour of the grapes intensifies and they grow softer and softer. They gorge themselves on sugar and the acid content

decreases. The relationship between the total sugar content and the total acid content is taken as an indication of the degree of ripeness.

Obviously, this last stage is crucial, because the degree of ripeness determines the date of the harvest.

The point at which the grapes reach their maximum sugar content is called the moment of "industrial ripeness". Although this is an important criterion, it is not the only determining factor. The decision also depends on the quality required; the point at which the grapes reach their maximum sugar

content, and are thus at their heaviest, is important. The best time to harvest the grapes depends on the type of wine for which they are to be used. Thus, in Champagne, if a Pinot Noir needs to be slightly acidic, it will be harvested before it is completely ripe. On the other hand, in Burgundy, it will be harvested later, in order to obtain more full-bodied wines.

So it is not only the point of maximum physiological ripeness that determines the time of harvest. This crucial decision is entirely at the discretion of each individual grower.

Following Page:
Medoc, Bordeaux, a
harvest lunch at Chateau
Margaux.

THE GRAPES

The two main constituents of a bunch of grapes are the stalks and the grapes themselves. Both these constituents play an extremely important role in wine-making.

In a way, the STALK is the framework of a bunch of grapes. Stalks constitute between 3% - 7% of the total weight of the harvest, depending on the type of vine and the year in question. They contain tannins, which are particularly soluble in alcohol. These lend astringency to the wine and give it better keeping qualities. Furthermore, the stalks have a high water content which can be used to dilute the alcohol, thus decreasing the alcoholic content.

The GRAPE itself consists of three main elements:

The skin, which contains almost all the colouring matter, i.e. the anthocyanes and flavones. It plays a vital role because the actual juice of the grape is colourless to begin with.

The skin is also covered in a waxy substance called the bloom, which contains the reserves of yeast that are so important in the fermentation process.

The pips contain both tannins and oils. They tend to give the wine an unpleasantly bitter flavour, and so they are removed and discarded.

The juicy flesh, or pulp of the grapes accounts for between 80% to 85% of the weight of the bunch. When the grapes are crushed, the flesh yields a liquid called the must. The contents of this liquid tell a basic truth about wine, namely that it consists mainly of water. The water content is about 80%, the sugar content is between 10% and 25% and finally there are the acids.

FROM THE GRAPES TO THE WINE

As soon as the harvest reaches the storehouse VINIFICATION begins, in other words, the process of turning grapes into wine. The method differs considerably from one wine to another.

VINIFICATION INTO RED WINE

The first two steps are nowadays performed by machinery. Firstly, the grapes are crushed to release the must. You no longer see grape-pickers up to their knees in grape juice; the old tradition of treading the grapes has died out. Today, the operation is carried out in a kind of enormous funnel with corrugated cylinders in the bottom that turn in opposite directions. The sugary juice then comes into contact with the yeast and colouring matter contained in the skins.

At this point, the stalks become detached from the grapes. They will be partially or totally removed, and this operation has a crucial effect on the wine in several ways. If the stalks are removed completely, the resulting wine is supple and the alcohol content completely undiluted. However, this is not considered appropriate if the must has a low sugar content or if the wine is to be kept for a long period of time. In such cases, only 70% to 90% of the stalks are eliminated.

When these two mechanical treatments have been carried out, the must is treated with sulphur. That is to say, a small amount of sulphur dioxide is added. This acts as an antiseptic and also protects the wine from oxydation. The maximum amount permitted is laid down by law in France.

At this point, the wine can be transferred to vats and ALCOHOLIC FERMENTATION can begin (see box). During this process, the pieces of grape-skin rise to the surface and form a "cap". This brings all the colouring matter together. In order to put sufficient colour into red wines, the "cap" needs to be immersed in the liquid a number of times. Alternatively, the must has to be pumped so that it washes over the "cap".

Medoc, Bordeaux. The grape-harvest arrives at the Pontet-Canet winery.

Medoc, Bordeaux, Alfred Tesseron, owner of Pontet-Canet, in his winery.

By the end of the fermentation process, the new wine lies in the bottom of the vat, still muddy-looking and gassy, whilst the murk, in other words the solid matter, floats on top. At this point, the new wine is siphoned off into another vat, or into barrels. At this stage it is called *vin de goutte*. The murk is then submitted to PRESSURE in order to obtain *vin de presse*.

The first batch of *vin de presse* is rich in flavour and tannins and may be added to the *vin de goutte*. Subsequent batches decline progressively in quality, becoming increasingly and unpleasantly tart. At this point, the wine is cloudy and slightly effervescent. So, once it has been tapped and transferred once again into vats or barrels, it has to undergo the following treatments: it is re-tapped a number of times in order to eliminate the lees which cover the bottom of the first receptacle; it is then clarified by means of FINING.

The best quality wines are then ready to begin the slow process of aging.

THE PROCESS OF ALCOHOLIC FERMENTATION

The first stage of this process is simple. Yeasts which are present in the bloom on the grape-skin react with the sugars in the flesh, thus producing alcohol and carbon dioxide. Some yeasts need 20-21 grams of sugar per litre in order to produce 1° of alcohol, whilst others only need 17 or 18 grams. The activity of the yeasts and their rapid multiplication which accompanies fermentation, is very obvious. The temperature of the must rises and it becomes frothy. At the same time, the flavour, colour and density of the liquid change. By the time fermentation is complete, the sugars in the must have all been turned into ethyl alcohol, glycerine and aldehydes. Furthermore, there has also been a change in the acid content. In addition to tartaric, malic and citric acids, lactic acid is also present now and has a most important role to play.

FINING

Fining is a clarification process, consisting of adding a mixture of substances of a higher density than the wine itself. These sink slowly to the bottom, taking with them even the smallest particles of impurities. Substances used for this purpose include gelatine, fish-glue, beaten egg-whites and minerals such as bentonite.

Medoc, Bordeaux, fermentation in stainless steel tubs.

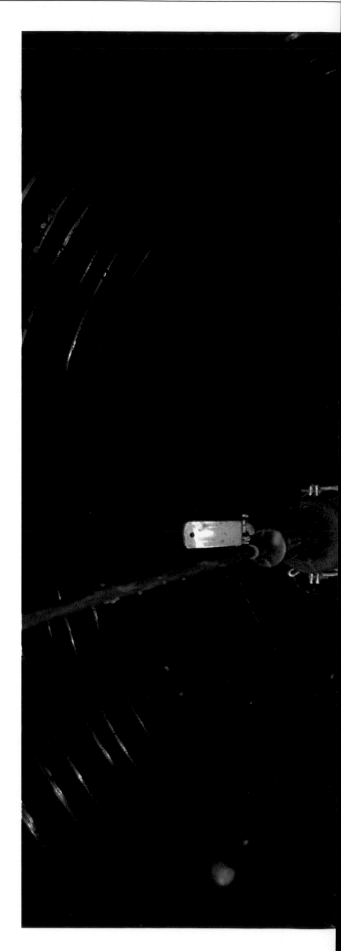

VINIFICATION INTO WHITE

White wine can be made from either red or white grapes. So during the vinification process of white wine, it is of the utmost importance to ensure that the grape-skins do not come into contact with the juice. The juice alone is fermented and there is no solid matter present at all.

The method consists of 4 stages:

First, the solid matter is crushed very lightly in order to bring out the must, a process known as EGOUTTAGE. Then, since at least a third of the juice is left behind in the murk, the solid matter is pressed gently in a process known as PRESSURAGE. The juice that emerges from the murk is sticky, so the bunches of grapes are left on their stalks, because the stalks are valuable for drainage purposes. Great care is taken to ensure that the stalks do not get crushed and release their tannins.

At this point, the juice still contains impurities, so these have to be separated out in a process known as DEBOURBAGE. The simplest method is to let the particles settle of their own accord in the bottom of the vat. However, the process can be speeded up by adding a large amount of sulphur dioxide, which has clarifying properties, or by using a centrifugal pump.

Next, comes the fermentation process which takes place in vats. It must be carried out at a relatively low temperature, between 8°C and 20°C, depending on the grower. If, by the time fermentation is complete, all the sugar has turned into alcohol, you get a dry wine. On the other hand, if there is some "residual sugar", the result is a sweet wine. There are two ways of causing this to happen. One is to interrupt the fermentation process artificially by adding large amounts of sulphur dioxide to kill the yeast. The other is to add sweetened grape-juice to a dry wine. Wine growers often prefer the latter method and, obviously, wine drinkers will always find it preferable.

Sauternes, Bordeaux, noble rot (botrysis), the world's most expensive grape, harvested at Chateau Eyquem.

THE WEIGHT OF THE SUGAR

The varying amounts of sugar which remain unconverted by the fermentation process determine the particular type of wine obtained. From 0 to 3 grams, the wine is dry, 3 to 10 grams produces a medium dry or sweet wine; 10 to 18 grams produces a mellow wine. Fortified wines contain between 40 and 200 grams of residual sugar.

"MIS SUR LIE" (ON THE LEES)

Once it has been fermented, white wine needs to be clarified. The most traditional method of doing this is to allow a rest period so that the lees have time to settle. In this case, the wine is said to be "mis sur lie" (put on the lees), and it usually turns out to be more supple and fruity.
However, this method is being abandoned to an increasing extent in favour of centrifugal pumps or filtration.

VINIFICATION INTO ROSE

It would be wrong to imagine that rosé wines are made from a mixture of white and red wines. They are, in fact, made from grapes with coloured skins, and the vinification process is midway between that for red and white wines.

The principle is a simple one. In the case of red wine, the longer it is left in the vat the darker it becomes. On the other hand, the shorter the maceration period, the paler it is. So, rosé wines are never left in the vat for very long, and the grape-juice alone is fermented. A distinction is made between:

Rosé de saignée (Bled rosé), macerated for 6 to 12 hours before it is racked (in other words, the vat is "bled").

Rosé de pressurage (Pressed rosé), the result of two pressings, the first almost colourless, and the second slightly coloured. The two musts are then fermented together.

Medoc, Bordeaux: blending at Château Prieuré Lichine.

BLENDING

Some wines are the product of a single variety of grape, for example, Burgundy, Sherry, Alsace and Barolo. However, most wines are the product of a mixture of grapes from different vineyards, producing a variety of wines of the same type and growing region.

Although grapes such as Pinot Noir and Riesling have not yet found an ideal match that will enhance their characteristics, most grapes gain from being used in combination and the resulting wine is more balanced and complex.

However, there are numerous types of combination, and it is necessary to distinguish between different practices:

EGALISAGE means blending the different vats from any one harvest in order to obtain the desired type of wine;

ASSEMBLAGE means blending wines of the same origin after they have been vinified separately;

CUVÉE is a blend of wines from different wine-growing communes of the same appellation;

COUPAGE means blending wines of different origins, a practice reserved for wines of poor quality.

It takes professional tasters to make a successful blend of wine. The art is to decide how the different characteristics of each wine will best blend and complement one another and then determine the right proportions so that the wine will have a rich and complex bouquet.

In other words, blending is a delicate art and needs to be tried out in small amounts first. Thus, the future of a great wine is determined gradually by trial and error. It is no good trying to hurry aristocrats in the making.

MALO-LACTIC FERMENTATION

This second fermentation is caused by bacteria that feed on the malic acid present in all wines, and takes place after the alcoholic fermentation. It converts the malic acid into lactic acid, thus giving the wine a much more mellow flavour. This is always desirable where red wines are concerned.
Malo-lactic fermentation is encouraged or even caused deliberately in the case of red wines, but it is avoided in white wines because acidity is one of their typical characteristics.

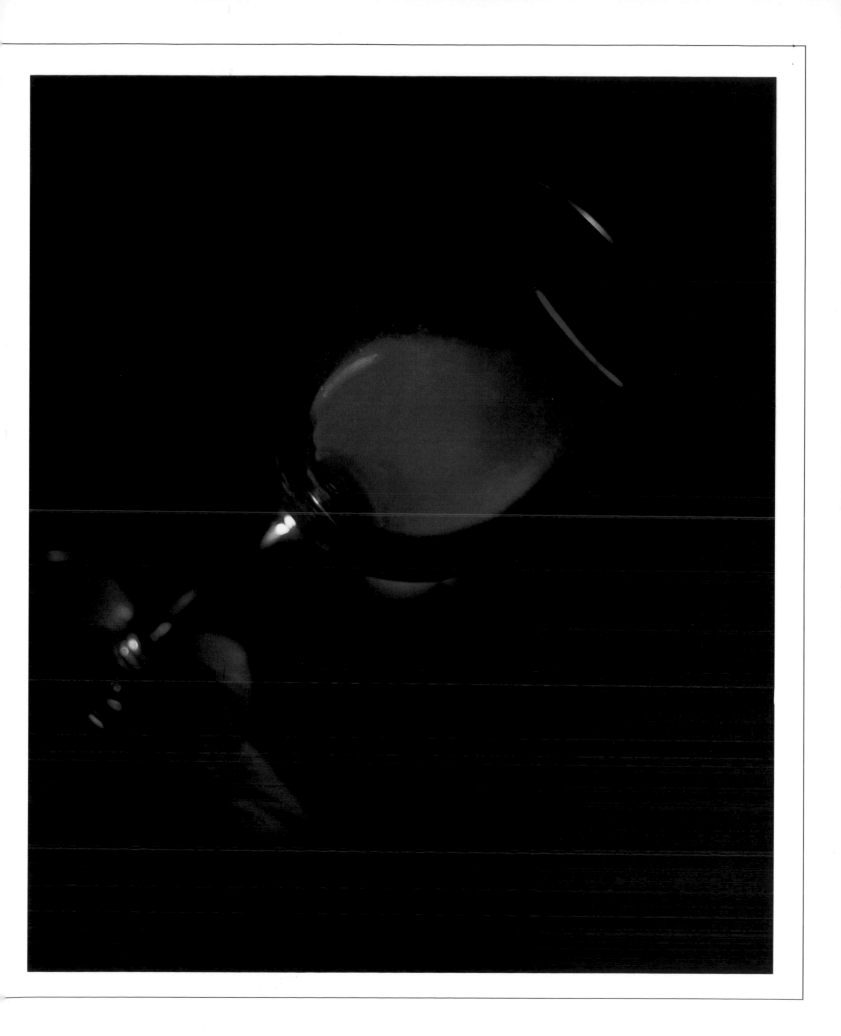

*Medoc, Bordeaux: stainless
steel vat.
Medoc, Château Margaux:
grape-picker.
Medoc, Château
Pontet-Canet:
harvesting machine.*

Medoc, Château Lynch-Bages:
the laboratory.

Napa Valley, California,
Chateau Clos Pégase.

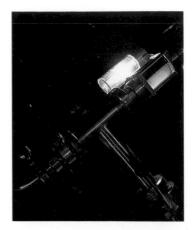

Napa Valley, California,
R. Mondavi Winery, automated
assembly line to fill the casks.
Stainless steel vat.

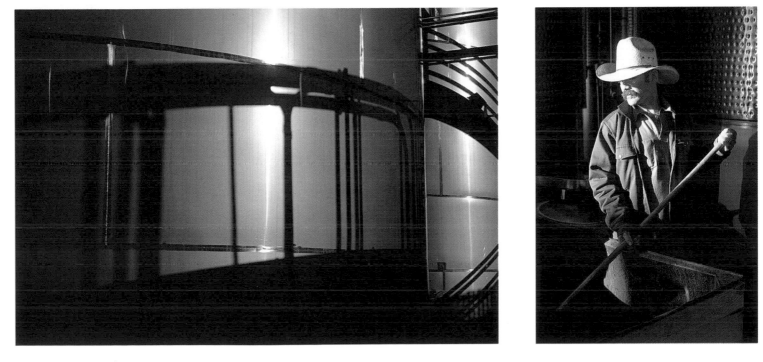

FROM YOUTH TO MATURITY

Wines, particularly vins fins, are not ready to be consumed as soon as the vinification process is complete. They need time to develop, or mature. Wine is a living substance. It is born and progresses through youth and maturity to old age and decline.

How does wine mature? In some cases, it is placed in barrels, in which case it comes into contact with oxygen from the air. In others, it is aged in the bottle and, therefore, has no contact with the air. The latter type of maturation is always preceded by the former, and is reserved for those wines which have a sufficiently robust constitution to be able to withstand contact with wood. More delicate wines would suffer from such contact.

Medoc, Bordeaux, the winery set up in a small house in Clerc Milon.
The new winery at Chateau Margaux.

THE PRESTIGE OF WOOD

Certain wines are matured in vats for periods ranging from six months to two years. These vats are made exclusively of oak, and not just any kind of oak. The cru and the terroir exist for wood just as they do for wines. The most prized oaks have a fine grain, mild tannins and smell strongly of vanilla. They say that, at one time, some craftsmen used to taste the wood before making a barrel.

However, it was not because of their influence on the flavour of the wine that barrels first came into use. In Roman times, before bottling was invented, barrels were just ordinary containers, and they were used simply because people considered them more practical for transportation purposes. Later on, however, regions such as Rioja and Bordeaux took to using smaller barrels with a 225-litre-capacity, and this was not just because they were easier to handle. The main reason was that their surface was ideal for making contact with the wine. So what happens inside a vat made of new wood? First of all, oxygen is constantly filtering slowly through the sides of the barrel and the pores of the wood.

This subtle aeration process intensifies and stabilises the colour of the wine. Furthermore, oak adds aroma and tannins. When the wine matures in vats, it has a pronounced woody flavour for the first few weeks. This gradually diminishes and all that remains of it is an aroma of vanilla or sometimes of toast. So the role of wood is not to assert itself but to reveal and then gradually fade from memory. Only mediocre wines let themselves be taken over by the wood. Great wines mellow and grow more complex.

WINE IS NOT MATURED IN JUST ANY WOOD

A good cask is not only made of oak, it must also be new. It takes only three years for the effect of wood to wear off completely. If the wood is constantly impregnated with wine, the flavour disappears and it becomes covered in sediment. Although the insides of the barrels can be scraped to uncover fresh, active wood, the best wine-makers do not hesitate to replace at least some of their barrels every year, despite the extremely high cost.

IS WOOD RESERVED EXCLUSIVELY FOR RED WINES?

Definitely not. Many white wines are worth maturing and fully deserve to be kept in casks for a while. This makes them smoother and more full-bodied. In actual fact, white wines need to be aerated, even though they are more prone to oxidization than red wines because they have no tannins to protect them. However, the aeration process must take place without the oxygen actually mingling with the wine. So, when white wine is put into casks, it is left on the lees in order to fix the oxygen. That is one of the secrets of white wines that have good keeping qualities.

Southwestern France,
a cooper.

Napa Valley, inspection
of the French casks at R.
Mondavi

LIFE IN THE BOTTLE

Whether it has been matured in oak or not, wine must be clear, wholesome and free of fermenting agents when it is bottled.

It either begins to age in the bottle, or else it continues the process of aging, but this time entirely without oxygen. Extremely complex reactions still take place, but extremely slowly.

Gradually, the colour changes from purple to carmine in the case of red wines and from greenish-yellow to gold in the case of white wines. At the same time, the wine becomes more fully rounded and loses some of its astringency as the tannins settle. Finally, the aromas blend with one another and the "bouquet" is formed, largely as a result of the conversion of acids into ethers.

Once they have been bottled, some wines need to be drunk quite quickly. On the other hand, the greatest wines from some vintages are capable of developing for decades before they start to deteriorate. For, just like a living creature, wine reaches a peak and then gradually dies.

FOR OR AGAINST THE HALF-BOTTLE?

Wine enthusiasts often criticise the half-bottle because they say it causes the wine to age too quickly. They are also wary of the magnum for the opposite reason. However, this particular characteristic of the half-bottle is not without its advantages, the main one being that it saves understandably impatient wine drinkers years of waiting.

CHOOSE YOUR CORK WITH CARE

An excellent cork is a must if you are to have a good bottle of wine. There is no substitute for cork, and good quality cork can never be too porous. A cork also needs to be very long, and it must be renewed every ten to fifteen years.

St. Emilion, the cellars of Beau-Séjour-Bécot.

CLASSIFICATION
AND LABELLING

To read a wine-label correctly, one needs to know the rules of classification which are, in turn, dictated by the systems of controls and protection which have had to be established in the interests of quality.

CURRENT SYSTEMS OF CLASSIFICATION

There is no world-wide system of wine classification. Countries such as the USA and Australia are currently setting up divisions into regions and territories. But in Chile, for example, wines may only be classified in terms of age.

So, the only global system of regulations in force for the time being is that of the EEC, and it is an umbrella for the individual systems of each member country. Under Common Market regulations, only two distinctions of quality are officially allowed, and these are:

Vins de table, which must be at least 8.5° proof. If the product in question is a blend of wines of different origins, the wines used must be from within the EEC.

VQPRD, or Vin de Qualité Produit dans des Regions Delimitées
(quality wines produced only in specific areas).
This category came into being in 1962. The following are taken into account:
The specific growing region;
The grapes used;
The growing methods;

The vinification methods;
The minimum degree of natural alcohol;
The yield per hectare;
The organoleptic properties of the wine.

In this way, minimum requirements are laid down and each member country of the European Economic Community is obliged to comply with them. As long as it does so, it is then free to decide upon, or continue with its own system of classification. Sometimes, the classification systems used by individual countries are so complex that they are not at all easy for the uninitiated to understand. Being a discerning drinker means being able to read the label on the bottle, and being able to interpret it correctly is the first step towards good drinking.

HOW THE LABEL REFLECTS THE WINE

It is impossible to get beyond the label before buying a bottle of wine because bottles do not let even the slightest aroma escape. The label may not be transparent, yet it constitutes a window, through which the wine may be viewed. Thus its main function is informative rather than aesthetic.

Furthermore, the information it contains is strictly codified. In 1979, the EEC passed a law based on the principle that "all unauthorised information is prohibited".

It lays down: COMPULSORY INFORMATION, which is confined to a few basic, but essential facts concerning:

The type of wine (eg. "Vin de table")

The metric volume of liquid contained in the bottle (eg. 75 cl);

The name and address of the bottler (and whether bottling was performed by him or on his behalf). The bottler may also indicate his status, for example viticulteur (wine-grower), négociant (wine-merchant) or propriétaire-récoltant (estate owner and harvester);

The name of the country of origin or some indication that the wine originates from within the EEC. Thus, a vin de table consisting of a blend of wines of different origins must bear the wording "Vin de differents pays de la CEE". (Wines from various EEC countries);

The degree of alcohol (in the case of vins de table).

OPTIONAL INFORMATION, left to the discretion of the individual producer. The most usual types of additional information are:

The type of wine, eg. medium-dry, sweet, sur lie (on the lees), etc.;

The vintage;

The grapes used, depending on the extent to which the variety determines a particular type of wine;

The name of the commune or other place of origin;

The brand-name;

The names of those concerned in the marketing process, eg. Selectionné par...("Selected by..."), Importé par... ("Imported by..."), etc.;

The name of the growers;

Any medals or other prizes awarded to the wine;

Advice to the consumer (eg., serve chilled).

Although a wine-label should be examined carefully, on the other hand it is not a good idea to pay too much attention to its appearance. The fact that a label is not much to look at does not necessarily reflect upon the contents of the bottle. The label on a bottle of Yquem is aristocratic in its simplicity, but not all the greatest names have such plain labels.

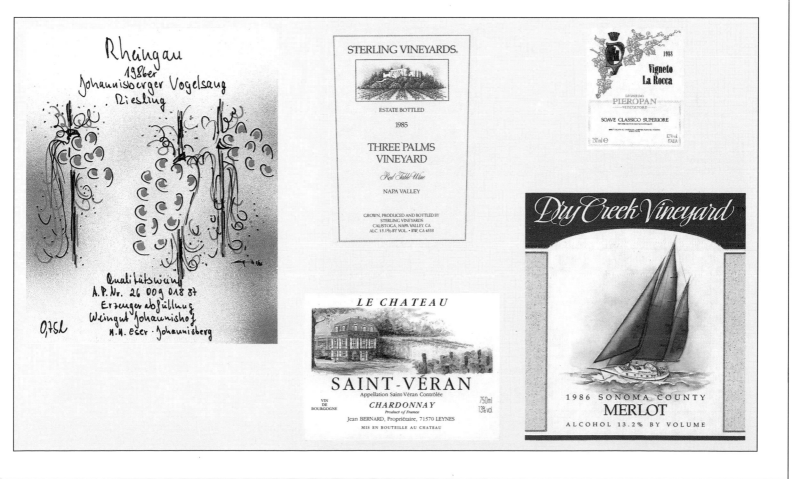

FRANCE

France is the wine-growing country par excellence, and many great French wines are universally extolled as models of perfection to be emulated.

The vine-growing tradition is an extremely ancient one, for the cultivation of vines, which was begun by the Phoenicians and Greeks, goes back to the 6th century BC. The great vineyards of France were planted under the auspices of the Romans during the 1st century BC. The positions of the hillsides and rivers determined the sites, and the best vintages are still to be found in the original localities, beside the great rivers of France, the Gironde, the Rhone, the Marne, the Loire and the Rhine.

No other country can offer such a wide range of climates and soils. Furthermore, all the great classic vines are represented here. An extraordinarily rich range of wines emanates from the 12 principle wine-growing regions, which are:

> *BORDEAUX, BURGUNDY, CHAMPAGNE, THE LOIRE VALLEY, ALSACE, COTES DU RHONE, JURA and SAVOY, PROVENCE, the SOUTH-WEST, LANGUEDOC and ROUSSILLON.*

The great phylloxera crisis hastened the introduction of a classification system which brought in distinctions of quality. It came into force at the beginning of the century. In France, the EEC category Vins de table has a subdivision, namely that of Vins de pays. These originate from a specific wine-growing area and are not subjected to coupage (i.e. the blending of wines of different origins). They have a minimum alcohol content of 10° proof. The second EEC category, that of VQPRD, is subdivided into:

> *Vins Delimitées de Qualité Superieure (VDQS) (Superior quality wines from a specific region). There are 48 such wines. They are subject to the same controls as AOC wines and have to be tasted and approved in just the same way. They come from regions whose wines have sufficiently distinctive characteristics to merit identification and protection.*
>
> *Vins à Appellation d'Origine Côntrolée (AOC) (Wines from a specific region, use of whose name is controlled). There are just over 300 of these, and they offer the best guarantee of quality because they are subject to controls relating to the region in which the grapes are grown, the variety of grape used, the yield, production methods and the percentage of alcohol. All great French wines belong to this category.*

Bordeaux, the village of Saint-Emilion

BORDEAUX

Bordeaux is one of the most important wine-producing areas in the world and, judging from the number of prestigious crus it produces, it must be gifted with some very special property.

The vineyards, which cover an area of 94,000 hectares (232,274 acres), form a kind of triangle which takes in the left bank of the Garonne and the right bank of the Dordogne, then grows narrower around the Gironde.

There is too much variety in the gravelly limestone and clay soils for the whole area to produce identical wines. The latter are usually the product of a mild maritime climate and of the use of particular kinds of grape.

The majority of Bordeaux wines are red, and the reds of the region are undoubtedly superior to the dry whites. Only the great sweet white wines can compete with them. There are three kinds of appellation, general ones such as Bordeaux and Bordeaux Supérieur, regional ones such as Médoc and those denoting the commune of origin, such as Margaux. In addition to this there is a regional hierarchy, partly the result of the famous classification scheme of 1855 and partly due to a combination of classification schemes introduced since then as well as to commercial practices.

Distinctions are made between the different châteaux. The term château covers the whole of an estate and all the plots of land within it, even if these are somewhat scattered. When you realise that there are nearly 3000 châteaux along the River Gironde, it becomes clear that the various gradings, which distinguish between 200 or so, are in no way superfluous despite their sophistication.

Medoc, Bordeaux: Château Mouton-Rothschild.

MEDOC

The name Médoc literally means "middle country" and, in fact, it covers an area of about 850 square miles with water on either side. It consists of a narrow strip of land only 3 to 6 miles wide and 44 miles long, stretching from the east bank of the Gironde to the Atlantic Ocean. The vineyards thus benefit from the presence of both the sea and the river, and these ensure sufficient humidity and keep temperatures at a moderate level all year round. Médoc is divided into two regional appellations:

BAS-MEDOC covers the northern part of the region. So many streams and canals run through the clay soil that the area is a little reminiscent of Holland. There are no crus classés (classic wines) in BAS MEDOC, but it does produce some reputable, quite full-bodied red wines.

HAUT-MEDOC, on the other hand, where there are plenty of gravel outcrops, produces wines of great breeding. These have such distinction and finesse that they are numbered among the great aristocrats of Bordeaux. Haut-Médoc is divided into six communal appellations, namely, from north to south: MARGAUX, MOULIS, LISTRAC, SAINT-JULIEN, PAUILLAC and SAINT-ESTEPHE; all names that reflect the best in wines.

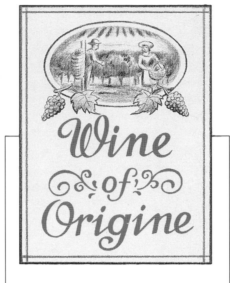

THE CLASSIFICATION OF MEDOCS

The classification scheme of 1855 identified 60 wines from Médoc, and hardly anything changed in 1973. The best wines established their position right from the start and have remained at the top.

PREMIERS CRUS

Château Lafite-Rothschild Pauillac
Château Latour Pauillac
Château Margaux Margaux
Château Mouton-Rothschild Pauillac
(classified in 1973)

SECONDS CRUS

Château Rausan-Ségla Margaux
Château Rauzan-Gassies Margaux
Château Léoville-Las Cases Saint-Julien
Château Léoville-Poyferre Saint-Julien
Château Léoville-Barton Saint-Julien
Château Dufort-Vivens Margaux
Château Gruaud-Laroze Saint-Julien
Château Lascombes Margaux
Château Brane-Cantenac Cantenac
Château Pichon-Longueville Pauillac
Château Pichon-Longueville Pauillac Comtesse de Lalande
Château Ducru-Beaucaillou Saint-Julien
Château Cos d'Estournel Saint-Estephe
Château Montrose Saint-Estephe

The classification also includes Troisième, Quatrième and Cinquième Crus.

MARGAUX

This appellation covers an area of 1060 hectares (2620 acres). It consists of the commune of Margaux itself, plus four neighbouring communes, ARSAC, CANTENAC, LABARDE and SOUSSANS. The majority of the actual châteaux are situated around the village of Margaux, but the vineyards are rather scattered.

Margaux has the stoniest soil with the highest gravel content in the subsoil of any area in Médoc. No doubt that is why the appellation has more crus classés than any other. Another crucial factor is that yields are wisely limited to an average of 40 hectolitres per hectare.

The resulting wines are discreetly complex and superbly harmonious. The greatest Châteaux Margaux are true works of art, but even the cinquièmes crus (wines from areas in the lowest grade of appellation) are still a great luxury.

THE GRAPES OF MEDOC

Since Médoc only produces red wines, only the appropriate Bordeaux grapes are found here. Cabernet-Sauvignon and Cabernet Franc predominate, but Merlot is also used and, to a lesser extent, Malbec and Petit Verdot.

MOULIS and LISTRAC

The two communes situated to the west of Margaux, more or less right in the centre of Haut-Médoc have been left out of the official classification systems, and rather unjustly so. They do not boast a single cru classé.

However, Moulis can pride itself on crus such as Château Chasse-Spleen. The vineyards of Moulis cover an area of 350 hectares (865 acres), and are partly situated on a large gravel ridge that rises above the hamlet of Grand-Poujeaux.

CRUS OF MARGAUX
PREMIER CRU
Château Margaux Margaux
DEUXIEMES CRUS
Château Rausan-Ségla Margaux
Château Rauzan-Gassies Margaux
Château Lascombes Margaux
Château Durfort-Vivens Margaux
Château Brane-Cantenac Cantenac
TROISIEMES CRUS
Château Kirwan Cantenac
Château d'Issan Cantenac
Château Giscours Labarde
Château Malescot-Saint-Exupéry Margaux
Château Boyd-Cantenac Cantenac
Château Cantenac-Brown Cantenac
Château Palmer Cantenac
Château Desmirail Margaux
Château Ferrière Margaux
Château Marquis-d'Alesme-Decker Margaux
QUATRIEMES CRUS
Château Prieuré-Lichine Cantenac
Château Pouget Cantenac
Château Marquis-de-Terme Margaux
CINQUIEME CRUS
Château Dauzac Labarde
Château du Tertre Arsac
CRUS OF SAINT-JULIEN
DEUXIEME CRUS
Château Léoville-Las-Cases
Château Léoville-Poyferré
Château Léoville-Barton
Château Gruaud-Larose
Château Ducru-Beaucaillou
TROISIEME CRUS
Château Lagrange
Château Langoa-Barton
QUATRIEME CRUS
Château Talbot
Château Saint-Pierre (Sevaistre)
Château Beychevelle
Château Branaire-Ducru
CRUS OF PAUILLAC
PREMIERS CRUS
Château Lafite-Rothschild
Château Latour
Château Mouton-Rothschild
DEUXIEME CRUS
Château Pichon-Longueville
Château Pichon-Longueville-Comtesse de Lalande
QUATRIEME CRU
Château Duhart-Milon Rothschild
CINQUIEMES CRU
Château Lynch-Bages
Château Croizet-Bages
Château Haut Bages-Libéral
Château Batailley
Château Haut-Batailley
Château Pontet-Canet
Château Grand Puy-Lacoste
Château Grand Puy-Ducasse
Château Mouton Baronne Philippe
Château Clerc-Millon
Château Pédesclaux
Château Lynch Moussas
CRUS OF SAINT-ESTEPHE
DEUXIEMES CRUS:
Château Cos d'Estournel
Château Montrose
TROISIEME CRU:
Château Calon-Segur
QUATRIEME CRU:
Château Lafon-Rochet
CINQUIEME CRU:
Château Cos Labory
CRUS OF HAUT-MEDOC
TROISIEME CRU:
Château La Lagune
QUATRIEME CRU:
Château La Tour-Carnet
CINQUIEME CRUS:
Château Belgrave
Château de Camensac
Château Cantemerle.

Listrac has a beautiful Romanesque church, but that is not its only treasure. It also has 500 hectares (1235 acres) of vineyards. The wines produced here are like those of Moulis, robust, but with a certain elegance.

SAINT-JULIEN

The vineyards of Saint-Julien cover an area of 740 hectares (1829 acres). In a

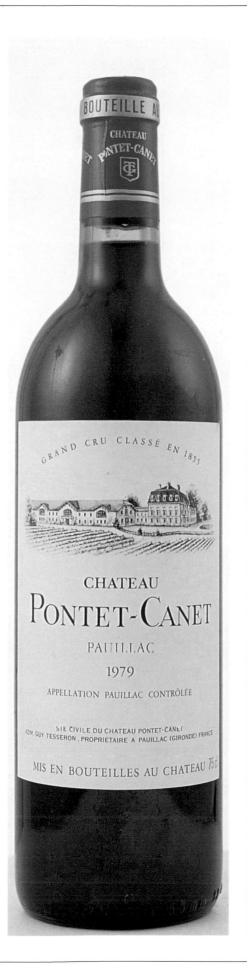

way that is not very much, but in another way it is, because much of the territory consists of crus classés. However, it has no premier cru estates. Saint-Julien occupies a gravel plateau with a well-drained clay subsoil, conditions so favourable to vine-growing that the resulting wines can easily compete with those of Margaux in grace and smoothness, whilst at the same time, they have more strength and solidity.

PAUILLAC

Pauillac is the largest commune in Médoc in terms of the numbers of inhabitants, due not to the vines, but to the fact that there is an oil refinery here. Despite this possible drawback, the town is surrounded by 950 hectares (2347 acres) of glorious vineyards growing in a gravelly, pebbly soil.

Pauillac has no less than three premiers crus, plus 15 other crus classés, and even the cinquième cru are of exceptionally high quality. The vigorous character of these wines makes them the most virile in Médoc, but they are also endowed with an exceptional degree of finesse and this balances their strength wonderfully.

SAINT-ESTEPHE

Saint-Estephe lies against a background of steep hills. It has the largest area of vineyards in Haut-Médoc, covering 1100 hectares (2718 acres). However, the soil here is also the heaviest in the region and has the lowest gravel content. Consequently, the wines are more colourful and robust, but they have less finesse. So Saint-Estephe has few crus classés. However, this is not to denigrate the quality of the wines of this locality, which is excellent.

HAUT-MEDOC

This appellation covers all the vineyards surrounding the six famous commune appellation areas. Consequently, the quality of the wines varies. Some are first-class, such as those from the commune of Ludon. Ludon lies in the south of the district, just 10 miles from Bordeaux; it can boast Château La Lagune and Château Cantemerle.

GRAVES

During the period when Aquitaine was part of the kingdom of England, all the famous Bordeaux wines came from Graves.

The Graves region is an extension of the Médoc. It is a strip of land between 6 and 9 miles across, which includes the city of Bordeaux itself and then stretches for 37 miles along the banks of the Garonne.

Urban development has banished all the vineyards from the town and its suburbs. Only three illustrious châteaux survive, namely, Haut-Brion, Laville-Haut Brion and La Tour-Haut Brion.

Why have these crus remained? Partly because, in Graves, forests and meadows vie with the vineyards for space. The vineyards are smaller than in Médoc and fewer in number. However, the main reason is that the best soils are in the north, mostly around the communes of Pessac and Talence (which are both extremely close to Bordeaux), Gradignant and Villenave d'Ornon, Leognan (which boasts six crus classés), Cadaujac and Martillac.

All the crus classés are to be found in the north where the soil is the same as in Haut-Médoc, in other words, it consists of sand, limestone and clay, with an abundance of siliceous pebbles ("gravel") in the subsoil. The gravel, which ensures that the soil is extremely well-drained, gradually disappears as one moves southward.

THE CLASSIFIED CRUS OF GRAVES

The classification system of 1855 only recognized Château Haut-Brion, placing it among the Premiers Crus. The classification system of 1959 singled out thirteen red crus and eight white crus but used no finer distinctions.

WHITE WINES CLASSIFIED IN 1959

Château Laville-Haut Brion Talence
Château Bouscaut Cadaujac
Château Couhins Villenave d'Ornon
Château Carbonnieux Léognan
Château Malartic-Lagravière Léognan
Domaine de Chevalier Léognan
Château Olivier Léognan
Château La Tour-Martillac Martillac

RED WINES CLASSIFIED IN 1959

Château La Mission Haut-Brion Talence
Château La Tour Haut-Brion
Château Haut-Brion (cru classified in 1855) Pessac
Château Pape Clement Pessac
Château Bouscaut Cadaujac
Château Carbonnieux Léognan
Château Fieuzal Léognan
Domaine de Chevalier Léognan
Château Haut-Bailly Léognan
Château Malartic-Lagravière Léognan
Château Olivier Léognan
Château La Tour-Martillac Martillac
Château Smith-Haut-Lafitte Martillac

The Graves region covers some 1500 hectares (3706 acres). It produces both white wines (AOC GRAVES in the case of dry wines and GRAVES SUPERIEURS in the case of sweet wines) and red wines (AOC GRAVES).

Almost all the great red wines come from the north. The best are to be found at the very edge of Bordeaux itself, and they are prefectly well-equipped to vie with their illustrious neighbours from Médoc.

THE GRAPES OF GRAVES

For white wines, a combination of the classic Sauvignon and Sémillon is used, with the addition in some cases of a little Muscadelle.

For red wines, the traditional Bordeaux grapes are used, namely, Cabernet Sauvignon, Cabernet Franc and Merlot, with the addition of small quantities of Malbec and Petit Verdot.

On the whole, although the red wines of Graves bear comparison with those of Médoc extremely well, they are considered to have slightly less finesse. It is also said that they do not mature quite as well, nor are they quite so typical of their terrain. These nuances may make a slight difference, but when it comes down to choosing between a bit less class and a bit more body, it is ultimately a matter of taste. Although white grapes are more widely cultivated in the south, white wines are to be found in northern Graves. The majority of these are dry and often prove to be extremely fresh and full of flavour with a subtle bouquet. They keep well and usually benefit from a period of aging. The sweet wines of the Graves Supérieur appellation come from the area close to the border with Sauternes and, on the whole, they are of extremely good quality.

SAUTERNES

The Sauternes region is a wedge-shaped enclave in the southern part of Graves. Its ridges and hills are covered with 2000 hectares (5000 acres) of vineyards. The appellation is reserved for the five communes of Sauternes, Bommes, Fargues and Preignac south of the River Ciron and Barsac on the opposite bank, at the point where the valleys give way to a plateau. Barsac actually has an appellation all to itself, AOC BARSAC. The River Ciron, a tributary of the Garonne, provides the high degree of humidity that is so vital to the wines of Sauternes.

THE CRUS CLASSES OF SAUTERNES

The classification system of 1855 established three gradings. Yquem stands alone at the top, followed by eleven Premiers Crus and thirteen Deuxièmes Crus.

GRAND PREMIER CRU

Château Yquem Sauternes

PREMIERS CRUS

Château Climens Barsac
Château Coutet Barsac
Château Haut Peyraguey Bommes
Château Lafaurie-Peyraguey Bommes
Château La Tour Blanche Bommes
Château Rabaud-Promis Bommes
Château Rayne-Vigneau Bommes
Château Sigalas-Rabaud Bommes
Château Rieussec Fargues
Château Suduiraut Preignac
Château Guiraud Sauternes

DEUXIEME CRUS

Château d'Arche Sauternes
Château Filhot Sauternes
Château de Malle Preignac
Château Romer du Hayot Fargues
Château Lamothe Sauternes
Château Doisy-Daëne Barsac
Château Doisy-Dubroca Barsac
Château Doisy-Védrines Barsac
Château Caillou Barsac
Château Broustet Barsac
Château Myrat Barsac
Château Nairac Barsac
Château Suau Barsac

The soil, which consists of siliceous gravel with a subsoil of clay, sand and limestone, is a crucial factor as far as quality is concerned. But the climate, characterized by early morning mists and sunny days, is equally important. The humidity is essential to the growth of a fungus called Botrytis cinerea which covers the surface of the grapes causing them to rot. This is the famous pourriture noble ("noble rot") which produces the sweet wines.

The best of these wines - and everyone speaks of the "lavish perfection" of Yquem, the king of them all - are of unmatched quality. As they mature, their colour changes from golden-yellow to light amber and they develop a bouquet of flowers, fruit and honey. Rich and mellow, they have a combination of finesse and strength. They are, quite simply, wines for special occasions. A good Sauternes is always expensive, and anyone who tries to sell one cheaply is not to be trusted.

There are several reasons why Sauternes is so dear. For a start, the grape-yield is limited to an average of 25 hectolitres per hectare (550 gallons per 2.5 acres) but even in the best years the actual yield is always lower than this. Then there is the fact that the pourriture noble does not affect the whole of a bunch of grapes at the same time. Consequently, it is necessary to pick the grapes selectively, one at a time, and this makes the harvest long and costly. The hyphae (microscopic threads) of the fungus penetrate the grapes in order to suck out the water, so as the fruit shrivels the juice becomes more concentrated. This causes the grapes to lose almost half their volume. Finally, the vinification process requires great care of a kind that only the best producers are able to provide. They give their wines plenty of time to mature in barrels and then in bottles before putting it on sale. That is the price of quality.

THE GRAPES OF SAUTERNES

Semillon is heavily predominant here, with the addition of Sauvignon and a little Muscadelle.

SAINT-EMILION

Saint-Emilion is a paradise for lovers of Bordeaux wines. Although the growing area covers only 5300 hectares (13100 acres) and is limited to eight communes, it produces more Grands crus than any vine-growing region of France.

Like Graves, vine-growing in Saint-Emilion has an extremely ancient tradition in the Bordeaux region. The fortifications surrounding the village of Saint-Emilion, and its narrow, cobbled streets are evidence of its great age and make it a great tourist attraction. The Château du Roy or the Cloître des Cordeliers are its most famous monuments, and the bakeries which make the famous macaroons are also not to be missed.

However, there would seem to be no chance of the village expanding because it is entirely given over to the production of red wines, and is therefore completely surrounded by vineyards.

THE CLASSIFIED CRUS OF SAINT-EMILION

PREMIERS GRANDS CRUS
A / Château Ausone
Château Cheval Blanc
B / Château Beauséjour (Dufau)
Château Beauséjour (Becot)
Château Belair
Château Canon
Château Figeac
Château La Gaffelière
Château Magdelaine
Château Pavie
Château Pavie
Château Trottevieille
Clos Fourtet
GRANDS CRUS
Château L'Angélus Château Fonroque
Château L'Arrosée Château Franc-Mayne
Château Baleau Château Grand-Barrail-Lamarzelle
Château Balestard-La-Tonnelle Château Grand Corbin
Château Bellevue Château Grand Corbin-Despagne
Château Bergat Château Grand Mayne
Château Cadet-Bon Château Grand-Pontet
Château Cadet-Piola Château Grandes-Murailles
Château Canon-La-Gaffelière Château Guadet-Saint-Julien
Château Cap de Mourlin Château Haut-Corbin
Château La Carte Château Haut-Sarpe
Château Chapelle-Madeleine Clos des Jacobins
Château Chauvin Château Jean Faure
Château La Clotte Château Laniote
Château La Clusière Château Larcis-Ducasse
Château Corbin Château Larmande
Château Corbin-Michotte Château Laroze
Château La Couspaude Clos La Madeleine
Château Coutet Château Matras
Château La Couvent Château Mauvezin
Château Couvent-des-Jacobins Château Moulin-du-Cadet
Château Croque-Michotte Château L'Oratoire
Château Cure-Bon-La-Madeleine Château Pavie-Decesse
Château Dassault Château Pavie-Macquin
Château La Dominique Château Pavillon-Cadet
Château Faurie-de-Souchard Château Petit-Faurie-de-Soutard
Château Fomplégade Château Le Prieuré
Château Ripeau Château La Tour-Figeac
Château St Georges-Côte-Pavie Château La Tour-du-Pin-Figeac
Clos Saint-Martin Château Trimoulet
Château Sansonnet Château Troplong-Mondot
Château La Serre Château Villemaurine
Château Soutard Château Yon-Figeac
Château Tertre-Daugay

There are no large estates in Saint-Emilion. The majority of vineyards cover no more than 2 or 3 hectares (5 to 7 acres) and few exceed 12 hectares (30 acres). The soil types are sufficiently differentiated for there to be two distinct zones:

the area known as the "côtes" which is situated for the most part on the escarpment surrounding the village. The soil is basically limestone but, for the most part, mixed with clay or silica. The best Saint-Emilion crus come from this area. The wines, which are a deep garnet colour, are well-constituted and powerful. The bouquet is often very rich, and develops beautifully as the wine matures.

The area known as the "graves" occupies a large plain which starts below the village and stretches as far as the Dordogne. The name (which is the French word for gravel) does not seem entirely appropriate because, in many parts, the gravel gives way to a siliceous soil with varying degrees of sand content. For that reason, the area is also sometimes known as "de plaine" (the plains) or "de sable"(the sands). It is further characterized by the presence of bands of clay and irons-tone as in Médoc.

The wines of this area have many characteristics in common with those of the Côtes de Saint-Emilion. However, they are more supple, less well-constituted and less suited to long periods of aging.

All the wines of Saint-Emilion are characteristically sound and clean. Although they improve greatly if left to

mature, they are fully rounded and drinkable with a well-established flavour right from the start.

It is not particularly easy to find your way around the vineyards of Saint-Emilion. The area has over a thousand châteaux with a total of 300 crus - by comparison, Médoc has only 60 in an area almost twice the size! So it is not surprising that Saint-Emilion has a classification system all of its own. It only dates back to 1954, for Saint-Emilion was not included in the classification system of 1855. There are three grades:

The Premiers Grands Crus Classés, with their two sub-categories, A and B;
The Grands Crus Classes;
The Grands Crus;
Clearly, the term Grand cru has a different significance here than in the rest of Bordeaux.

The first two categories are reviewed every ten years and tend to stay pretty much the same. However, the third is compulsorily reviewed every year. In early summer, usually in June, every estate that wishes to be considered for approval must submit samples of its wine, and these are tasted by a jury. The wines are then accepted, referred or else rejected.

The Grands crus sometimes achieve an extremely satisfactory quality, but, unfortunately, this is not a regular occurrence.

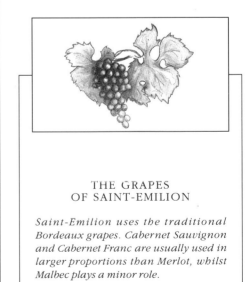

THE GRAPES OF SAINT-EMILION

Saint-Emilion uses the traditional Bordeaux grapes. Cabernet Sauvignon and Cabernet Franc are usually used in larger proportions than Merlot, whilst Malbec plays a minor role.

POMEROL

The appellation Pomerol covers a mere 750 hectares (1853 acres). It is situated north-west of Saint-Emilion, close to the town of Libourne. The only additional appellation is that of Lalande-de-Pomerol, which belongs to a small neighbouring commune. But the vineyards there are small.

Visitors would hardly be drawn to the sleepy village of Pomerol by a desire to see the sights. It is completely different from Saint-Emilion except for the fact that it is encircled by wine-growing country. The vineyards have squeezed out all other crops and, despite the fact that they cover a fairly small area, over 150 wine-growers operate there. Many of them cultivate two hectares or even less.

UNCLASSIFIED WINES AND YET...

Although the wines of Pomerol are not officially graded, the following unofficial classification scheme exists:

PREMIER CRU

Château Pétrus

PRINCIPAL CHATEAUX

Château Beauregard
Château Gazin
Château Certan de May
Château Lafleur
Château La Conseillante
Château Lagrange
Château La Croix
Château Latour-Pomerol
Clos L'Eglise
Château Nenin
Château L'Eglise-Clinet
Château Petit-Village
Château L'Evangile
Château La Pointe
Château Feytit-Clinet
Château Rouget
Château La Fleur-Gazin
Château Trotanoy
Château La Fleur Pétrus
Vieux Château Certan

The area is dedicated exclusively to the production of red wines, and since the soils vary, the wines vary too. The gravel beds of the south-east give way to a sandy soil in the west. Between these two areas stands a plateau which has a pale clay subsoil mixed with dark packed clay, shot through with iron.

Thanks to these soil properties Pomerol has a distinctive character all of its own. Since the best soil in the appellation has a clay base, the Merlot is the predominant

grape, and the Cabernet Sauvignon, which reigns supreme in Médoc, has a rather low profile here.

The combination of soil and grapes yields a deep ruby-red wine with a remarkably velvety quality. The wines of Pomerol have the finesse of Médocs combined with the rich generous character of Saint-Emilions. In addition to these qualities,

they have a unique ability to develop quickly, revealing, in many cases a distinct aroma of truffles. The wines of Pomerol often achieve their full power after five years. However, they still continue to improve if aged for longer periods of time. Another peculiarity of Pomerols is the fact that they have never been officially classified. Nevertheless, the world-famous Château Petrus is considered by all to be a Premier Grand Cru, and it is followed by a string of other châteaux who are worthy runners-up. Thus the wines of Pomerol are the subject of a kind of unwritten classification system, upon which all the experts are agreed.

THE GRAPES OF POMEROL

The predominant grape, namely Merlot, is used in conjunction with Cabernet Franc and a smaller proportion of Cabernet Sauvignon. There is no Petit Verdot at all in Pomerol, but small amounts of Malbec are used.

BORDEAUX MINOR REGIONS

The vineyards of Bordeaux are sufficiently extensive to accommodate a number of so-called "minor" regions. Some of these bear comparison with the most prestigious appellations. So if you are visiting the area, it is worth making a detour, especially as the output from the minor areas is considerable and here and there there are excellent bottles which have the additional advantage of being very reasonably priced.

Geographically, the minor appellations are divided into two large areas:

Le Centre (The central region) is situated between the rivers Garonne and Dordogne. Most of this territory is taken up by the appellation ENTRE-DEUX-MERS which takes in - from north to south along the banks of the Garonne - PREMIERES COTES DE BORDEAUX and BORDEAUX-SAINT-MACAIRE, LOUPIAC and SAINTE-CROIX-DU-MONT, and along the banks of the Dordogne in the north-east of the region, GRAVES DE VAYRES and SAINTE-FOY-BORDEAUX.

The right bank of the Dordogne. From the Gironde southwards, there are COTES DE BLAYE and COTES DE BOURG, then FRONSAC and CANON-FRONSAC and, finally, COTES DE CASTILLON and COTES DE FRANCS.

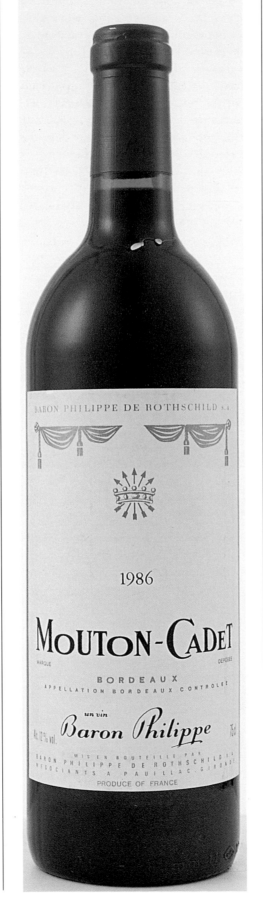

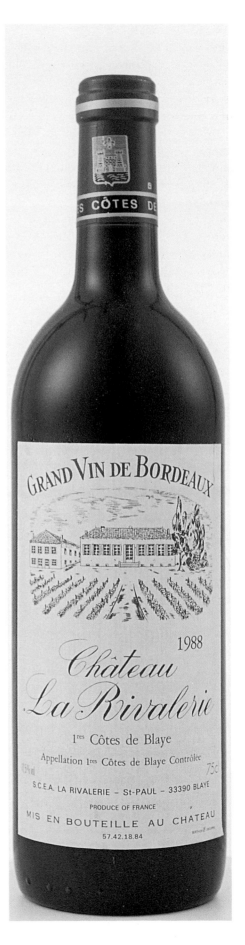

ENTRE-DEUX-MERS

The name means "between two seas", but it is really between two rivers, the Garonne and the Dordogne. The region is an extensive one, resembling an immense garden of vineyards dotted with historic monuments and archaeological remains. It produces both red and dry white wines. Nowadays, the sweet wines form only a small proportion of the total production.

Only white wines are permitted to bear the appellation ENTRE-DEUX-MERS. The red wines are divided into two categories, AOC BORDEAUX and AOC BORDEAUX SUPÉRIEUR.

It is rare in Bordeaux for a basic AOC to have two gradings in this way. This phenomenon merits closer examination for more than one reason. Firstly, there is the size of the appellation. At 48,000 hectares (118,608 acres), it represents half the vineyards in the Gironde area. Consequently, there is a whole host of minor Bordeaux wines. What is different about the Bordeaux Supérieurs?

Firstly, there are far fewer of them. They only occupy 9600 hectares (23721 acres), i.e. one-fifth of the territory. Secondly, although the grapes used are more-or-less the same as those used for minor Bordeaux (about 55% Merlot to 25% Cabernet Sauvignon, 15% Cabernet Franc and 5% Petit Verdot), the yield is more limited. In many cases, it is as low as 50 hectolitres per hectare (1100 gallons per $2^{1}/_{2}$ acres).

The wine-growers of the region have come to an arrangement whereby they submit their wines to a kind of qualifying examination. It is carried out at the Maison de la Qualité (Quality House) at Beychac-et-Caillau near Bordeaux. This establishment has a cellar that is well worth a special visit. Wines are approved or rejected on the basis of a blind tasting process. It would mean ruin, more or less, for any wine-grower if he were refused permission to use the appellation. So everyone tries extremely hard to earn the right to use, not only the appellation Bordeaux, but also to become part of the elite of Bordeaux Supérieurs. That is why, fifteen years on, Bordeaux Supérieurs deserve their name to an ever increasing extent but, at the same time, the prices remain extremely reasonable.

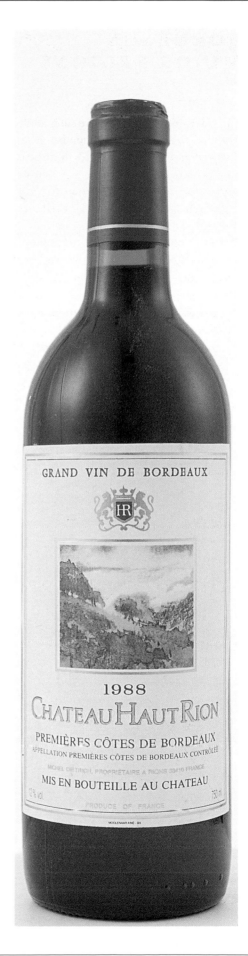

PREMIERES COTES DE BORDEAUX AND COTES DE BORDEAUX SAINT-MACAIRE

These two regions occupy a long narrow strip of land that stretches for 60 kilometres (37 miles) along the right bank of the Garonne, downstream from Bordeaux.

The northern area is given over to red wines and the southern area to white wines. The red wines are full bodied and vigorous. The white wines may be either sweet or dry. The sweet wines come from the extreme south.

One category of sweet wine is the appellation known as CADILLAC, an enclave whch produces heady, rich, fruity wines. It is less common to find such quality in Côtes de Bordeaux-Saint-Macaire. The white wines of this appellation, which range from medium-dry to sweet, have less body and bouquet.

LOUPIAC AND SAINTE-CROIX-DU-MONT

These two appellations form an extremely small enclave surrounded by Premières Côtes de Bordeaux. They are close neighbours of Sauternes, and use similar combinations of grapes. However, a higher yield is permitted in Loupiac and Sainte-Croix-du-Mont.

The sweet wines of Sainte-Croix-du-Mont achieve the higher quality. At harvest time, pourriture noble is allowed to develop, and the wines, which are less rich and full-bodied than those of Loupiac, have more finesse and richer aromas.

GRAVES DE VAYRES AND SAINTE-FOY-BORDEAUX

These two neighbouring appellations, situated to the north-east of Entre-Deux-Mers on the right bank of the Dordogne, produce both mellow and dry white wines (the dry wines, however, are never as dry as those of Entre-deux-Mers). They also produce a few reds, the best feature of these being their suppleness.

COTES DE BLAYE

Only the Gironde estuary - which is quite wide-separates this appellation from Médoc. If the red wines of Côtes de Blaye deserve a mention, the whites never seem to have achieved memorable quality.

COTES DE BOURG

The ancient fortified town of Bourg stands at the point where the Garonne meets the Dordogne. The rolling terrain that surrounds it is almost entirely covered in vineyards.

The white wines are scarcely worthy of attention, but the reds are attractively supple and rounded.

FRONSAC AND CANON-FRONSAC

The fortified village of Fronsac lies on the outskirts of Libourne, against a background of hills. The appellation AOC FRONSAC covers the wines produced on two-thirds of these hills. The remaining third, which enjoy more exposure to sunlight, belong to the appellation AOC CANON-FRONSAC.

The region is completely given over to the production of red wines, and the results are admirable; full-bodied, robust, spicy wines with plenty of flavour, wines that easily deserve to be allowed to age.

In fact, this district is the elite of all the secondary appellations of Bordeaux.

COTES DE CASTILLON AND
COTES DE FRANCS

The first of these appellations is a continuation of the Saint-Emilion district, but neither the soil nor the subsoil are of such good quality.

Furthermore, although the red wines produced here are sometimes very respectable, they cannot compare with their prestigious neighbours. In the same way, the wines of Côtes de Francs, the small adjoining region, have a rich constitution but lack finesse.

THE SATELLITES OF SAINT-EMILION

Since 1936, a few communes to the north and east of Saint-Emilion have been permitted to put the name Saint Emilion after their own names.

Five communes enjoy this privilege, and their appellations are:

Saint-Georges-Saint-Emilion
Montagne-Saint-Emilion
Lussac-Saint-Emilion
Puisseguin-Saint-Emilion
Parsac-Saint-Emilion

The best of these wines are reputedly Saint-Georges-Saint-Emilion and Montagne-Saint-Emilion, which are held to be almost as good as the produce of their prestigious neighbour. However, many growers throughout the "satellite" communes manage to produce rich, full-bodied wines with good keeping qualities,

worthy of comparison with those of Saint-Emilion. Cabernet is the predominant grape. However, where a greater proportion of Merlot is favoured, the resultant wines are at their best after aging for two years.

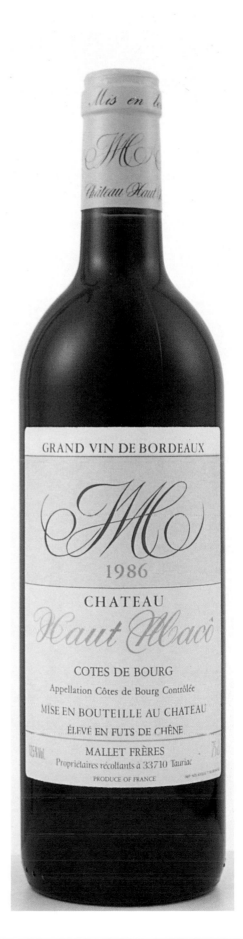

BURGUNDY

Many travellers are content to drive through Burgundy without seeing it, as they pass by on the motorway linking Paris and Lyon. In order to discover the mysteries of Burgundy, you have to turn off at Auxerre and take the minor roads.

Burgundy is probably one of the most fascinating wine-growing regions in the world. This is partly due to the region's magnificent castles and monasteries which bear witness to its glorious past, and partly on account of the vineyards (38,000 hectares (93,898 acres) of AOC vines), laid out like some huge mosaic. This peculiar characteristic, much in evidence in the départements of Yonne and Côte d'Or, becomes less pronounced as you move south into Saône-et-Loire and Rhône. In Yonne and Côte d'Or, it seems as if every little patch of suitable hillside had been carefully selected for vine-growing. This jig-saw puzzle produces a fabulous variety of wines. The fact that only two grape stocks - the Pinot Noir for red wines and the Chardonnay for white - predominate in this region, makes it seem all the more mysterious. The semi-continental climate seems to suit these grapes amazingly well. In any case, combining them with a great variety of predominantly limestone soils has something of a miraculous effect.

Yonne, the Chablis wine region.

CHABLIS

The département of Yonne covers northern Burgundy. The main appellation here is Chablis, which is exclusively reserved for dry white wines.

At one time, Chablis consisted of a vast area of 40,000 hectares (98,840 acres) of vineyards, situated between the towns of Auxerre and Tonnerre. The wines produced here were greatly appreciated by the aristocracy, and it was easy to transport them to Paris via the Yonne and the Seine. Consequently, the wine flowed so successfully that more and more had to be produced and the vineyards expanded at the expense of quality.

Then came the railways and with them a huge influx of wines from the south, which suddenly caught the Parisians' fancy. As if this were not bad enough, the phylloxera disaster then struck. Then came a series of spring frosts which the growers did not yet know how to combat. All this was enough to discourage many of the wine-growers in numerous localities around Chablis.

But the wine-growers in Chablis itself persevered. To make their products more profitable, they decided to cultivate only the best terrain. So the appellation was reduced to some 400 hectares (988 acres). This rigorous selection process produced some convincing results in terms of quality, and the wines of Chablis became even more renowned than before.

Thus the Chablis region , which now occupies 1600 hectares (3954 acres), has turned successive crises to its advantage, to such an extent that, outside France, the name is almost synonymous with great white wine. Yet another danger now confronts Chablis, namely bogus labelling and poor imitations. After all, there are so-called "American Chablis", "Australian

THE CLASSIFICATION OF CHABLIS

CHABLIS GRAND CRU

Blanchots
Bougros
The Seven Great
Les Clos
Wines of Chablis
Grenouilles
Preuses
Valmur
Vaudésir

CHABLIS PREMIERS CRUS

Monts de Milieu
Côte de Léchet
Montée de Tonnerre
Beauroy
The Fourchaume Vaucoupin
best-known Vaillons Vosgros
Montmains
Les Fourneaux
Mélinots

CHABLIS

PETIT CHABLIS

Chablis" and "Argentinian Chablis". These are but pale copies. The only thing they have in common with the authentic Burgundy wine is the grape. The Chardonnay vine is by no means everything, and even within the confines of Chablis, it gives rise to wines with highly individual personalities.

There are four different grades of Chablis. First come the Grands Crus then the Chablis Premiers Crus, followed by plain Chablis and Petit Chablis. The best Chablis comes from grapes grown in soil which is half limestone. The Upper Jurassic Kimmeridgian soils produce the crus.

A good Chablis is greenish-gold in colour. When fermented in vats, it is light and fresh. When fermented in casks, it is richer and more full-bodied. Most Chablis have a floral bouquet, but sometimes they also offer aromas of apples, almonds, hazelnuts or hay. They are vigorous, and have a characteristic bite to them.

THE GRAPES OF CHABLIS

All the wines of Chablis are made from Chardonnay grapes.

THE GRANDS CRUS

These are grown on plots of land covering a 100 hectares (247 acres) site in north-eastern Chablis. These "climates" are called:

BLANCHOTS
BOUGROS
LES CLOS
GRENOUILLES
PREUSES
VALMUR
VAUDESIR

These seven crus have incomparable status. To these should be added Chablis Moutonne. La Moutonne (a private label) straddles Preuses and Vaudesir.

On all of these plots, the yield is limited to 35 hectolitres (770 gallons).

It should also be noted that the appellation Chablis Grand Cru on a bottle label may be followed by the "climate" of origin.

THE PREMIERS CRUS

The "climates" of origin all lie within a two-and-a-half mile radius of Chablis. There are 29 in all, 11 main districts which, in turn, include 18 localities. The districts are as follows:

MONTS DE MILIEU, in the communes of Fyé and Fleys;
MONTEE DE TONNERRE, divided into Chapelot and Pied-d'Aloup, in the commune of Fyé;
FOURCHAUME, divided into Vaupulent, Côte de Fontenay, Vaulorent and L'Homme-Mort, in the communes of La Chappelle-Vaupelteigne, Poinchy, Fontenay and Maligny;
VAILLONS, which is divided into Châtains, Séché, Beugnons and Les Lys, in the commune of Chablis;
MONTMAINS, which is divided into Forêts and Butteaux, in the commune of Chablis;

MELINOTS, which is divided into Roncières and Les Epinottes, in the commune of Chablis.

COTE DE LECHET, in the commune of Mily.

BEAUROY, which is divided into Troesmes, in the communes of Poinchy and Beine;

VAUCOUPIN, in the commune of Chichée;

VOSGROS, which also includes Vaugiraut, in the commune of Chichée;

LES FOURNEAUX, which is divided into Morein and Côtes des Prés-Girots, in the commune of Fleys.

In the case of these Premiers Crus, the yield is limited to 40 hectolitres per hectare (880 gallons per 2¹/₂ acres), and the appellation Chablis Premier Cru may be followed by the name of the area of origin.

CHABLIS

The vineyards which produce ordinary Chablis are also situated around the town itself, but further out. They were able to expand into these outlying districts after the various crises that reduced the region to a few hundred hectares.

Even though the yield is limited to 40 hectolitres per hectare everywhere, the final product depends very much on the producer. There are a number of light, vigorous extra dry wines of very good quality.

PETITS CHABLIS

"Petits" Chablis deserve their name mainly on account of the mediocrity of the soils from which they come. They grow on the plots of land that are furthest away from Chablis, and are also the furthest removed from other Chablis in quality.

COTE D'OR

Côte d'Or begins just south of Dijon. It is an extraordinary mosaic of vineyards which looks as if it has been carefully arranged on a ribbon of land stretching for 50 kilometres (31 miles) along the banks of the Saône. At no point does the land measure more than a few hundred metres across.

Côte d'Or is divided into two major appellations, each occupying a distinct geographical area:

in the north there is COTE DE NUITS;

in the south there is 'COTE DE BEAUNE.

The great red and white wines for which Burgundy is famous all over the world come from this region.

As for Côte dijonnaise, which was once cultivated right up to the edge of the city of Dijon, it has almost disappeared, pushed out by advancing urbanisation. Only the communes of Marsannay and Couchay survive, and they produce red and rosé wines that make a pleasant prelude to Côte de Nuits.

Côte d'Or, the most fascinating wine-growing region.

COTE DE NUITS

The Côte de Nuits terrain stretches for 20 kilometres (12½ miles), from Fixin in the north to Corgoloin in the south. The slopes face east and overlook the Saône. The soils are extremely varied, but the subsoil is always limestone and marl.

APPELLATIONS COMMUNALES AND GRANDS CRUS OF COTE DE NUITS

Fixin
Gevrey-Chambertin Chambertin
Chambertin-Clos de Bèze
Charmes-Chambertin
Chapelle-Chambertin
Griotte-Chambertin
Latricières-Chambertin
Mazis-Chambertin
Ruchottes-Chambertin
Morey-Saint-Denis Bonnes Mares (part only)
Clos Saint-Denis
Clos de la Roche
Clos de Tart
Clos des Lambrays
Chambolle-Musigny Musigny
Bonnes Mares
Vougeot Clos de Vougeot
Flagey-Echézeaux
Vosne-Romanée Romanée-Conti
Romanée
Romanée-Saint-Vivant
La Tâche
Richebourg
Nuits-Saint-Georges

The Pinot Noir reigns supreme, and there is scarcely a white wine to be found anywhere in the region.

Every commune here is a Grand cru or a Premier cru. Some of these are so prestigious that they are known the world over. From north to south, the appellations are as follows.

FIXIN

The commune of Fixin may not be internationally famous, but it makes a splendid introduction to Côte de Nuits. It has nine Premiers Crus which all

**THE GRAPES
OF COTE DE NUITS**

*All the wines of Cote de Nuits are made
from Pinot Noir grapes.*

connoisseurs of wine agree are worthy of comparison with their prestigious neighbours from Gevrey-Chambertin.

GEVREY-CHAMBERTIN

This is the most important appellation area in Côte de Nuits. It consists of 430 hectares (1962 acres) of vineyards with 20 Premiers Crus and no less than eight Grands Crus. The finest of these, Chambertin and Chambertin-Clos de Beze, are often described as "divine" on account of their colour, bouquet, finesse and velvety texture. As for the surrounding vineyards, the wines produced here are close relatives and, on the whole, deserve the right to add their names to that of Chambertin. Hence, we have Chappelle-Chambertin, Charmes-Chambertin, Griotte-Chambertin, Latricière-Chambertin, Mazis-Chambertin and Ruchottes-Chambertin, all of them magnificent Grands Crus. Furthermore, the Premiers Crus are a worthy accompa-niment. Take Clos-Saint-Jacques, Lavaux, Les Combottes and Varoilles, for example.

MOREY-SAINT-DENIS

This area has 100 hectares (247 acres) of excellent vineyards and four Grands Crus which, strangely enough, are not very well known. It is a surprising and unjust anomaly, for Clos Saint-Denis, Clos de la Roche, Clos de Tart, Clos des Lambrays and part of Bonnes-Mares produce full-bodied, rich red wines of superb breeding. Furthermore, the 18 Premiers Crus make a pleasing accompaniment.

CHAMBOLLE-MUSIGNY

"Silk" and "lace" are two words often used when describing Chambolle-Musigny, in particular the two Grands Crus, Musigny and Bonnes Mares. These wines are like a dream, they have such finesse, grace, subtlety and delicacy. However, it should be remembered that the 200 hectares (494 acres) of vineyards that go to make up Chambolle-Musigny also include 19 Premiers Crus, including Amoureuses and Charmes, all of which vie with one another in elegance and bouquet.

VOUGEOT

The commune of Vougeot has 90 hectares (222 acres) of vineyards but only one Grand Cru, namely Clos de Vougeot which, alone, occupies 50 hectares (123 acres). Although it is surrounded by walls, dozens of growers own land within them with the result that, even though some of the wines produced there are magnificent, the quality varies from one grower to the next. At one time, the wines of Clos de Vougeot were fit to be served up to princes, but this is no longer the case.

FLAGEY-ECHEZEAUX

This commune has no appellation of its own. Nevertheless, it produces two Grands Crus, Echézeaux, which covers an area of 30 hectares (74 acres) and Grands Echézeaux. The latter occupies only 9 hectares (22 acres), but the wines it produces are of a higher class. Note that, since the wines of Echézeaux come under the appellation Vosne-Romanée, they may be labelled Vosne-Romanée Premier Cru.

VOSNE-ROMANEE

The appellation area of Vosne-Romanée covers 200 hectares (494 acres) and includes five Grands Crus. One of these is the famous Romanée-Conti, which occupies an area of only 1.8 hectares (about 4½ acres). Romanée-Conti is a legendary wine. It is prohibitively expensive and extremely rare. The estate only produces from 5000 to 10000 bottles each year, and only a few privileged people will ever get to drink them. Romanée-Conti is said to be pure velvet,

perfectly balanced and with an extra-ordinary persistence in the mouth. The praises flow, and we shall have to be content with those.

At least it is possible to get close to the king of wines, for near Romanée-Conti are Richebourg (8 hectares (20 acres)) and La Tache (6 hectares (15 acres)), which belong to the same owners. There are also La Romanée (1 hectare (2.47 acres)) and Romanée-Saint-Vivant (9.5 hectares (23 acres). All these Grands Crus are excellent and are sold at less exorbitant prices.

There are also 12 Premiers Crus which include treasures such as Grande-Rue (1.5 hectares (4 acres) adjoining Romanée-Conti) and Malconsorts (2.5 hectares (6 acres)). They too have to mature for a long time, though not as long as Romanée-Conti-about eight to ten years-and they are still rare. The vineyards of Vosne-Romanée are only big in terms of quality.

NUITS-SAINT-GEORGES

The 375 hectares (926 acres) of this appellation extend to the neighbouring commune of Prémeaux.

The southern plots produce the most robust, full-bodied wines. Although there is no Grand Cru, there are nearly 40 Premiers Crus. Connoisseurs of wine usually agree that the best of these is Saint-Georges (7.5 hectares (18 acres)), which produces powerful, well-rounded wines, and Vaucrains (6 hectares (15 acres)). Both of these are wines that keep well.

COTE-DE-NUITS-VILLAGES

This is a sub-regional appellation, a kind of consolation prize awarded to five communes situated at either end of Côte de Nuits. It consists of Fixin (which also has its own appellation) and Brochon in the north, and Prissey, Comblanchien (which is also famous for its marble) and Corgoloin in the south.

In all, there are 320 hectares (790 acres), from which the yield is limited to 35 hectolitres (646 gallons) per hectare. Red wines predominate, and these are fruity and relatively light.

COTE DE BEAUNE

Côte de Beaune is a long strip of land, a continuation of the Côte de Nuits which also hugs the banks of the Saône . The vineyards cover the hillsides and occupy an area of 3000 hectares (7413 acres), nearly double that of Côtes de Nuits.

The landscape here is less austere, with its gently sloping hills. Some areas have a pebbly clay and limestone soil, coloured with iron salts, and this makes them extremely suitable for producing red wines. In other areas, there are light-coloured marls, ideal for white wines. Accordingly, one finds both Pinot Noir and Chardonnay stocks.

Here we have the two foremost grapes in Burgundy, and yet they only produce two Grands Crus, Corton (red) and Montrachet (white). Yet this does not mean Côte de Beaune is a kind of poor relation. To say that would be to dismiss too hastily the many Premiers Crus. These include some extremely great red wines and, more important still, dry white wines, which are reputed to be the best in the world.

However, the wines of Côte de Beaune are not very approachable. The number of plots is enormous, and it is difficult to find one's way around them, a problem which is exacerbated by the fact that there are scarcely any signs. How can one tell where one Cru ends and another begins? There are no signboards to tell you. However, as in Côte de Nuits, each commune has its own mosaic of vineyards with definite frontiers. From north to south these are.

APPELLATIONS COMMUNALES AND GRANDS CRUS OF COTE DE BEAUNE

Ladoix- Corton-Charlemagne Corton
Aloxe-Corton*
Aloxe-Corton Corton Corton
Corton-Charlemagne
Charlemagne
Pernand-Vergelesses* Corton Corton
Corton-Charlemagne
Charlemagne
Savigny-les-Beaune*
Chorey-les-Beaune*
Beaune
Pommard
Volnay
Monthélie*
Auxey-Duresses*
Saint-Romain*
Meursault*
Puligny-Montrachet* Montrachet
Chevalier-Montrachet
Bâtard-Montrachet
Bienvenues-Bâtard
Montrachet
Chassagne-Montrachet* Montrachet
Bâtard-Montrachet
Criots-Bâtard-Montrachet
Saint-Aubin*
Santenay*
Cheilly-les-Maranges*
Dezize-les-Maranges*
Sampigny-les-Maranges*

* The red wines of 15 appellations of Cote de Beaune may be sold under the appellation of Côte de Beaune-Villages. Those in question have been marked with an asterisk.

LADOIX-SERRIGNY

This commune marks the beginning of Côte de Beaune. It is also the beginning of the Grand Cru of Corton. The name of the latter is sufficiently prestigious to have eclipsed that of its first place of origin.

In any case, Ladoix-Serrigny is condemned to modesty. The four Premiers Crus, namely, La Maréchaude, La Toppe-au-Vert, La Coutière, Les Petites Lolières and Les Grandes Lolières, now bear the name of Aloxe-Corton instead.

ALOXE-CORTON AND PERNAND VERGELESSES

The majority of the wines of Corton come from these two communes. The Corton group is a prestigious one. It consists of red wines plus some rare, but quite extraordinary whites. The white wines are Corton-Charlemagne, Charlemagne and the extremely rare Corton wine.

As far as red wines are concerned, the only appellation that exists is Corton followed by the name of the cru of origin, for example, Corton-Clos du Roi, Corton Bressandes and Corton-Renardes.

Now that these landmarks have been indicated, all that remains is to wish all wine lovers the privilege of tasting these wines. Firstly, the white wines. These come from vineyards which, unusually, have a southern exposure. These white wines are powerful and full-bodied and a beautiful gold in colour. They have a splendid bouquet, which often contains a scent of almonds. Red Cortons are also

THE GRAPES
OF COTES DE BEAUNE

All the wines of Cote de Beaune are made from Pinot Noir grapes.

among the most illustrious wines of Burgundy. They are always a deep garnet colour and prove to be rich, powerful and full-bodied, with aromas of ripe or cooked, soft fruit.

Many of these wines could put a Premier Cru in the shade, and what is more, their excellent quality is enhanced by being decidedly more affordable.

SAVIGNY-lès-BEAUNE

The vast majority of the wines of Savigny-lès-Beaune are red, but there are a few white ones too. The area covers 380 hectares (940 acres) and is divided into two distinct areas, situated to the north and south of a small river called the Rhoin. The wines produced in the south, and therefore closer to Beaune, are light and reputed to be of inferior quality to those produced in the north, which is closer to Aloxe-Corton. The latter are a lovely pale ruby-colour. They are rich and full-bodied, particularly if they come from certain plots such as Lès Vergelesses, Les Dominodes, Lavières and Les Marconnets, which have a good reputation.

CHOREY-les-BEAUNE

This little commune, which stands to the east of Savigny-lès-Beaune is distinguished first and foremost by its beautiful château. But there are no crus here. The vineyards are situated on a plain and are exposed to too much sunlight to enable them to produce great wines, although the wines do have a certain charm.

BEAUNE

As far as the wines of Burgundy are concerned, Beaune is the historic capital and also a major trading centre. It is a town to be visited, and not just for the famous hospices. That would mean ignoring the 500 hectares (1235 acres) of vineyards. The crus of the north near Savigny, in particular, produce red wines of extremely good breeding. Especially noteworthy are Beaune-lès-Grèves, Les Marconnets, Clos du Roi, Clos des Fèves, Les Cent Vignes and Les Bressandes.

However, the more southerly vineyards, near Pommard, also deserve a mention. The pale colour of the wines produced here is in keeping with their suppleness and delicate, fruity flavour.

POMMARD

At one time, the English were so taken with the wines of Pommard that neighbouring communes used to sell wine to them under the same appellation, and the name became almost a synonym for red Burgundy.

The 340 hectares (840 acres) of vineyards are, in fact, worthy of a good deal of attention. Let us begin with the vineyards of Les Epénots and Rugiens, situated to the west of the motorway, which produce exceptionally powerful wines.

Despite their rich constitution and high alcohol content, the other Premiers Crus (21 in all) are usually a little more delicate and their character a little less definite.

VOLNAY

Just as a Corton is assertive in its power and robustness, a Volnay plays on its femininity, elegance and delicate nature. Basically, it is to Côte de Beaune as Chambolle-Musigny is to Côte de Nuits, in other words, the finest of its jewels.

The 220 hectares (544 acres) of vineyards do not include a Grand Cru. Nevertheless, Les Caillerets perhaps deserves the title, as do certain other Premiers Crus, for example Champans, Bousse d'Or and a host of others.

The wines of Volnay have one other virtue. They can be drunk while still quite young and rather fresh.

MONTHELIE

Monthelie, with its 130 hectares (383 acres) of vineyards, deserves to be much better known. It boasts one veritable jewel, namely Champs-Fulliot, which forms an extension of Les Caillerets and is one of the best crus in Volnay.

AUXEY-DURESSES

This appellation grows two-thirds Pinot Noir to one-third Chardonnay stocks in a total area of 160 hectares (395 acres). The vineyards face directly southwards. On the one hand, the area produces red wines that are rather reminiscent of Volnay but on the other, it produces white wines that are almost a prelude to the great wines of Meursault.

The best terrains in the area are Les Duresses, Reugne and La Chapelle.

SAINT-ROMAIN

The village of Saint-Romain, which huddles beneath the ruins of its own castle, is extremely pretty, but, unfortunately, it does not produce a single Premier Cru, even though the quality of the white wines is more than respectable. This should be remembered if you notice the name Saint-Romain on a Côte de Beaune-Villages label. The commune is permitted to use this appellation.

MEURSAULT

This area, with its 420 hectares (1038 acres) of vineyards, is the home of some fabulous white wines. So, it does not really matter that the best plots, namely Genevrière, Perrières, Charmes, Goutte d'Or and Les Poruzots, do not enjoy the status of Grands Crus. They are famous just the same for their luxurious, bright, greenish-gold wines. These are both dry and mellow. The aromas are intense, those of hazelnut and almond predominating.

Red wines are rarer in Meursault, and most of them are legally sold under the name of Volnay.

PULIGNY-MONTRACHET AND CHASSAGNE-MONTRACHET

Although these two communes both belong to the illustrious Montrachet family, they are not identical. The first produces mainly white wines, while the second is dedicated mainly to reds.

The two communes share some Grands Crus, but the rest belong exclusively to one or the other.

The following belong entirely to Puligny:

Chevalier-Montrachet (7 hectares (17 acres)), a perfectly balanced white with a subtle bouquet.

Bienvenues-Bâtard-Montrachet (3 hectares (7 acres)), also has great finesse, but the flavour is perhaps slightly less concentrated.

The following belong to both Puligny and Chassagne:

Montrachet (7.5 hectares (18 acres), often described as the greatest white wine in the world. The vines grow half-way up the hillsides, and the soils, which are of silica, clay and limestone, are reddened with iron oxide. They yield a distinguished, light-coloured wine with plenty of bouquet. It manages to be mellow and vigorous at the same time. In other words, a true aristocrat.

Bâtard-Montrachet (12 hectares (30 acres) is situated just below Montrachet. Although not so subtle and well-rounded, the wines produced here are equally rich and powerful. The bouquet is characterized by the aroma of toast.

Finally, the following belongs entirely to Chassagne:

Criots-Bâtard-Montrachet (1.5 hectares (3¹/₂ acres)) produces a single white wine, which is powerful and fruity just as it should be, given that the vineyards face due south.

These great wines should not be allowed to overshadow the Premiers Crus, particularly those of Puligny, for example, Folatières, Clos de la Garenne, Les Colombettes and Les Pucelles.

SAINT-AUBIN

The commune of Saint-Aubin and the neighbouring village of Gamay produce mainly red wines. Simple and light, they are sold under the appellation Côte de Beaune-Villages.

SANTENAY

The vineyards of Santenay occupy an area of 400 hectares (988 acres). The bulk of the production consists of enjoyable red wines. Although not especially full, these have a pleasantly robust character. A number of the Grands Crus are most attractive, such as Les Gravières, La Comme and Les Maladières.

CHEILLY, DEZIZE AND SAMPIGNY-les-MARANGES

The last three villages in Côte de Beaune share a Premier Cru, that of Maranges. They produce well-structured, colourful red wines almost all of which are all sold together simply under the name of Côte de Beaune-Villages. However, many of them are as attractive in quality as they are in price.

COTE CHALONNAISE

This area is usually called the "région de Mercurey" nowadays, because the town of Châlon is no longer a great wine-shipping port as it was in the days of the Empire, and Côte Chalonnaise does not exist as an appellation. Nevertheless the region, which stretches for 25 kilometres (15½ miles) beyond Côte de Beaune, has a number of interesting vineyards.

The vineyards are more scattered than in Côte de Beaune, and they do not keep to the eastern slopes of the hills to such a great extent. However, the soil characteristics are quite similar to those of Côte de Beaune, so the red and white wines of both regions are closely related.

Five communes have their own appellations:

RULLY
Situated in the north of Côte Châlonnaise, this commune produces extremely good red wines, though it owes its reputation mainly to whites. Made from a mixture of Aligote and Chardonnay, the latter are quite acid, and therefore suitable to be subjected to a second in-bottle fermentation or "prise de mousse", as a result of which they make excellent quality "crémants", or slightly-sparkling wines.

MERCUREY

This appellation covers 600 hectares (1483 acres) and is spread over two communes. The bulk of the production consists of red wines. These are of excellent quality because they come from Pinot Noir grapes grown in a soil which consists of clay, limestone and iron. Thus they have the same characteristics as many Côte de Beaune-Villages.

GIVRY

Like Mercurey, this commune is basically dedicated to the production of red wines. The appellation area is far smaller than that of Mercurey and far less famous, but the wines it produces are important just the same. In some cases, they even turn out to have a higher tannin content than the wines of Mercurey, and this makes them more suitable for keeping.

MONTAGNY

The white wines of Montagny are exclusive to this one commune. Made from Chardonnay, they are usually light, and some of them have a considerable degree of finesse. Several areas have the right to call themselves Premiers Crus, but they modestly and discreetly refrain from putting this on their labels.

MACONNAIS

This appellation stretches from Tournus to Macon, a distance of nearly 50 kilometres (31 miles). It is a transitional area just before south Burgundy. The vineyards are situated on hillsides, surrounded by meadows and forests. Many of the villages have beautiful Romanesque churches and this makes the region even more attractive. Maconnais is known first and foremost for its white wines, and justly so. Made from Chardonnay, some of them are excellent. The red wines, on the other hand, do not have such a good reputation. Some are made from Pinot, some from Gamay and some from a mixture of the two.

So the region has a varied output, and this explains why there are five specific appellations.

The first three apply to both red and white wines and are listed in ascending order of quality:

> *Macon*
>
> *Macon Superieur*
>
> *Macon + the name of any one of 43 authorised communes*

The other two appellations apply exclusively to white wines, and the fame of Maconnais rests entirely upon them. They are as follows:

> *The POUILLY wines, from the communes of POUILLY FUISSE, POUILLY LOCHE and POUILLY-VINZELLES.*

Produced exclusively from Chardonnay stock and grown in a limestone soil, the Pouilly wines are pale gold tinged with green. They are extremely dry, and yet silky at the same time. Furthermore, they are quite vigorous, and will keep for two to three years. The best ones, which come from Pouilly Fuissé, will keep for even longer.

SAINT-VERAN

The appellation SAINT-VERAN applies to the dry, light white wines of eight communes. Although produced in the same conditions as the wines of the Pouilly group, these are lighter and do not have such a characteristic bouquet. They are simple wines and should be consumed while young and fresh.

BEAUJOLAIS

The inhabitants of Lyon are always quick to say that their city has a third river besides the Rhône and the Saône, namely the Beaujolais. And it is true that the wine of Beaujolais flows like water. It is usually served in pitchers.

Beaujolais is, in fact, the largest wine-growing area in Burgundy. It covers an area of 22000 hectares (54,363 acres), that is to say just over half the total area of AOCs. The crests of the hills are covered in vineyards all the way from south Macon to the outskirts of Lyon.

CLASSIFICATION:

Beaujolais wines are graded into three levels of quality, which is ascending order, are as follows:
BEAUJOLAIS
BEAUJOLAIS SUPERIEUR;
BEAUJOLAIS-VILLAGE;
THE CRUS:
Brouilly,
Chénas,
Chiroubles,
Côte de Brouilly,
Fleurie,
Juliénas,
Morgon,
Moulin à Vent,
Régnié,
Saint-Amour.

There are two types of terrain:
> *"Haut-Beaujolais" (Upper Beaujolais) in the north has a soil composed of granite and fragments of schist. It is here, in the area of the Villages and Crus, that the best wines are produced.*
> *"Bas Beaujolais" (Lower Beaujolais) in the south, on the other hand, has a clay and limestone soil. It is here that the more humble Beaujolais are made.*

All over the region, white and rosé wines are relegated to the role of extras. Beaujolais is completely dominated by red wines, all of them made from the Gamay Noir à jus blanc (Gamay Noir with white juice) grapes.

The Gamay yields purplish, pleasantly fruity wines. These are so light that Beaujolais has long been the French vin de café par excellence, served in bottles and carafes in all the bars in France.

The current fame enjoyed by Beaujolais is due to the combined astuteness of wine-growers and marketing experts. First of all, the growers had the idea of perfecting a special vinification process that would use the Gamay to the best advantage. It is a method largely based on the principle of

THE GRAPES OF BEAUJOLAIS

A single grape variety is used for the Beaujolais wines, the Gamay Noir.

carbonic maceration.

Not only does this method ensure that the Gamay retains all its fruitiness, it also makes for speedier production, and the resultant wines, the famous "Beaujolais Primeurs" are best consumed very young. They may be sold from November 15 of each year, a date which is now joyfully celebrated thanks to blatant but astute marketing techniques.

The advertisements scream out all over the world that the Beaujolais Nouveau has arrived! Whole planeloads take off for London, Brussels and New York, and the festivities commence.

However, to be more precise, it is Beaujolais Primeur, (not Beaujolais Nouveau) which is consumed on November 15 and which may remain on sale under that appellation until January 31. The term "Beaujolais Nouveau" more usually applies to Beaujolais which may be sold in the year following the harvest, up until August 31. Inevitably, the success of Beaujolais means that the quality has become erratic to say the least. At best, it is the simple, lively wine for festive occasions. At worst it will give you a terrible hangover! At any rate, such is the case with ordinary Beaujolais and Beaujolais Superieurs. The quality of the 10 crus of Beaujolais is much more consistent, and that of Beaujolais-Villages even more so. There are no less than 35 of the latter, and they are to be found distributed here and there among the crus.

THE CRUS OF BEAUJOLAIS

The yield here is limited to 40 hectolitres per hectare (880 gallons per 2½ acres), as opposed to 50 (1100 gallons) or more for the bulk of ordinary Beaujolais. The wines produced are capable of maturing for between two and five years. Each cru has its own distinctive personality. From north to south, they are as follows.

SAINT-AMOUR

The wine is as alluring as its name. It should not be kept waiting more than about two years, after which time it is at its most supple and fruity.

JULIENAS

The fruity wine of Julienas is one of the most robust Beaujolais. The tannin content enables it to age for longer than the wine of Saint-Amour.

CHENAS

Like Juliénas, this wine is very full-bodied and can appear surprisingly vigorous.

MOULIN-A-VENT

There is no village of this name and the cru is, in fact, divided between the communes of Chénas and Romanèches-Thorins. Its wine has enough class to suggest, as it ages, a thoroughbred Burgundy and it stands out as the most corpulent and flavoursome of the Beaujolais crus.

FLEURIE

This wine is as elegant and fresh as its name suggests and indeed has a very floral bouquet. Light and delicate from its first year onwards, as it ages it acquires a very gentle smoothness. However, it is too enticing for impatient enthusiasts to wait two or three years before drinking it.

CHIROUBLES

A supple, fruity and balanced wine, which is generally regarded as being of reliably good quality.

MORGON

This wine has substance and is particularly well suited to laying down.

REGNIE

Formerly a "village", Régnié has been admitted to the ranks of the crus since 1988, a promotion it deserves on account of its supple fruitiness.

BROUILLY

This is an extensive cru with a high level of production. The wine has undeniable vigour and all the flavour characteristic of the Gamay vine. It needs to be aged for two years.

COTE DE BROUILLY

Harvested on the slopes of the Mont Brouilly, the wine testifies to the sunny aspect of the terrain in its full-bodied character, which finds its best expression after three to four years in the bottle.

THE JURA
AND SAVOIE

This region, which lies to the east of Burgundy, is probably better known to the public at large for its cross-country skiing than for its wines. The vineyards were established at the time of the Roman Conquest and cover an area of 1200 hectares (2965 acres), divided up into a large number of small plots scattered among forests and pastureland.

THE APPELLATIONS
OF THE JURA

There are five regional AOC's: Côte du Jura, Arbois, Arbois Pupillin, L'Etoile and Château-Chalon (which only produces vin jaune).

JURA

The vines are planted on limestone hills at an average height of 1000 feet, and are well enough exposed to tolerate the rigours of winter. Their production remains very diversified. One finds, for instance, fairly pale red wines, made from Poulsard stock, sometimes with the addition of Pinot Noir. There are also some rosés, but, above all, there are dry whites and sparkling whites from Chardonnay vines (which are called the "Melon d'Arbois" here) and two very unusual specialities of the region, vin jaune (yellow wine) and vin de paille (straw wine).

Vin jaune, which is rare and expensive, because it is produced in small quantities, is a speciality of the Jura. It originates mostly from the Château-Chalon district, it is made from the Savagnin (or "Naturé") vine and is subjected to a process of vinification similar to that of sherry. After the normal vinification into white wine of the grapes - which are harvested at a state of advanced ripeness, the wine obtained is transferred into barrels which have previously contained vin jaune. It remains there for at least six years, during which the film of yeast which forms on the surface protects it from oxidation. At the same time, the colour develops as does a

very characteristic taste, the "goût de jaune", which is very reminiscent of walnuts. Vin jaune is sold in small bottles with a capacity of 62 cl (slightly more than one imperial pint or 1¼ American pints). It is best served at room temperature and proves to be of exceptional longevity, retaining its qualities after more than a century.

THE GRAPES OF THE JURA

For the reds:
Poulsard, Trousseau and Pinot Noir.
For the whites:
Savagnin, Chardonnay and Pinot.
For the "yellows":
Savagnin (also called Naturé).

As for vin de paille, it owes its name to the fact that, after a late harvest, the white grapes are placed on racks (formerly made of straw) in a ventilated room. In three to four months, the bunches of grapes lose nearly 50% of their weight and their sugar content becomes concentrated. After the pressing, a very slow fermentation produces a syrupy wine, sold in 32.5 cl (nearly half an imperial pint or just over half an American pint) bottles, and also capable of being kept indefinitely.

SAVOIE

Along the course of the Rhône, from Lake Geneva to the Val d'Isère, 1500 hectares (3706 acres) of vines are scattered over the foothills of the Alps to the great delight of the skiers.

The Mondeuse is the local vine which is nowadays grown with Pinot and Gamay to produce fairly plain red wines which should be drunk slightly chilled. However, the whites usually form the greater part of the production. For these, the Roussette (or "Altesse") is the dominant vine, but the Jacquère, the Molette, and the Chasselas (the Swiss "fendant") should also be mentioned. Many of the mainly dry and lively white wines produced in Savoie are often sparkling or "perlant", in other words, they have a natural tendency to effervescence.

THE COTES
DU RHONE

Many great French rivers accommodate great vineyards along their banks. This is also true of the Rhône, whose steep slopes are covered with vines over a distance of 200 km (124 miles) and an area of 42,000 hectares (103,782 acres), from the commune of Vienne to that of Avignon.

This vineyard is one of the oldest in France, since the Phoenicians, followed by the Romans, grew vines in the Rhône valley, a traditional route for invasions and trading. However, in modern times, the wines of the region have sometimes suffered from a less than flattering image. This is quite unjustified. Fortunately this tendency has been reversed today and many enthusiasts now pay homage to the strength and richness of the Grands Crus, which deserve to be included among the best wines of France.

The vineyards are divided into two regions corresponding to quite different types of soil and climate:

The Northern Côtes-du-Rhône, from Vienne to Valence, have predominantly granite soil, hot summers and autumns and a significant degree of humidity regulated by the river.

About 25 miles further south, around Avignon, Orange and Châteauneuf-du-Pape, the southern Côtes-du-Rhône have sandy soil containing an abundance of gravelly alluvial deposits and drift boulders. This is an area of summer drought, exacerbated by that violent wind, the mistral.

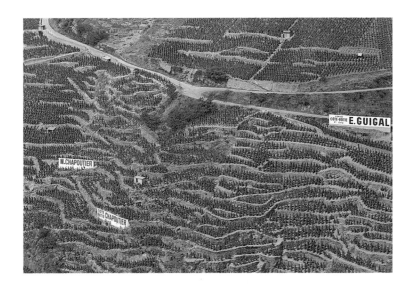

Côtes du Rhône, the Cerdon vineyard.

THE NORTHERN VINEYARDS

The wine-growers of this region have one thing in common, namely their unbending loyalty to the Syrah, the only vine used for all the red wines. It produces a dark, tannic wine with concentrated aromas. As for the whites, they are produced either from the Viognier vine alone, or from the Marsanne and the Roussane, usually combined. Almost all the glories of the Côtes-du-Rhône are represented here, with ten AOC's, some of them quite capable of competing with the most prestigious vineyards of the Bordeaux region or Burgundy.

THE "VILLAGES" OF THE COTES-DU-RHONE

The following communes benefit from a "Villages" appellation:

In the département of Vaucluse: Beaumes-de-Venise, Cairanne, Rasteau, Roaix, Sablet, Seguret, Vacqueyras, Valéras, Visan.

In the département of Drôme: Rochegude, St Maurice-sur-Eygues, Rousset-les-Vignes, St Pantalon-les-Vignes.

In the département of Gard: Laudun, Chusclan, St Gervais.

COTE ROTIE

This vineyard which covers an area of 70 hectares (173 acres) lies on the west bank of the Rhône, four miles from Vienne and above the village of Ampuis. It is divided into terraces on the steep slopes of two quite distinct hills: the Côte Brune and the Côte Blonde. Both are mainly planted with

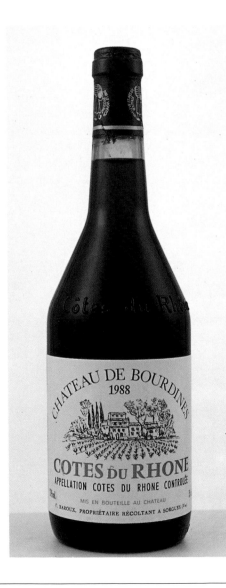

the Syrah vine, though, paradoxically, a little room is left for Viognier, a white vine which brings a little suppleness and delicacy to the bouquet.

Dark red, heady, strong wines with sumptuous bouquets are created by blending and aging in oak casks. It is considered heretical not to leave them for at least five years and preferably more.

CONDRIEU AND CHATEAU GRILLET

Three miles from Ampuis, the commune of Condrieu controls 12 hectares (30 acres) of vineyards on steep terraces. These are planted exclusively with the Viognier vine, which produces a magnificent white wine here. Sometimes dry, sometimes medium-sweet, it displays a golden colour and presents a fine bouquet of flowers and spices. In fact, its only fault is its rarity, since production is limited and almost monopolized by the great restaurants of the region.

Rarer still is Château Grillet, which is confined to 2 hectares (5 acres) enclosed within the area of the Condrieu appellation. The wine is said to possess a greater level of finesse, but it is difficult to confirm this. The sole proprietor sells almost all his bottles singly.

HERMITAGE AND CROZES-HERMITAGE

Formerly the favourite of the great and powerful of this world, Hermitage manages to maintain an excellent level of quality. Its 125-hectare (309-acre) vineyard, is planted in terraces above the commune of Tain-L'Hermitage. The grape varieties are Syrah, producing generous red wines with substance, and Marsanne and Roussanne for the whites. Mellow and dry without acidity, the latter may, like the reds, be kept for a long time.

As for the 500 hectares (1235 acres) of Crozes-Hermitage surrounding the preceding appellation area, they also produce reds and whites which, although lighter, are quite often similar to the Hermitage wines.

SAINT-JOSEPH

On the west bank of the Rhône, opposite Hermitage and planted with

THE GRAPES OF COTES DU RHONE

The Syrah is the only vine used for the red wines. The whites are made from the Viognier, Roussane and Marsanne vines.

the same vines, lie some 150 hectares (370 acres) of vineyard occupying less granitic and less steep terrain. The reds and whites are thus lighter and more supple, so that they can easily make do with only five years of aging.

CORNAS

This vineyard opposite the town of Valence in the foothills of the Cévennes is limited to 55 hectares (136 acres) planted with the Syrah vine. Its wine, which is very dark if it has been well vinified and indeed a little hard when still young, generally has a corpulence which makes it an ideal accompaniment for game.

SAINT-PERAY

Very close to Cornas, on some arid hills, the 56 hectares (138 acres) of Saint-Péray are planted with Marsanne and Roussane, producing an effervescent white wine, more rounded and fruitier than many Champagnes. Since it is still rare, this excellent aperitif wine is not very widely known.

CLAIRETTE DE DIE AND CHATILLON-EN-DIOIS

On the north bank of the Drôme, this vineyard produces an effervescent white wine from the Clairette and Muscat vines. It is called "traditional" (not to be confused with the "brut"), and proves to be a very pleasant aperitif with a marked aroma of apples. Upstream of Die lies Châtillon, a recent AOC which produces simple and light red and white wines.

THE SOUTHERN VINEYARDS

Between Montélimar and Avignon, everything changes - not only the soil and climate, but even the vines grown here. The region is the domain of the Côtes-du-Rhône and the Côtes-du-Rhône-Villages. All the prestige thus falls to a small number of key appellations, essentially Châteauneuf-du-Pape and Gigondas.

CHATEAUNEUF-DU-PAPE

Its 3,000 hectares (7,413 acres) make Chateauneuf-du-Pape the largest appellation district in the Côtes-du-Rhône. The popes of Avignon were originally responsible for introducing the cultivation of the vine on these vast hills, on which the soil is buried beneath a layer of drift pebbles suited to the accumulation of heat. Unusually, 13 types of vine are authorized here. Although the yield for both red and white wines is limited to 35 hectolitres (770 gallons), the vineyard is vast enough to provide an abundant production, encompassing both the best and the not-so-good. The fact remains that a traditional Châteauneuf-du-Pape is an ample, rich and full wine, which gains greatly in smoothness as it ages. Thus the present tendency of some producers to make use of carbonic maceration is regrettable; even if they are more immediately pleasing, such wines nevertheless lose in presence and body.

GIGONDAS

This vineyard covers an area of 1,000 hectares (2471 acres), whose soil presents characteristics similar to those of Châteauneuf-du-Pape. Thirteen types of vine are also authorized here, but only Grenache, Cinsaut, Syrah, Mourvèdre and Clairette are actually used. The reds, which constitute the great majority, are not unlike those of Châteauneuf-du-Pape, though with less richness and complexity.

Among the other southern AOC's LIRAC and TAVEL are noteworthy as dry rosés with a fine bouquet when they are carefully produced. Finally, among the Côtes-du-Rhône Villages, special mention should be made of RASTEAU, particularly for its sweet aperitif wines, and BEAUMES-DE-VENISE for its magnificent Muscat.

THE 13 GRAPES OF CHATEAUNEUF-DU-PAPE

The most widespread are Grenache and Cinsaut. Next come Syrah, Mourvèdre, Clairette and Picpoul, followed in turn by the Muscardin, Vaccarèse, Cournoise, Piccardin, Roussane, Terret Noir and Bourboulenc.

PROVENCE
AND THE MIDI

From Toulon to Marseille and Aix-en-Provence, the heat of the Mediterranean climate stimulates the thirst to such an extent that most wine-growers devote themselves as a priority to the production of rosé wines to be served well-chilled. In fact, nothing sells better during the peak tourist periods.

Thus the vast vineyard of the Côtes-de-Provence, which covers nearly 20,000 hectares (49, 420 acres) and was recently granted the status of an AOC, has increasingly reduced its production of reds. The recent effort by some owners to introduce vines from the Bordeaux region must be welcomed, because some promising reds have thus been produced. There are four important appelations for the whole of Provence, despite their restricted area. Firstly there is BANDOL, covering 500 hectares (1235 acres) and dominated by the Mourvèdre vine. It

produces the most harmonious tannic red wines of the region. On the other hand, CASSIS, near Marseille, is notable mainly for its dry, fruity white wine. The small (20 hectare (50 acre)) area of PALETTE, near Aix-en-Provence, also produces some fresh and distinguished whites, as well as some well-structured reds. Finally, BELLET (40 hectares (98 acres) overlooking Nice) produces red, white and rosé wines which are superior in their finesse to those of the surrounding district.

CORSICA

In the 1960s, after the Algerian War, the wine production of Corsica, which is also known to the French as the Ile de Beauté (island of beauty) underwent a revival when expatriate French settlers arrived on the island. The local Sciacarello and Niellucia vines now stand side by side with Grenache and Cinsaut, producing full-bodied reds and rosés with a strong constitution. More rarely, it is possible to find a few dry whites of good quality.

Of Corsica's seven AOC's, Patrimonio is the oldest and is still the best.

THE GRAPES OF PROVENCE

Many of the vines of the Côtes-du-Rhône are to be found in this region also. The Carignan, Cinsaut, Grenache and Mourvèdre vines are responsible for the red and rosé wines. As for the whites, they are made from the Sauvignon, the Clairette and the Ugni Blanc varieties.

LANGUEDOC-ROUSSILLON

France's largest wine-producing area extends from the Rhône delta to the Spanish border, along the arc of the Mediterranean coastline.

Until the mid-60s, the most of the production consisted of red vins ordinaires, which were as light in colour as they were in alcohol and were mainly destined for blending. However, for the last fifteen years or so, the region has been aiming at quality with increasing resolution, first by uprooting a large amount of the high-yielding vines and the selection of aromatic stocks, and secondly by the increasing use of carbonic maceration in the vinification process. This method is suitable for young wines since it accentuates their fruitiness. In view of increasing competition from elsewhere in Europe, this trend is tending to accelerate.

The region now has no less than 97 vins de pays and about 20 VDQS wines.

In this last category, the vast area of the Corbières (which stretches from Narbonne to Carcassone right up to the outskirts of Perpignan) merits particular mention because of its pleasant, popular red wines. The Corbières nevertheless have a direct rival in the Minervois, where merchants such as Chantovent have opened up the way to voluntary selection and are setting an example in terms of quality.

We must also mention the Costières du Gard (to the south of Nîmes) and, within the vast area of the Coteaux du Languedoc, vineyards like La Clape and Saint-Chinian. However, it is the regional AOC's which are the most deserving of attention. The most famous apply to the Vins Doux Naturels (sweet red wines) produced at BANYULS, MAURY and RIVESALTES,

THE GRAPES OF LANGUEDOC-ROUSSILLON

For the white wines:
Clairette, Picpoul, Mauzac, Ugni Blanc, Listan, Bourboulenc and Terret.
For the red wines:
Grenache, Carignan, Aramon, Cinsaut, Syrah, Mourvèdre, Alicante and Bouchet.
For the sweet and syrupy wines:
Grenache, Malvoisie, Maccabéu and Muscat.

three wines which have achieved excellence. Although in France itself these wines suffer from being sold almost exclusively in the larger supermarkets, one should not be misled by their poor image, because they actually deserve the prestige of the greatest port wines. Muscat d'Alexandre, Malvoisie (Malmsey), Maccabéu and Grenache are the four grape varieties which ensure the richness of their bouquet.

The other gems of this region are the Muscats. The best come from the AOC's of FRONTIGNAN, LUNEL, MIREVAL and SAINT-JEAN-DU-MINERVOIS. Based exclusively on the Muscat grape, these sweet wines are excellent both as an aperitif and with dessert.

There are also two AOC's for the red wines of FITOU and COLLIOURE, robust wines with a deep garnet colour with a full-bodied quality that surpasses their finesse. The whites also have three AOC's. Apart from CLAIRETTE DE BELLEGARDE and CLAIRETTE DU LANGUEDOC, an unusual wine should also be mentioned. It is BLANQUETTE DE LIMOUX, a good sparkling wine made from the Mauzac vine, sometimes marked by fruitiness and elegance.

THE SOUTH WEST

The various vineyards of south-western France are scattered over a wide area from the east of Bordeaux to the south near the Spanish border. They have original and strong personalities and generally benefit from a generous amount of sunshine. These wines have enough body to accompany the rich local cusine, dominated by the famous goose or duck preserve and foie gras. Although some are close neighbours to the wines of Bordeaux, they are in no way copies of them, and this is especially true in the southernmost areas, which have their own types of vine.

BERGERAC

The small town of Bergerac, near Bordeaux, is surrounded by a large vineyard which has nine AOC's all to itself. For three centuries, Bergerac, like its illustrious neighbour, took advantage of the brisk trade afforded by the English occupation and was thus long looked upon as an undesirable competitor.

At the time, most of its success was based on mellow or syrupy white wines. Today, despite the fact that they have generally fallen out of favour with the public, some AOC's, headed by MONBAZILLAC, continue to produce them from the vines of Bordeaux (Sémillon, Sauvignon and Muscadelle). If they are well made, their bouquet of honey and flowers and their suitability for laying down make them wines of a very good quality.

The reds produced by the AOC's of BERGERAC and PECHARMANT are generally ample and generous wines. On the other hand, the dry whites of Bergerac or the MONTRAVEL AOC are of less interest.

COTES DU BUZET

The Bordeaux vines (Carbernets, Malbec and Merlot) in the département of Lot-et-Garonne, around the town of Agen, are also grown in this fine vineyard which covers undulating hills. In this region, almost all the wine producers have formed cooperatives and mainly produce red wine, whose quality/price ratio makes them most attractive.

CAHORS

For the last 15 years, this vineyard, which lies downstream from the town of Cahors, on both banks of the Lot, has been developing a policy of quality which is now bearing fruit. The Malbec is the dominant vine here. It gives the wine its dark, almost black, colour. This wine, which used to be very tannic, has now been deliberately made more supple, so that it can be served slightly chilled and does not need to age for more than two or three years.

GAILLAC

East of the delightful town of Albi, on either side of the Tarn, this vineyard offers a variety of wines, reds, rosés and whites, some of them sparkling. Here the Bordeaux vines have largely given way to indigenous varieties, such as Duras and Braucol for the reds, and Ondenc and Mauzac for the whites. On the whole, the wines of Gaillac, which should be served young and slightly chilled, enjoy an attractive quality/price ratio.

COTES DU FRONTONNAIS

This vineyard is situated north of Toulouse, not far from Gaillac. It is planted with the Négrette vine, and produces mostly red wine, with some rosé. This supple wine should be drunk young and fresh. It is as familiar to the inhabitants of Toulouse as Beaujolais is to those of Lyon.

MADIRAN

This vineyard, north of the town of Pau, produces a wine that is almost black, like that of Cahors. However, here it is the Tannat vine, accounting for half the vines grown, which is responsible for the colour. The wine gives it a robust corpulence and, though it is not outstanding in terms of finesse, it does prove to be exceptionally full-bodied. This type of wine may be kept for ten years and more.

JURANÇON

Planted mainly with those rare vines the Gros Manseng and the Petit Manseng, this vineyard to the south of Pau is devoted mainly to syrupy whites, but also produces some dry whites. The former are the most noteworthy, with their bite and firmness, as well as their bouquet of spices, hey are great wines, which can be kept for well over ten years.

Finally, mention should be made in passing of the trustworthy AOC of IROULEGUY, the less interesting VIN DU BEARN, and the VDQS TURSAN.

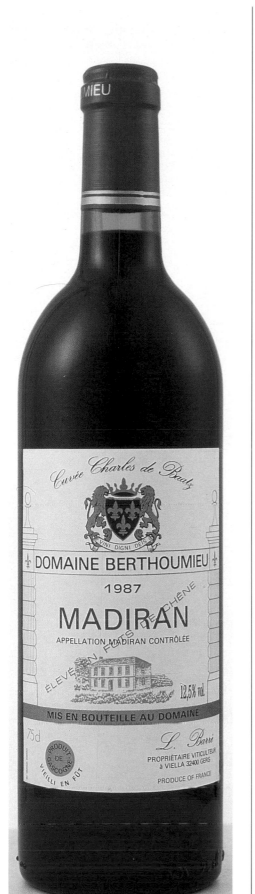

THE LOIRE

The Loire provides confirmation of the harmonious combination of vines and great rivers. Here, more than 400 kilometres (250 miles) of vineyards punctuate the course of the river, from its mouth right up to the town of Nevers.

The whole of this region, which has been called the "Garden of France", has an air of opulence and tranquility, with a freshness that is naturally reflected in the wines.

However, there is no uniformity in this vast territory, especially since the Loire basin consists of a succession of diverse regions which are related to one another principally by the river. Here and there are traces of the monks who used to devote themselves to the perfection of these wines, which history tells us were the favourite wines of the kings of France.

Despite the variety in the types of wine produced, the whole of the Loire region may be divided into four large and homogenous wine-producing areas:

NANTAIS, ANJOU-SAUMUR, TOURAINE, NIVERNAIS.

These areas all offer - in red, rosé, white, sparkling and syrupy wines - a range extensive enough to satisfy every gastronomical requirement and to provide a varied accompaniment to a tour of the famous châteaux of the Loire.

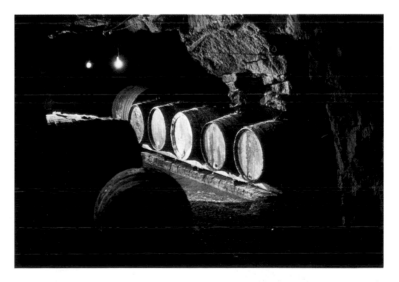

Touraine, the Chateau of Chenonceaux has been producing a very good wine for several years.

NANTAIS

This vineyard on the left bank of the Loire, to the south of Nantes, has an oceanic climate, both mild and humid. Its main distinction is the vine variety used, the Muscadet, which gives its name to these dry white wines and remains the sole vine allowed for the production of the AOC's (MUSCADET DE SEVRE ET MAINE, which is the most widespread, MUSCADET DES COTEAUX DE LA LOIRE and generic MUSCADET).

The best Muscadet is that which has undergone vinification "sur lie" (on the lees), because this technique retains its fruitiness and finesse. Nevertheless, Muscadet is a pale-coloured wine which, being very refreshing and musky, provides an ideal accompaniment for shellfish and seafood.

As for the GROS PLANT vine, the VDQS of the same name produces smaller quantities of a very dry, slightly acid white, to be served well chilled.

Finally, the COTEAUX D'ANCENIS, the VINS DU HAUT-POITOU and the VINS DU THOUARSAIS are three VDQS brands, producing plain red, white and rosé wines to be served young and chilled.

ANJOU-SAUMUR

This undulating vineyard east of the Nantes region, is divided into two regional appellations: ANJOU and SAUMUR. Though these two regions share a climate of the oceanic type, their soils are different. Schist and clay predominate in Anjou, while chalk holds sway in Saumur, to such a point that deep, cool cellars have been dug into it, as in Champagne. All this is enough to produce wines which are quite different from each other, although they are made from the same grape variety.

Although the Anjou vineyard has long suffered from over-production on account of the success of its wines in the export market, there nevertheless remains a good number of great bottles. The greatest of these is the group of mellow white wines from the COTEAUX DU LAYON AOC.

This vast vineyard owes its name to the Layon, a tributary of the Loire, which flows through it. In the range of whites it produces, the mellow wines from the Chenin vine should be tried in particular.

The frequent autumn mists encourage the development of pourriture noble here and, in the best production areas, the grapes are harvested when they are overripe, having been selected on successive occasions. This is the case in several communes which are authorized to add their name to that of Côteaux du Layon, those of Chaume, Rochefort, Saint-Aubin de Ligné, Saint-Lambert du Lattay, Beaulieu, Rablay and Faye.

With their fine golden colour, the mellow or syrupy wines, with their

THE GRAPES OF ANJOU-SAUMUR

The Chenin Blanc is the predominant white grape variety, accompanied by the Sauvignon and the Chardonnay. For the reds, the Cabernet Franc easily outnumbers the Cabernet Sauvignon, the Pineau d'Aunis and the Gamay.

wonderful bouquet of fruit and honey, combine richness with smoothness. The chance should not be missed of tasting the two grands crus of the region, BONNEZEAUX and QUARTS DE CHAUME, which are perfectly able to compete with the greatest Sauternes.

Closer to Angers, two vineyards produce some quality dry, or medium-dry white wines, the COTEAUX DE L'AUBANCE and the COTEAUX DE LA LOIRE. For its part, SAVENNIERES, which offers a full-bodied, sappy white wine, possesses two outstanding crus, "La Roche aux Moines" and "La Coulée de Serrant".

As for the bulk of the Anjou wines, these comprise a whole range of wines including light reds to be served chilled, rosés ranging from medium dry to sweet, and whites some of which are effervescent, like the Crémant de Loire.

For its part, the whole of the regional appellation of SAUMUR produces mainly dry whites, most of them effervescent. They may not have the finesse of Champagne, but they sell at a more modest and convincing price. An exception in this region is the AOC of SAUMUR-CHAMPIGNY, which devotes itself exclusively to reds. Ruby in colour, these are tannic and lively wines, though they are now threatened by their dazzling success in Paris.

THE GRAPES OF TOURAINE

The Chenin is the dominant white vine, accompanied by the Arbois and the Sauvignon. For the reds, the Cabernet Franc leads the way, followed by the Grolleau, the Pineau d'Aunis, the Gamay, the Pinot Noir and the Cot (Malbec).

TOURAINE

This vineyard of ancient reputation - it was in existence by the 4th century - produces two main types of wine, reds to the west of Tours and whites to the east; they have a very high reputation.

On the north bank of the Loire, the AOC's of BOURGUEIL and of SAINT-NICOLAS DE BOURGUEIL , covering a total area of 1300 hectares (3212 acres), produce red wines mainly from the Cabernet Franc vine, called the "Breton" here. They are deep red in colour and have a marked aroma of raspberries and blackcurrants.

On the opposite bank of the Loire, alongside its tributary, the Vienne, the CHINON AOC is a more fragmented vineyard of 1000 hectares (2470 acres). Here the Cabernet Franc produces a ruby wine with substance, which is ready to drink earlier than a Bourgueil.

The VOUVRAY AOC to the east of Tours, consists of 1600 hectares (3954 acres) of vines growing on chalky soil and split into eight communes . These wines, some of which are still and dry, some mellow, some effervescent are produced solely from the Chenin vine. Although all these are quite respectable, the sweeter wines are of the highest quality , because they are made from the best grapes, rich in pourriture noble. These great wines have a strong bouquet. The MOUNTLOUIS AOC,

not far from Vouvray, produces a range of similar wines over an area of 300 hectares (741 acres). The various appellations of the TOURAINE AOC, particularly AMBOISE, AZAY-LE-RIDEAU and MESLAND, provide light red, white and rosé wines, to be served young and chilled.

NIVERNAIS

Five small quality vineyards are grouped together near Nevers. Two of them, QUINCY and POUILLY-SUR-LOIRE, are devoted exclusively to white wines from the Sauvignon vine. The latter AOC produces, with Pouilly Fumé (not to be confused with the Burgundian Pouilly Fuissé!), a dry and distinguished wine with a spicy bouquet, which has established itself as the best in the region. However, it is the SANCERRE AOC that enjoys the greatest fame. Here, the Sauvignon and Pinot Noir are responsible for a range of dry whites, reds and rosés, fresh and pleasant wines, but of unequal quality now that Sancerre has become intoxicated with its own success. The same production is to be found at REUILLY and MENETOU-SALON. Here too, the wines cannot be aged and are served chilled. Finally, five VDQS wines complete the region's production. These are COTES DE GIEN, VINS DE L'ORLEANNAIS, CHEVERNY, VALENCAY and COTEAUX DU VENDOMMOIS.

THE GRAPES OF NIVERNAIS

Of the white varieties, the Sauvignon reigns supreme here, while the reds are made mainly from the Pinot Noir.

CHAMPAGNE

The eponymous wines of Champagne carry a celebration in the mere mention of their name. For Champagne is the wine of joy par excellence, the wine that makes all people beautiful, a wine that epitomizes a whole art of living. Furthermore, there is no other name more shamefully plagiarized all over the world.

Yet the only Champagne is Champagne. The vineyard overlooked by the towns of Rheims and Epernay covers more than 20000 hectares (49,420 acres) to the north-east of the Paris basin. Its primary distinctive feature is its soil, which consists of a layer of chalk thick enough to accommodate the miles of tunnels in which the bottles are stored.

Only three varieties of grape are grown. These are the Chardonnay (25%), the only white vine of Champagne, very much in fashion today because of its finesse and its elegance; the Pinot Noir (30%), which gives structure and sap to the wine; and the Pinot Meunier (45%), a less noble vine, so-called because its young shoots are covered with fine white down. These different vines possess complementary qualities so it is easy to see that one of the most important secrets of Champagne lies in the art of blending.

A snow-covered vineyard in Champagne.
The "dégorgement" always a spectacular operation.

CHAMPAGNE

The proportion of vines varies according to the locality. The wine-growing area can be divided into four regions:

The MONTAGNE DE REIMS, in which the Pinot Noir predominates, includes the crus of Ambonnay, Bouzy, Louvois, Mailly-Champagne, Sillery, Verzenay and Verzy.

The VALLEE DE LA MARNE is mainly devoted to the Pinot Meunier. It is marked by crus such as Avenay, Ay, Mareuil-sur-Ay, Hautvillers, Damery, Boursault, Verneuil and Venteuil.

The COTE DES BLANCS, where the Chardonnay still reigns supreme, possesses in particular the crus of Avize, Cramant, Oger and Mesnil-sur-Oger.

The VIGNOBLE DE L'AUBE, which used to be despised, is now starting to produce more decent wines.

THE BOTTLES

Champagne is bottled in a wide range of sizes. These are Quart (quarter bottle), Demi (a half-bottle), Bouteille (75-cl or 24-fl oz bottle), Magnum (two bottles), Jeroboam (four bottles), Rehoboam (six bottles), Mathusalem (Methuselah) (eight bottles), Salmanazar (Shalmanezer) (twelve bottles), Balthazar (sixteen bottles) and finally the Nabuchodonosor (Nebuchadnezzar) (twenty bottles).

HOW TO DRINK CHAMPAGNE

Champagne is above all an excellent aperitif wine which should be served at 7°C to 10°C, i.e. not too cold.
It can only be sampled to full advantage in flute or tulip glasses, which enable the rising bubbles to be admired.
The use of wide, shallow champagne glasses is a heresy.

"CHAMPAGNIZATION" OR THE METHODE CHAMPENOISE

For a long time, red wines were the major product of Champagne and sparkling wines were not to be found there at all. Champagne as we know it today did not came into being until as late as the end of the 17th century thanks to an invention by Dom Pérignon, a cellarer monk at the Abbey of Hautvillers.

How then is Champagne obtained? The first requirement is careful harvesting, because it is important to discard any damaged grapes. Next, the bunches of grapes are cleaned (EPLUCHAGE). The pressing (PRESSURAGE) is then performed quickly and gently, so that the black skins of the grapes do not "stain" the juice with their pigment. Once the undesirable solid matter has been removed, the must is decanted into casks with a 205-litre (45-gallon) capacity or into vats. This produces a still wine of marked acidity. It is at this point that champagnization proper begins, by means of a series of specific operations.

FORMATION OF THE CUVEE.

This consists in blending different wines in the special vats in which they will be fermented. Sometimes wines from the same commune are blended, and sometimes wines from different crus and vines. Blending can also involve either just the wines of the year likely to become vintage Champagne, or additions of vins de réserve , reserve stocks from earlier harvests. In this way, the consistency of the flavour peculiar to each brand is attained.

TIRAGE ("DRAWING OFF").

A saccharose solution, called liqueur de tirage, is added to the vats (25 g per litre of wine), along with some natural yeast. After the fermenting, the wine is "drawn off" into bottles. These are corked with a temporary stopper and are stored in cellars, where they lie on laths.

PRISE DE MOUSSE (FORMATION OF THE BUBBLES).

The yeast causes a second fermentation to occur. The sugar is turned into alcohol and carbon dioxide, which is responsible for the formation of the bubbles. The deposit resulting from this fermentation continues to enrich the wine for at least a year.

REMUAGE ("TURNING")

At the end of their stay in the cellar, the bottles are placed on racks and gradually inclined so that the deposit slides slowly into the neck. Remuage then consists in turning each bottle daily through one-eighth of a revolution, combining this movement with a slight vibration. Once the deposit has completely descended into the neck, the bottles are all stored upside-down.

DEGORGEMENT (DISGORGEMENT)

Today, ice is used to remove the trapped deposit. The bottle necks are soaked in a

refrigerated bath at -20°C, so that an ice stopper is formed around the deposit, which is then ejected by the pressure of the gas.

FILLING AND MIXING

The gap which the dégorgement leaves in the bottle is filled with a liqueur d'expédition, a mixture of old Champagne mixed with sugar. The proportion of sugar corresponds to the type of wine required, from brut to sec, demi-sec, or doux.

All that remains is to cork the bottles and put on the muselet (the wire which holds in the cork), before covering the neck with foil and labelling.

THE GRAPES OF CHAMPAGNE

Only three vines are authorized in Champagne - Chardonnay, Pinot Noir and Pinot Meunier.

PARTICULAR TYPES OF CHAMPAGNE

BLANC DE BLANCS Champagne. This is made exclusively from white grapes and thus from the Chardonnay. It usually comes from the Côte des Blancs and its crus. This Champagne possesses more grace, finesse and lightness than traditional Champagne.

The BLANC DE NOIRS, on the other hand, is made exclusively from black grapes, producing richer wines with more structure.

ROSE. Pink (Rosé) Champagne is usually made by blending white wine with a small quantity of red wine from the Pinot Noir. The result is a pleasant increase in fruitiness.

CREMANT. This is a lightly-sparkling wine to which only a half-measure of liqueur de tirage has been added, so that the gas is reduced by half and the wine is correspondingly less sparkling.

CHAMPAGNE MILLESIME (Vintage Champagne). Only the best quality Champagne from the harvest is classified as vintage (millésimé). The wine must be able to do without vins de réserve and deserve distinction on its own. This Champagne is aged for longer than the non-vintage varieties and cannot be sold before its third year.

CUVEE SPECIALE. Champagnes bearing this wording have a variety of brand names, some of which are very prestigious. They represent the best wines from each big firm.

BRUT ZERO or BRUT INTEGRAL. These are bottles which have been topped up with wine alone and to which no sugar has been added.

THE CHAMPAGNE FIRMS

Since the Champagne production process requires considerable financial resources, most of the production and marketing is in the hands of a few large companies.

Among the most famous are:

> In Rheims: Besserat de Bellefon, Charles Heidsieck, Mumm, Heidsieck Monopole, Henriot, Krug, Lanson, Louis Roederer, Piper-Heidsieck, Pommery, Ruinart, Taittinger, Veuve Clicquot-Ponsardin.
> In Epernay: Moët et Chandon, Perrier-Jouët, Pol Roger, De Venoge.
> In the vineyards: Bollinger, Canard-Duchêne, Deutz, Laurent-Perrier.

Each Champagne firm gives its name to the wine it sells. It is quite logical that this name should figure prominently on the label, since each brand imparts particular

characteristics to its wines and strives to keep these constant. The following initials appear at bottom of the label, in much smaller print:

N.M., which stands for négociant-manipulant (merchant-processor): In this case the grapes have been bought from the wine-growers, but the processing of the wine has been carried out by the merchant.

R.M., which stands for récoltant-manipulant (harvester-processor). In this case, the wine-grower has processed his own wine.

C.M., which stands for coopérative de manipulation (wine-processing cooperative). In this case, the wine-growers have brought their grapes to a cooperative which has done the processing into Champagne.

ALSACE

This region of eastern France is not merely picturesque, with its quaint, half-timbered houses and their flower-filled balconies. It also produces some great wines, still insufficiently well-known by the French themselves, even though the wine-growers are doing their best to promote their produce. They are doing this so effectively that to pretend to be unaware of them now is to verge on being ridiculous. The policy of quantity, formerly forced upon the region by the successive invasions and annexations by Germany, has given way to one of quality; abundance has now yielded to class and distinction.

The vineyard, which is hardly more than 2 to 4 km (1 to 2½ miles) wide, occupies a strip of land which does not run beside the Rhine, but beside its tributary, the Ill. It covers about 12000 hectares (30000 acres), from Marlenheim in the north, near Strasbourg, to Thann in the south, near Mulhouse.

LATE HARVESTING AND SELECTION OF NOBLE GRAPES

If the summer has been particularly hot, the grapes become exceptionally rich in sugar. If, in addition, the autumn brings with it the "noble rot", pourriture noble, the grapes are subjected to a careful process of selection. Only the "noble" grapes are retained, which, thanks to the action of the Botrytis fungus, are capable of attaining 15° alcohol in the case of Riesling and 16.4° in the case of Gewurztraminer and Tokay. This strict selection results in wine that is quite wonderful, but only a few years have managed to attain this perfection. They include 1976, 1983, 1985 and 1988.

The vines grow on the south and east foothills of the Vosges, at an altitude of 600 to 1200 feet. They are thus protected from the humid westerly winds by the peaks and the forests. The continental climate, with its hot summers and harsh winters, is also characterized by particularly dry autumns. This near-absence of rain in September and October is a considerable advantage since it makes late harvesting possible. As for the soil, it varies from granitic rock to gneiss and sandstone, though the best crus come from limestone hills.

GRAPE VARIETIES

The diversity of vines used in Alsace has a consequential effect on the wines , most of

THE GRAPES OF ALSACE

Among the white vines used in Alsace, the most "noble" are Gewurztraminer, Muscat, Pinot Gris or Tokay and Riesling. Pinot Blanc or Klevner, Sylvaner and Chasselas are also used. The only red vine used is the Pinot Noir.

which have a strong and rich character. They were introduced a long time ago. Proof of their presence exists from the 15th century, at least as far as the best, or "noble", vines are concerned. There are four of these.

GEWURZTRAMINER

Of all the Alsatian vines, this is the easiest to identify, on account of its marked aroma of musk and spices. It produces full-bodied wines, dry or mellow in the good years, and develops an exceptionally strong fruity bouquet.

MUSCAT

Alsace is one of the few regions in which the Muscat grape produces a perfectly dry white wine. This wine has a delicate flavour, creating the impression of drinking fresh grape juice. With its subtle elegance and graceful perfume, it proves to be, among other things, a wonderful aperitif.

PINOT GRIS OR TOKAY D'ALSACE

This produces ample, heady wines, yellow-gold in colour with a powerful bouquet. The wines are generally opulent rather than refined and graceful.

RIESLING

This is the lord of the vines of Alsace, capable of producing the most thorough-bred of wines - very dry whites, whose pale colour is tinged with green, wines which, though they develop an intense bouquet, possess finesse and sensitivity.

Next to these aristocrats are varieties of lesser rank:

PINOT BLANC or KLEVNER: This produces a wine that is light, though without great finesse, a frank and simple wine pleasant to drink when young and chilled.

SYLVANER: The white wine from these grapes sometimes has the defect of being excessively thin. It is a wine to be drunk without ceremony, young and well-chilled, for example as an accompaniment to a hearty dish of sauerkraut.

To this list may be added:

CHASSELAS: This is the vin ordinaire of the vineyard. Its sole interest rests in providing light wines which are useful for blending.

PINOT NOIR: The only red grape in Alsace which is used to make light red and rosé wines.

All these vines, apart from the Chasselas, have lent their names to the various wines they produce. The EDELZWICKER appellation does not therefore correspond to a particular vine; it is the name given to the wines made from a blend of the white grape varieties of Alsace.

THE APPELLATION SYSTEM IN ALSACE

Although it has become more sophisticated in the recent years, the appellation system in Alsace remains relatively simple.

A distinction is made between:

The regional appellation "ALSACE" or "VIN D'ALSACE"

Prior to 1975, only the name of the grape variety used, such as Tokay or Riesling, was optionally added to this designation. For these generic Alsace wines, the regulations allow a generous yield of 100 hectolitres per hectare (2200 gallons per 2 1/2 acres).

The appellation "VIN D'ALSACE GRAND CRU"

This is applied exclusively to wines from defined terroirs and made only from the "noble" vines: Gewurztraminer, Muscat, Pinot Gris and Riesling. For the grands crus, the authorized yield may not exceed 70 hectolitres per hectare (1540 gallons per 2 1/2 acres), but the best producers deliberately limit themselves to 50 or 60 hectolitres (1100 to 1320 gallons). Finally, the grands crus must undergo a tasting session and the grape variety and vintage must be indicated on the label.

The appellations of the communes and localities.

Since 1975, fifty defined terroirs have been authorized to place their names on the label in addition to the above-mentioned designations. For example, the commune of BERGHEIM with the locality of Altenberg, RIBEAUVILLE with Kirchberg or Zahnacker, RIQUEWIHR with Sporen or Schonenburg, GUEBWILLER with Kitterle, THANN with Rangen, etc.

The appellation CREMANT D'ALSACE.

This is reserved for sparkling wines made from the white wines of Alsace using the méthode champenoise. The Pinot Blanc is the main vine used.

Finally, there are also two VDQS wines: The COTES DE TOUL, which produces a light, slightly acid wine, either red, white, or gris (light rosé), and the VIN DE MOSELLE, red or white, which is generally light and faintly-coloured.

GERMANY

At first glance, there is nothing that predisposes Germany to being a wine-producing country.

It is situated too far to the north, the climate is too cold and there are late frosts and rainy autumns which ought to have discouraged the Germans from growing vines. After all, vines do not take kindly to adverse conditions, even the commonest German varieties - the extraordinary Riesling, the prolific Sylvaner, the very resistant Müller-Thurgau, Gewürztraminer and Ruländer. Each vine-growing area seems to have been chosen two thousand years ago with infinite care, to provide the best micro-climate. These include the warmest banks along the Rhine, the Moselle and their tributaries, rivers which capture warmth and rediffuse it during cold spells by means of mists and fogs. The objective has always been to produce not just wine, but fine wine. Over the centuries, the Germans have acquired the art of developing dry or mellow white wines. These wines are rather light (10°-11° proof), fruity and refeshing, with that hint of acidity which is their great attraction. Their clear colour, aroma and distinction have become legendary.

The 100,000 hectares (247,100 acres) of vineyards constitute 1% of all the agricultural land of the German Federal Republic. The vineyards are situated in south-western Germany between Lake Constance and Bonn, the capital of the Federal Republic. Incredibly, this is the same latitude as Labrador and Mongolia. White wine constitutes 85% of the 9 million hectolitres (198 million gallons) produced annually. Typical of the German wines, collectively called "hock" in the English-speaking world, are the great wines of the Rhine Valley. In this almost fairytale part of the country, the vines grow on steep crags topped by gothic castles and the village taverns are full of young girls in peasant costume. Yet the Rhineland is only one of the ten wine-growing areas of Germany.

There are at present 90,000 German wine producers, most of whom work part-time because since the days of Napoleon, German vineyards have been worked in very small plots, rarely larger than one hectare (about 2½ acres). The vine-growers consequently deliver their grapes or musts to cooperatives for processing.

The history of German wine is closely linked to the Rhine and the Moselle. It was in these two river valleys that the Romans left their strongest imprint, and particularly the wine-growing tradition. When the Empire fell, as elsewhere in Europe, vine-growing became the prerogative of the monasteries.

Rudesheim on Rhine.

Quality control was introduced as early as the 18th century, in the form of uprooting campaigns in the Rheingau and Moselle, to replace older grape stocks with Riesling. It was at this period that the practice was introduced of laying down fine wines and great vintages in small cellars, the famous Kabinett Keller or Prädikat Kabinett of today. The first mention of this practise concerns Schloß Vollrads and dates back to 1728. Another key date is 1775, marking the birth of late harvesting (Spätlese), which produces fuller, richer wines. According to legend, these wines were actually the result of the carelessness of a cleric, the Abbot of Fulda. It was in that year that he simply forgot to order the harvesting. When he realised his omission, it was too late. The grapes had rotted on the vine. All he could do was abandon them to his peasants, who made the magnificent wine which is now so well-known.

In the late 18th century, wine began to be estate-bottled. Thanks to lithography, Senefelder's invention, labels could be printed to distinguish each bottle of wine from its fellow. Napoleon's occupation of Germany, beginning in 1803, had the effect of secularising the wine trade which hitherto had been the exclusive prerogative of the church. Another result of the Napoleonic conquest was that the introduction of the Napoleonic code as the legal system caused the fragmentation of land upon inheritance, since property had to be divided equally among the heirs. The result was 30000 names of Crus which were reclassified and reduced to 2600 in 1971.

The cooperatives developed in the 19th century, as did the classification of regions for the marketing of their "natural" wines (those which are not chaptalized in any way). The regions, including Moselle, Saar, Ruwer and Rheingau, auctioned their wines. In 1910, the Verband des Deutscher Prädikats- und Qualitätsweingüter (Association of German Prädikat and Fine Wine Producers) or VDP was established at Trier. This was a guarantee of quality for natural wines sold at auction which the law of 1971 transformed into a system of Prädikats. Today, the Verband has only 171 members drawn from all the regions. Very strict regulations are imposed, which have won an international reputation for German wines. Should German wines be sugared or unsugared? The climatic conditions under which the vines grow are such that, in some years, the grapes need to undergo chaptalization (or Gallization, after its inventor, Gall) a process whereby sugar is added to the must before fermentation to counterbalance too great an acidity or a lack of alcohol. However, the regulations are very strict. This has nothing to do with the sweet wines produced by late harvesting. Leaving grapes on the vine after they have fully ripened so that they are attacked by the "noble rot", is a completely different process, one which in France produces the great Sauternes and in Germany the wonderful Trockenbeerenauslese and Beerenauslese wines. At this stage, each grape is meticulously hand-picked, which makes these mellow wines extremely expensive.

A property near Bonn.

MOSEL-SAAR-RUWER

The Mosel River, which rises in the Vosges mountains in France, is responsible for several VDQS wines in the French province of Lorraine and then becomes the frontier between the Grand Duchy of Luxembourg and the Rhineland-Palatinate (Pfalz). The wines of this district have a generosity and surprising freshness (see Luxembourg). However, it is in the heart of Germany, having passed through Trier and the schistic soil of the Rhineland hills where the river is swollen by two tributaries, the Saar and the Ruwer, that the vineyards attain their worldwide reputation before the Mosel rejoins the Rhine at Koblenz.

The white wines of the Mosel are incomparable. They are fruity and delicate, elegant, aristocratic, very aromatic and with a hint of sharpness. Experts on wine consider the Mosel Rieslings to be unrivalled. The reason for this is the Riesling's liking for slate. Slate breaks down very slowly in the soil, always leaving a cultivatable stratum without exhausting the nutrients in the soil. Clearly, the vines are particularly fond of this valley caused by the bends and meanders of the river, with its precipitous banks. Slate is everywhere, fossilising the flora and fauna left behind by the sea which covered the area in prehistoric times. Down the centuries, the Mosel carved out its bed leaving sheltered micro-climates along its course, which were protected from the wind and which captured solar energy which the river would convect during cold spells. This is why wine has been produced here since Roman times, not, of course, from Riesling which did not exist then, but from a variety very similar to the modern Elbling grape variety. Elbling produces a light, neutral wine, which is very acid and is mainly used for making sparkling white wines (Sekt). It is still cultivated in the Upper Mosel. The cultivation of Riesling was only decreed as compulsory in 1787 by the Prince-Bishop of Trier, Clement Wenceslas.

Mosel-Saar-Ruwer is the fourth-largest wine-growing region of Germany. It covers 12700 hectares (31380 acres) and only produces white wines. Of these, 57% are made from the Riesling grapes which grow on the steepest slate banks, and 23% from Müller-Thurgau grapes which occupy the flatter ground. There are 11000 wine-growers who cultivate plots of just over a hectare (2½ acres) in size. Half the production is marketed by large firms, one quarter is sent to cooperatives (which have 5000 members) and the rest is sold directly by the vine-growers.

In Mosel, wine-producers use gigantic oak barrels called fudern, which hold 1000 litres, 1333 bottles or 111 cases of wine. Each vine-grower owns his own fuder in which he ages his best wines. The vines follow the Mosel Valley from Trier. The heart of the wine country is at Middle Mosel between Trittenheim and Traben-Trarbach, including the communes of Piesport, Bernkastel, Graach, Wehlen, Zeltingen and Brauneberg. Five districts (Bereiche) are recognized. These are Zell (Lower Mosel) between Coblenz and the village of Zell known for its Schwarze Katz (black cat) vineyards, the world-famous Bernkastel (Middle Mosel), the districts

of Saar and Ruwer which includes the vineyards around Trier and finally Upper Mosel (Obermosel) and Moseltor, the gateway to the Mosel region.

MIDDLE MOSEL
(BEREICH BERNKASTEL)

One side of the river bank of the Mosel in this area is very steep, where the river has forced its way through the strata of slate. The opposite bank consists of gently-sloping hills, which are banks of alluvial soil that have built up during flooding. The very steep hills produce wines which are dryer and more aristocratic; wines from the alluvial bank are lazier and full-bodied. The finest wine in the Bereich is undoubtedly a Trockenbeerenauslese, a golden wine of an incomparable richness which concentrates all the perfumes of the Mosel wines. Each grape used to produce it has been hand-picked after reaching a the perfect degree of overripeness. This is such an arduous task that it makes the wine incomparably expensive.

Bernkastel was founded in 1291 by the Emperor Frederick Barbarossa. It is a little medieval town with a population of 10000, whose harvest festival in the first week of September draws huge crowds. Its vineyards have the highest reputation in Germany. The Bernkasteller Doctor vineyard overlooks the town to the south-east of it.

The name derives from the fact that the wine is alleged to have cured the Prince-Bishop of Trier of an illness in the 14th century. Chancellor Adenauer gave 50 bottles of the Feinste Auslese, considered to be the best wine in Germany, to President Eisenhower on his birthday.

The vines from this vineyard are exceptional, the slate gives them a flinty, spicy taste with a slight smokiness. The southern exposure gives the wine its roundness and richness. In poor years, Bernkasteler Doctor is sold as Badstube. The vineyards of Kues, opposite Bernkastel, are on the gentler slopes of the left bank of the river. For this reason, the soil is more alluvial and the wines (Kardinalsberg and Rosenberg) lack the elegance which the slate gives to Bernkastel wines. On the opposite bank of the Mosel, the Brauneberg (brown hill)

slopes are responsible for elegant, fruity wines (Großlage Kurfurstlay, the best Juffer crus, Juffer-Sonnenuhr and Kammer).

The Mosel has its golden mountain. It is the hill of Erden which with Doktorberg is the equivalent of a Premier Cru. In the district itself, it is said that the Erden wines are more virile (Bube) than those of Wehlen which are considered to be more feminine (Mädel). The best vintages are Prälat, Busslay and Herrenberg.

The best-known of Wehlen's wines is Wehlener Sonnenuhr, a wine whose finesse and elegance are legendary. Some people consider it superior to Bernkastel Doctor. The vineyards of Wehlen date from 1084. Prior to 1802, when they were secularized by Napoleon, they belonged to the Cistercian abbey of Klöster Machem. The present owners are the Prum and Bergweiler families.

The Graach vineyard of the Großlage Münzlay has a south-western exposure. The vines are grown on the stony hillsides (Graach comes from an old Gallic word for gravel). The soil is a mixture of slate and clay giving the wine body and roundness. In dry years, Graach wines, Himmelreich, Domprobst, Josefshofer, are exceptionally good. Josefshofer (along with Schloß Vollkach and Schloß Johannisberg) is one of the few German wines which is sold without an indication of origin.

The Piesport wines of the Mosel (including Goldtropfchen, Günterslay, Falkenberg, Grafenberg, Schubertslay) have a remarkable distinction and balance, and are both aromatic and delicate. In the very great years, they attain peaks of perfection Urzig (from the Großlage Schwarzlay) has two Crus, Goldwingert and Würzgarten (spice garden). These wines are very fruity and unusually spicy. The two reasons for this are the full southern exposure of the vines and the soil on which they are grown, a mixture of slate and volcanic rock.

Lower Mosel (Bereich Zell-Mosel), the

section between Zell and Koblenz, where the Mosel and Rhine merge, produces good wines, though they do not have the quality of Bereich Bernkastel. However, they are pleasant and very drinkable.

The Schwarze Katz estate at Zell supplies Germany with one of its most popular wines. According to legend, the original Schwartze Katz or black cat was a cat which was able to determine the best barrel (fuder) for the wine by going to sleep on top of it!

After leaving Zell, the visitor ought to take a trip to the villages of Alf and Beilstein and Bullay, where vineyards are grown on the steepest slopes in Europe, as well as the little town of Cochem. The landscape is magnificent, with its medieval villages, half-timbered houses and gothic churches, against a background of rolling hills covered in vineyards. Upper Mosel (Bereich Obermosel and Bereich Moseltor) is upstream of Trier and is dominated by the Elbling grape variety, which was brought here 2000 years ago as part of the Roman impedimenta. Ruländer and Pinot Gris are also grown here. The slate which is so good for Riesling gives way here to a more calcareous soil. The wines are not great wines but they have a certain charm, especially as they are priced a great deal lower than the other Mosel wines. The Saar-Ruhr (Bereich Saar-Ruhr) wines are produced from the vineyards around Trier, the oldest city in Germany, founded by the Romans. The vines grow on the banks of the River Saar and the Ruwer, a tiny stream.

The wines attain a perfect balance between too much acidity and an exceptional fruitiness. In the very best years, the Saar wines outclass those of the Mosel. The slow-ripening grapes take on an elegance and a bouquet reminiscent of blackcurrant with a hint of nutmeg which one encounters nowhere else in Germany. The best Crus are Kupp, Herrenberg, Schloßberg, Braune Kupp, Rausch and Bergschloßchen.

RHEINGAU

There is no doubt that this little section of Hesse produces the best white Rieslings in the world (though it shares this distinction with Mosel). Riesling is said to have been born in the Rheingau; at any event, it has been almost a compulsory crop since the 17th century. Today, it represents 80% of the vineyards.

The Rhinegau extends along the length of the Rhine Valley between Wiesbaden and Bingen, where the Rhine encounters a spur of the Taunus Mountains. It is a strip 45 kilometres (28 miles) long and 8 kilometres (5 miles) wide, about 30 kilometres (19 miles) from Frankfurt. The vineyards face the Rhine sheltered by the foothills of the Taunus Mountains, which are made of schist and are only 2650 feet at their highest point. The Rhine is 800 yards wide and forms an east-west bend here, providing the vines with a wholly southern exposure. The Riesling grapes are thus protected from cold winds by the Taunus and can benefit from the heat of the sun which the waters of the Rhine diffuse during cold spells. This climate brings the autumnal mild, moist weather essential for a late-ripening grape variety.

Harvesting is late in the Rheingau, beginning in the second half of October and even lasting into November, which gives the wine the elegance and freshness so typical of the best Rieslings. Autumn wine festivals are held in the villages where there are numerous stalls at which one can sample the local vintages. Harvest time is an ideal season for travelling along the Riesling Route, a 70 kilometres (44 miles) stretch which links the 24 villages between Hochheim and Lorchhausen.

The wine-growing history of the Rheingau began in the Roman era. However, according to legend, Charlemagne was contemplating the scenery from his palace at Ingelheim on the opposite bank of the Rhine (in Rhinehessen) when he noticed that the snow was melting early on the Johannisberg. He took this as a good sign for vine cultivation.

The vines did not, in fact, really prosper in this part of the world until the Middle Ages, under the influence of the Bishops of Main and the monks of the monasteries of Johannisberg and Eberbach who deforested the banks of the Rhine. "Whoever breaths the Rheingau air is a free man", it was said at the time, because the serfs who helped to uproot the forests and plant the vines were given their freedom and acquired the first civil rights in

Germany, in exchange for their assistance. Rheingau is almost synonymous with Riesling. The first mention of the place in history is on March 13, 1435, in an invoice from the firm of Klaus Kleinfisch concerning the delivery of a quantity of Riesling to the fortress of Russelsheim.

In the 17th century, the Pinot Noir vines, which had been brought from Burgundy by the Cistercian monks, were uprooted and the vineyards replanted with Riesling. It was in the same period that late harvesting was discovered accidentally. In 1736, the first Cabinet-Keller (a little wine-cellar in which the best vintages were laid down) was established at Kloster Eberbach. The wines aged in this way were later called Kabinettswein. By the early 19th century, the international reputation of Rheingau Riesling was finally established.

Today, the Rheingau has 2700 hectares (6672 acres) of vines, producing 200,000 hectolitres (4,400,000 gallons) of wine annually, 80% of which is from Riesling grapes. The Rheingau's 1500 or so vine-growers have plots which average 2 hectares (5 acres) in size. They tend to sell their own wines direct, like the major estates (of which there are over 100). The latter sell through a guild of wine-brokers founded in the 14th century which auctions the wine each year.

There are also about a dozen large cooperatives and an association of 33 estates who have formed the Vereinigung Rheingauer Weingüter, a collective which includes the elite of Riesling producers.

In the Rheingau, the Riesling grape is transformed into an entire range of subtle variations, which depend on the soil type, topography and exposure of the vineyards.

The steep hillsides of Rüdesheim in the Middle Rheingau and those in the bend of the river, at Lorch and Assmannshausen produce wines that are sharper-tasting, more acidic, perhaps less smooth but always refined. The vineyards on the gentler slopes produce wines that are more full-bodied and fruity. The geology of the region consists of mainly of marl-and-clay soils. The northern and central Rheingau at Erbach, Markobrunn and Kiedrich have a mixture of sand and gravel soil covered

THE GRAPES OF RHEINGAU

Rheingau produce the best Riesling in the world.
For the white wines:
80% of Riesling, 6% Müller-Thurgau, 5% of Spätburgunder, 3% of Ehrenfelser and 2% of Kerner.

with loess. The upper Rheingau has soils that are warmer, and based on limestone, loess and clay-loam at Geisenheim, Östrich, Eltville and Hattenheim. In the west, the soil is a mixture of slate and clay, and there is also sandstone and quartz. According to the experts, in a good year, the best wines are Rauenthal, then the famous Erbach-Hattenheim-Hallgarten triangle, in third Johannisberg (Schloß Vollrads), Winkel (Winkler Hassensprung) and Rüdesheim.

The Rheingau appellation applies to the vineyards of Hochheim at the eastern extremity of the Rheingau where the Main flows into the Rhine.

The terrain is flat here and the very special climate ripens the grapes two to three weeks earlier than elsewhere.

This is of considerable benefit in the production of Kirchenstück and Domdechaney, the excellent fruity, aromatic Rieslings which are considered to be among the best in the Rheingau. Ever since Queen Victoria visited the region in 1850, Hochheim Riesling, which the English have shortened to "hock", has become the generic British name for German wine. In honour of the royal visit, there is a vineyard with the name of Königen-Victoriaberg (in the Grosslage Daubhaus).

At the western end of the Rheingau, Assmanshausen is famous for its red wine, Höllenberg, which is among the best in Germany. There are two reasons for its success, the sedimentary soil and the grape variety, a Spätburgunder (Pinot Noir) brought from Burgundy in the 12th century by Cistercian monks. It is a lighter version of the original Burgundy, a velvety wine with a slight taste of almond. Not far away to the north-west, the steep slate hills of Lorch and Lorchhausen produce very elegant Rieslings which are sufficiently acid to render them slightly sparkling (Spritzig). The best vintages are Bodental-Steinberg, Kapellenberg and Pfaffenweis.

The greatest vineyards in the Rheingau begin south of Wiesbaden where the Rhine curves westwards. Rauenthal, on the heights of the Taunus range, has terraced vineyards and steep hills which in sunny years produce the best wines in Germany. These are incomparable fruity, spicy Rieslings which have all the best qualities for aging well. The best

Cru is Baiken (Großlage Steinmächer). Others are Gehm, Wülfen, Rothenberg, Nouvenberg and Langenstück. After Eltville, a major wine-producing centre on the banks of the Rhine where Gutenberg stayed in the late 15th century, there is the little village of Marcobrunn (St. Mark's Spring) halfway between Erbach and Hattenheim. The wines produced here (Großlage Deutelsberg with Hohenrain, Rheinhell and Siegelsberg) are among the best of the Rheingau, slightly more full-bodied than those of Rauenthal. These are splendid, aromatic and generous Rieslings which have acquired an international reputation thanks to a visit by Thomas Jefferson in 1788.

The village of Hattenheim which follows is associated with several famous institutions. The first of these, Kloster Eberbach, is a Cistercian abbey and one of the Grands Crus of the Rheingau. Its legendary Steinberg vineyard produces Rieslings which are extraordinarily fresh and delicate. The 32 hectares (80 acres) vineyard was planted by the monks of Eberbach in the 12th century and is surrounded by a wall as was the custom in Burgundy. Today the vineyard belongs to the State. Kloster Eberbach has become the cultural centre of wine-growing in the Rheingau and is the headquarters of the German Academy of Wine and the Rheingau Wine-Growers Association. Its magnificent Roman basilica is used for classical music concerts as well as for the Erutedankefest a ceremony held on the first Sunday in December at which 4000 bottles of Riesling are auctioned for charity. Eberbach is also the home of the Cabinet-Keller. There is an invoice dating from 1773 for the joinery work done at Kloster Eberbach in the Kabinettkeller. Certain documents prove that the first bottles stored in the little cellar were those of the 1712 harvest (or at least, the best of them). Other important vineyards in the area are Mannberg, Nußbrunnen, Wisselbrunnen and finally those of Hassel, Pfaffenberg and Schützenhaus.

Further to the west lies Johannisberg

which is quite a surprising place. The castle and the historic vineyard overlook the town. The terrace, from which one has a superb view, lies exactly 50°N, on the same latitude as Labrador and Mongolia. The cellars of the castle are among the largest in the world and date back to the 11th century. The town has an ancient history. Louis the Pious, son of Charlemagne, related that the harvests of 817 A.D. yielded 6000 litres (1312 gallons) of wine. Schloß Johannisberg was originally a Benedictine monastery dedicated to St. John the Baptist. After it was confiscated from the church in 1803, it passed successively to Napoleon, the Prince of Orange, and then to the Emperor of Austria who presented it to Metternich, the great diplomat who organized the Congress of Vienna in 1816, for services rendered. It still belongs to descendants of Prince Metternich.

The vineyard is of historic interest for more than one reason. From 1720 onwards, Riesling was to be the only grape variety grown there. In the year 1775, the vine-growers who worked for the Abbey of Fulda waited a long time for the epistle from the Abbot authorizing the grape harvest to begin. They waited so long that when the letter finally arrived, it was too late. The grapes had rotted on the vine. The sequel is famous. The grapes were harvested nevertheless and, to everyone's surprise, made excellent wine. Late harvesting (Spätlese) had been discovered.

The biggest estates in the area belong to Fürst von Metternich-Winneburg, Schloß Johannisberg, and G.H. von Mumm. The best Crus are Hölle, Hansenberg and, of course, Schloß Vollrads, an exquisite, fruity, elegant, slightly sharp wine. It is a neighbour of Steinberg and Schloß Johannisberg. The name is associated with the Schloß Vollrads, belonging to the Greiffenclau family. The first trace of Vollrads dates back to 1291. The present owner is Erwin, Count Matuschka-Greiffenclau who still lives in the magnificent baroque palace built by his family in the 17th century. The last stage

of a trip through the Rheingau should be Geisenheim, between Rüdesheim and Johannisberg. It is famous for its Viticulture and Œnology Research Institute. It was here that in 1882, Dr. Herman Müller von Thurgau crossed Riesling and Sylvaner to create the very resistant grape variety that bears his name.

THE PALATINATE (RHEINPFALZ)

This region is part of the state of Rhineland-Palatinate and is the second-largest and most productive wine-growing region of Germany, with 21000 hectares (51,900 acres) of vines. It lies west of the Rhine, bounded n the north by Reinhessen and in the south by Alsace. Its main advantage is a southern microclimate with 1800 hours of sunshine annually and an average temperature of 11°C. The winters are extremely mild.

The Palatinate owes its sunny climate to the Haardt Mountains, a sandstone range which is an extension of the Vosges in the north and which rises to a height of 2200 feet, sheltering the vines in its lea from cold winds and rain.

This hilly region was once considered the wine-cellar of the Holy Roman Empire. Its name comes from the Palatine Hill, one of the seven hills of Rome on which Augustus built his palace which was thus called the palatium, a name which came to be applied to all royal residences. The count palatinate (Pfalzgraf) was the senior dignitary of the Holy Roman Empire who was the hereditary administrator of the

palaces. There are about 150 million vine plants covering the low hillsides of the Haardt right up to the fertile plains which meet it east of the Rhine. The vineyards cover 150 square kilometres (94 square miles) on both sides of the Deutsche Weinstrasse, the German wine route, created in 1934, whose southern part is famous worldwide as the Bereiche Mittelhaard Deutsche Weinstrasse between Bad Durkheim and Neustadt.

The 1150 vine-growers of the Palatine whose plots average only 3 hectares (7½ acres) produce 2.5 million hectolitres (55 million gallons) of wine a year. Forty per cent of them make their own wine, which they market direct to the public.

Proceeding northwards along the wine route, one encounters a landscape of hills and orchards, vineyards and villages, all looking like something out of an old print. Every house has exposed beams inside and an illuminated inn-sign outside. Schweigen, with its stone gateway, is at the start of the German wine route which ends at nearby Alsace, the French border.

At the northernmost end of the Palatinate, after leaving Zellertal and Bockenheim behind, the wine route starts after Grünstadt with Dackenheim, Herxheim and Freinsheim. Freinsheim is a little fortified town whose gothic church and half-timbered houses are a major tourist attraction. The white wines produced there are very acceptable. There are also a

few good red wines from Portugieser and Spätburgunder stock. After leaving Kallstadt, one enters the best section with four centres of attraction - Ungstein, Bad Durkheim, Wachenheim and Forst. The local delicacy of this district is Saumagen, pig's tripe stuffed with a mixture of spiced meat and potatoes. The name "Saumagen" means "sow's belly". The next village is Ungstein, whose sweet, pleasant-tasting wines have the reputation of reviving the dead, as shown on the village's coat of arms. The wines made here are Weilberg, Nubriegel and Herrenberg. Bad Durkheim is one of the most popular villages in the Palatinate, famous for its unique Crus, Spielberg, Michelsberg, Fronhof, Abtsfronhof and Fuchsmantel and its collective Crus, Feuerberg (a mellow, heady red wine), Hochbenn and Schenkenbohl. The annual Durkheim Wurstmarkt, the sausage fair, is held in September. Despite its name, this is actually the biggest wine fair in Germany. Another tourist attraction is the famous Durkheim barrel which originally contained 1,700,000 litres (371,875 gallons) and is now used as a restaurant!

The wines of Wachenheim - Rechbachel, Goldbachel, Gerumpel and Luginsland - have the solid reputation of being rich, heady, and full-bodied. An excellent dry sparkling wine, known in Germany as Sekt, has been made from Riesling since 1888 by Schloß Wachenheim.

Forst and Deidesheim have been locked in competition for generations vying for the title of the best wine-producer of the Palatinate. The soil at Forst consists of basalt, a volcanic rock which holds the heat from the sun. This means that the grapes can be harvested later than elsewhere. There is also clay in the soil, which makes it heavy and has the advantage of retaining water, an essential quality during a dry spell. The best wines are Kirchenstuck, Jesuitengarten and the other wines sold under the name of Großlage Mariengarten.

Deidesheim has a lighter soil, giving its wines more elegance and fruitiness. The best wines are Hohenmorgen, Leinhohle,

THE GRAPE OF PALATINATE

Riesling accounts for 14% of the Palatinate vineyards and is generally of excellent quality. The wines are elegant, full-bodied - even superb! Sylvaner is losing a lot of ground. It now constitutes only 9% of the stock whereas in the early 1960s, it was 40%; the wines made from it are sweet and aromatic. The largest variety is again Müller-Thurgau (a cross between Riesling and Sylvaner) with 24% of the vines. The 40% of dry wines of the Palatinate have a reputation of being very drinkable, harmonious and palatable.

Kieselberg, Herrgottsacker and the Großlage Hofstuck. Deidesheim also boasts one of the oldest inns in Germany, the Gasthaus Zur Kanne, founded in 1160. It is also home to the three B's, the biggest wine-growing estates of the Palatinate, Dr Burklin-Wolf, Reichsrat von Buhl and von Bassermann-Jordan The association of eight villages around Neustadt in very centre of the Mittelhardt has become the biggest wine-producing commune in Germany, owning 2000 hectares (4942 acres) of vines. An autumn festival is organized every year at which a queen of the wine is crowned. The best wines are Erkenbrecht, Monchgarten and Grain. The southern wine route (Südliche Weinstrasse) begins south of Neustadt and Mount Kalmit, the highest point of the Hardt. The landscape here is just as picturesque. The main villages are Maikammer, Edesheim and particularly Rhodt-unter-Rietburg, known for its famous, 300-years-old Traminer vineyard and for the home of King Ludwig of Bavaria, the Schloß Ludwigshohe which dominates the town.

RHEINHESSEN (HESSIA)

Rheinhessen which borders on the Rhineland-Palatinate has 25000 hectares (61,775 acres) of vines growing in 160 vineyards, making it the largest vine-growing area of Germany. It is a hilly district bounded in the north and east by the Rhine, in the west by the valley of the Nahe and in the south by the Palatinate.

The vines arrived with the Roman legions. Their other legacy was the Roman road linking the two major wine-growing centres, Mainz and Alzey. After the fall of the Roman Empire, Rhenish wine is not mentioned again until the 8th century. A certain Nierstein vineyard called Glöck was offered by Charlemagne's uncle to the bishopric of Würzberg. Hesse or Hessia, which became the Grand Duchy of Hesse, later annexed by Prussia, had two principal sources of wealth - wine, and the sale of the famous Hessian mercenaries, mainly to the English.

Rheinhessen is divided in three Bereiche or wine-producing districts. The most westerly of these is Bingen which extends as far as Mainz;in the south there is the Wonnegau district around the city of Worms and finally, "the Rhenish front" or the "Rhineterrasse" and the famous village of Nierstein which symbolizes the whole area. Two factors favour the vineyards of Rheinhessen, a particularly mild climate with dry autumns and few late frosts and a soil consisting of marl, quartz and limestone. Schist is found at Bingen on the Rhine as it is in Mosel, and a sort of red limestone was deposited during the Ice Age glaciation between Nierstein and Nackenheim. If the Rheinhessen wines are generally mild and supple, they are not wines for laying down (with the exception of the Beerenauslesen), though they are distinctive. The Riesling and Sylvaner wines from the Rhenish Front are fruity, distinguished and expansive, comparable to the best of the Rheingau wines. Bingen, on the left bank of the Rhine, is at the junction of four major districts, Rheinhessen, the Nahe Valley, the middle Rhine and the Rheingau.

It was famous in Roman times for the vineyards of Bingen-Kempten and Bingen Büdesheim; today, the best wines come from the vineyards of Scharlachberg, Rosengarten, Schloßberg-Schwärtzerchen, Kirchberg and Osterberg. In Bingen, people still confuse a corkscrew with a pencil, the famous Bingen pencil, the subject of an amusing tale. The Bishop of Mainz is alleged to

have asked his assembled clergy for a pencil. Eager to oblige, all fumbled in their cassocks and simultaneously withdrew - a corkscrew! One of the most beautiful parts of Germany, the Rhineterrasse, begins south of Mainz. The first village is Nackenheim, whose baroque church dominates the Rhine, rising out above vine-covered hills. The reddish soil consists of a mixture of clay and sandstone (Rothliegaide). The wines produced here - Rothenberg, Engelsberg, Schmitts-kapellchen and Spiegelberg - are very similar to those of Nierstein and for a long time they were used for blending. Nierstein, of course, needs no introduction. Everyone has heard of Niersteiner, an elegant, full-bodied Riesling with a superb bouquet. The most famous Crus are Glöck, Orbel, Hipping, Kreuzberg, Brückchen, Bildstock, Schloß Schwabsburg, Heiligenbaum and Pettenthal. In Roman times, Nierstein was the frontier between Frankish territory and the lands of the other Germanic tribes. The wines of Oppenheim are more powerful and more mellow than those of Nierstein, and are even better than the latter in warm, dry years. The best Crus are Paterhof, Herrenberg, Daubhaus, Kreuz and Zuckerberg. Further south, the flat vineyards of Ockenheim and Gau-Alsheim produce excellent Müller-Thurgaus in good years. Gau-Algesheim was the site of a big annual wine fair in the Middle Ages; today it is a new wine festival, held in the second week of October. The limestone soil of the two villages of Ingleheim and Weinheim is particularly well-suited to German red wines. Charlemagne built a fortress in the vicinity and one winter's day, he noticed that the snow had begun to melt on a nearby hillside. He ordered a vine to be planted there, a variety now known as Schloß Johannisberg. The southern vineyards of Guntersblum, Alsheim and Osthofen, north of Worms, grow on very gentle slopes in a loess soil which produces harmonious and fruity wines. Guntersblum is worth a visit, because of its Kellersweg, or "Cellar Route", a one-kilometre (800-yard) stretch

THE GRAPE OF RHEINESSEN

Müller-Thurgau predominates, accounting for 24% of the vineyards of the Rheinhessen. However, it is diminishing in area, since it accounted for 33% of vine-stock in 1964. The same applies to the 14% of Sylvaner vines which 20 years ago constituted 47% of the crop. A cross between a Sylvaner and a Riesling, called Scheurebe, comprises 10% of the vines and Kerner, a cross between Trollinger and Riesling, occupies 7% Finally, there is Riesling with only 5%. Rheinhessen is one of the few parts of Germany to produce fine red wines (especially at Ingelheim). They seem to have the same qualities as the whites. They are fruity, markedly acid, and low in alcoholic content and tannin. The red wines are made from two varieties of grape, Spätburgunder (Pinot Noir) and Portugieser (Blue Portuguese), but they represent a total of barely 4% of all the grapes grown in the region.

which seems to include all the village's wine-cellars. The city of Worms is famous on several counts. It was the Edict of Worms issued in the cathedral which pronounced Martin Luther a heretic, and one of its churches, the Liebfraukirche, has given its names to one of the most popular of German wines, the Liebfraumilch, a Qualitätswein. The Liebfraumilch appellation has been used since 1910 for all the best Rheinhessen, Palatinate, Nahe and Rheingau wines, on condition that they are made from the permitted grape varieties - Riesling, Müller-Thurgau, Sylvaner and Kerner - though the variety is not stated on the label. These wines may never be dry (trocken) or semi-dry. The best-known Liebfraumilch wines are Crown of Brown, Blue Nun, Madonna and Goldener Oktober.

BADEN

Baden, in the state of Baden-Württemberg, is the third-largest wine-growing region in Germany with 15000 hectares (37,000 acres) of vines. This sun-kissed land has been blessed by the gods. It starts on the shores of the Bodensee (Lake Constance), runs along beside the rolling hills of the Black Forest, lingers between France and Switzerland then turns north following the course of the Rhine, exactly parallel to the vines of Alsace on the opposite bank. The Baden vines end on the Neckar just south of Heidelberg.

Baden has a great wine-producing history. Before Phylloxera destroyed half the vines, the Grand Duchy of Baden was the biggest wine-producer in Germany. The Duchy had barely recovered from this catastrophe when it had to deal with a law which insisted that any hybrid variety had to be uprooted. The consequences can be measured today by the considerable improvement in the quality of the wines, which also owes something to modern growing and production methods. Almost the entire yield is vinified in cooperative cellars. The white grapes predominate (77%), especially the Müller-Thurgau variety which alone accounts for 40% of the vines. Baden wines, especially the vins ordinaires, are now the most popular wines in Germany.

A tour through Baden should begin at Lake Constance in the Bereiche Bodensee, to discover the famous Seeweine (lake wines) made from Spätburgunder (Pinot Noir), Rülander and Gewürztraminer grapes. Each lakeside port at which the little Lake Constance steamers call seems to rise up from among the vineyards, with the snow-capped peaks of the Alps in the background. This is region where the Föhn blows, a warm wind which sets animals and humans on edge but which has the advanage of ripening the grapes very fast. The state of Baden owns the magnificent Meersburg estate, consisting of a castle 1300 years old and one of the greatest vineyards of the Bodensee Bereich.

Following the Rhine south-westwards, to the frontier between France and Switzerland, one comes to the Bereich Markgräflerland (the Margrave's land) which has been planted with Gutedel (Chasselas) vines from Vevey since the late 18th century . Today, Müller-Thurgau predominates in the region. Further north, opposite Alsace in the direction of Freiburg im Breisgau, there is a sort of conical mount, actually an extinct volcano, covered in vines. This is the Kaiserstuhl-Tuniberg Bereich. The soil of the Kaisterstuhl is a mixture of volcanic lava and clay, which is perfectly suited to Müller-Thurgau (whose wine is amber-

THE GRAPE OF BADEN

The predominant variety is Müller-Thurgau, which today represents 40% of the vines, although 30 years ago it accounted for barely a quarter of them. Spätburgunder (Pinot Noir) covers 22% of the area, followed by Ruländer (Pinot Gris) with 12%. As for Gutedel (Chasselas, or Fendant in Switzerland) originally from Vevey, in Switzerland, it is disappearing, though it has been planted in the region since the 18th century.
Riesling and Sylvaner are hardly grown at all in the region, because they do not do well here.

coloured here), Spätburgunder and to Ruländer. The crus are excellent. Moving further north, the Breisgau Bereich produces lighter wines. Weißherbst made near Freiburg is definitely one of the best wines in Baden.

The most interesting area in terms of quality is Bereich Ortenau, and especially a narrow strip of land situated between the Rhine and the mountains over which the Ortenburg Forest extends to Baden-Baden. This decaying granite soil produces the best Rieslings, Traminers and Spätburgunders in the state. Every village - Durbach, Ortenberg, Neuweier - is fascinating to visit. An unusual feature is the shape of the wine bottles, the flagon-shaped Bocksviertel, which are used mainly in Franconia.

ITALY

Wine has been made in Italy for three millenia, so it is hardly surprising that the Italians are very enthusiastic about wine and vineyards. Furthermore, Italy is the only country in the world where wine is produced everywhere.

Not content with being the first producers and exporters of wine, outstripping France, the USSR and Spain and producing an astronomical 77 million hectolitres (1,700,000,000 gallons) - a quarter of world production - the Italians are also the greatest wine-drinkers, consuming an average 82 litres (143 pints) per capita per year.

Pliny, writing in the days of the Roman Empire, listed 91 different grape varieties; today there are 2000 types of wine. Most of them are vins ordinaires, heavy, heady, woody, the whites being subject to oxydation. The wines may be coarse and poorly-fermented but they are never devoid of interest. Fortunately, mentalities are changing and traditional methods are being replaced by modern viticulture. Italy can be said to have made the most progress in the past 15 years, with the United States and Australia following close behind.

The variety of soils and climates of the Italian peninsula have produced a unique range of grape varieties. If one divides the Italian boot into transverse sections like a Neapolitan ice cream, one finds the Ugni Blanc and Sauvignon predominate from the Alps to south of Rome, then come Bombino Blanco and Montepulciano. Each grape variety has been acclimatized to the region in which it grows, and some have been grown in the same region for thousands of years. For instance, Lambrusco has been used to make wine in southern Italy since the days of the Etruscans and of Ancient Greece. Perhaps because love is blind, it has caused the Italians to protect their wines by means of totally obscure regulations. Deciphering the label on an Italian wine bottle will reveal neither the content nor the origin of the wine. It may be a D.O.C., a D.O.C.G., a "Classico", a "Reserva" or "da Tavola". One might be dealing with a wine which is the finest of its type, such as a Barbaresco or Barolo from Piedmont, a Brunello from Montalcino, the famous Chiantis from Tuscany or tavern wines. It is best to rely on a few bottlers with a high reputation who produce and market their own wines. From one extremity to the other of the Italian boot, there are 18 great wine-producing regions which are divided administratively along the lines of the outstanding geographical features. The Alps shelter the vast Plain of the Po, then come the Appenines, lying like a 1300 kilometres (812 miles) spinal column down the centre of Italy. The provinces on either side of the chain are Liguria, Emilia, Tuscany (the land of the Etruscans), the Marches, Umbria, and so on, names redolent of sun and of history. Let us begin in the north, in the foothills of the Alps, where the best wines are made in Piedmont.

The village of Barolo in Piedmont

TUSCANY

Tuscany is famous for its beautiful landscapes (the incomparable Tuscan Hills!) the unrivalled cultural history of its major cities - Florence, Leghorn (Livorno), Carrara, Pisa, Sienna - and its most famous wine, Chianti. This magnificent region in the north-west of the Italian peninsula, is bounded in the south by Latium, and is the second biggest wine-growing area of Italy, with an annual production of 5 million hectolitres (110 million gallons). Although this sounds a lot, it is nothing compared with the ocean of Chianti which swamps the world annually! So how can one distinguish between real Chianti and pizzeria plonk? The only way is the origin. There is only one real Chianti-producing district, the 70,000 hectares (172,970 acres) between Florence and Sienna. Outside that area, anything goes! Real Chianti has the word "Classico" on the label. Chianti Classico has a D.O.C.G., the highest distinction that can be granted to Italian wine. One should also check to ensure that the label shows a black cockerel on a red background or with a red circle round it, and the words "Consorzio per la Difesa del Vino Tipico di Chianti". Chianti is made in an area of steep hills covered with vines and cypresses, whose fortified villages are a legacy from the battles between the Florentines and Siennese. The Chianti League was formed in 1376, to protect the local inhabitants from incursions from Sienna. Today, the League would seem to be even more necessary to protect the name of Chianti from all those who abuse it!

THE CHIANTI APPELLATION:

The most famous Tuscan wine is Chianti (D.O.C.G.). There are various types of Chianti but only those from the Chianti Classico district have the right to use the appellation.
Brunelo de Montalcino (D.O.C.G.) is the youngest of the European tres grands crus. It is surely the greatest wine in Tuscany.

If Chianti is such an outstanding wine it is because of the soil on which it is grown. If a Chianti is well-produced it is heady, tannic and powerful. The aroma of violets and liquorice comes from the soil, which is a mixture of schistic clay, sand and stones covered with a layer of limestone. A young Chianti can be fizzy (sparkling) if fermented grape-juice is added to it. The traditional composition of Chianti is 80% Sangiovese to give it body and a bouquet supplied by 5% Canaiolo. Trebbiano and Malvasia are added to lighten the colour and Colorino gives it brilliance.

There are 14 different appellations of origin, which include Chianti Colli Aretini, Chianti Colli Fiorentini, Chianti Colli Senesi, to name but a few. All of them come from districts around the Chianti Classico district.

The cheap, coarse trattoria Chianti, in its distinctive, squat, round-bottomed bottles encased in raffia, are tending to disappear. Today, hand-blown glass bottles and raffia casing costs too much. A good Chianti is something rare and expensive. It is generally sold by the bottle, and in any case it ages better that way.
Brunelo de Montalcino (D.O.C.G.) is, with Barolo and Barbaresco, one of the youngest of the great European wines. It is produced from a hillside vineyard of barely 900 hectares (2224 acres) in the Sienna region, near the little town of Montalcino. Without the addition of Biondo-Santi, Brunello would not exist.

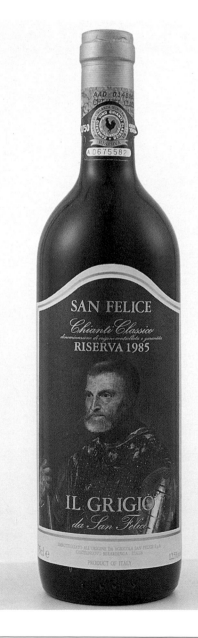

THE GRAPES OF TUSCANY

The five great varieties of Tuscan grapes traditionally used to make Chianti are Sangiove, Canalolo, Trebbiano, Molsavia, Colorino.

Before it existed, prior to 1888, the district merely produced good Chianti. When Ferrucio Biondo-Santi, a biologist, amateur painter and friend of Garibaldi came back from the wars, the Italian nation had just been born. It needed a wine to rival the greatest French vintages. This was the work of Ferrucio Biondo-Santi. Contrary to Tuscan tradition, he made his Brunello using only Sangiovese grapes. He cultivated this variety for years, selecting it to obtain small, thick-skinned grapes, rich in colour and flavour. "A ruby-red wine, almost garnet-coloured, with a characteristic and intense perfume, a taste both dry and warm, perhaps a little tannic when young but harmonious, full and persistent", is how Franco Biondi-Santi, Ferrucio's grandson, described the wine. When harvested, each grape is

individually sorted. The rejects are used to make an honest red wine, Rosso de Montalcino (D.O.C.). The family still owns 12 hectares (30 acres) of vines. Only bunches of grapes from the best vines, those which are more than 25 years old, are reserved for Brunello "Riserva", that is 12000 out of the 60,000 bottles produced each year. These bottles are laid down for 10, 20, and even 50 years in cellars and they are priceless! Vines which are at least 10 years old are used to make Annata and Greppo, two wines which are less special. The example of Biondi-Santi has now been followed by another 138 producers. A consortium has been set up whose members are investors from Milan and even Americans; it includes all the growers except the Biondi-Santis.

If you are ever in Tuscany, try and get hold of a bottle of Vino Santo (the wine of the saints), a golden dessert wine whose sweetness masks its alcoholic strength. Some wine-makers still produce it by hanging up the heavy bunches of Trebbiano and Malvasia grapes from the roof-beams of their attics to dry them. As the liquid in the grapes evaporates, the sugar becomes more concentrated. When pressed, the liquid obtained is poured into casks until they are three-quarters full. They are then sealed and left in a warm place for four years before filtering. The fortified wine thus obtained has a dark-brown colour like Sherry and the same delicious walnut aroma.

In the 18th century, the poet Francesco Redi said of Montepulciano "of all the wines, it was the king". Today, its fame remains only in the D.O.C.G. title of Vino Nobile de Montepulciano. The town of Montepulciano lies 50 kilometres (31 miles) south of Sienna. The wine was made only by a few aristocrats who produced it from Sangiovese grapes. Today, it is a ruby-red wine which is rather light and produced on the clay soil of the hills around the town. When young it is coarse, but it blossoms with age.

The island of Elba, where Napoleon spent his first exile, is also part of Tuscany. Elba wine is made from Procanico and Canaiolo grapes and is a light, straw-coloured wine. A more aromatic red is made from Sangiovese grapes. Aleatico di Portoferraio is also worthy of note; it is a warm, full-bodied red which is often excellent.

PIEDMONT

Piedmont is a region at the foot of the Alps. To the north and west of it, the mountains form a huge arc containing the highest peaks in the range which serve as the frontiers of France, Switzerland and Austria. To the east are Lake Maggiore, Ticino (the Tessine) and the plains of the Po and to the south there are the Appenines. Vines grow everywhere, producing 15% of Italian wines. They are to be found mainly in southern Piedmont in the Monferrato Hills and the Langhe Hills in the province of Alba. In this area, the mountain seems to have become tamed and rounded and the countryside is covered with vines which dominate the landscape.

APPELLATION

The two greatest wines of Italy are : Barolo and Barbaresco, which have had a D.O.C.G. since 1981. Piedmont also produces Asti Spumante.
Other Italian wines of repute are : Barbera, Freisa d'Asti, Gattinara, Grignolino d'Asti, Nebbiolo d'Alba, Dolcetto and Ghemme.

The villages are perched high on the hillsides which are dotted with magnificent hunting-lodges built by the princes of Savoie. Piedmont is also the region of Italian gourmet food, of grisons (wind-dried, paper-thin slices of goat meat), the famous white truffles and true Gorgonzola cheese. It also produces Barolo and Barbaresco (both D.O.C.G.), the best red wines of Italy.

The capital of Piedmont is Turin, also the capital of the Italian automobile industry and of Vermouth. This region produces 5 million hectolitres (110 million gallons) per year, making it the fifth-largest wine producing province of Italy. Eighty

THE GRAPES OF PIEDMONT

Freisa is grown in Piedmont and likes high altitudes, dry soil and an exposed location. Its wines are sugary and acid, a little out of fashion, and can be drunk slightly sparkling. Dolcetto, as the name indicates, produces a fruity wine with a sweet taste; the grape ripens four weeks before Nebbiolo. Dolcetto provides Piedmont with seven D.O.C. wines which should be drunk young. These wines, and Barbera, are the Piedmontese everyday wines. Nebbiolo is the wine for special occasions.

per cent of the crop comes from Monferrato and Langhe. The local grape variety, Nebbiolo (meaning "mist"), does extremely well on the local soil, a mixture of clay and limestone, producing wines which are marvellously complex, almost a work of art. They combine a range of aromas which are not particularly fruity but contain a hint of bitterness which is very characteristic. They are tannic, it is true, but contain a hint of acidity which makes them exceptionally good.

The ancient Piedmontese city of Alba, south of Turin, boasts the vineyards of Barolo and Barbaresco on its surrounding hills. These two wines are so prestigious that, by unanimous agreement, they were the first to receive the D.O.C.G classification, the highest appellation they could be granted. If Barolo is more masculine and powerful, Barbaresco is more supple and feminine, a touch more harmonious. The strong tannic properties of these wines are attenuated by maturing for between two and four years in oaken barrels. The huge barrels, blackened with age, were cut long ago from oak trees in the forests of Slovenia.

As the wines age, they lose their harshness, attaining their full subtlety in the bottle. Barbaresco is deep red in colour; Barolo is almost black when poured but as soon as it makes contact with the air the colour changes until it is as pale as brown onion skin. Both go extremely well with red meat, game and pasta. The Barolo appellation covers 1300 hectares (3212 acres) around Barolo, Castiglione, Falleto, Monforte d'Alba, Serralunga and la Morra. The major wine-producers include Moscarello, Bartolo, Rinaldi Francesco and Renato Ratti.

These bottles are easily recognizable by the blue label decorated with a golden lion. The 500 hectares (1235 acres) of Barbaresco lie south-west of the village of Barbaresco and the three communes of Cuneo. The label depicts the ancient tower of Barbaresco. Angelo Gaja is the producer who best symbolizes Barbaresco. He has become famous throughout the world. In Angelo Gaja, Italy probably has the most gifted wine-producer of his generation.

The sparkling wine of Asti has been given many names, such as Muscat Champagne, Italian Champagne, and so on, ever since Charles Gancia brought the secret of its manufacture from France to Canelli in 1860. Today it is known throughout the world under its appellation Asti Spumante* or Moscato d'Asti (D.O.C.). The range of Asti sparkling wines are sparkling, very sparkling, dry or sweet and lightly fruited, and are between 7° and 9° proof. They have a high proportion of residual sugar. Although still very popular - partly because of their low price - they are drunk less than before. Asti is produced by 53 communes around the little town of Asti on the banks of the Tanaro River. However, in view of the growing fashion for drier wines, more and more Pinot and Riesling are being planted, their wine being sold under the names of Pinot Spumante and Gran Spumante.

The other wines of Piedmont generally bear the name of the grape variety from which they were made without an indication of origin. Carema (D.O.C.) is a Nebiollo, delicate and velvety and less bitter than Gattinara. It is grown in the Asti Valley.

Nebbiolo d'Alba (D.O.C.) is very well known and like Roero (D.O.C.) it is a very pale red wine with a scent of violets. Brachetto d'Acqui (D.O.C.) near Alessandria and Asti produces pale-coloured wines which are slightly sugary and which are found effervescent (sparkling) or slightly sparkling. The same area produces Barbera, strong red wine with a ruby colour. It is rather hard when young and improves by aging for a few years. Ghemme (D.O.C.) is a very aromatic blended wine with a beautiful garnet colour. It is a mixture of Nebbiolo, Vespolina and Bonarda. It has a hint of bitterness and improves with age.

*The bottles are stamped with a likeness of the patron saint of Asti, San Secondo, on horseback.

LOMBARDY

Lombardy is bounded by the Alps to the north, Lake Maggiore in the west and Lake Garda in the east. It is a region of wines and the vines grow right into the suburbs of Milan. The best wines are made in Valteline, a glacial valley near the Swiss frontier, only 30 kilometres (19 miles) from the Swiss mountain resort of St. Moritz. The vines are grown on the south-facing slope of the deep valley of the Adda between the Alps of the Grisons and the Alps of Bergamo.

WINE OF THE HIGH TERRACES:

Four red wines which are very similar in type come from vines grown on the high moutain terraces of Valtelina : Fracia, Sassella, Grumello, Inferno. Franciacorta rosso (D.O.C.), which is made from Cabernet, Barbera, Nebbiolo and Merlot grapes and Franciacorta-Chardonnay (D.O.C.), both originate from the province of Brescia.

The superb mountain landscape, said to be haunted by werewolves, has changed little over the centuries. No machinery is used here, it could not be brought to the vines on the precarious alpine slopes. The yield is low 27000 hectolitres (594,000 gallons)

annually. Four red wines are made from Nebbiolo which is called Chiavennasca here. They are Fracia, Sassela, Grumello and Inferno. These are pleasant, fresh wines which are sometimes sparkling. Valtellina Superiore (D.O.C.) whose label indicates its place of origin is more tannic and warmer. Like Sfursato, it can be made from raisins. If, as in the Riserva quality, it is left to age for four years or more, it becomes remarkable.

THE GRAPES OF LOMBARDY

In Valtelina, the Nebbiolo grape grows everywhere, and is known as Chiavennasca. The Lugana wines are made from Trebbiano and Vernaccia. As for Frecciarossa wines, these are made from Riesling, Pinot noir, Bonarda and Barbera.

Lugana is made much lower down, between Lake Maggiore and Lake Como, from Trebbiano and Vernaccia grapes. It is a light red or a rather yellowish white wine, which is unfortunately allowed to age for too long. Among the D.O.C. vines that prosper around Lake Garda, there are Tocai di San Martino della Bottaglia, an excellent white wine and Riviera del Garda Bresciano, which can be red or rosé.

Casteggio near Pavia, right on the border of Piedmont, is the home of the Frecciarossa estate which owns 28 hectares (70 acres) of vines grown on the low hills. The varieties grown are Riesling, Pinot Noir, Bonarda and Barbera, which produce about 2000 hectolitres (44,000 gallons) a year. Unusually for Italy, the wines are estate-bottled. There are whites (Bianco), semi-sweet whites (Ambrato), dry reds (Rosso) and rosé semi-dry wines (Saint-Georges).

Two other D.O.C.s are produced in the foothills of the Brescian Alps. They are Franciacorta Rosso and Franciacorta Chardonnay. They should be drunk young. Rosso is a dry, well-structured wine made from Cabernet, Barbera, Nebbiolo and Merlot.

Also noteworthy are the sweet and sparkling Muscats known as Moscato di Casteggio Spumante.

VENETIA

The vineyards of Veneto nestle between the Venetian Alps, the plain of the Po and Lake Garda. The wines are not great but are sufficiently attractive and fresh to be appreciated throughout the world. Veneto is the third-largest wine-producing region of Italy, with an output of 8.5 million hectolitres (187 million gallons) of wine a year. Most of the vines are grown between Verona and Venice, with a tendency to concentrate around the shores of Lake Garda, the Italian Riviera. There are four well-known Venetian wines. They are Soave, a dry white wine as suave as its name indicates, and three reds, Valpolicella, Bardolino and Valpentena.

VALPOLICELLA
THE REGULATIONS GOVERNING IT.

This wine is made by 19 communes. The grapes used are Rondinella, Rossignola, Molinara, Negrara, Corvina and Pelara.
No more than 90 hectolitres (1980 gallons) may be produced per hectare (2¹/₂ acres).
Other wines from Veneto are :
Soave, white and suave, Bardolino and Valpeuteux, both reds.
Valpolicella, Recioto della Valpolicella and Amarone are all D.O.C. appellations of Valpolicella.

These are dry and light, to be drunk young so as to be appreciated. They are also encountered as rosés under the name Chiaretto.

There is nothing like a light Valpolicella, with a little "fizz", drunk in a little café in one of the alleyways of Verona near the arena on an opera night. Your glass will contain all the subtlety of a flower combined with a hint of acid-drop and the memory of an unforgettable summer's night.

What, then, is the origin of this enormous quantity of Valpolicella to be found on the wine-lists of every Italian restaurant in the world? Only 19 communes make it from Rondinella, Rossignola, Molinara, Negrara, Corvinon and Pelara grapes. The vineyards extend 30 kilometres (19 miles) north of Verona to the shores of Lake Garda. The legislation is quite clear, only 90 hectolitres per hectare (4900 gallons per acre) can be produced. So what is going on? Recioto della Valpolicella is another famous Veneto wine. The word Recioto

THE GRAPES OF VENETIA

The grape varieties of Veneto. A Valpolicella contains six types of grape: Rondinella, Molinara, Rosignola, Negrara, Corvinon and Pelara.

comes from "recia" meaning "ear", because only the ripest grapes from the top of the bunch (the ear) can be used to make the wine. The grapes are dried on racks which increases the sugar content. The result, Amarone (D.O.C.) is a very dry, very concentrated red wine with a high alcohol content which ages wonderfully. The other Recioto wines are semi-sweet, sweet or spumante (sparkling).

Bardolino, made from Corvina, Molinara, Negrara and Rondinella grapes comes from the south-eastern shores of Lake Garda. It is a dry, very light red with a beautiful ruby colour. The vineyard from which it comes has been very much extended in size, despite the word "Classico" on the label. Fortunately, nowadays it is left to ferment for a much shorter time than was traditionally the case, producing a lighter, fresher wine that is most pleasant.

The 6000 hectares (14826 acres) of Soave, Recioto di Soave and Soave Classico (D.O.C.) lie between Soave and Monteforte, 25 kilometres (16 miles) east of Verona. The wine is straw-coloured with greenish reflections and a typical flavour, a most delicious wine.

Two other wines are worthy of mention, Prosecco di Conegliano and Prosecco di Valdobbiadene, both dry, fruity wines produced 50 kilometres (31 miles) north of Venice near Treviso.

FRIULI VENEZIA GIULIA

Friuli-Venezia-Giulia has been an autonomous region since 1963. The treaty of Saint-Germain-en-Laye made it part of Italy in 1919, although for four centuries it had been part of the Austro-Hungarian Empire. The Carnic Alps are to the north and serve as the frontier with Austria, the Julian Alps and the Gulf of Trieste are to the south-east, and the Yugoslav border is to the east.

AN UP-AND-COMING REGION:

The region produces excellent white wines which continue to improve.
These are made from :
Pinot blanc, Pinot gris, Traminer, Tocai, Picolet, Sauvignon, Riesling, and even Chardonnay.
Friuli is best known for its red wines made from :
Merlot, Cabernet-Franc, Refosco, Pinot noir, Malbec.

This tiny, mountainous region has a mild climate and produces the astronomical amount of 1 million hectolitres (22 million gallons) of wine annually. Almost every grape variety is grown on its terrain. The reds include Merlot, Cabernet-Franc, Cabernet-Sauvignon, Refosco, Pinot Noir, Ribolla Nera, Tazzelenghe, Malbec and Schioppettino. The whites include Pinot Blanc and Pinot Gris, Chardonnay, Riesling, Müller-Thurgau and Verduzzo. When approached from the Plain of the Po, one can see the hillsides covered with vines following the contours of the foothills of the Alps and climbing gently towards the Yugoslav frontier. The wines are mainly varietal. If you stop at a wine-grower, he will offer you the choice of his Sauvignon, Chardonnay, Pinot Grigio or his Tokay. In general, wines from this region name the grape variety on the label. The whites are of a surprising freshness and vivacity. The reds, with the exception of Refosco which is rather harsh, have the freshness and fruitiness which is so typical of the region, especially the Cabernet, Gamay and Merlot varietals. The Adriatic

THE GRAPES
OF FRIULI, VENEZIA, GIULIA

This region is best-known for its red wines made from Merlot, Cabernet, Sauvignon and Refosco grapes, the last being a local variety which can be found in France under the name Mondeuse de Savoie. The whites are no different to those found in Austria and Yugoslavia. There is Tocai, which makes a fairly full-bodied wine, not very aromatic but with a slightly floral bouquet. Other varieties are Picolit, Sauvignon, Chardonnay, Pinot Blanc and Pinot Gris (Grigio), Riesling and Traminer.

coast, near the Yugoslav frontier, produces Aquileia and Collio, excellent white wines which benefit from the favourable micro-climate near Gorizia. Latisana is a red wine grown along the Tagliamento River, as is the better-known Collio Orientali di Friuli, sold like the other D.O.Cs under the name of the grape variety from which it was made.

TRENTINO AND ALTO ADIGE

This autonomous region of northern Italy extends over the Valley of the Alto Adige, part of the Dolomites and southern Tyrol. Unlike their Austrian neighbours just to the north who have developed wonderful white wines from Welschriesling, Ruländer, Pinot Blanc and Traminer grapes, the 6000 Italian vine-growers of the area have remained faithful to the traditional reds which constitute the majority of the 4 million hectolitres (88 million gallons) of wine produced annually. Fortunately , mentalities are changing and thanks to new techniques being applied, especially in Trentino, the wines are improving. The aim is to achieve the same quality as the Swiss and Austrian wines.

Upper Trentino has always been the scene of bitter national conflict. It belonged to Austria until the Treaty of Saint-Germain-en-Laye in 1919, when it was ceded to Italy. The inhabitants are still German-speaking; this area of South Tyrol has had equal rights and cultural freedom since

THE ITALIAN TYROL:

Riesling del Trentino (D.O.C.) is easily comparable with the best Austrian or German Rieslings.
The Austrian influence in this region called Trentino or Alto Adige is very strong:
Kalterersee called Caldaro (D.O.C.), Santa Magdalener (or Sankt Magdalener), now known as Santa Magdalena (D.O.C.), the best red wine of the region, Lagreinkretzer, known under the name of Lagarino Rosato D.O.C.

THE GRAPES OF TRENTINO AND ALTO ADIGE

The Austrian influence is clear in the Riesling and Traminer grapes, but there is also French influence in the Pinot types, the Cabernet and the Merlot.
Schiava Grossa is the most important local variety in Trentino and Alto Adige. It is grown over an area of 3,500 hectares (8,648 acres). In Germany, it is called Trollinger, and it comes from Würtemburg. It is a robust, fruity wine used to make Santa Magdalena and is the main ingredient in "vino da tavola locale".

1946. It is generally agreed that the best wines (which are white) are produced in the northernmost section of the Upper Adige. The best red wines are made around Trento in an extraordinary ring of mountains and all along the major route through the Dolomites, the Brenta Pass, right up to the sun-drenched shores of Lake Garda.

Riesling di Trentino (D.O.C.) from the Alto-Adige sometimes attains the same standard as the best Austrian or German Rieslings, although the Italians have the bad habit of fermenting their wine in cask for too long. It is a wine of the heights which flourishes in a rather cold climate. Traminer del Trentino (D.O.C.) which is not as good as Riesling is still the best in Italy. It is a pleasantly-scented, slightly spicy wine. As for the red wines, Santa Magdalena (D.O.C.) is clearly the best. It is made around Bolzano from Schiave and Lagrein grapes, and has a delicious taste with a slight aroma of almonds.

Caldaro (D.O.C.), also known under the German name of Kalterersee, takes its name from Lake Caldaro in the Adige Valley. However, so much of it is in evidence that the provenance may be somewhat in doubt. Real Caldaro has a beautiful garnet colour and is a harmonious wine which is very pleasant to drink.

Vino Santo di Trentino (D.O.C.) resembles the sweet wines of Tuscany. It is made from dried Malvasia and Trebbiano grapes. As for the vins ordinaires, the best is a red called Val d'Adige made from vines grown on the banks of the Adige River near Trento. It is a blend of Schiave, Lambrusco, Pinot and Teroldego grapes. Terlano (D.O.C.) is a white wine from the Alto Adige, and is made from Terlano grapes as the name indicates. It has a slightly greenish tinge. The famous Lagreinkretzer (or Lagarino Rosato D.O.C.) is a sparkling rosé. Marzemino del Trentino (D.O.C.) is a red which has to be drunk young. All these wines as well as Pinot Bianco (D.O.C.) and Cabernet del Trentino (D.O.C.) are generally quite good and never uninteresting.

EMILIA ROMAGNA

Emilia Romagna is one of the most fertile plains of Italy and extends between the Po River in the north to the Appenines in the south, and from the Adriatic Coast in the east. It includes the little republic of San Marino, on one of the peaks of the Appenines. Although this is an important agricultural area, one does not see large vineyards, though the vine is omnipresent. A few plants spring up in odd corners and receive no particular care, climbing over trees, walls and poles.

Emilia Romagna is the home of Lambrusco, the famous red wine which is slightly sweet and slightly sparkling which is drunk young. The Etruscans called it Lambrusca. It is still trained over trellises as it was in ancient times. It provides the region with four D.O.C.s. There are 60 sub-varieties of Lambrusco grape, covering the various regions of Italy as far south as Sicily, and it is also grown in the United States.

However, mentalities are changing and nowadays there are 5000 hectares (12355 acres) of disciplined cultivation. The numerous "wine routes" which criss-cross the region allow one to taste a multitude of little vintages which go admirably with the local dishes.
Emilia Romagna is the home of Lambrusco, one of the most popular Italian wines (and the most exported, especially to the U.S.A.). Its slight fizziness is a wonderful accompaniment to the cookery of the Bologna region, which is reputed to be slightly heavy. Lambrusco dates back to Roman times and its long history means that every whim has been catered for. It can be white, red, dry, pleasant, rather harsh and even sweetish. The bubbles produce a foam which is a surprise to those seeing it for the first time. The Lambrusco appellation includes five

THE GRAPES OF EMILIA ROMAGNA

The white grape varieties of Emilia Romagna are Sauvignon Blanc, Pinot Gris and Pinot Blanc, Tokay and Riesling. Other reds include Merlot, Cabernet Blanc and Pinot Noir.

D.O.Cs from the region of Modena and Reggio Emilia. They are Lambrusco di Sorbara, di Castelvetro, Grasparossa and Salamino di Santa.
If Lambrusco and Albana grapes make the best wines, the most commonly-grown variety is Sangiovese. The province produces 9 million hectolitres (198 million gallons) of wine from this grape per year, mainly in the form of Sangiovese di Romagna, a dry, strong, almost bitter wine with a wonderful ruby colour.
Albana di Romagna (D.O.C.) can be encountered all along the mountain road from Bologna to Rimini. It is a golden-yellow wine which may be secco (dry) or amabile (mellow). Galla Placidia, regent of the Roman Empire, stopped near Albana in about 435 A.D. and was served a glass of wine from an earthenware jug. When she tasted it, she exclaimed, "You deserve to be drunk from gold!". This is how the local wine, Bertinoro ("Drink you in gold") got its name. Trebbiano di Romagna is found in the districts of Bologna, Forli and Ravenna. It is a dry, straw-coloured wine which is also vinified as sparkling. Also of interest are the Colli Bolognesi di Monte San Pietro, varietal red or white wines made from Pinot Blanc, Merlot or Sauvignon grapes.

UMBRIA

South of Tuscany, half-way between Florence and Rome lies Umbria, ancient land of the Etruscans, which extends over both sides of the Tiber Valley. It is a very mountainous region with a calcareous soil. Vines cover 12000 hectares (29650 acres) producing a million hectolitres (22 million gallons), mostly of the local wine, Orvieto Blanco (D.O.C.), a limpid and pleasant white wine flecked with gold which is sometimes slightly sweetish. It is made from Trebbiano Toscano and a little Verdello, Grechetto, Drupeggio and Malvasia grapes. Of the 10000 hectolitres (220,000 gallons) produced of the wine, one third is Classico. Torgiano (D.O.C.) is another Umbrian wine produced south-east of Peruggia. About 100,000 hectolitres (2,200,000 gallons) of pleasant, fruity red and white wines are made annually. The grapes are harvested around the Tower of Janus. There are two other interesting wines, Colli del Trasimeno (.D.O.C.) from near Lake Trasimeno in the northern Appenines, and Colli Altotiberini (D.O.C.) made from Trebbiano, Sangiovese and Merlot grapes. A total of 350 hectares (865 acres) produces 25000 hectolitres (550,000 gallons) annually.

THE MARCHES

The Marches get their name from the time when they were the southern border of Charlemagne' Empire. They consist of a wild, mountainous region, a zone of fertile, clay hills (where most of the 4 million hectolitres (88 million gallons) of local wine is produced) and a coastal plain fringed with beaches.
The wines produced here are not good enough for export. However, when

THE GRAPES OF THE MARCHES

The most famous variety of the Marches is Verdicchio (dei Castelli di Jesi) which has been grown here since the 14th century, especially in the Ancona region. Its name ("yellow-green") comes from its colour. The wine is spirited and acid which makes it indispensable in sparkling wines.

passing through the capital, Ancona, it is worth tasting Verdicchio Castelli di Jesi (.D.O.C.). a cool, straw-coloured white wine which may be dry or semi-dry. It is the best wine of the Marches, but be careful since it has an alcohol content which may go as high as 14°. It is produced in the regions of Cupramontana, Monteroberto and Castebellino. The title "Classico" is only given to wines from the southern part of Jesi. The best red wine is Rosso Piceno (D.O.C.) made from Sangiovese and Montepulciano.
Bianchello del Metauro (D.O.C.) is a light, dry white wine made from Bianchello and Malvasia grapes. However, it is only of interest because it is made on the Metauran Hills, where the Romans beat the Carthaginians in one of the greatest battles of antiquity.

LATIUM

Latium includes Rome and the Roman provinces. The region is bordered in the north by Lake Bolsena, in the south by the Tyrrhenian Sea and in the east by the Abruzzi. Ninety per cent of the wines made here are dry and semi-dry whites which are quite lively and very popular with Romans and tourists alike. The most famous of them is made near Lake Bolsena in the province of Viterbo. It is called Est! Est!! Est!!! di Montefiascone. The legend goes back to the 12th century. A certain bishop called Fugger was travelling from his native Germany on the way to Rome. He was in the habit of sending his servant along ahead to prepare the way for him, which in his case meant trying the wines before the bishop patronized the taverns. If the wine was good, the servant would write "est!" on the door of the tavern; if the wine was bad, he would write "non est!". On arriving at Montefiascone, he found the wine so extraordinary that he wrote "Est! Est!! Est!!!" before returning to the wine-cellar to await his master.

If you stop at a trattoria in Rome, there is no point in indicating that you would like a Frascati, a Colonna or a Colli Albani, because the proprietor has his own wine-merchant, but what he serves you will rarely be disappointing. Almost all the wines comes from Castelli Romani which produces enormous quantities of dry, sweet, or semi-dry wines made from Malvasia and Trebbiano grapes. They are recognizable by their straw colour.

Frascati (D.O.C.) found on all the menus of Roman restaurants is drunk dry or semi-dry. If it is sweet, it is called Canellino. Frascati, a rather vigorous wine, is produced from three grape varieties, Malvasia, Greco and Trebbiano.

South of Rome there are plenty of surprises. Colli Albani (D.O.C.) which comes from Albano and Aricca is a strong, golden wine with a delicate bouquet. Marino, produced between Lake Albano and Rome, produces a straw-coloured dry wine or a mellow, lightly-fruited one. The Aprilia wines

THE GRAPES OF ABRUZZI

White Trebblano di Abruzzo.
Red Montepulciano di Abruzzo.
Rosés using the appellation Cerasuelo d'Abruzzo.

from Trebbiano are straw-coloured or rosé. They are dry when they are made from Sangiovese and robust and garnet-coloured when made from Merlot.

THE ABRUZZI

The Abruzzi is in the central area of the Appenines. The region is arid and poor and is dominated by the 9000 feet San Sano peak. There is also a narrow coastal strip beside the Adriatic.

The vines grow on the soft limestone rock known as karst, which gives the wines a piquant acidity. Montepulciano d'Abruzzo is produced in large quantities in the Chieti region by the Adriatic Sea. It is a robust red wine 12° proof, vinified with a little Sangiovese.

Chieti, Aquila, Pescara and Terano are ruby-red wines which are slightly sweetish and may be Cerasuolo (made with fermented must) or Vecchio (more than two years old).

Trebbiano d'Abruzzo is a dry, straw-coloured white 11° proof wine.

It is made in 57 communes in the provinces of Chieti, Aquila, Pescaro and Terano.

CAMPANIA

If one day in Naples, or anywhere else in the world in an Italian restaurant, you are served a dry white wine with pale gold reflections from a grape harvested on the southern slope of Vesuvius, think of this, one of the loveliest legends about wine. A very long time ago, Satan was chased out of Paradise, so he settled, in a flurry of thunderclaps and volcanic eruptions, in the Bay of Naples, a wonderful spot just at the gates of Paradise. As might have been expected, the city and its surroundings soon became a place of sin and debauchery. Christ, who liked to

THE GRAPES OF CAMPANIA

Vesuvio is a very popular red wine made from Aglianico, Piedirosso and Olivella grapes.
Greco is obviously of Greek origin, and may be the vine which produced the famous Falernum praised by Horace. Here it is called Greco di Tuffo, and it gives a rich, dry white, straw-coloured wine. It is one of the grapes used to make Lacrima Christi.

meditate on the slopes of Vesuvius, overlooking one of the most beautiful bays in the world, saw that his earthly paradise had become a hell. A tear fell from his eye to the ground. At this very spot, a vine sprang up, which was therefore dubbed Lacrima Christi - Christ's Tear. Although today the Lacrima Christi vineyards are planted with Greco and Fiano grapes, they remind the Neapolitans of the original vine with its taste of paradise lost.

Modern Campania is a fertile sunny region, the Campania Felix ("happy countryside") of the ancients. It includes Naples, Herculanum, Pompeii, the Sorrento peninsula, and the islands of Capri and Ischia. In Roman times, it produced the famous Falernum whose praises were sung by Pliny and Horace as an immortal wine, one of the wonders of the world.

Today, one is sadly disappointed! The local wine is a vin ordinaire made with Falanghino grapes for the white and Aglianico for the red. It is made in abundance at Capua, Campi, Flegrei, Sessa Aukunca and Mondragone. However, it is still better than the acid Taurasi (D.O.C.) which is only drinkable after long aging, or Greco di Tuffo (D.O.C.) a dry wine with a good flavour and a golden-yellow colour

which is also to be found in sweet and even sparkling types.

The wines of Capri have an international reputation. In fact, they are typical Campania wines - heady, lively and dry. They go wonderfully with seafood, or sipped as an aperitif in the shade of a trellis. The grape varieties used are Greco and Falanghina, but the wines have not yet been honoured with a D.O.C. However, the neighbouring island of Ischia has had one for a long time. Ischia Bianco or Rosso are made from Forastera and Biancolella; they are pleasant, light-coloured wines with a delicate bouquet.

SICILY

Sicily is the largest island in the Mediterranean. It lies south-west of the Italian peninsula and is separated from Calabria on the mainland by the Straits of Messina. Sicily owes its name to its first inhabitants, the Siculi who were of Asian origin. With its magnificent beaches and vegetation, hills and mountains covered with olive trees and vines, the great plain of Catania dominated by the volcanic Mount Etna, Sicily is doubtless the most beautiful island in the Mediterranean. It was occupied by the Phœnicians and colonized by the Greeks from the 8th century B.C. The Greeks brought viticulture to the island and covered it with temples, theatres and ancient cities. After Roman rule, the Vandals conquered it and were in turn beaten by the Byzantines. The Arabs held it briefly but were soon chased out by the Normans. In 1194, it was conquered by Germany. In the 13th century, the islanders revolted against French rule (in the notorious incident known to history as "the Sicilian vespers"). Sicily was ceded first to Spain then to Austria. It was not until the 19th century that the island became part of Italy.

Sicily is thus a museum of European culture and since Greek times it has been a land of vines. They cover an area of 90,000 hectares (222,390 acres) and produce 9 million hectolitres per year. Most of the wine produced is exported (mainly to France) to be used in blending.

Sicilian viticulture has come a long way. Two measures saved it:

A considerable reduction in the acreage of Grillo grapes devoted to the making of the version of Marsala produced on the western side of the island, a strong, dry wine whose alcohol content may be as high as 18°. The area has partly been replanted with Trebbiano, Catarratto

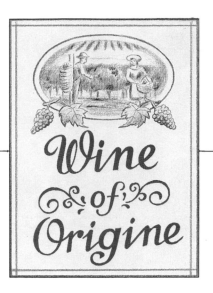

Today, 80% of Sicilian wine is produced by a hundred or so cooperatives. They include Corvo in Palermo, Settesoli near Agrigente and Villa Grande at the foot of Mount Etna. This is one of the reasons why the wines of Sicily are so successfully exported.

THE GRAPES OF SICILY

Nero Mascalese is used in Sicily to increase the alcohol content and improve the colour of other wines. It is used to make Faro near Messina and is added to the Etna wines, which generally age well.
Monica is of Spanish orign and is the most widely-grown variety in Sardinia. It produces very ordinary wines, with very few exceptions.
As for whites, the famous Marsala wines of Sicily, which may be dry or sweet, are made from Grillo and Catarratto Blanco varieties.

and Inzolia to produce dry white wines and mostly with Sangiovese for the red wines.
Earlier harvesting, starting in early September to retain the fruitiness, acidity and freshness of the wine. The must no longer spends long periods in vats and the wine is bottled before Christmas.

The best-known Sicilian wine is the fortified version of Marsala, a sweet wine with a good amber colour, in which the fermentation of the must is stopped by the addition of spirits. The grape varieties used to produce this Marsala are Grillo, Catarratto and Inzolia and the district is strictly delimited. Marsala is classified according to its glucose content. It may be Fino (17° alcohol, 5% sugar), Superiore (18° alcohol, 10% sugar) or Vergine 18° alcohol and no additional sugar, made in the same way as Sherry. Mamertino is a golden white wine with a very aromatic

bouquet. It is grown on the slopes near Messina. Cæsar had it served to him during a banquet to celebrate his third term as Consul. Corvo di Casteldaccia is a fresh, dry white wine from Trebbiano, and Faro is a good red wine made near Messina. It has a D.O.C. and is up to 14° proof. However, the best Sicilian table wines come from the slopes of Mount Etna. All are D.O.C. and have a high alcohol content. The whites are made from Carricante (Superiore if they come from the commune of Milo) and Catarratto. The reds and rosés are made from Mascalese. The Rosso is a powerful wine that needs aging for several years to reveal its true aroma.

The Syracuse region produces Moscato di Noto (D.O.C.), a very pale yellow wine with a slight scent of honey.

One should not leave Sicily without tasting Malvasia delle Lipare (D.O.C.) the famous sweet Malmsey wine made from raisins. It is the speciality of the string of islands called Salina, Stromboli, Lipari and Pantellina, a superb dessert

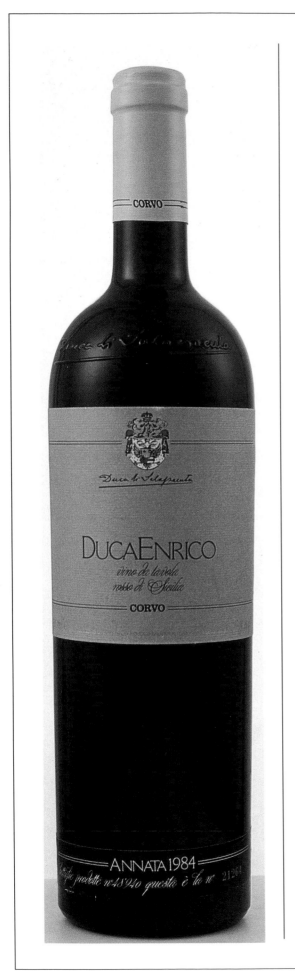

SARDINIA

Sardinia is one of the largest islands in the Mediterranean. It lies parallel to central Italy in the Tyrrhenian Sea and is very mountainous, the average altitude being 3000 feet.

The island is difficult to understand because so many questions remain unanswered.

For instance, who built the Nuraghi, those large conical towers?

Were they tombs, watchtowers or fortresses?

So far, no one has been able to discover the truth nor discover the exact origin of the population of Sardinia.

The island has recently become a major centre of tourism, thanks largely to the investment by the Aga Khan, who spent large sums to develop the Costa Smeralda. Sardinia also produces 2 million hectolitres (44 million gallons) of wine annually.

Once known for its powerful, sweet wines, Sardinia followed Sicily in completely overhauling its wine production in the 1960s. It introduced new grape varieties, earlier harvests and new vinification techniques.

The vineyards of Sella and Mosta, north of Algherro, are the most commonly quoted successful example; they are owned by the Italian government.

The wines produced here are light, perfumed and slightly spicy. They are made from Torrelata, a Spanish variety.

Vernaccia di Oristano (D.O.C.) is the best known Sardinian wine. It is up to 16° proof and with its amber colour it bears a close resemblance to Sherry.

It is made mainly in the Tirso Valley near Oristano in the Gulf of Oristano. It is aged for up to 30 years.

The northernmost part of the island, the Santa Teresa region, produces a very dry, straw-coloured wine called Vermentino di Gallura D.O.C. Another important region is Cagliari, known for its heady wines. They include Malvasia (Malmsey)

THE GRAPES OF SARDINIA

In Sardinia there are also Vermentino Corso, Nugarus brought by the Phœnicians whose name is similar to that of the Nugharo towers (see above), the spirited and full-bodied Torbato and Nasco, whose flavour is mellow with a pronounced walnut flavour.

(14.5° proof), Monica, a very full-bodied red wine and Moscato. Moscato (Muscat) is made in Dolce Naturale (natural sweet) and Liguoroso Dolce Naturale (liqueur natural sweet), and Giro di Cagliari, a fortified wine similar to Port.

It is also found in dry and slightly mellow forms.

It has a ruby-red or pink colour and must age for at least a year in casks.

It is also found in the form of a liqueur wine. Nugarus (D.O.C.), also from the Cagliari region, is an excellent table wine and accounts for 10% of Sardinian production.

Malvasia di Bosa (D.O.C.) is a white wine with a faint flavour of hazelnuts which is produced on the west coast. It is easily 17.5° proof and is compulsorily aged for at least two years in casks.

BASILICATA, APULIA, CALABRIA

Basilicata, the ancient Lucania, is one of the poorest, most mountainous and wild regions of southern Italy. The slopes of Monte Vulture produce a warm red wine, Aglianico del Vulture (D.O.C.) with the flavour of its volcanic soil. It is a wine which ages well. After three years in cask, it becomes Vecchio (old) and after five years Riserva (reserve). Muscat and Malvasia, which also abound in the Monte Vulture area, produce excellent dessert wines thanks to what Italians call Passito, the trick of drying the grapes before vinification.

Apulia, also known as Puglia, lies to the east of Basilicata. It is the heel of the Italian boot, between the Appenines and the Adriatic. The region consists of a series of plains and plateaus intersected by valleys. Wheat grows in the fertile regions, leaving the rest to the olive trees and the vines. Under a burning sun, Apulia produces 11 million hectolitres (242 million gallons) of wine a year, most of which is vin ordinaire, the rest being used to make Vermouth.

The pleasantest wines include Locorotondo, made near Fasano, a yellow-green wine produced from Verdeca and Bianco di Alessano grapes. While waiting at Brindisi for the ferry to Greece, it is a good idea to try the local Martina Franca which is drunk very cold. Castel del Monte (D.O.C.) from the Bari region and Moscato di Trani (D.O.C.) are naturally sweet wines. Martina is produced at Lecce in the heel of the boot. It is made partly from Negro Amaro grapes which give it a faintly burnt taste.

If Apulia is the heel of the boot, Calabria is the toe. It is a very poor and very mountainous region known for its legends and its bandits. Tourists visit the coastal region which has orchards of

THE GRAPES OF BASILICATA

Aglianico del Vulture is a very concentrated wine which has the slight aftertaste of strawberries and raspberries. It is made, of course, with Aglianico grapes, a variety of Vitis hellenica. This is a wine of sun and a dry climate, being very tannic when young and requiring long aging in the bottle. Muscat and Malvasia grapes are also found in the region.

THE GRAPES OF CALABRIA

Apart from Muscat, Gaglioppo represents 60% of the acreage. This variety originates from Greece and produces Ciró, a very red, very heady wine, which needs aging. Greco di Gerace is a wine subjected to passerillage - the process whereby the grapes are harvested late and left to shrivel on the vine to increase the sugar content. The wine is used for largely for Catholic rites.

orange and lemon trees and acres of olive trees. Yet Calabria's volcanic soil also makes it an important wine-producing region. However, the wines are disappointing with a few surprising exceptions. These are Ciró (D.O.C.) produced east of Cosenza, whose pale straw colour comes from Greco Bianco and Trebbiano grapes. The warm and powerful reds and rosés are made from Gaglioppo, Greco and Trebbiano grapes. Finally, there is the rare Greco di Gerace, from a little town in Appenines. This wine was very popular with the Ancient Romans, and it remains superb, with an aromatic bouquet and a golden colour reminiscent of nectar.

LIGURIA

Liguria is the extension of the French Côte d'Azur into Italy. Its coastline consists of a succession of seaside resorts, behind which the Alps straddle both sides of the Gulf of Genoa. Most of the 400,000 hectolitres (8,800,000 gallons) of wine produced annually are of mediocre quality, grown under very difficult conditions. In some places, they can only be accessed on foot. The two exceptions to the rule of mediocrity are Rossesse-di-Dolceacqua (D.O.C.), a pleasant wine with a 12° to 14° alcohol content, which is said to have been liked by Napoleon, and Cinqueterre-Sciacchetra (D.O.C.). The latter is the best Ligurian wine, and is made from Bosco and Vernaccia grapes. It is a white wine with a beautiful amber colour which, as its name indicates, comes from five terrains, the communes of Vernazzi, Campiglia, Riomaggiore, Monte Rosso and Biassa. It is produced in dry and semi-dry versions and is found both as an apperitif and a dessert wine. In the latter case, it is made from partially dried grapes and is 17° proof.

THE GRAPES OF VALLE D'AOSTA

Donnaz and Enfer d'Arvier are the two best-known wines made from Petit Rouge and from Nebbiolo vines. The latter is called Picotener in this region

VALLE D'AOSTA

Valle d'Aosta is dominated by the highest peaks of the Alps. It is the smallest in size and population of all the Italian regions and is situated between Switzerland to the north and France to the west; Piedmont is to the south and east. The Valle d'Aoste D.O.C. includes 15 different types of wine, of which the best known are Donnaz and Enfer d'Arvier. The vines are grown on the mountainsides around Donnaz and in the communes of Paloz, Bord and Pont St. Martin, on narrow terraces. They produce sweet, garnet-coloured wines made from Nebbiolo grapes which are called Picotener here. Enfer d'Arvier is also a red wine made from Petit Rouge grapes with a little Vin de Nus, Negret and Dolcetto added. This wine ages very well in casks, and is recognizable by its hint of bitterness.

The wines of Liguria: Cinqueterre-Sciacchetra (D.O.C.), a dry or semi-dry white wine made from Vernaccia grapes, Dolceaqua (D.O.C.), a red from Rossese, Vermentino ligure, made from Vermentino grapes as well as from the Bosco and Brachetto varieties.

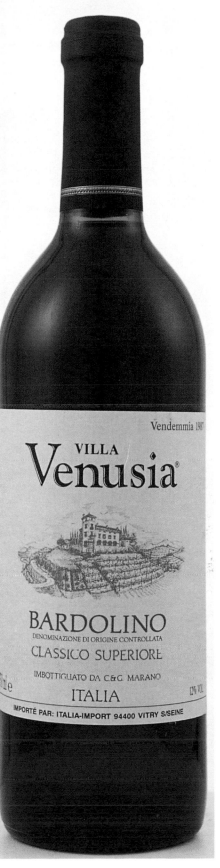

SPAIN

Until recently, only a few Spanish wines such as sherry escaped widespread mistrust. Wine produced in Spain conjured up images of excessive sunshine and thus excessive alcohol. Quantity was suspected of always taking precedence over quality. These over-simplifications are in urgent need of correction.

In the first place, the total quantity of wine produced in Spain is still much lower than the country's actual potential. In this respect, Spain is only in third place among the countries of Europe, whereas it is in the leading position as far as the extent of its vineyards is concerned. This contradiction is explained both by the excessive aridity of the soil and by the low level of mechanization used in vine-growing.

However, wine-growers are increasingly forming cooperatives, while large bodegas (cellars) are now provided with high-performance equipment. Not only does the modernized equipment allow careful vinification, but an increasingly rigorous selection of vines has accompanied a general tendency towards improved quality, of which the Rioja wines are eloquent examples.

Andalusia, working the vineyards, the sherry is stored and kept cool in the Bodegas.

RIOJA

No other wine-growing region of Spain enjoys such a wide and flattering reputation. Rioja has recently won several international competitions, thereby increasing its exports to more than sixty countries, with Great Britain as the biggest customer.

RIOJA

The denominación is subdivided into
RIOJA ALTA,
RIOJA ALAVESA,
RIOJA BAJA,
in descending order of quality.

It was at the end of the 19th century that this region's vocation as a wine producer was confirmed, under the aegis of the first large modern bodegas. Taking advantage of the temporary commercial decline of the Bordeaux wine industry, these bodegas were wisely inspired by its methods. They thus foreshadowed the vast bodegas of today which have benefitted from the confidence of the financiers and have thus been able to afford to install advanced technology.

It is therefore no surprise to learn that Rioja was the first region of Spain to set up a system of quality control. In 1926, a Consejo Regulador (Regulatory Council) was created to lay down strict regulations and supervise their implementation.

The Rioja vineyards of northern Spain consist of nearly 45,000 hectares (111,200 acres) on both banks of the Ebro, covering a strip of land about 120 kilometres (75 miles) by 40 kilometres (25 miles). The soil consists of a mixture of limestone, iron, clay and alluvial deposits. On the whole, the climate is a temperate one, with warm but not torrid summers and mild winters. While the common hallmark of the Rioja wines has long been a strong aroma of oak due to prolonged storage in casks, modern producers are tending to adapt themselves better to international taste. Aging in the bottle is now favoured, so that the intrusive aroma of the wood is beginning to give way to a richer and more complex bouquet.

THE RANGE OF WINES AND GRAPE VARIETIES

Whether they are red, white or rosé, all the Rioja wines are produced by blending.

In the case of the white wines, the vine which dominates 90% of the production is the Viura, better known under the name of Macabeo. Its success stems mainly from its generous yield. In addition, its fairly fruity juice has the advantage of being fairly impervious to oxydation. Although the Viura has almost ousted the other white vines, the best producers continue to combine it with a little Malvasia, which gives the wine more flavour and subtlety. Some bodegas also resort to a little Garnacha Blanca, the main advantage of which is the ability to increase the degree of alcohol.

The reds rely mainly on the Tempranillo, which is unquestionably the vine-king of Rioja. According to professional wine-tasters, it is not unlike that noble French vine, the Pinot Noir of Burgundy. In any case, it produces wines of a deep colour, which remain unspoiled even after a long period of aging. Although it also has the advantage of a good yield, it has one notorious defect, its low acidity. It is therefore necessary to combine it with vines like Garnacha, Mazuelo and especially Graciano. The latter is the most aromatic of the red vines of the Rioja, adding a rich and delicate flavour to the wine.

These vines produce two types of red wine, Clarete (claret), a light-coloured wine, once very popular but increasingly giving way to Tinto, which has a strong colour and a better structure. It is also fruitier, very well suited to aging and has a fine smoothness.

As for the whites, they are generally very dry and barely exceed 11°. Most of the bodegas have now decreased the amount of time they leave the white wines in oak casks. Some have even dispensed with the casks altogether, so as to bring out the primary aromas.

This is true in particular of Recentie, which must be drunk within the year. The other whites generally benefit from a few years'

aging in the bottle. The region is divided into three distinct areas.

THE RIOJA ALTA

This covers the south of the Ebro, where thirty-odd bodegas handle about 17,000

THE GRAPES OF RIOJA

For the whites, the Viura (or Macabeo) is combined with only a little Malvasia and Garnacha Blanca.
The reds are dominated by Tempranillo, to which a little Garnacha, Mazuelo and the very aromatic Graciano are added.

hectares (42,000 acres) of vines. Nearly half of these firms are grouped around the small town of Haro, while the others are divided between Cenicero, Fuenmayor and Navarrete.

The high altitude at which the vineyards are planted, the iron-and-clay soil and the adequate humidity all contribute to the success of the Rioja Alta wines. They are certainly the best in the whole region, with their bouquet, their solid structure and their suitability for lengthy aging.

THE RIOJA ALAVESA

This is the northernmost region, covering nearly 7000 hectares (17300 acres) of the north bank of the Ebro. The vineyards are planted on hillsides in a mainly limestone soil.

The principal bodegas are to be found in the communes of Abala, Elciego, Labastida, Laguardia, Oyón and Villabuena. The wines produced are mainly light and supple reds with a strong aroma.

THE RIOJA BAJA

Almost 20000 hectares (4942 acres) of vineyards are planted with too high a proportion of Garnacha for the wines to aspire to the finesse of their neighbours. These robust wines with a high alcohol content are mainly useful to add to the blends produced in the other areas.

CATALONIA

Although Catalonia is only fifth-largest in Spain in terms of the area of its vineyards, it is in second place for quantity. There is no better way to illustrate the work put in by the Catalan wine-growers.

This north-eastern region of Spain forms a triangle bounded in the north by the Pyrenees and in the east by the Mediterranean. The mountain vineyards are terraced to an altitude of 21,000 feet. The winters are generally mild and the constant summer heat is tempered by sea breezes.

THE D.O.'S OF CATALONIA

Seven D.O.'s produce the diversified range of Catalan wines. They are Ampurdan-Costa Brava, Alella, Penedés, Conca de Barbera, Tarragona, Priorato and Terra Alta.
The reds and sparkling whites of Penedés are the finest wines of the region.

A large number of wine-growers have formed cooperatives, which supply some of the bodegas with wine intended for future blending.

A range of grape varieties is used to produce the wines of Catalonia, but as in Rioja, the Macabeo predominates in the whites, combined with the Malvasía and the Garnacha Blanca. Two local varieties are also used, the Parellada and the Xarel-Lo, which compensate for a lack of acidity. Similarly in the reds, the Tempranillo, which is called Ull de Llebre here, crops up again, as well as the Garnacha, the Monastrell and the Carinena. This latter is much appreciated for its high yield.

The variety of the soil types and of vine stocks enables Catalonia to offer the most complete range of wines to be found in Spain, including reds, rosés and dry, sparkling or syrupy whites.

This diversity of Catalan production is also reflected in the seven D.O.'s which are officially defined here.

ALELLA

This coastal area to the north of Barcelona is suffering increasingly from its proximity to the big city. In fact, with the advancing urbanization, the *denominación* area, which, was as by as 1500 hectares (3700 acres) ten years ago, is no larger than 500 hectares (1235 acres) today. Nevertheless, the many owners of the plots of vineyards are striving to produce mainly white wines, some of them dry with a marked acidity, some of them medium-sweet and more attractive.

AMPURDAN COSTA BRAVA

Set sufficiently back from the coast and the crowds of tourists, this most northerly area benefits from a very recent denominación. Swept by the mistral and the tramontana winds, its 5000 hectares (12355 acres) of vines produce mainly rosé wine. The Vi Novell is a newly-introduced light red wine, modelled on Beaujolais primeur.

THE GRAPES OF CATALONIA

The Macabeo predominates in the white varieties, combined with the Malvasia and the Garnacha Blanca. The Parellada and the Xarel-Lo add acidity.
Among the reds, the Ull de Llebre (or Tempranillo) plays the leading role, despite the presence of the Garnacha Tinta, the Cariñena and especially the Monastrell.

CONCA DE BARBERA

This is the most recent D.O. and covers 10000 hectares (24710 acres) of hilly vineyards producing a table white wine from the Macabeo and Parellada vines. The more acidic wine is sold in the Penedés region for the manufacture of sparkling wine. This D.O. has another distinctive feature. It is here that the Bodega Torres has begun some successful experiments with the introduction of two "noble" French vines, the Cabernet Sauvignon and the Pinot Noir. Developments should be watched closely.

PENEDES

The Penedés is a central coastal region between Barcelona and Tarragona Some 25000 hectares (61,775 acres) of vines cover the limestone hills of the hinterland up to an altitude of 2100 feet. It is to the dry whites that Penedés owes a good part of its reputation. The more acidic versions include some very decent sparkling wines produced by the méthode champenoise. The production is dominated by the bodegas, which are grouped around the comunes of Villafranca del Penedés and San Sadurní de Noya.

The sparkling wines of Penedés are

divided into two categories:

the CAVAS, which undergo a second fermentation in the bottle and which attain the highest level of quality, and the GRANVAS, naturally sparkling wines whose second fermentation takes place in vats.

The quality of the cavas should not however eclipse that of the red wines. With their body and their fruitiness, some of these are in fact quite able to compete with the best produce of Rioja.

PRIORATO

This D.O. is an enclave of 3700 hectares (9143 acres) of hillside vineyards within the larger area of the Tarragona denominación. The volcanic soil, planted largely with the Garnacha vine, produces wines that are almost black, very full-bodied and with a high alcoholic content. The district also produces a golden white wine which, with oxidation, develops into the Rancio type.

TARRAGONA

The cooperatives which own this vast 25000 hectares (61,775 acres) produce a robust red with a high alcoholic content, which is mainly useful for blending.

Tarragona's main contribution to œnology consists of its sweet wines which are aged according by the solera system

TERRA ALTA

This recent D.O. consists of some 1600 hectares (39,536 acres) of hillside vineyards centred around the town of Gandesa in southern Catalonia. Robust red and white wines, mainly intended for blending, are produced here.

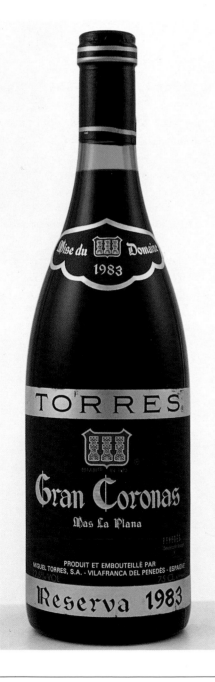

GALICIA

Galicia is a fertile region of northern Spain, like an extension of Portugal, bordered by the Atlantic Ocean, with consequent relatively high humidity. Only its two most southerly provinces, Pontevedra and Orense, produce wine to any great extent, but this does not prevent the whole region from occupying first place in per capita consumption. Galicians drink an average of over 140 litres (31 gallons) a year, three times more than in the rest of Spain.

On the other hand, the quality, perhaps for this very reason, is often disappointing. Yet, the climate, granitic soil and methods of cultivation are all similar to prevailing conditions in northern Portugal. The vines grown along the banks of the Minho river are also identical. These include the Albarino, which produces very dry white wines, and the Treixadura.

These two predominant vines only give moderately satisfactory results in the province of Pontevedra, notably in the D.O. of Val de Salnes, Condado de Salvatierra and El Rosal at the mouth of the Minho. Some decent sparkling wines are produced here, though they do not attain the standard of the Portuguese Vinho Verde. It is true that the few cooperatives have inadequate equipment and that they are outnumbered by a large number of smallholders who practise vinification very much in the style of a cottage industry.

THE GRAPES OF GALICIA

Tempranillo and Garnacha, with a little Sonson and Mencia, are responsible for the reds. The whites are made mainly from Albarino, but also from the Palomino and Godello varieties.

The province of Orense contains three other D.O. Valdeorras, in the east, produces a white from the Palomino grape and a deeply-coloured red mainly from the Garnacha, both of these wines being simple and rustic. Ribeiro, in the west, attains a more satisfactory degree of quality in both red and white. This area has Galicia's largest cooperative, which strives to make judicious use of the local vines, the Godello for the whites and the aromatic Sonson for the reds. Monterrey, on the Portuguese border, produces mainly robust and alcoholic red wines under a scorching sun. The rest of the region's production is mainly used for blending or is sold in the neighbouring region of the Asturias, which produces too little to satisfy the needs of the local population.

D.O.'S OF GALICIA

Despite a fairly average overall level of quality, Galicia has no fewer than six D.O.'s. These are Ribeiro, Monterrey, Valdeorras, Val de Salnes, Condado de Salvatierra (also called Candado de Tea) and El Rosal.

ANDALUSIA

Andalusia, at the southern tip of Spain, can take pride in some famous wines. Sherry (Jerez) is the best-known and sets an example of quality for Montilla-Moriles and for Malaga.

Wine of Origine

Due to their method of production, the sherries are never given vintages. However, it would be wrong to restrict the finos to being drunk as aperitifs. The best, which attain the level of the great Burgundian whites, can provide an excellent accompaniment to fish in sauce and white meat.

JEREZ

It was the English who made the name of Jerez world-famous in the 15th century, ensuring its commercial prosperity. Even today, the United Kingdom remains the leading market for sherry, whose popularity does not appear to be declining. It is thus not surprising that the name of Bristol, formerly the biggest English port for sherry, continues to appear on many labels as a symbol of quality. The 15,000 hectares (37,065 acres) vineyard is situated a little inland from the Bay of Cadiz, between two rivers, the Guadalquivir to the north and the Guadalete to the south. The three main wine-producing centres are Jerez de la Frontera, the coastal town of Puerto de Santa María and Sanlúcar de Barrameda at the mouth of the Guadalquivir.

The whole of the region benefits from a large amount of sunshine throughout the year and a very low average rainfall. This is enough to give the wines a uniformity, despite the three different types of soil. The best terrain is albariza, a clay containing a high percentage of chalk and which is mainly to be found in the north and west. The less chalky barro absorbs less humidity, while the sandy arena is being increasingly abandoned.

The chalky soils are reserved for the vine-king of Jerez, the Palomino, which now accounts for 90% of the vineyard and easily reaches a yield of 80 hectolitres per hectare (1,760 gallons per 2½ acres). The only additional varieties are the Pedro Ximénez and a little Muscatel. The very average quality of wines produced by the Palomino indicates the importance of blending and of aging, thanks to which the mediocre can achieve excellence.

THE GRAPES OF ANDALUSIA

Although Palomino is the dominant variety in the Xeres vineyard, Pedro Ximénez is the leading grape in Montilla-Moriles. Muscatel is almost the only other variety grown.

THE CREATION OF SHERRY

The wines of Jerez are not protected from the effects of oxygen, as is normally the case, but on the contrary they are left in uncovered casks and left exposed to the air. It is here that the new wines reveal their character. The best soon develop a thick layer of white yeast: this is the flor, the main property of which is to protect the wine from oxidation. This wine is legitimately called fino. Oloroso sherry, which is more robust and has a higher alcohol content, is distinguished from fino by its lesser ability to produce flor. As for raya sherry, it produces none at all.

However, this is not all. The various wines produced by this type of maceration are hardly ever sold at this stage. The bodegas perform blending operations, the aim of which is not only to obtain the uniformity peculiar to each brand, but also to sweeten the wine, which is originally very dry. To this end, sweetening wines are used, such as Dulce Pasa, Dulce Apagado, or pure Muscatel, obtained from grapes that have been dried in the sun so that the sugar becomes concentrated in them. Arrope, a wine reduced by cooking, can also be used as a sweetener.

For the blending operations, the bodegas use the solera system, which consists of gradually mixing the new wines with wines from previous harvests.

It goes without saying that raya is never used by the best producers and it is regrettable for the brand image of Jerez that some blenders sometimes give in to this temptation.

THE VARIOUS TYPES OF SHERRY

Apart from the two main types of sherry, fino and oloroso, the other main ones to be found are:

Amontillado: was originally a fino, but one which was much more generous and concentrated, because this sherry has the benefit of a period of aging after the removal of the flor. As for the Fino-Amontillado, this is merely a fino tending towards the Amontillado type.

Manzanilla: This is the name given to sherries nurtured beside the sea in the bodegas of Sanlúcar de Barrameda, where they acquire a peculiar iodized flavour.

Cream Sherry: This is a dessert wine, usually based on sweetened oloroso. However, in its Pale Cream version, it consists of fino combined with dulce apagado.

MONTILLA MORILES

This vineyard lies very close to that of Jerez, south of Córdoba, and produces wines of the same type. This is possible because, despite the even more intense heat, the chalky soil is similar. There are only two important differences. One is that the predominant vine in this area is the Pedro Ximénez; the other is the clay jars, called tinajas , which look like immense amphorae and are used for the fermentation. This wine, like sherry, produces varying amounts of flor. The finos are of matching quality, both dry and mellow.

MALAGA

The vineyard occupies the sunny hills set back from the Costa del Sol, where the Muscatel grape vies with the Pedro Ximénez. Here the amphorae give way to cement fermentation vats. Muscatel grapes produce the most aromatic wines which can achieve excellence when blended using the solera system. Lagrima (the "tear" of the grapes) is the best quality. It is obtained by means of very gentle, non-mechanized pressing. Dulce color, is the poorest quality, containing a high porportion of arrope, must, which has been concentrated by evaporation in the sun.

OLD CASTILE LEON

Old Castile, with the former kingdom of León, represents one of the most extensive vineyards in the country. The land is arid and harsh winters follow torrid summers. Under these conditions, the influence of the River Duero is no doubt decisive, as its banks are home to the two D.O.'s, Ribera del Duero and Rueda. Similarly, almost all the wine-producing areas worthy of attention, though not yet officially defined, are near the river or its tributaries. Old Castile produces a very varied range of wines and its reputation is continuing to spread, thanks in particular to red wines which are able to compete with the best Riojas.

RIBERA DEL DUERO

This D.O. runs alongside the Duero from north-west of Valladolid to Penafel and into the province of Burgos. Its fame comes from its red wines produced mainly from the Tinto Fino and the Tinto Aragones vines. These fruity and well-structured wines are very well suited to aging in oak casks, which adds still further to their depth and richness. The Vega Sicilia sets an example of outstanding quality.

Further north, starting from Aranda del Duero, the Ribera de Burgos, an extention of the denominación, produces mainly good-quality clarete, though these have less structure and fullness than their French counterparts.

RUEDA

The second D.O. of Old Castile, which lies south-east of Valladolid, extends around

THE GRAPE OF OLD CASTILE LEON

The main varieties used in Old Castile are Tinto Fino and Tinto Aragonés for the red wines, while Verdejo produces the whites.

the commune of Rueda. Its chalky clay soil produces a remarkable amber wine from the Verdejo, a white grape which is capable of producing a flor as abundant as that of the best sherries.

However, it is possible that Rueda will soon cede pride of place to a dry, full-bodied and spirited white wine, the recent and very promising result of new vinification methods.

Several districts in Old Castile which still do not have a D.O. are also worthy of attention:

> *TORO lies between the communes of Rueda and Zamora. It produces a dark, very strong red wine, much appreciated by the Spaniards when it is not being used for blending.*
> *CIGALES, to the north of Valladolid, owes its reputation to its clarets, produced from a mixture of red and white grapes.*
> *EL BIERZO and VALDEVIMBRE, in the province of León, produce light reds and dark, well-balanced rosés.*

THE D.O.'S OF OLD CASTILE-LEON

Although only two D.O.'s, Ribera del Duero and Rueda, have been defined, the region has several other promising wine-growing districts which are worthy of attention.

NEW CASTILE LA MANCHA

New Castile is an arid region in central Spain. The middle and south is covered by the vast expanse of La Mancha, immortalized by Don Quixote.

The very dry climate, characterized by sweltering summers and freezing winters, is the initial explanation for the high alcohol content of the wines. Irrigation is forbidden.

The vineyard, owned by a multitude of wine-makers grouped together into more than 400 cooperatives, stretches as far as the eye can see. In La Mancha, it is almost entirely planted with the Airen, a white vine appreciated above all for its great vigour. Although it produces mainly whites, it is often combined with the Cencibel, whose dark wines it renders less thick and heady. Despite an unexciting level of quality, New Castile has five D.O.'s.

MENTRIDA

This 32000 hectares (79,000 acres) vineyard in the province of Toledo, south-west of Madrid produces a robust red wine, high in alcohol content and mostly used for blending.

LA MANCHA

The area of the denominación proper covers an immense calcareous plateau in the middle and south of the region. The almost 500,000 hectares (1,235,500 acres) of vineyards planted with the Airen produce a white wine which is high in alcohol and of mediocre fruitiness, but which is tending to be

THE D.O.'S OF NEW CASTILE

Although the wines of New Castile are of relatively mediocre quality nowadays, five regional D.O.s have been defined. These are Mentrida, La Mancha, Valdepeñas, Manchuela and Almansa.

VALENCIA

The Levante, the region of Valencia which runs along the Mediterranean coast in the east of the peninsula, is one of the busiest wine-producing areas of Spain. Although it has no prestigious wines, this region includes five D.O.'s where the Mediterranean climate favours the production of full-bodied, generous wines.

VALENCIA

Not far from the town, this vast vineyard, formerly called Cheste, mainly produces a coarse white wine with a high alcohol content. It is thus best to use the attractive town of Valencia as a base for visiting the rest of the region.

UTIEL-REQUENA

West of Valencia and almost immediate extension of it, this hilly vineyard is planted almost exclusively with black grapes, of which the most important is the Bobal, which produces a pitch-black wine. The small proportion of Cencibel and Garnacha which are added does not lighten it in any way, with the result that, after a long maceration of the skins, the wines are as full of colour as they are of tannin. This is what produces the very typical vino de doble pasta. The word "doble" is used because the proportion of skins added to this liquid is doubled.

However, much juice is left over which has had only the briefest contact with the skins and this is used to make a most pleasant light rosé.

ALICANTE

The area of the denominación is divided

THE GRAPES
OF VALENCIA

Black, or almost black, wines abound in the region of Valencia. They are made from Bobal, Cencibel, Garnacha and Monastrell vines.

in two, corresponding to particular types of wine. The coast, where the vineyards are planted with Muscatel, produces a sweet wine of fine quality, while the hills set back from the sea are mostly devoted to the Monastrell, which produces both a vino de doble pasta and a light rosé. There are also some white wines made from Verdil stock.

JUMILLA

South of Alicante in the province of Murcia. This D.O., with its chalky soil, strives to extract from the Monastrell a wine that is less dark and alcoholic than is usually the case.

UECLA

This area, which is immediately adjacent to the preceding one, inevitably yields closely-related products, in other words, dark, robust wines.

THE GRAPES
OF NEW CASTILE

The Airen is the dominant white vine. As for the reds, they are made from Garnacha Tinta, Monastrell and Cencibel. This last is so dark that it has to be mixed with Airen.

improved by the adoption of modern methods of vinification.

VALDEPEÑAS

The peculiar feature of this southern D.O. from the province of Ciudad Real is that it produces mainly red wine while its main vine is the white Airen. In fact it is mixed with the Cencibel, which produces such a dark wine that it is enough to add a proportion of 10% of it to give colour to white grape-juice. The light ruby wine thus obtained is called aloque. It lacks sufficient structure and acidity.

ALMANSA

Bordering the Levante, west of Albacete, this 10000 hectares (24710 acres) vineyard is planted mainly with Monastrell and Garnacha Tinta, which produce thick, very dark wines, usually used for blending.

MANCHUELA

East of La Mancha and south of Cuenca, the production of this vineyard consists almost entirely of clarets, or else extra-ordinarily thick reds sold in bulk.

THE D.O.'S
OF VALENCIA

The five D.O.'s of the Valencia region are developing fast enough and well enough to deserve a great deal of attention. They are Alicante, Valencia, Utiel-Requeña, Jumilla and Uecla.

PORTUGAL

Situated on the western edge of the Iberian Peninsula, Portugal, a name derived from the Roman name for Oporto, "Portus Cale", has always been a major wine producer. Well before the Roman occupation, vines were cultivated in the valleys of the Douro and Minho rivers, benefiting from the sandy soil and the temperate Atlantic climate.

Perhaps it was an omen that in the 12th century, Henry of Burgundy should have been the first ruler of an independent Portugal. At the time, wine was already being exported to Britain. Treaties and trading alliances were long to link the two countries. Wool from England was exchanged for Portuguese wine.

The 15th and 16th centuries were Portugal's golden age. Vasco da Gama rounded the Cape of Good Hope. A fabulous empire was founded, stretching from Brazil to Africa . Wherever the Portuguese went, they planted their vines.

In 1765, port was officially protected, having already attained its definitive character. This was the first wine-growing region of the world to be legally restricted in this way.

The saying goes, "a million Portuguese live on wine" and it is true that per capita consumption is very high, at 95 litres (166 litres) per year. Vines cover an area of 350,000 hectares (864,850 acres), giving an annual yield of more than 10 million hectolitres (220 million gallons) of which 2 million hectolitres (44 million gallons) are exported. Three quarters of the output consists of red wine.

The 15 wine-growing regions are very strictly regulated. They produce three types of wine, the famous fortified wines, Port and Madeira (280,000 and 80,000 hectolitres or 6,160,000 and 1,760,000 gallons respectively), demarcated wines, particularly the famous Vinhos Verdes (3 million hectolitres), and finally table wines.

Porto: "After five years of aging, a sort of crust forms on the edges of the cask; the ruby-red colour of port becomes clearer."

PORTUGAL PORT

It is impossible not to wax lyrical about the extraordinary story of Port. It is amazing to think that one of the lesser, harsher wines of the upper Douro valley should have become one of the greatest fortified wines, drunk and enjoyed all over the world. This is undoubtedly a superlative case of alchemy, with Man and Nature working in harmony. Three factors were involved, an exceptional climate, schistic soil and a unique method of vinification. Yet there was still a certain something missing - the "English palate" which refined it and established the name of "Port".

In 1703, England was in conflict with France, and so forbade the wines of Acquitaine from entering her territory. Portugal then became the favourite supplier.

Of course, as is fitting, it was an Englishman, Joseph James Forrester, who came to Oporto in 1831 and was the first to think of transporting the casks from the upper Douro to Oporto. Because the wine did not travel well, he added alcohol, and port was born. In recognition of his services, the Portuguese made him a baron.

Imagine thousands of terraces worked into the very ravines, beaten by the sun. It is from here, on this schistic soil, that Port takes all its character. The gorges of the upper Douro are a truly superb spectacle which men have worked and moulded for generations to make use of the smallest patch of land.

About twenty varieties of grape are grown (Port is a blended wine). The very painstaking harvests start at the end of September or the beginning of October.

Quick fermentation is to be avoided at all costs. The bunches of grapes are therefore pressed in mechanical crushers, instead of in the traditional way. The crucial moment is when a proportion of about 20% of spirits (brandy) is added to the raw wine, just before fermentation. The amount added decides how rich in sugar the must

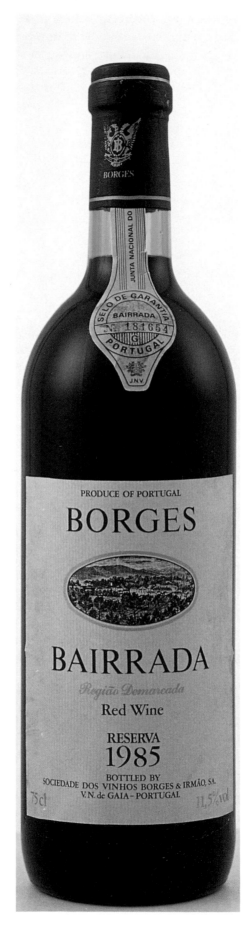

will be, and therefore whether the resulting wine will be sweet or dry. The must is then kept cool in huge storerooms. In the spring, the wine goes on its way to the wholesalers not on the rabelos, those famous raft-like, flat-bottomed sailing craft which used to navigate the hazardous Douro, but by land to Vila Novo de Gaia (opposite Oporto). There, it is decided whether they merit entry into the prestigious family of "vintages Port" or whether they will become "port blends",

THE GRAPES OF PORT

Nine types of superior grapes must constitute at least 60% of the content of a red port. They include:
Touriga Nacional, the best grape variety, which has small fruit and produces few grapes per vine. It makes a potent and deeply-coloured wine which tastes of blackberries.
Touriga Francesca, much used for making port, has a high yield and a potent aroma.
Tinta Barroca is mainly used to sweeten the port blends.
The white ports must contain at least 60% of six varieties, Verdelho, which gives port its alcohol content, the rather acid Esgana-Çáo, Rabigato, one of the better Douro varieties, Folgazão, which is fairly bland, Malvasia Fina and Viosinho.

known as Tawny, a skilful blend which will age for three years in the cask. Each Port has its classification. It can be extra dry or dry (for the whites), medium or sweet (for the reds). A full (retinto) port will go from dark red to ruby red (or tinto alvirado), tan brown (alvirado) and light brown (alvirado claro). As for the white, there is an infinity of colours from pale white right through straw, golden and "onion-skin" to light golden. It takes 20 or 30 years for a good Port (a Vintage) to reach perfection. It should be drunk at the end of a meal, with cheese or dessert. Chilled, extra dry port is sometimes served as an aperitif in France.

THE DEMARCATED WINES
VINHOS VERDES

The famous Vinhos Verdes are called "green" because they are young, not because of their colour. They are produced in north-western Portugal between the Douro and the Minho, a region with a pleasant climate, thanks to the proximity of the Atlantic Ocean. The vines grow freely beside trees which protect them from the sun and the heat. The grapes are harvested early, before they are completely ripe. The wine is fresh, fruity and light, with a hint of a sparkle due to secondary fermentation in the bottle. The whites are the best. They should be drunk within a year, served chilled as an aperitif or to accompany fish. Examples are Monção, sold in brown bottles, Agulha, Gatão, or Lagosta, which is a common export brand.

REGULATIONS AND CONTROLS ON PORTUGUESE WINE

The Portuguese have one of the most stringent systems in Europe. Each wine must bear a certificate of origin. The best are entitled to an "appellation" (Denominação de Origem), for example Port and Madeira and also Vinhos Verdes, Colares, Dão, Carcavelos, Douro, Bairrado, Algarve, Bucelas, etc. Each wine producer's output and number of barrels is monitored and he is then granted the exact number of seals for the quality awarded.

There are two official bodies in charge of these operations, the Instituto do Porto for Port and the Instituto da Vinha e do Vinho in Lisbon for the other wines.

DAO
Red Dão comes from the triangle formed by the towns of Viseu, Guarda and Coimbra in the centre of northern Portugal, one of the wildest and most mountainous regions of the country. The vines grow on terraces in the granite-and-schist soils, trained high on poles and among the trees, which leaves the ground free for cultivation of other crops. The Dão wines are somewhat reminiscent of Côtes du Rhone, with their tannic taste, great versatility and smoothness. They keep for several years in a wine-cellar.

COLARES
This is wine of the dunes. The vines, protected by low dry stone walls, grow on sandy soil (which enables them to avoid phylloxera) from the ocean right up into the Sintra Mountains. Byron adored it, calling the region the Eighth Wonder of the

World. The wine made from Ramisco grapes is a slow-maturing, potent wine with a good bouquet. The best Colares can age for as long as 14 years in mahogany and sequoia casks.

BUCELAS

This area lies north of Lisbon on one of the banks of the Tagus estuary. Bucelas was very popular with Englishmen from Wellington to Dickens at the time when it was a sweet, amber wine. The Bucelas of today is a dry, light, straw-coloured wine which should be drunk well-chilled.

THE RED GRAPES

Mourisco Tinto, found in the Douro, produces a pleasant and very tonic wine. Tinta Amarella recognizable by its lovely colour and very high yield. Baga is the most common red variety in Portugal, its thick-skinned grapes being high-yielding. The wine has a good colour, but lacks finesse.
Ramisco, which grows on the sandy soil of Colares in the south, produces an excellent wine with all the qualities favouring good ageing.

THE WHITE GRAPES

The outstanding variety is Alvarinho, the single variety used for Vinho Verde. It is only permitted in the Monção region. The alcohol content is higher and the aroma gives it the advantage over the other Minho wines.

PORTUGAL
MADEIRA

The island of Madeira is part of a vast volcanic archipelago 400 miles off the coast of Morocco. When Henry the Navigator's seafarers discovered it 500 years ago, they called it "Madeira" (wood) because it was covered in a forest so impenetrable that pathways had to be burned through it. For seven whole years, the forest burned, and Malvasia vines from Cyprus were planted from seashore to mountaintop. Thanks to the vine, Madeira once again became an oasis of green in the Atlantic that we know today.

In the 18th century, someone had the idea of adding, "a bucket of brandy to every cask" before shipping. This had the remarkable effect of actually improving the Madeira as it travelled, helping it to gain an unrivalled reputation everywhere. It was said to be the only immortal wine.

It became the Americans' favourite wine, for patriotic reasons. All the ships bound for the Americas used to call at Funchal to take on supplies and Madeira. This was a regular practice until the disaster of 1852, when oidium and phylloxera attacked the vines. Madeira has never really recovered from that disaster.

THE GRAPES OF MADERA

Jacquet is the hybrid most commonly grown in Madeira, having replaced the vineyards devastated by phylloxera. Its yield is average but it has plenty of saccharine and a splendid dark red colour. There are three main white varieties, Verdelho, giving Madeira its alcohol content and characteristic colour, Bual, becoming rarer and rarer, the richest and most sought after Madeira, and Sercial, a well-loved variety. It ripens late but gives Madeira its subtlest aromas and an incomparable radiance.

Today there are plenty of average Madeiras but very few really good ones. The best is Sercial, which is also the driest (it comes from Rheinriesling stock). The colour is pale to golden, with plenty of nose and a hint of harshness (for drinking as an aperitif). Verdelho is very similar to Sercial, with perhaps a little more versatility, and a slightly duller colour. Malmsey (Malvasia) is exceedingly rich and fruity and blessed with a superb dark-brown colour. It is at its best served with a dessert. As for the paler and lighter Rainwater, it is an altogether more common blend. Like Port, Madeira can be decanted.

GREECE

Ancient Greece had well-developed vineyards and the wine, whose virtues were praised by Hippocrates, a follower of Dionysus, continues to occupy a dominant position in the agriculture of modern Greece.

The vineyards extend from the coast to the mountain slopes, an area of about 95,000 hectares (234,745 acres). Planted in mainly rocky and limestone soil, they have to tolerate a very dry environment and a large amount of sunshine. These conditions, which encourage a high sugar content and a strong degree of alcohol, explain the abundance of both sweet wines and robust, full-bodied reds.

RETSINA

The name of Retsina is given to all white or rosé wines which have had their taste modified by the addition of pine resin to the must during fermentation.
This process perpetuates a practice which was common in ancient times when, in order better to preserve the wine, jars and amphorae were coated with resin, the technique known in French as poissage.

By relying on a large variety of indigenous vines with high yields, Greece maintains an annual production in excess of five million hectolitres (105 million gallons), making it the ninth largest producer in Europe. However, wine exports remain low, accounting for only 10% of production.

While it is true that quality control is a recent phenomenon, it has been rigourously applied since Greece joined the EEC. Thus, 26 districts of "controlled appellations of origin" (AOCs) or VQPRD as they are known in Greece, have now been defined, covering eight large wine-producing regions.

THE PELOPONNESE

This vast vineyard, covering an area of 65,000 hectares (160,615 acres) provides more than one quarter of the country's total production. Patras is the viticultural centre of the region and it is surrounded by four appellation districts. Three of these take their names from the vines from which they are made. These are Mavrodaphne, which produces a dark, syrupy red wine, high in alcohol, the Muscat of Patras and Muscat Rion, sweet white wines with a fine golden colour. Finally, the Patras appellation produces a light white wine.

Two mountain vineyards are also noteworthy. These are Nemea, which makes a robust red, almost black, wine from the Agiorgitiko, and Mantinia, where the Moschofiler produces a light and dry white wine.

ATTICA

This very arid region derives great commercial advantage from its proximity to Athens. Savatiano is the dominant vine and is responsible for the whole range of the very famous Retsina wines. However, its fame should not be allowed to obscure either the red Mandilaria grape, or, more importantly, Pallini, which produces the best white wines in the country.

THE GRAPES OF GREECE

The best vines which produce the power-ful Greek red wines are Mavrodaphne, Xinomavro, Mandilari and Liatiko.
For the whites, the Savatiano (used for the Retsinas) predominates, followed by Rhoditis, Robola and Assyrtico. Then there is the range of Muscat vines, of which the best is the Muscat d'Alexandrie.

CRETE

The island has retained a wide variety of vines and produces mainly strong and generous red wines, which are now of very decent quality.

MACEDONIA AND EPIRUS

Thanks to a higher rainfall than in the rest of the country, these areas of production rely mainly on the Xinomavro, a vine that produces the excellent tannic and fruity red wine, Naoussa. Another centre of interest is the Porto Carras estate, which has turned to two French vines, the Cabernet Sauvignon and the Cabernet Franc, to produce the excellent Côtes de Méliton appellation. Finally, two appellations in Epirus are worthy of attention, Zitsa, for its sparkling white, and Metsovo, for its well-structured red.

THE IONIAN ISLANDS

Here the white wine of Robola shares the limelight with the Muscat and the Mavrodaphne of Cephalonia. As for the white wines of Xante, Leukas and Corfu they pride themselves mainly upon the Verdea appellation.

THE AEGEAN ISLANDS

The Muscat of Samos is protected by strict regulations and attains the highest level of quality. Blending is forbidden and no other Greek wines may be brought on to the island. The Muscat of Lemnos faithfully copies this example of quality.

THE DODECANESE

Only Rhodes still maintains a tradition of wine production, dating back to the Knights of the St. John.

The production is divided between generous reds from the Amorgiano grape, and dry whites from the Athiri variety, such as those of Lindos. The Muscat of Rhodes is produced in very limited amounts.

THE CYCLADES

In the volcanic soil of Santorini, the Assyrtico grape produces both a dry white and a very alcoholic sweet white, the Vino Santo. The wines of Paros are produced from a mixture of two vines, red and white.

ENGLAND

Few people are aware that wine has been made in England since the Roman occupation. Indeed, in the 9th century, the wine lobby was so powerful that Alfred the Great passed a decree granting compensation to vinegrowers for any damage to their vines. At the time of the Norman Conquest, vines were growing in monasteries as far north as Lincolnshire. The decline set in when Henry II married Eleanor of Acquitaine in 1152; with the acquisition of the lands of Acquitaine came the wines of Bordeaux. This was the beginning of an enduring passion.

Until World War II, vines were ornamental plants - just the thing to adorn a sunny wall. But, in 1952, one man was to return English vines to their former glory, Sir Guy Salisbury-Jones of Hambledon, in Hampshire. His example inspired others, and the English Vineyards Association was formed in 1967.

Warning: the words "British wine" (as distinct from English wine, which is grown and produced in England, and contains 11.5° alcohol) are used to describe wines containing 15° alcohol, made in Britain from imported raisins or grape juice.

THE GRAPES OF ENGLAND

Such red wine as there is consists mainly of Pinot Noir; the climate favours whites. The commonest varieties of grape are Müller-Thurgau (150 hectares (375 acres)) and Reichensteiner. Seyval Blanc, a very robust French hybrid, has produced excellent results since its introduction in 1952 by Sir Guy Salisbury-Jones. Chardonnay, Austrian Schönburger and Triomphe d'Alsace are also grown. In all, there are about thirty varieties, the majority of which are German hybrids.

Today England has 25 vinegrowing areas, chiefly located in the southern counties and East Anglia, and comprising a total of 450 hectares (1100 acres); each vineyard owner cultivates an average of half a hectare (roughly one acre) and there are more than 270 registered growers. It should be noted that almost all the grapes produce white wine, chosen for their quality of early ripening.

The four best vineyards are :

> *Lamberhurst in Kent, owned by Sir Kenneth MacAlpine.*
> *Carr-Taylor, near Hastings in Sussex (60,000 bottles from 6 hectares (15 acres)).*
> *The famous St George's of Sussex marketed by Gay Biddlecombe.*
> *Sir Guy Salisbury-Jones' Hambledon vineyard in Hampshire.*

LUXEMBOURG

This little country wedged between Belgium to the west, France to the south and Germany to the east, produces light, fruity white wines which are not well-known, and which resemble the wines of Alsace. Most of the vineyards are on the left bank of the Moselle river which runs through the Grand Duchy. They are bathed in sunlight in the mornings and protected from the west winds by the thick forests that cover the hilltops. Luxembourg

THE GRAPES OF LUXEMBOURG

There are about thirty wine-producing districts. The best vineyards are planted with Riesling grapes on the limestone and clay soils of Remich, Grevenmacher and Ehnen. The wines produced from them are very similar to the German Moselle wines, being elegant with a hint of acidity in rainy years. They are wines that need aging. Rülander (Pinot Gris), Pinot Blanc and Auxerrois produce wines that are coarser but lacking in bouquet (from Wellenstein, Remerschen and Schengen). Traminer wines are velvety and spicy; they are produced from vines in Ahn and Wellenstein.

THE RULES OF LUXEMBOURG

Prior to 1935, Luxembourg wine was of mediocre quality.
It was marketed under the name of Elbling and used only for blending Since then, with the establishment of a viticulture research station at Remich, the vineyards have been entirely replanted, with quality taking precedence over quantity. One of the functions of the station is to supervise the Appellations d'Origine which appear on the bottles. Taking their example from Alsace, Luxembourg wines - almost all of which are white - are designated by the name of the grape variety.

drinks 70% of its own production, which amounts to 170,000 hectolitres (3,740,000 gallons) from 1000 hectares (2470 acres) of vines. Thus, very little wine is left to export. Vines have been grown on the banks of the Moselle since Roman times. The first really bad year recorded was 370, as black as the years 1866 and 1944, when Von Rundstedt counterattacked across the Ardennes. The monks who had owned the vineyard since the Middle Ages were dispossessed by the French Revolution. The vineyard was then split up so that today there are 1000 plots of vines averaging half a hectare (about an acre) in size.

CENTRAL AND EASTERN EUROPE

As the wind of democracy sweeps through this ancient bastion of "the Russian Empire", as nationalism and religious wars are beginning to sour this newfound liberty, it is strange to note that viticultural imperialism is spreading from the West.

Chardonnay, which is very widely grown in Georgia, Moldavia and the Ukraine is replacing the traditional Russian grape varieties - the Rkatsiteli and Saperavi - to an ever greater extent. It is perhaps unfair to give so little space to the huge vineyard of the USSR (twice as large as France and Italy combined) but very few westerners today get the opportunity to drink good Russian wines.

The same policy is being pursued in Bulgaria, where Cabernet-Sauvignon and Merlot are tending to push out Melnik and Pamid. The Hungarians, on the other hand, have actually been spreading their local varieties which are used to make their famous Tokay. Furmint is grown throughout eastern Europe, as is Harle Velü and Kékuaplü, to say nothing of Kadarka, a red grape of Albanian origin.

Romanian grape varieties are gaining in importance. Thise include Feteasca, Tamlîoasa and even Weltschriesling. Yugoslavia is too stretched between Italy (the Adriatic coast), Greece (Macedonia) and Austria. Austria is also known for its white wines of Germanic origin - Riesling, Müller-Thurgau, Sylvaner, Gewürztraminer and some local grape varieties such as Rotgipfler and Grünen Veltliner.

Vineyard of the Wachau: Spitz on the Danube, a village of vintners built around a single, large vineyard, called the Tausendeimerberg.

SWITZERLAND

Switzerland has been a confederation of cantons since the end of the 13th century. It has two mountain ranges, the Alps and the Jura, separated by a depression called the Swiss plateau. The Alps occupy 60% of the surface area of the country. Switzerland also happens to be surrounded by four great wine-producing nations, France, Italy, Germany and Austria. The borders of the wine-producing regions of Switzerland naturally fall within the linguistic and cultural frontiers of the regions. There is the eastern or German-speaking part of Switzerland (Ostschweiz), the western or French-speaking part and the Italian-speaking canton of Ticino (the Tessine). Of the total area of 14000 hectares (38,000 acres) of vines, French-speaking Switzerland has 11000 hectares (27181 acres), German speaking Switzerland 2200 hectares (5450 acres) and Italian-speaking Switzerland 850 hectares (2100 acres). Total production is one million hectolitres (22 million gallons), three-quarters of which is white wine.

THE WINE STATUTE

Swiss wines are governed on a federal level by the Law Concerning Agriculture, the Wine Statute and the Regulation Concerning the Wine Trade. The quantity of grapes harvested must be declared and production is controlled. The area of wine production is carefully mapped and there is a list of authorized grape varieties. A whole series of provisions have been implemented, covering cellaring, blending, designation of origin, grape varieties, the vintages and permitted additives, which make Swiss wine one of the most highly-regulated in the world.

Vineyards are to be found in practically all the cantons, surviving from the great medieval vineyards which were partially destroyed by the epidemics of the 18th and 19th centuries. Only a few barrels of Swiss wine ever cross the frontiers and Swiss wine is thus the object of curiosity. This is understandable because there is quite a contrast between Dezaley and Grand Vaux, which are cultivated on the sunny slopes around Lake Geneva, and the Vispertermin which is produced in the canton of Valais at an altitude 3700 feet, a European record.

FRENCH-SPEAKING SWITZERLAND (LA SUISSE ROMANDE)

This is by far the largest wine-producing region of Switzerland with 11000 hectares (27181 acres), half of them in Valais. Vines are to be found around the lakes of Geneva and Neuchâtel and on the steep banks of the upper reaches of the Rhône. The white vine most cultivated is the Chasselas Doré. In some cantons it bears a generic appellation, such as Fendants du Valais (the best-known Swiss wines), which are generous and thoroughbred, the Perlans around Geneva and the Neuchâtels at Neuchâtel. In the Canton of Vaud (around Lake Geneva), wines are offered under their appellations d'origine with all the prestigious names of the villages. These are Mont-sur-Rolle, Féchy, Bonvillars, Epesses, Saint-Saphorin, Dezaley, etc. The Chasselas is a somewhat neutral vine and therefore draws all its originality from the terrain.

Every self-respecting inhabitant of Valais has his own vine. The result is 20000 wine growers who share 5000 hectares (12355 acres) of vines on the steep slopes of the Rhône Valley. Few wines are named by cru, apart the famous Sion. However, there are 12 local production regions which are distinguished by a new development, the introduction of red varieties, including Gamay and Pinot Noir. For example, Dôle wine obtains its vigour, bouquet and its ruby colour from the Pinot Noir, and its freshness and fruitiness from the Gamay. It works wonders on the calcium-rich soil of Sierre. The third great wine of Valais is Johannisberg, made from the Sylvaner vine and with a higher alcohol content than Fendant. It is pleasant, fine and mellow and is mainly to be found on the alluvial cones of the mountains of Lower Valais.

To complete the picture, the vines of more distant origin should be noted. They include the white specialities such as Arvine, a proud and virile white for laying down, with a fruity and well-balanced bouquet, which should be served chilled as an aperitif or with dessert; Amigne, a dessert wine with a brilliant golden colour; Malvoisie (Malmsey) from the Pinot Gris, which is 14° proof, and Païen, a dry and pleasantly acidic wine made from vines growing at an altitude of 3700 feet near Visp. The rosés of Valais include Œil de Perdrix, a strong, well-structured wine from the Pinot Noir. All these specialities are remarkable wines, but be warned, they are rare!

The Canton of Vaud is divided into five regions. The slopes from Geneva to

Lausanne mark the end of the gentle foothills of the Jura facing the snow-capped Mont Blanc. The wines here are lively, light and often sparkling. The gentle landscape contains a succession of estates and châteaux.

Lavaux, between Lausanne and Montreux, is known for its terraced vineyards and its famous wines, such as Butry, Villette, Dezaley, Vevey, Montreux and Saint-Saphorin. The wines of Chablais are wines from the rocky terrain which have the "flinty" taste so typical of the region.

Geneva is surrounded by a horseshoe-shaped ring of vineyards. Mandement, a light, dry white tasting of hazelnut, is the best-known wine. Satigny is famous for its priory and its vineyards, which date from the first century A.D. Neuchâtel is the region of the Jura lakes (Neuchâtel, Bienne, Morat). Here, the vineyards, which are divided into small plots, often suffer from frost. While the Chasselas is dominant, cultivation of the Pinot Noir, the only authorized red vine, is on the increase. The vines are still grown in a traditional manner trained over poles and are pruned using the goblet cut, a bunched-up shape. "Vin de Neuchâtel" comes from 18 wine-producing communes which are named on the label. Only three cantonal crus are entitled to their own appellation:

Château Vaumarcus, Domaine de Champréveyres and Hôpital Pourtales. Another speciality is the "Œil de Perdrix", a delicate rosé, easy and pleasant to drink, made from the Pinot Noir.

EASTERN SWITZERLAND

Eastern Switzerland, with its 2,200 hectares (5436 acres) of vineyard, includes all the German-speaking cantons, Zurich, Schaffhausen, Aargau, Thurgau, St-Gallen, and Graubünden (Grisons) along the valley of the Rhine. Demand greatly exceeds supply and the German crus are much sought after. They are light and fruity wines, made with a great deal of expertise. The Pinot Noir (Klevner) is said to have been introduced into Graubünden during the Thirty Years' War by the Duke of Rohan. This region of the Bündner Herrschaft in the upper reaches of the Rhine has been called as the "Little Burgundy of the Alps".

TICINO, ITALIAN-SPEAKING SWITZERLAND

Of the 7,000 hectares (17300 acres) of vines which existed in 1900, only 800 hectares (1977 acres) remain today. However, Ticino is a land blessed by the

THE GRAPES OF SWITZERLAND

Of the 14000 hectares (34,600 acres) of Swiss vineyards, 6000 hectares (14826 acres) are planted with the Chasselas vine. It has an extraordinary history. It originated in southern Lebanon and was very probably the first vine to be cultivated by man (its distinctive leaf is represented on the mural paintings of the temples of Luxor, in Egypt). It appears to have been introduced to Europe by the Phoenicians. On the other hand, it is known for a fact that it was one of Louis XV's generals called Courtier who transplanted it to Valais. Its cultivation in Switzerland is a delight. In Valais, it produces a supple, dry and fruity Fendant, with little aroma, but made more lively by a hint of crispness. It is called Dorin in the canton of Vaud. There are magnificent Chasselas vineyards between Lausanne and Vevey, where the wine it produces combines finesse with a slightly smoky aroma. The vine produces the slightly-sparkling Perlan in the canton of Geneva. The Chasselas, which has an excellent yield, has the added advantage of ripening just after the Riesling-Sylvaner (Müller-Thurgau), just another of its many good qualities.

gods. The climate is mild, the lakes are blue and all the slopes seem to face the sun. The old vines were the native ones, Bondola or Piedmontese. Since World War II, the Merlot, a red vine from Bordeaux, has been producing some of the most popular wines in Switzerland. The prestigious Ticino Merlot, which is smooth and fruity, benefits from the "Viti" label, a mark of quality instituted by the government.

1988
RÉCOLTE DU DOMAINE

CHÂTEAU DU CREST
JUSSY 1ᵉʳ CRU
PRODUCTION LIMITÉE

YVES MICHELI-PROPRIÉTAIRE
MIS EN BOUTEILLE DANS LES CAVES DE VIN-UNION GENÈVE & SÉTD

AUSTRIA

Austria, which was once the heart of the Austro-Hungarian Empire, possesses one of the finest vineyards in Europe. Eighty per cent of Austrian territory consists of the Alps and the Pre-Alps. The famous "blue" Danube flows through the north-east, in the Bohemian massif, and the great Hungarian plains begin in the east. As in Bavaria, it was the monks who, from the 10th century onwards, reconstructed the vineyard which had disappeared with the collapse of the Roman Empire. Otto I granted the producers the right to sell their wine free of taxation (Eigenbauwein), a right which has continued until today.

When a wine-maker wanted to sell his new wine, all he had to do was hang a branch on the door of his house. This custom of "aushängen" (hanging outside) gave its name to a type of wine (the Hengelweine) which is still drunk today in the famous Heuringen, the new wine taverns of Grinzing, a suburb of Vienna.

The largest vineyards are situated in the east of the country in five big wine-producing regions. In lower Austria, the areas of Vienna and Wachau are the best known. The other regions are Burgenland, near the Hungarian border, the Wienviertel north of the Danube and southern Styria near Yugoslavia.

There are about 56,000 wine-producing concerns spread over 58,000 hectares (143,318 acres), most of them not exceeding two hectares (less than an acre). The production consists of three million hectolitres (66 million gallons) per year, 80% of which is good quality white wine. Every wine-maker keeps his harvest

in his own cellars, with the excess going to cooperatives who take care of the vinification and marketing. The Austrian vineyards can barely cope with local demand, which is as much as 37 litres (65 pints) per inhabitant annually. Most of the red wine is thus imported from France and Italy.

Lower Austria, the granary of the country, also contains three-quarters of the vines. It is a wonderful region of baroque monasteries and churches and fabulous castles. Here, the Grüner Veltliner, a local white vine, accounts for 40 % of Austrian production. The mild climate of the valleys of the Danube, the Kamp and the Strauer and the loess soil provide ideal conditions for the cultivation of the vine. The Wachau, which extends from Melk to Mautern, is often considered one of the most beautiful valleys in the world. On the steep slopes of the Danube, vines are cultivated in terraces. The wines of Wachau are distinguished by their freshness and fruitiness; they are aged for several years in cellars. Krems, where a wine fair takes place each May, is mainly famous for its immense cellars and its viticultural museum. The valley of Langenloin is reputed for Heiligenstein, one of the country's grands crus.

At Klosterneuburg in Lower Austria, where Augustinian prelates have been growing vines for 200 years, there is the oldest school of viticulture in the world.

The Wienviertel region next to the Bohemian massif northeast of Vienna produces light and pleasant wines. Here the Veltliner gives a wine which leaves a bitter, spicy and peppery taste with a very refreshing touch of acidity. There have been some great vintages.

The vineyard of Thermen is one of the warmest in Austria. The stony limestone soil produces the first-rate Gumpoldskirchen, a sweet wine made from grapes which have been harvested very late. Seventy-five per cent of the red wines come from the Burgenland, once a Hungarian province. The distinctive climate of the region, situated between the Danube and the Neusiedlersee, produces

THE GRAPES OF AUSTRIA

Of the 200 vines grown, 30 benefit from the title of "quality wines" (Qualitätswein). These include Grüner Veltliner which represents one third of the production. This is an Austrian wine par excellence. Fruity, slightly effervescent, with a slight spicy, peppery taste, it produces some great vintages. Neuburger tastes of walnuts and has a delicate bouquet. It is found mainly on the limestone soil of lower Austria. Riesling and Gewürztraminer are light and fruity wines which are very common in Burgenland. The Zierfandler produces the famous Gumpoldskircher, a vigorous and thoroughbred wine of substance, one of the best in the country. The late-ripening Weltschriesling should not be omitted from the list. Müller-Thurgau is a sweet wine with a hint of Muscat which can be found throughout Austria.

white wines of excellent quality, which are well-structured and very well-balanced. Styria, in southeast Austria near the Yugoslavian border, where the famous White Horse Inn is situated, has an almost Mediterranean climate and volcanic soil. The vineyards are all on the southern slopes between 750 and 2000 feet. They produce the famous Gewürztraminer, which is known all over the world.

Vienna, the capital, is surrounded by woods, meadows and vines which produce Heinigen, a "new" wine which is lively and full of charm (though a little tart). It is drunk from carafes on the terraces of the taverns and cafés. Heinigen, in fact, refers both to the new wine from the most recent harvest and the wine-maker's inn. It was on these same hills, where the vines now grow, that the Turkish invasion was halted in 1529.

HUNGARY

Hungary is closely associated with Tokay, one of the rare wines in the world which is unquestionably legendary. It is the "Vinum regum, rex vinum", the wine of kings and the king of wines. However, the Hungarians pride themselves on producing other excellent wines. Hungary is the largest wine-producing region in Eastern Europe. The climate is continental. In the north, a mountainous region contrasts with the plains of Trans-Danubia and the sandy soil between the Danube and the Tisza. To the east lies the great Hungarian plain (the Puszta). The cultivation of the vine existed well before Stephen I, Hungary's first king, crowned in the year 1000 A.D., but it was in the 17th century, with the arrival of the Walloons and the Lorrainese, that the Hungarian vineyard really started to develop.

Hungary has the most rigorous vinification standards in Eastern Europe. The checks are continuous and very strict. The first laws governing the guarantees of origin and the various types of grape were promulgated in 1893.

Today, Hungarian wine production is being greatly increased. Current production is 5 million hectolitres (110 million gallons) per year from 190,000 hectares (296,520 acre) of vines. Sixty per cent of the grapes are of the Welschriesling type, a strong white wine with a powerful bouquet. The four big wine-producing regions coincide with the natural borders of the country. The large central plain, the Alföld, stretches between the Danube and the Tisza as far as the Romanian border. It alone accounts for 65% of Hungarian wines. It is responsible for excellent white wines, such as the Kecskemeti Leangka, cultivated on a former desert dotted with quicksands. The hilly region, or Badacsóny, is on the northern shore of Lake Balaton. As long ago as the Roman occupation, its wines filled the imperial cellars of Rome. Everything combines to produce some remarkable white wine, the micro-climate around the lake and the terrain, consisting of basalt covered with loess. The vineyards are planted mainly

with the Szürkebarát (grey monk) and the Kéknyelü (blue stem) varieties. On the neighbouring hills of Balatonfüred Csopak, the Olaszrizling (Italian Riesling) is grown, along with Traminer, Sylvaner and Muscat grapes, producing much sweeter and richer wines. Further south, the small volcanic mountain of Somlö dominates the Trans-Danubia plain. From

the Furmint vine, an excellent, full-bodied dessert wine is made whose reputation matches that of Tokay. The Habsburgs' appreciated it for its regenerative properties. The region of Szekészárd northeast of Pecs and 60 km from

THE GRAPES OF HUNGARY

Many white vines prosper in Hungary. The most famous, which is associated with Tokay, is the Furmint, from the old French word froment meaning "wheat", because of its golden straw colour. It is robust and gives Tokay its fire, but it is a little acidic. On the other hand, the Harslevelü (also known under its German name of Lindenblättriger, or linden leaf), the other vine, gives this legendary wine all its spicy aroma. Other important vines are the Kéknyelü (blue stem), the Szürkebarát (grey monk), a sort of grey Pinot, and the Ezerjö ("thousand benefits"), which produces a dry, light and frank wine between the Danube and Lake Balaton. As for the red vines, the most commonly cultivated is the Kadarka, which originated in the Middle East. It occupies 17% of the Hungarian vineyard, mainly in the plain. It produces a dry, tannic and spicy wine, with a somewhat pale colour

Budapest is well-known for its Fleuré de Pecs, its Szekészard Riesling and its red wines from Kádárka, which age well in the bottle. Finally, in the north, the mountainous region (northeast of Budapest) of Gyöngyös, a wine-producing centre, includes the villages of Abasàr, Visorita, Waskaz, Douroszló and Verpelet. These produce a white wine as sweet as honey from the Chasselas vine. Farther east is the very beautiful Baroque city of Eger. The large wine-producing area surrounding it gives Hungary its two best red wines, Bikavér (Bull's Blood) and Egri Kádarika, full-bodied mellow wines which can be laid down for a long time. This region ends near the Carpathians and the Soviet Ukraine, with the extraordinary Tokay vineyard.

TOKAY

Here, at the foot of the Carpathians, where the Bodrog and the Tisza rivers converge, is the wine-producing region of Tokay Hegyalja ("mountain spur" in Hungarian), a vineyard of 6000 hectares (14826 acres) with an annual production of 200,000 hectolitres (440,000 gallons). No one knows how long it has been cultivated. However, it existed when the Magyars settled there more than one thousand years ago. Its international reputation dates back to the Council of Trent in 1562, but it was Louis XV's famous remark to Madame de Pompadour, as he offered her some Tokay, which immortalized it: "Madame, it is the king of wines and the wine of kings". Everything seems to work like magic here. There are two main vines varieties, Furmint and Hàrslevelvü (Lindenblättriger). The volcanic soil is a mixture of kaolin and porphyry covered with a layer of loess, which the wind has accumulated over the millennia, There are dry, sunny autumns which are beneficial to passerillage (drying of the grapes on a bed of straw). The grape harvest starts late, at the end of October, and lasts until early December. By then, the grapes have reached their maximum degree of sweetness. They are shrivelled and have been affected by the mould Botrytis cinerea. They have lost their water content (hence the name Aszu, which means "dried out"). The must obtained is stored from the onset of

fermentation in small casks called gönci and placed in those famous cellars whose walls are covered with a film of black mould of the Cladosporium cellare species, which helps the wine to mature. It is said that only low cellars make good Tokay and therefore, as the saying has it, you must bow before Tokay. It is bottled 5 to 15 years later in characteristic half-litre bottles with a long neck. There is a Cru d'Origine, Szamorodni, which is sold as Edes (sweet) or Szaraz (dry), containing 13.8° alcohol. Aszu Tokay is something quite different. It is a Premier Cru, and a marvel of sweetness. It is rare and expensive, and one can see why. Each grape is selected by hand when it has been completely infected by noble rot. When the grapes are pressed, a sort of paste is obtained which is added to the must from ordinary grapes which have already been

pressed. The percentages are indicated on the label. In Hungary, the term puttonyos is used; a puttonyo is a 15-kilogram (33-pound) basket. Thus, the more puttonyos there are (up to six and with an alcohol content of 15°), the better the Tokay is. The very best of all comes from a small place called Tallya (from the French word "taille"). The fine bouquet, unforgettable flavour and golden colour make Tokay one of the greatest wines in the world.

YUGOSLAVIA

Yugoslavia covers the north-western tip of the Balkan peninsula. It is on the same latitude as Italy and both countries are on the Adriatic Sea. Vines grow almost everywhere, covering a total area of 250,000 hectares (617,750 acres) which yield 7 million hectolitres (154 million gallons) a year. This puts Yugoslavia in seventh place in the European wine-producing league.

Label 1990

REGULATION

There are about 300 grape varieties in Yugoslavia, but quality is becoming more and more of a priority, and it has been improved by the introduction of Gamay and Cabernet stocks. Vintages mean nothing here, because all the wines are produced by blending. Vinification and marketing are undertaken by the large cooperative cellars. Quality and origin have recently tended to be better defined in law. The label on the bottle should indicate the grape variety and the place of origin, which would appear to be essential in the case of exports.

Yugoslavia was formerly part of the Austro-Hungarian Empire and consists of six republics joined in a federation. This country, which is both Mediterranean and Balkan, can trace the origins of its viticulture to the Thracians who crossed the mountains of Macedonia 4000 years ago. The numerous amphorae and other Greek remains which have been found here prove that wine was being produced in Dalmatia and Istria under the Greek occupation, and in Slovenia under Roman occupation. Even the vocabulary used for wine is of Greek and Latin origin. The wine trade flourished in the Middle Ages, but was suppressed throughout the centuries of Turkish rule.

Today, Serbia and Croatia alone account for two-thirds of Yugoslav wine. Macedonia produces 20%, Slovenia 8% and Bosnia-Herzegovinia 3%.

Most Serbian wine is made from the Prokupac grape, a local variety which is being replaced by Gamay and Cabernet. Most of the vines are to be found in the valleys of the Danube and the Morava rivers and further south in the highlands of the autonomous province of Vojvodina, where the Hungarian and Romanian frontiers meet those of Yugoslavia. The largest vineyards are at Fruska Gora and quite good white wine is

made from the Weltschriesling, Sémillion and Sauvignon grapes. A little red wine is stil produced in memory of the Karlovice Rothwein for which it was once famous. Suboticka Pescara is a sandy extension of the great Hungarian plain between the Danube and the Tisza. In addition to Hungarian varieties found here, there is also a local white wine called Kevedinka. The autonomous province of Serbia called Kosmet, which borders on Albania and Macedonia, is known abroad for its red wines made from Cabernet and Pinot Noir. In central Serbia, the Zupa area, around Aleksandrovac and Vençáç-Oplenac on the Morava, produce red wines from the Prokupac grape which are rich and high in alcohol content. Oplenac, from the same region, is a rosé which is very popular with the Yugoslavs.

In Croatia, there are two clearly-defined wine-producing areas. Firstly, the great plain of the Danube which extends as far as Zagreb between the Drava and the Sava rivers, produces quite pleasant, light wines such as Plejesivica, Vinica and Varazdin. Northern Croatia is influenced by Austria and grows mainly Traminer, Riesling, Sauvignon and Sémillon.

The second wine-producing area of Croatia is the former Italian province of Istria and the famous Dalmatian Coast. The Borra wind rises from the Adriatic and sweeps the vine-covered slopes from which tannic, full-bodied, heavy wines are produced. They are so strong that the Dalmatians are in the habit of adding water to them. They are made from the local grape variety of Plavac Mali, and are called Bol, Vis (meaning "island") Brela, Lastovo and Dingác. Excellent rosés are sold under the name Opol. As for the white wines, the best known is Grk (pronounced "Gerk"), an amber-coloured white wine from Split and the island of Korcúla. Two other wines are noteworthy, red Blatina and white Zilavka, both strong and dry, harvested in the Rostar region. There are no great vineyards here, but little plots wedged between two large rocks, no cooperatives but individual growers who make their own wine.

THE GRAPES OF YUGOSLAVIA

Although Yugoslavia has been invaded by the grape varieties of Riesling, Merlot, Cabernet and Chardonnay, it has managed to retain the local Plavac, either Beli (white) or Zulti (yellow). Like Marastina, it is cultivated in Slovenia on the sandy soil of the islands off the Dalmatian Coast and around Dubrovnik. The aroma is not strong and it must be mixed with Weltschriesling. Plavac Mali ("Little Plavac"), the red equivalent of Plavac, makes a good, strong wine for laying down. It is cultivated along the Dalmatian Coast. Prokupac produces a coarser wine; it is the commonest grape variety in Yugoslavia and is one of the grapes used in the blended local wines.

Istria, which is very near Italy, mixes vines with other crops. The best wine is Malvazya (Italian Malvasia or Malmsey). The wine-growing area of Slovenia is the home of the famous Ljutomer (better known as Lutomer Riesling), produced in the Drava river basin. Despite its name, it is made not only from Riesling but also from Sylvaner and Sauvignon grapes with the addition of Sipon, a local variety. According to the grapes from which it is made, the colour varies between gold and green. It is strong and spicy with a superb bouquet.

The ancient Illyrians grew vines in Macedonia. Since World War II, its 30,000 hectares (74,130 acres) have made it an important wine-producing area. The vines, which cover an area between the Mediterranean and central Europe, produce Vranac, an excellent red wine which is heavy, rich and mellow, and two excellent white wines are made in Zilavartea and Smederevka.

ROUMANIA

Roumania is the ancient Roman province of Dacia which, over the centuries, has retained its original Latin-based language and its long tradition of viticulture. Wine has always been made in the foothills of the Carpathians long before the Greeks colonized the Hellespont (the Black Sea). In the Middle Ages, the Roumanians sold their wines to Russia, the Venetian Republic and even Poland. Nowadays, they produce 8 million hectolitres (176 million gallons) a year, of which 11% is exported. The acreage under vine cultivation is 300,000 hectares (741,300 acres) and is constantly being increased. Roumania is now the fifth-largest producer of wine in the world, ranking between Portugal and the Federal German Republic. The country has everything to produce the finest wines, the same latitude as France, a continental climate with hot, dry summers tempered by the Black Sea and the Carpathians, and soil which is generally calcareous consisting of gentle slopes and hills with a suitable exposure.

Three categories of wine are recognized under Roumanian law. These are "Calitate superiora" (V.S.) and "Calitate superiora cu denumire de origina" (V.S.Q.) with guarantee of origin and the long-winded "Calitate superiora cu denumire de origina si trepte de calitate" a V.S.O.C. with a level of quality. CMD = late harvest, CMI= Premier Cru and SCB = Superior Wine of the First Drop (a superior table wine).

THE GRAPES OF ROUMANIA

Feteasca Alba, known in German as Mädchentraube ("maiden grape") is the predominant white variety which is found mainly in Banat and Transylvania. It is similar to Gewürztraminer, and is a very fruity wine with peach and apricot flavours. Unfortunately, however, it lacks acidity to balance the bouquet. The Grasa cultivar brings mellowness to the Cotnari wine and gives it the qualities it needs to allow it to age so well. Ruländer (Pinot Gris) produces strong, heady wines.

Of the black varieties, Feteasca Neagra is best known for its light and fruity wines which should be drunk young.

An increasing amount of Cabernet and Pinot Noir vines are being planted, and these produce wines of excellent quality.

The largest Roumanian vineyards are to be found in the southern and eastern Carpathians; which are divided into six regions. One of the most interesting and ancient Roumanian vineyards is in the Carpathian foothills, in the northeast, extending into Soviet Moldavia.

The grape variety grown produces an excellent dessert wine which has a very high alcohol content and contains more than 50 grams per litre of residual sugar. The colour of the wine is as deep as that of Furmint, a wine which has excellent keeping qualities. The Dealul Mare ("big hill") vineyard is situated on the southern flank of the Carpathians and extends over more than 60 square kilometres (37 square miles). It produces full-bodied, velvety red wines made from Pinot Noir and Cabernet-Sauvignon grapes, including Valea Calugareasca, the most popular wine in Roumania. The vines grown on the hills of Murfatlar near Bessarabia, by the Black Sea, where the gentle sea breezes have a favourable effect on the climate, produce a pleasant dessert wine flavoured with a hint of orange-flower. The Vrancea district, in the centre of the country, is the largest wine-growing area of Roumania, best-known for its table wines. The Banat region in the heart of the Carpathians consists of plains and hills. The wines here are white with greenish tints. Kadarka is a fine red wine which is produced from vines grown on the stony terraces of Minis. The Tirnave vineyards are situated in Transylvania. The dry wines are obtained from the Feteasca grape (the famous "perle de Tirnave") and from Riesling, and the demi-sec and sweet wines are made from Sauvignon and Traminer grapes. The Otonel Muscatis a noteworthy wine, spicy with a subtle fruitiness which leaves a delicate taste in the mouth.

CZECHOSLOVAKIA

Few countries have had as eventful a history of viticulture as Czechoslovakia. There is good reason to believe that wine was being made in Bohemia from the 9th century. Emperor Charles IV introduced vines from Burgundy in the late 15th century, making Prague into a flourishing viticultural centre until the devastation wrought by the Thirty Years' War. Vines were thus planted and replanted over again. In the late 19th century, the phylloxera plague arrived and destroyed all the vineyards. They were not re-established until the 1920s.

Today, this former province of the Austro-Hungarian Empire has more than 46,000 hectares (113,666 acres) of vines producing more than a million hectolitres (22 million gallons) of wine, though this is less than Czechoslovakia's neighbours.

There are three major regions. These are Slovakia, which produces two-thirds of the wines, Moravia which produces a little less than the remaining third and Bohemia, which produces the rest. The Bohemian vineyards are very similar to those of Germany, especially as it is on the same latitude as the Rheingau-Palatinate. So it is hardly surprising to find Riesling, Traminer and Sylvaner around Prague, as well as the Blauer Burgunder red vine. The best vines are to be found north of Prague at Melnik in the Elbe Valley, just west of Velké Zernoseky and at Brezanky. Moravia is irrigated by the tributaries of the Danube. It is bordered in the south-west by Znojmo district, in the north-east by Mikulov, and by Hustopeçe-Hodonin on the Austrian frontier, facing the Viennese vineyards of Krems. As in Austria, there is a lot of Vetliner, Rheinriesling and Weltschriesling, the last constituting 20% of the vineyards. The white wines are fresh, light and aromatic - in fact, very similar to Austrian Grüner Vetliner.

Slovakia is the main wine-growing province, and the principal districts are around the towns of Malá Trna and Nové

THE GRAPES OF CZECHOSLOVAKIA

Most Czech wines are vinified in cooperatives and sold under their brand names. It is important to be aware that the place of origin and the grape varieties are not always indicated. However, the law requires the labels to differentiate between blended wines and pure wines. The best wines are divided into three categories. The first contains the white wines, such as Rheinriesling (Rizlink Rynsky), Lindenblüter (Lipovina), yellow Muscat (Muskat Zluty), Welschriesling and Vetliner. The second category consists of Tausendgut (Ezerjo) and the third of Portugieser Madeira.

Mesto, in the extreme east of the country, near Hungary and its legendary Tokay. The same varieties of grape are grown on both sides of the border - Furmint, Lipovina and Muscat. However, here they are less successful. The best Slovakian wines grow from vines planted at the foot of the Tatra mountains and around Bratislava, Modra and Pezinok.

BULGARIA

The Thracian ancestors of the Bulgarians were the earliest wine-makers in that part of the world. Like all the Balkan states, Bulgaria's frontiers have tended to be rather elastic. Today, the Danube serves as the northern border, the Black Sea as the eastern frontier and Macedonia and Greece form the southern boundary. Most of Bulgaria is covered by two mountain ranges, the Balkans which stretch from west to east, an extension of the Carpathians, and the Rhodope range, to the south, extending to the Ægean sea. The vines are to be found on the pre-Balkan plain and in all the valleys in between these two mountain ranges.

Bulgaria is on the same latitude as Tuscany

The first regulatory laws were promulgated in the 10th century but current legislation only dates back to 1978. It distinguishes between two categories, "standard" wines and "quality" wines. The quality wines are divided into a "declared geographical origin" and "Region Controliran", the Bulgarian equivalent of "appellation contrôlée". The two best wines in these categories constitute the so-called "Reserve" wines.

and grows 63 grape varieties. It well deserves to be the second-largest European wine exporter. Viticulture was revived at the end of World War I after five centuries of Turkish rule. Today, thanks to a tradition which was never entirely eradicated and modern methods of production, the 450,000 peasant wine-growers produce 4 million hectolitres (88 million gallons) of wine a year, 60% of which is exported, mainly to the U.S.S.R. Three-quarters of the production is vins de table. There are six wine-growing districts in Bulgaria but the names and places are not very important because wines are classified by grape variety.

Dimiat is the predominant local white vine. It is very similar to Chasselas and is the equivalent of the Serbian Smederevka, high-yielding and of good quality (in fact it is the second most widely-grown grape,

THE GRAPES OF BULGARIA

Pamid is the most popular Bulgarian red grape variety, though its 9000 hectares (22239 acres) fall far short of the acreage of Cabernet-Sauvignon and Merlot. It produces wines which should be drunk soon after production and whose quality is variable.

Dimiat is a white variety similar to Smederevka in Serbia. It is a flexible wine with the aroma of ripe fruit. Its 8000 hectares (19768 acres) make it the second most popular white grape after the U.S.S.R.'s Rkaziteli. Misket, with a bouquet of Muscat and vinified in the same way can be found all over Bulgaria and is also worthy of note.

after the U.S.S.R.'s Rkaziteli). Dimiat flourishes along the Black Sea littoral. It is golden and harmonious and the white wines it produces are light and of good quality. They are quite acidic and thus easy to export. The Valley of the Roses in the Kazanlyk region produces Rosenthaler Riesling and a sort of amber Muscat called Misket is produced in Karlovo.

Melnik, a rather pleasant sweet white wine, is cultivated around Sandanski in the south-west. In Thrace, the vines border the Marica river. They are mainly for producing such red wines as Pamid, Pirinsko and Trakia. However, the Gamza is by far the most popular grape variety. It is grown in the Danube Valley and produces a white wine with a remarkable bouquet.

Mavrud (meaning "black") is a strong, dark local red which is aged for several years in cellars. However, local varieties are increasingly being replaced with Cabernet Franc and Cabernet-Sauvignon grapes.

One cannot speak of Bulgarian wine

without mentioning the sparkling wines (Champanski), marketed under the name "Iskra", from the northern part of the country.

USSR

Wine is produced throughout southern Russia, from the Roumanian frontier in the west to the Chinese frontier in the east. However, the three largest wine-growing areas are the Caspian Sea basin, the Crimea/Azov Sea area and Armenia. The vine has always prospered in this part of the world. Noah landed on Mount Ararat when the flood subsided, and when he left his Ark he planted the first vine in what is today Armenia. Later, the ancient kingdom of Van covered the whole of Armenia and the Caucasus and it based its prosperity on wine. In the days of Herodotus (460 b.c.), Armenian wines had a considerable reputation. It is astonishing to realise that sulphur was already being used to treat wine in those early days. In the Odyssey, Homer goes into raptures over "the bright and scented wines of Colchis, the land of the golden grapes". (The land of the Golden Fleece, nowadays known as Georgia).

REGULATION

The authorized appellations of origin in the Soviet Union are grouped into thirteen categories. These are:
wines from the Abrau-Dursso, Krasnodar, Massandra, Crimea and Bessarabia (Moldavia) conglomerates;
Wines of the Tempelhof collective;
Wines from the republics of the Ukraine, Azerbaidjan, Georgia, Armenia, Uzbekistan, Kazakhia, Kirghizia, Tadjikistan and Turkmenia.
The Russian authorities allow the appellations "type of Port, Madeira, Tokay, Sherry, Samos, Cognac and Champagne".

This illustrates the importance of viticulture throughout Russia. In the past 60 years, the government has quadrupled the vine-growing area, especially between the Black Sea and the Caspian Sea in Armenia, in Azerbaidjan, Georgia and the Crimea. Today, production amounts to 35 million hectolitres (770 million gallons) from an area of 1.4 million hectares (3.5 million acres) under cultivation. This puts the USSR in third place in the wine-producing league, after Italy and France. Despite these figures, production remains

inadequate, and the government is forced to import 7 million hectolitres (154 million gallons) a year, in an attempt to use wine to replace vodka consumption. The Russians are the heaviest drinkers of spirits in the word, but their wine consumption is only 13 litres (22³/₄ pints) per capita annually.

So vine cultivation is extensive, modern production techniques are used and there are large cellars, as visitors to the country will have seen. Wine production is controlled by state enterprises and kolkhozes (collective farms). About 200 grape varieties are used, including European types imported by Peter the Great. A wide variety of wines are made, liqueur and dessert wines, distilled wines of the brandy type, Sherry, Madeira, Port, Tokay and the famous sparkling wines of the Crimea.

East of the Azov Sea in the Valley of the Don, red and white wines are made from the local grape called Donski. The

GRAPES OF USSR

In addition to the classic grape varieties of western Europe such as Cabernet-Sauvignon, Riesling and Merlot, the USSR has 190 of its own cultivars, of which 16 are of great interest.

Of the red varieties, Saperavi which means "dyer" because its colour improves the reds of blends, smells of plums and can age for many years in cellars. It is a late-ripening grape with a high saccharine content. The most famous Saperavi wine is Yuzhnoberezbny on the Crimean coast, which is very rich in alcohol and very concentrated.

The Khindogny stock comprises 70% of the vineyards of Karabakh. It is a rather sour, tannic wine, mainly used in blending.

Tsimlyansky Cherny is a grape used mainly to make sparkling wines, especially in the Don region, where Tsimlyanskoe, the famous sparkling red wine, is made. Rubinavy Magaracha is a wine made from a cross between Cabernet-Sauvignon and Saperavi, a very promising plant.

The most important white grape variety in the USSR (18% of all the vineyards, outstripping White Ugni) is Rkatsiteli which comes from Georgia (the word means "red vine" in Georgian). This is the second most-cultivated variety in the world. Its wines are lively with a spicy aroma which is somewhat remiscent of wine from Alsace. Rkatsiteli is used to make dessert wines of the Port, Madeira, Samos and Sherry types and even to make Brandy because it also does well in oak casks.

Mtsvane is definitely the best variety in the country. It comes from Kakhetia and Georgia, and produces a wine which vinifies at low temperature after long distillation. If drunk young, it is a fruity, very aromatic wine.

Tsimlyanski Cherny (black) is used to make a sparkling red wine, called Tsimlyanskoe.

Crimea is the premier wine-growing region of the USSR, and has 30% of all its vineyards. Vines grow around Sebastopol and Simferopol on the Black Sea and extend as far as the eye can see. This whole region developed thanks to the introduction of French wine-producers in the early 20th century. Massandra is now the best-known wine in Crimea and even in the whole USSR. It is a vinous, Madeira-type wine with a beautiful golden colour. Other important wines are Livadia, a warm Muscat, Oreanda, a dry white made from Sémillon grapes, and dessert rosés such as Alupka. Yuzhnoherezhny, a concentrated wine with a high alcohol content is made from the Saperavi stock. If Crimea is known for its sweet and dessert wines, the most popular of its wines are the sparkling types such as Kaffra and Krimskoje, which must be the best in the land.

Soviet production grew considerably when Moldavia, the ancient Romanian province in Bessarabia, was annexed in 1940. A great deal of wine (20% of total production) is produced there around the Moldavian capital, Kishinev, which lies at the mouth of the River Dniester. Wine is also produced in the Bielgrad Dniestrovsky region, formerly known as Akkerman and now in the Ukraine. Excellent table wines are made from Pinot, Traminer, Riesling and other Aligoté grape varieties. One cannot mention the Ukraine without recalling the famous vineyards of Odessa, Ismalia and the Carpathians. The hybrids planted after the phylloxera epidemics have now been replaced by European stocks.

Georgia, between the Black Sea and the Caspian, has the oldest vineyards in Russia; the best wines are produced in the Kakhetia region. Two of these wines are quite well-known abroad, Myshako Riesling and Ghurdjurni. Less well-known are Napureouli, Mukuzani and red and white Mzvanes. The white Rkatsiteli grape originates from Georgia and constitutes more than half the harvest. Wines made from it are refreshing with a floral, almost spicy, scent. If wine can be said to have a homeland, it is surely Armenia, the

smallest of the federal republics of the USSR, situated between Anatolia and the Iranian plateau. It has a number of important wine-producing centres such as Oktemberian, Vedin, Echmiadzin and Ashtarak which produce natural wines, fortified wines and brandies. The Krasnodar region, which has given its name to a sparkling wine, lies east of the Black Sea and the Azov Sea. Anapa and

Novorossivsk are the wine-producing districts. Their good quality dry wines are made from Riesling and Cabernet vines. Abrau-Dursso, by the Black Sea, produces ones of the best Rieslings in the country. To complete the picture, mention must be made of Azerbaidjan (near the Iranian border) where viticulture only dates back to 1960s. It is known for its table wines called Matrassa. Turkmenistan produces a Tokay-type wine from irrigated vines. Other central Asian regions such as Tadjikistan, north of Pakistan and Kashmir, and the huge Kazakhstan republic which stretches from the Caspian sea to Mongolia, are also now producing wine.

THE LEVANT

Although it is the cradle of viticulture, Turkey produces very little wine. Less than 10% of the Turkish grape harvest is vinified. In Lebanon, the famous Beka'a Valley is still producing some respectable wines, such as Chateau Mussard, despite 15 years of civil war. Its vineyards, like those of its invasive neighbour, Syria, are mainly planted with "Cinsant", Cabernet-Sauvignon and Syrah, which have replaced Meroue and Obaideh, the two traditional white varieties. As for Israel's young wine-making industry, it is organized and has developed along French lines, although it can trace its origins back to the Bible.

Cappadocia in Turkey is one of the oldest wine-growing regions in the world.

TURKEY

The word Turkey conjures up such familiar names and dates as the Byzantine Empire, the fall of Constantinople in 1453, the Ottoman Empire, etc. But Turkey is above all the viticultural cradle of the world. There is every reason to believe that the vine grew wild in the mountains of Anatolia. The first tangible proof of vinification was the discovery, in a village in central Anatolia, of barrels at least 4,000 years old.

The Turkish vineyards prospered until the Greco-Turkish conflict after the First World War. Its wines were drunk and appreciated throughout Europe. Unfortunately, upon the departure of the important Greek communities of Thrace, wine production plummeted and the grapes were either eaten fresh or as raisins.

In 1927, the Turkish government decided to nationalize the wine industry. From a peak of three million hectolitres (110 million gallons), production had decreased to 20,000 hectolitres (440,000 gallons). After 1935, the Kemal Ataturk did everything to encourage a resurgence of wine-growing vineyard and promote internal consumption.

Today, while Turkey is has the fifth-largest vineyard in the world, only 5% of the harvest is made into wine. The internal market is very small and consumption barely exceeds 7 litres (12 pints) per capita per year.

The best wine is produced in central Anatolia, in Asia Minor. Three-fifths of Turkish production comes from Thrace

TURKEY

Most wine growers sell their harvest to cooperatives, which are still governed by the 1927 monopoly, but sales are also made to private companies who take care of the vinification. The wine has low acidity, so sulphur dioxide has to be added to it to enhance its keeping qualities (this is very strictly controlled). The government has undertaken a huge project to delineate administrative wine-growing zones, lay down selection standards and define grape varieties. The future looks promising.

and the coasts of the Aegean Sea. Two other regions are famous for the quality of their wines, the Sea of Marmara and the slopes bordering the Black Sea, beyond the Bosphorus.

Turkish wines are generally good.

Those that are dry and pleasant to drink include the deep-red Buzbag from Anatolia, Doluca, Kavakldere, Marmara, and the famous Thracian Trakya.

This last is also found in a white form from the Sémillon vine. Izmir is an excellent, fruity white wine, to be served cool. There are also muscat and sparkling wines.

LEBANON AND SYRIA

The Lebanon, which derives from the name Jebel Liban, "the white mountain", and Syria on the eastern shore of the Mediterranean, are the heirs of the famous Phoenicia. This region of the world was one of the first to produce wine. The wine of Helbon, particularly Chalybon, was the favourite of the kings of Persia. It was exported by the Syrians and Phoenicians to places as remote as China. The name has been handed down through history as being one of the great wines of antiquity. Ezekiel even specifies that it was a cooked white wine. Since Lebanon and Syria are predominantly Moslem countries, they have always left the production of wine to

THE GRAPES OF TURKEY

Apart from the well-known red vines, there is also a considerable variety of regional vines. The best known are the Papazharasi from Kimklareli in Thrace, Kalecik and the Cubuk from the Ankara region, Dimrit and Horozkarasi in Anatolia. Among the white vines, the best wines are produced from the Emir of Hasandede and Nerince of Anatolia.

THE GRAPES OF LEBANON AND SYRIA

Before the arrival of the vines imported from France - Cinsault, Cabernet, Sauvignon and Syrah - the white vines, such as the Meroné and the Obaideh, which have a very low yield and bear some resemblance to Chardonnay

their Christian populations.

The French troops stationed in Syria before and during the World War II were an essential element in the development of viticulture.

There remains a vineyard of 100,000 hectares (247,100 acres), cultivated in the hilly region of Aleppo and Homs near Damascus. In 1857, the Jesuits in Lebanon created the famous wine-producing estate of Ksara which produces the first-rate Château Musard.

Despite a permanent state of war, the country continues to maintain a 19000 hectares (46,949 acres) vineyard centred in the Beka Valley in the south.

However, the grapes face increasing competition from the cultivation of the poppy. Most of the harvest is used for raisins and table grapes; the rest produces vins ordinaires with a low degree of alcohol, and some sparkling wines.

ISRAEL

One name is intimately linked to the history of wine in Israel, that of the Baron de Rothschild. In 1882, well before the creation of the State of Israel, the first Zionist settlements were established in Palestine. Those financed by the Baron planted the first vines. These were vitis vinifera vines (Alicante, Carignan, Petit Bouchet) planted in Samaria and in Galilee. In only a few years, there was overproduction, but then all the vines were exterminated by a phylloxera plague. The baron not only taught the wine-growers the technique of grafting on to American root-stock, but also offered them his cellars at Rishon-le-Zion near Tel Aviv and Zikhron Yaacov, south of Haifa. These are still the country's two main centres of production.

The Israel Wine Institute was established in 1957. It selects and tests the best grape varieties and the best wines adapted to the climate and soil. Thanks to its great degree of technological advancement, the young Israeli vine certainly has a promising future.

In the land of the Bible, the history of the vine dates back to Genesis. After the flood, which is dated at 3000 BC, the first thing Noah did was to plant a vine. A clay tablet dating back to 1800 BC reports that wine was commoner than water in ancient Israel and covered the whole country. The wine growers' imagination was limitless. Wine was mixed with honey or pepper, it was boiled with asparagus, it was used as a disinfectant and to dye cloth.

By the beginning of the Christian era, the wines of Judaea were so greatly appreciated that they were exported as far away as England. When the crusaders disembarked in the Holy Land, despite the Moslem presence, they found vines grown by Christians on Mount Carmel, and around Bethlehem and Nazareth.

Since 1948 and the massive arrival of new immigrants, wine-growing has been developing constantly. Today, the production is 350,000 hectolitres (7,700,000 gallons) from an area of

cultivation of 3000 hectares (7413 acres)*. The "Société coopérative vigneronne des grandes caves" owns two main vineyards which account for 60% of production.

GRAPES OF ISRAEL

All the great vines suitable for a hot and dry country are to be found in Israel. For the red wines, there are the Alicante, Grenache and Carignan varieties (though the latter is tending to be replaced by Colombard and Cabernet Sauvignon, which produce the best wines).
In the whites, there are Clairette, the Muscat, the Sémillon, Ugni Blanc and Dobuki, a local vine. At the present time, quality takes precedence over quantity.

These are Zichron Yaakov, on the slopes of Mount Carmel, southeast of Haifa and Rishon-le-Zion, near Tel-Aviv. They are well-known for their rosés and whites, produced using the French methods introduced by Baron de Rotschild. In Galilee, in the north of the country, a new vineyard is producing excellent dry white and red wines, Gamla and Yarden, respectively. In central Israel, in the Zebulun Valley, the Gezer district produces red wines. Vines have also recently been planted near Jerusalem and the results are said to be promising.

Almost every type of wine is produced in Israel, including sweet wines of the Tokay type, Muscats and slightly-sparkling and sparkling wines. Of these, 70% are table wines. Some of the names once borrowed from the great European vineyards have been translated into Hebrew.

They include Adom Atic, Primor (previously Pommard), Mont Rouge, Carmelith, Chateau Windsor, Chateau Rishon, etc.

* Of which 10% are exported (kosher wines) to the United States and Great Britain by the Carmel Wine Company.

CYPRUS

This great eastern Mediterranean island off the Syrian coast has been inhabited since the Mycenaean era. Both Greeks and Phoenicians founded major settlements here. Cyprus has been a land of wine ever since the time of Aphrodite, the goddess of love, who is reputed to have been born on this island. To this day, 10% of cultivated land is given over to viticulture, with a production of 200,000 tonnes.

The best vineyards are on the southern slopes of Mount Troodos, between Limassol (known as the Bordeaux of Cyprus) and Paphos. Ever since the days of Homer, this has been the home of the legendary Commandaria, made from dried grapes. Due to fear of phylloxera, which has not so far affected the island, the varieties have remained very traditional. There are three main grapes: red Mavron (80% of production), white Xynisteri (a local variety) and Muscat d'Alexandrie. The Mavron gives a dry, vigorous and very tonic wine, for example Afamès and Othello. Kokkineli, also found in Greece, is a very dry, deeply-coloured rosé. It is made from Mavron grapes and should be drunk well chilled to accompany a meal.

It is a matter of great pride to the islanders that Cypriot vines were used in the 15th century to plant the prestigious Madeira vineyards, although Hungarian Tokay and Sicilian Marsala varieties were also used.

In the beginning there was Nama, that famous wine of antiquity, mentioned by Hesiod, and made from dried grapes. It was drunk in abundance on annual pilgrimages to the temple of Aphrodite. Years passed. During the Crusades, King Richard the Lionheart captured Cyprus. Before handing it over to the Knights Templar, he discovered this wonderfully sweet and golden wine, unchanged since the days of Homer.

The Knights Templar, who also enjoyed it, changed its name to "Commandaria". History tells us that it was served at the "Feast of the Five Kings" in 1352, and it is also said that Sultan Selim II conquered the island in 1571 in order to possess it.

This legendary wine is still as famous today. About twenty villages on Mount Troodos (Olympia) are authorized to produce it. It is always made from a mixture of Mavron and Xynisteri (red and white grapes). Some producers still maintain the ancient tradition of drying the grapes in the sun. The storage jars are smeared with pitch mixed with ash and goathair. They are then laid down and new

wine is added each year.

A true Commandaria is a wine turned a dark golden colour by the sun. It has a velvety texture, brimming with sweetness, since it contains four times as much sugar as port. Sometimes it is so concentrated that it needs to be diluted for drinking.

A more ordinary Commandaria is a pleasant dessert wine, very reminiscent of sherry.

MALTA

What can one say about Malta, that little island of 120 square miles in the middle of the Mediterranean, south of Sicily? The torrential rain in May and scorching hot summers do not favour the production of good quality wine. Nevertheless, Malta has devoted 1000 hectares (2,470 acres) to the cultivation of the vine and produces 19,000 hectolitres (418,000 gallons) of wine every year. Most of the vineyards are on the south coast. They produce very average red and white wines which lack smoothness. Two wines, however, rise above the mundane - the white Ghirgentina and the red Gellewza. The government's efforts to produce a quality Muscat for export are also worthy of note.

GRAPES OF CYPRUS

Having escaped phylloxera, Cypriot vineyards depend on two main varieties:
Red Mavron: 80% of cultivation. It produces a robust medium or dry wine which is potent but lacks finesse.
Xynisteri, the local white variety. Chiefly used for Commandaria, it is also used to make a rather bland and deeply-coloured white wine.

NORTH AFRICA

The temperate Mediterranean coastline is the only part of the African continent (apart from South Africa) suitable for vine cultivation.

The three countries which constitute the Maghreb (the name means "the west" or "where the sun sets") all make wine. Morocco. Tunisia and Algeria lie between the Mediterranean and the Sahara and are bounded in the west by eastern Libya and the Atlantic Ocean. Viticulture began in the 12th century b.c., when the Phoenicians first established trading posts along the coasts. By the time the Romans conquered North Africa two centuries before the birth of Christ and turned it into Roman provinces, vines were already well-established. They continued to prosper thanks to ingenious irrigation systems.

The Arab conquest in the 13th century united North Africa under a single faith, which also had the effect of stopping the expansion of grape-growing in its tracks. The vines progressively dwindled until the arrival of the French colonists in the 19th century. Within the space of a few years, the whole of north Africa was once again covered in vines, the same Alicante, Bouschet and Carignan vines which still grow here. For instance, at the time of Algerian independence in 1962, Algeria was producing 16 million hectolitres (352 million gallons) of wine annually. Today, Algeria, Tunisia and Morocco devote about 200,000 hectares (500,000 acres) to growing grapes, to produce about 4.5 million hectolitres (99 million gallons) of wine a year. These three countries have traditionally been the main suppliers of cheap wines for blending, but are now aiming at producing fine wines and are starting to regulate the wine trade more strictly.

Morocco produces heady red wines with strong bouquets.

ALGERIA

Here we have a great paradox, a North African Moslem country and former French colony which, on gaining independence in 1962, inherited one of the largest vineyards in Europe. Despite large-scale uprooting campaigns, Algeria still produces three million hectolitres (66,000,000 gallons) of wine from an area of 100,000 hectares (247,105 acres). Almost all the production is exported because the Algerians, being Moslems, are strictly forbidden to drink it.

REGULATION

Algeria, following the example of France with its V.D.Q.S., has imposed a classification system based on its Vins d'Appellation d'Origine Garantie (V.A.O.G.), an appellation conferred by the Institut Algérien de la Vigne et du Vin (I.V.V.). These wines come from defined regions and are bottled at their place of production. Since 1970, the Algerian authorities have recognized seven large wine-producing regions, three in the Algiers district and four in the Oran district.

The history of Algerian wine dates back to the time when Algeria was a province of the Roman Empire. After the Moslem invasion, only table grapes were left and it was not until the arrival of the French in the 19th century that Algeria regained its vineyards. In fact it was the phylloxera epidemic, which, having laid waste the French vineyards, encouraged the ruined wine-growers to settle there from 1842 onwards. The vines they brought with them were Pinot, Cabernet, Chasselas and Grenache. These were soon replaced by the Alicante-Bouschet and the Carignan grafted on to American root-stock, when Algeria in turn was hit by phylloxera. When Algeria became independent in 1962, the country was producing 16 million hectolitres (352 million gallons) of wine, which were used as a basis for blending into a fair number of French

wines. Forty percent of the Algerian workforce was employed in the vineyards. Today, the vineyards have been greatly reduced. Sixty per cent of production consists of red wine, dark in colour and high in alcohol content (up to 15°). Thirty per cent of production is white, which is unexportable because its colour suggests it is oxydized. The remaining 10% consists of rosé wines. The authorities are increasingly encouraging quality wines with the status of Vins d'Appellation d'Origine Garantie (V.A.O.G.). They are made from vines inherited from the colonial period and from the two former French départements of Oran and Alger. The Vins d'Appellation d'Origine Garantie are divided into seven areas.

THE ALGIERS DISTRICT

Côtes du Zaccar (near the town of Miliala) and particularly the Château Romain, which produces a substantial, strongly-coloured red wine from Pinot Noir and Syrah grapes, at Ain-Bessem, a mountain-

THE GRAPES OF ALGERIA

The main vines originate from the colonial period and have all been grafted on to American root-stock. They produce deeply-coloured wines with a high alcohol content.
Vines used for the red wines of the plains include Carignan, Cinsault, the Grenache and Morrastel. The varieties used on the slopes are mainly Cabernet, Mourvèdre, Pinot and Syrah.
The white wines are produced from Farrana (Coteaux de Tlemcen), Clairette, Ugni Blanc and Aligoté. Sometimes the colour leads one to suspect oxidation.

ous and very wild region south of Algiers. The vineyard covers a high plateau as far as Bouira and produces some excellent rosés and well-balanced red wines. Further west lies Médéa, a vineyard planted up to an altitude of 4000 feet, a world record for grape-growing.

THE ORAN DISTRICT

alone produces two-thirds of the harvest. Coteaux du Mascara has all the elements for the production of the best wine in Algeria. It has a continental climate, sandy and sandstone soil and an altitude of between 1800 and 2700 feet.

Coteaux de Tlemcen to the southwest of Oran and the region of Dahra also produce excellent wines. The latter was where the great wine-growing estates were situated prior to independence.

These are Taoughrite (formerly Paul Robert), Ain Merane (formerly Rabelais), Mazouna (formerly Renault) and Khadra Achaacha (formerly Picard). Also worthy of note is Mostaganem, that fine and fruity wine from the slopes.

MOROCCO

Morocco, as the westernmost country in North Africa, has a coastline bordered in the west by the Atlantic Ocean and in the north by the Straits of Gibraltar and the Mediterranean. The history of wine began when the Phoenicians set up their first trading post at Lixus (Larache) in the 12th century BC. Transformed into a Roman province after Carthage was defeated, Mauritania Tingitana, as the Romans called Morocco, sent its best wines to Rome. This tra-dition was interrupted by the Arab invasion, when all vines for wine-making disappeared for one thousand years.

REGULATION

Since 1956, the year of independence, the Moroccan authorities have regulated the quality and marketing of the wines. The law which has been in existence since the French Protectorate, requires all wines, even those intended for export, to be "sound" and to be at least 11° proof (the minimum for a country in which red wines can be anything up to 15° to 19° proof). On the other hand, the appellations contrôlées are very vague. The appellation d'origine shown on some labels is more likely merely to indicate a better-quality wine.

In 1912, the French Protectorate was established. Viticulture developed with the arrival of the French colonists until it covered 45,000 hectares (111,200 acres). Since independence, production has stabilized at around 500,000 hectolitres (11 million gallons), of which 80% is consumed locally, the rest being exported to Europe for blending.

Heady wines are made, whose strong bouquet is somewhat lacking in finesse. They come from high-yield vines, such as Cinsault, Carignan, Grenache, Alicante-Bouschet and, to a certain extent, Cabernet. The rosés, which should be drunk when young, are pleasant and very popular. The white wines from the Clairette, Macabeo, Grenache and Xim-énez vines are not well-suited to the hot climate and tend to oxidize quickly. However, there is a pleasant surprise south of Casablanca and east of Marrakesh, dry and fruity vins gris , produced by the two old-established vineyards of El-Jadida and Demnate.

The two great wine-producing regions of Morocco are situated on the plain. They are Berkane and Oudjda around Meknès and Fez and the region of Rabat and Casablanca.

Other vineyards are to be found in the south of Morocco in the region of Mogador and on the slopes of the High Atlas range. There are no Grands Crus. The best rosés

come from Berkane in the northeast. Taza, in the centre of the country, is known for its strong wines which are used for blending. Fez produces reds, whites and rosés. The best red wines in Morocco are produced in the Meknès and Rabat region. They have a good colour, are very full-bodied and their flavour is characteristic. Also worth mentioning are the slopes of the Daïet (Roumi) and, farther north, the Dar bel Hamri around Sidi Slimane.

There is one cause for regret. It would be worth laying down these red wines so that they could age and attain their full maturity, but, unfortunately, they are drunk too soon.

THE GRAPES OF MOROCCO

The red vines planted by the French between 1929 and 1935 are high-yield vines of the plains, the Cinsault, Carignan, Cabernet, Mourvèdre, Grenache and Alicante-Bouschet varieties. For the white wines, there are Clairette, Macabeo, Ximénez and Grenache vines. Local stocks which are still cultivated are Rafsaï grown in the Rif and the Plant X (or what remains of it after the ravages of phylloxera). Both produce table grapes and are also used in vinification.

TUNISIA

Tunisia is the easternmost of the North African countries of the Maghreb. This small country of eight million inhabitants has an unusual history. When the Phoenician trading posts became emancipated in the 6th century BC, Carthage became the capital of an immense maritime empire. The vine, which was already present, was developed, especially after the Punic Wars and the victory of Rome, thanks to an ingenious irrigation system which transformed the country into a superb vineyard admired throughout the empire. It was a Carthaginian called Magon who wrote the first manual of viticulture in the 4th century BC. The Muslim invasion put a stop to this

REGULATION

In 1957, the Tunisian government imposed an appellation system and a system of definition by region. Three types of wine are recognized. All are analysed and subjected to blind testings by experts from the classification commission. The first category covers the best wines which must contain between 11° and 13° alcohol and be at least one year old. The second category covers the Muscats. Since 1965, the appellation of "Vin de Muscat de Tunisie" has been restricted by origin on the condition that it is made from the Muscat d'Alexandrie, Frontignan or Terracina Muscat grapes. The third category applies to appellations such as the wines of Radès, Kelibia and Tebourda.

expansion. It was not until the French protectorate period (1881-1953) that the Tunisian vineyard arose from the ashes. Today, it covers 38,000 hectares (9400 acres), with a production of 600,000 hectolitres (13,200,000 gallons). The two most important regions are Cap Bon, due east of the Gulf of Tunis, and the valleys of the Medjerda and the Oued Miliane near Tunis. The vines are of European origin, including Carignan and Alicante Bouschet for the red wines. The climate, which causes the grapes to ripen too rapidly, tends to alter the colour of the wine and cause it to oxidize.

The Pedro Ximénez, Sauvignon and Sémillon vines are being increasingly cultivated for the whites, as are Pinot Noir, Cabernet and Mourvèdre for the reds.

From the Alicante Grenache, Tunisia produces one of the best rosés in North Africa, which should be drunk young,

before it oxydizes. Almost all the wines come from the Tunis-Mateur-Bordj Toum triangle and from Khanguet, Grombalia, Kelibia to Cap Bon. The best wines are those from the slopes of Utique, Carthage, Mornag and Tebourda. However, Tunisia

is best known for its Muscat wines from Kelibia, Rads and Thibar. These powerful, heavily-scented sweet types contain up to 18° alcohol and have no less than 70 grams (2¹/₂ oz) of sugar per litre.

THE GRAPES OF TUNISIA

As in Morocco and Algeria, the Carignan, the Alicante-Bouschet and the Cinsault vines are cultivated. These high-yielding varieties produce red wines which have a tendency to oxidize very quickly. For a certain number of years, the government has been encouraging quality rather than quantity, so these vines are gradually being replaced by Sauvignon and Sémillon for the whites, and Cabernet, Pinot Noir and Mourvèdre for the reds. The Muscat grapes are Muscat d'Alexandrie, Frontignan and Terracina. Two local vines are still cultivated: the Nocera (red) and the Beldi (white).

THE UNITED STATES

Whenever anyone, anywhere in the world, mentions American vines, one immediately thinks of California.

This huge country is the sixth-largest wine-producer in the world, placed just after the USSR. The vineyards of the land which has welcomed so many European immigrants have the same image as the population - a "melting-pot" of various European viticultures. The list of wines is a long one, including Californian Tokay, American Port, Chianti, Burgundy, Champagne, Sauternes, Chablis, and so on. Today, with the unbelievable boom in American wine, Californian viticulture is in the process of creating its own traditions and producing wines comparable to the best European vintages. In 1976, when the United States celebrated its bicentenary, a French wine merchant organized a blind tasting in France of Californian Chardonnay and Cabernet-Sauvignons, plus clarets and white Burgundies. The Californian wines won the taste test. The news came as a bombshell. In 1980, US wine consumption exceeded that of whisky.

There are two types of vine on North American soil. The native vines, which are generally of the variety Vitis riparia, grow wild more or less all over the country, and then there are the European varieties of the Vitis vinifera type which constitute the basis of American viticulture.

An old map drawn in the 15th century and preserved in Basle, Switzerland, shows land beyond Iceland and Greenland. This is the very first representation of North America, which had been discovered by the Vikings in about the year 1000 a.d., four centuries earlier. They named the new land Vineland because they found so many grapevines growing wild. It was not until 1562 that the first American wine was produced. It was probably made in Florida by Huguenots who used the Scuppernong variety of Vitis rotundifolia.

The name Scuppernong was used by the Indians to describe both the vine plant itself and the region in which it was discovered. According to legend, the scent of the Scuppernong was so powerful that it intoxicated those arriving by ship even before they had entered port! The pilgrim fathers who arrived on the "Mayflower" drank their first American wine in 1623 at the first Thanksgiving celebration.

Its quality was immaterial. It can be said that the first drinkable wine produced on the East Coast was the result of the accidental cross between a local variety and a European plant.

Napa Valley, California, young vines.

It was called Alexander, after its creator, John Alexander, who worked as gardener to William Penn, the English Quaker who founded Pennsylvania and the city of Philadelphia. It was the result of the difficulty of acclimatising Vitis vinifera, a European vine, to American soil. "It is useless to waste time and sweat by insisting on planting foreign vines. Centuries will pass before they will take. Let us rather develop native plants," wrote Jefferson. He was both right and wrong. He was wrong because a few decades later, California growers managed to grow Vinifera vines successfully.

He was right because of a tiny insect by the name of Phylloxera vastatrix , which attacked the roots of the fragile Vinifera seedlings, destroying any new plantings in the space of a few months. When Phylloxera crossed the Atlantic and reached Europe in 1863 it caused such a disaster that in a few years it had entirely destroyed every vineyard. In 1880, an œnology and viticulture department was established at the University of California at Davis, with the aim of halting this terrible epidemic. A partial solution was found by grafting Vinifera stocks onto the very robust Labrusca* which was phylloxera-resistant, like all American grape stocks. The vineyards destroyed by Phylloxera had hardly been re-established when a new catastrophe hit American viticulture - Prohibition.

The Volstead Act passed into law on October 28, 1919, forbidding the manufacture and sale of any alcoholic drink, except for religious or medicinal purposes. A mass of state legislation along similar lines followed. These laws were to have major repercussions on wine consumption. It explains the American taste for very strong drink, the quick "shot" drunk secretly with all the enjoyment of forbidden pleasures. By the time the Volstead Act, the Eighteenth Amendment to the Constitution of the United States, was repealed on December 5,1933, a coach and horses had been driven through it.

Both during and after Prohibition, wines were hurriedly "aged", destroying forever the palate of a generation who were unaccustomed to the subtleties of fine wine. It was not until the G.I.s returned home from Europe after World War II and the discovery of the Old World by American tourists that the American mentality began to change. "Over there", they had learned to drink wine with meals, something which had previously been unthinkable. It was not until the late 1960s that, for the first time since Prohibition, the consumption of table wine exceeded that of fortified wines (Sherry, Port and Muscat). Amazingly, it was only then that Americans began to recognize the quality of their own wines. In 1968, there were only 40 wineries. Now there are 1500, and most of them are concerned mainly with quality.

*Unfortunately, Vitis Labrusca may be phylloxera-resistant, but it is said to have a "foxy" taste. Some people detect the flavours of blackcurrant, raspberry and wildfowl, others perceive the smell of wet fur!

Napa Valley, California

CALIFORNIA

The Californian statistics speak for themselves. Of all the wines bought in the United States, 70% come from California. Today - and this is an important development because the vineyards have grown in size by 300% between 1970 and 1990 - there are more than 300,000 hectares (741,315 acres) devoted to growing grapes, more than half of which are for wine-making.

It is estimated that soon one-sixth of the agricultural area of this state will be covered with vines. Here, grapes are big business, worth billions of dollars, which is why 65% of Californian vines are owned by several large conglomerates such as Seagrams, which owns Paul Masson, Nestlé which owns Beringer, Heublein of United Distillers, Almadén, Inglenook and Beaulieu. The owners may well change tomorrow at the whim of investment policy. So why has there been this incredible rush towards California, emphasised by the fact that for eight years in the recent past, a Californian president has sat in the White House? California is a miracle of nature, the climate and soil make it one of the greatest wine-producing regions of the world. However, this realisation did not come about suddenly.

Napa Valley, California, Sterling Vineyards.
Sonoma County, Buena Vista winery.

CALIFORNIA

In 1524, Cortes had just conquered Mexico and he decided to transform the New World into a huge vineyard. He was so successful that a few years later, there was fatal overproduction of Spanish wines. To protect the vineyards of the mother-country, the King of Spain ordered the systematic uprooting of all the vines in the new colonies of the Americas. Fortunately, Baja California was so remote that it escaped the effects of this decree. It is recorded that a Jesuit, Father Juan Ugarte, planted the first vines on the west coast

REGULATION OF THE WINE TRADE

When will there be an end to those pale imitations of Sherry, Port, Tokay, Burgundy, Chablis, Sauternes, Beaujolais and Champagne (this last appellation is still legal) which are the daily output of the Californian wineries? Fortunately, with the arrival of excellent grape varieties, the Californian wine-producer is increasingly tending to name the grape variety from which the wine was made.

Thus, since 1983 the so-called "varietal wines" must, by law, name the grape variety if the wine consists of at least 75% of this grape (the remaining 25% can be anything, Thompson Seedless or Concord, for instance).

There is one exception, the Labrusca, with its peculiar "foxy" taste, which need constitute only 51% of the blend.

There is another improvement, the strictly-controlled use of the term "Estate-bottled", indicating that all the vinification has taken place on the site of the vineyard.

Another important improvement is the classification of the wine-producing regions by geographical and climatic features which is now being perfected.

The BATF (Bureau of Alcohol, Tobacco and Firearms) is the regulatory body. Thus wine of controlled appellation of origin must contain at least 85% of wine from the defined region.

The best known such regions are the Napa Valley and Sonoma County in California and Finger Lakes in New York State. In the land of consumerism, where consumer protection is deemed so important, it will be interesting to see whether the wine label will list the 50 or so permitted wine additives, which range from sugar to sulphur dioxide and other preserving agents.

around the mission of St. Francis Xavier. This vine of European origin came to be called the Mission grape, a name it retains to this day. In 1769, a Franciscan monk of Majorcan origin, Miguel José Serra planted a Mission vine at San Diego de Alcalá. The harvests were wonderful and the wine excellent. Fifty years later, there were 21 missions strung out along the Pacific coast, right up to Yerba Buena (modern San Francisco) and even as far north as Sonoma, at the end of the road linking them together, the Camino Reál ("the royal road", still a major highway in California). One of the biggest tourist attractions of California today is the San Gabriel Mission, in the suburbs of Los Angeles, where one can see "the original vine" and the little adobe hut in which the Indians trod the grapes. A new chapter opened in 1850, when the Mexican government decided to secularize the missions. It was the start of another story, that of the pioneers. An immigrant from Bordeaux with the highly fortuitous name of Louis Vigne settled on the site of the present Union Station, the Los Angeles railway station, in the centre of town. He was the first to advise the planting of the major French grape varieties which he imported via Boston and Cape Horn. Later, a trapper from Kentucky, William Wolfskill - who was also the first man to grow oranges on a commercial scale in California - became known for his vast wine-cellars which could hold 4000 hectolitres (88,000 gallons). Two immigrants of German origin, Charles Kohler and John Frohling, probably opened the first wine-shop in San Francisco.

Prior to the arrival of the father of Californian viticulture, Colonel Haraszthy, the hardy and high-yielding Mission grape dominated southern California; the wines of the north were mediocre and characterless. The legend of Agoston Haraszthy, a Hungarian aristocrat and a colonel to boot, began in 1851, on the day he decided to begin the large scale importation of European vines, and especially the famous Zinfandel which was planted for the first time in San Diego.

It took him 30 years to establish the dry red wine which is one of the great Californian varieties. The Colonel bequeathed his 2400 hectares (5930 acres) ranch to the Buena Vista Vinicultural Society, leaving it about 300 varieties of grape all planted around San Francisco. Thanks to his work, it was discovered that excellent wine could be produced in this part of the world on non-irrigated land.

The Gold Rush brought real prosperity to the vine-growers and a benevolent legislature constantly encouraged them to plant more and more vines. This major expansion was halted in its tracks in 1870 by the phylloxera epidemic which ravaged the vineyards. Help was extended to the growers in the form of experimental stations and organizations. It was at this time that the first standards of quality were introduced. The vines had hardly recovered from the phylloxera epidemic when they were hit a second time by the Volstead Act, the law that imposed Prohibition. In 1920, production plummeted from 2.3 million hectolitres (over 50 million gallons) to barely one million (22 million gallons). It took 30 years for the market to recover.

Yet this involuntary slimming cure had its advantages. Firstly, it helped to reduce the role of the Mission grape in the north of the country in favour of Cabernet-Sauvignon, Pinot and Chardonnay. Secondly, it showed that the high yields offered by the Carignane and Alicante-Bouschet varieties were not an end in themselves but that it was more important to concentrate on quality. Two œnologists from the University of California, helped bring about this new development. Professor A.J. Winkler and Dr. Maynard Amerine were the first to establish a relationship between climate and the quality of the wine (according to grape variety) from various regions of California. In their opinion, temperature was the only climatic factor which affected vine cultivation.

They divided California into five climatic

regions, based on mean daily and average temperatures above 10° between April 1 and October 31.

Region 1 : less than 2500 degree days.

Region 2 : between 2500 and 3000 degree days (Sonoma).

Region 3 : between 3000 and 3500 degree days (Napa Valley).

Region 4 : between 3500 and 4000 degree days.

Region 5 : 4000 + degree days.

The best wine regions were 1, 2 and 3.

THE GRAPES OF CALIFORNIA

The white wine boom of the 1980s has had major repercussions on Californian vineyards.

Although the red varieties increased by 15% in the same period, the area planted with white varieties doubled! French Colombard became by far the most popular variety, with more than 30,000 hectares (74,130 acres). It was followed by Chenin Blanc and Chardonnay, with 10000 hectares (24710 acres). Other white varieties include Sauvignon Blanc, Sémillon, Pinot blanc, White Riesling (Johannisberg Riesling), Sylvaner and Traminer.

The most important of the red varieties is Zinfandel, "Zin" as it is often called here, which covers 11000 hectares (27000 acres). It is the most European of the Californian varieties. How did it originate? No one knows! It is slightly looked down on as a good red carafe wine, whether white or full-bodied and is used to make every type of wine, from light wines and dry wines to Port or Sherry. It is drunk as "Zinfandel nouveau" or as a Classified Cru. But where it is grown and vinified under the best conditions (in regions 1 and 2), Zinfandel produces an excellent dry, red wine with a rather high alcohol content, good acidity, and many extracts and aromas which give it a wonderful bouquet when it has been allowed to age. Unfortunately, 40% of Californian Zinfandel is grown in the central valley, a very hot area which makes this wine almost undrinkable and as a result, has caused it to become more and more unpopular.

Other red wine varieties which are meeting with increasing success are Cabernet-Sauvignon (here called Cabernet), Gamay, Beaujolais, Pinot Noir, Grenache and Barbera. The hybrids developed at the University of California at Davis include Ruby Cabernet, a cross between Cabernet-Sauvignon and Carignane. The vine is high-yielding and resistant to high heat; it has a pronounced taste of Cabernet-Sauvignon.

THE GREAT WINE REGIONS

California is divided into six major wine-growing regions. These are the northern coast, the valleys of Sacramento and San Joaquin, the southern coast and San Luis Obispo. The northern coast produces the best wines in the whole of the United States. It extends north and south of San Francisco Bay especially in the three valleys parallel to the coastal mountain range. The summers here are hot and rainfall reduced. There are eight major districts, Napa, Sonoma, Livermore, Mendocino, Santa Cruz, San Benito, Santa Clara and Monterey.

NAPA

In entering the Napa Valley, you are entering the heart of the most prestigious American vineyards. You leave San Francisco via the Golden Gate Bridge and travel north for one hour. Napa, whose name means "abundant soil" in the local Indian language, is a valley 40 kilometres (25 miles) long with Mediterranean vegetation. There are 12,000 hectares (30,000 acres) of vineyards covering the slopes and the narrow strip of land only 5 to 6 kilometres (3 to 3 1/2 miles wide) at the bottom of the valley, where the soil is alluvial, consisting of a mixture of sand and clay. Napa's annual production averages 90,000 tonnes of grapes. The yield is relatively low, only 50 hectolitres per hectare (2718 gallons per acre), due to the poverty of some of the soils. In 1838, a certain George C. Yount, an explorer from North Carolina, planted one of the first vines in Napa, in the locality today known as Yountville. It was a Mission vine. The European varieties did not begin to arrive until 1850. It was then at St. Helena that the pioneer Charles Krug founded what was to become the biggest vineyard in California. In Napa, one grape variety reigns

supreme, Cabernet-Sauvignon, which is aged for up to four years in barrels. It covers one quarter of the acreage and particularly the cooler parts of the valley. Here, each vine-stock is worth a fortune. It is warmed in winter and humidified drop by drop in the hot season. Although mechanical harvesting was born in California, it is used sparingly in Napa and only if the terrain is suitable.

With the exception of the biggest estates, and unlike the practise in Europe, a distinction is made here between the grower and the wine-maker. The winery is the place where the wine is processed and aged. Thus, numerous vineyards which do not have their own winery make their wine in cooperatives, benefiting from the advanced technology available on a larger scale. The Napa Valley is divided into two areas, the upper and the lower valley. The upper valley, whose capital is St. Helena, covers an area of about 10 square kilometres (6 square miles) between Calistoga in the north and Rutherford and Oakville in the south. It differs from the lower valley by having stonier soil and a dryer climate and the fact that the vines are grown on the slopes. The lower valley area, which is more fertile but cooler because it is closer to San Francisco Bay, surrounds the town of Napa. It consists of the valley bottom and extends up to Sonoma.

Beaulieu is a 400-hectare (990-acre) vineyard, one of the most beautiful of the Napa vineyards, situated in the centre of the Valley. It produces Chardonnay, Pinot Noir, Sauvignon Blanc and even Muscat de Frontignan. However, its Cabernet-Sauvignon is unrivalled. The Georges de Latour Private Reserve is the greatest red wine in the United States. Beaulieu owes its history and its reputation to two men, Georges de Latour, a Frenchman who founded this estate near Rutherford in 1900 and André Tchelistcheff, who was of Russian origin but raised in Czechoslovakia. Tchelistcheff fought with the White Russians and became a refugee in France where he became assistant to the professor and œnologist, Paul Marsais. He was hired by Georges de Latour in 1938 and performed miracles in his cultivation of Cabernet-Sauvignon, Pinot Noir and Chardonnay. Today, the Beaulieu estate belongs to Heublein, the big distillers.

Beringer Brothers must be visited by every tourist to Napa. This winery of Rhenish inspiration was established in St. Helena by Frederick and Jacob Beringer in 1876. It is now part of the Nestlé empire. Château Montelena has a magnificent vineyard and produces wonderful wines from Zinfandel, Cabernet-Sauvignon and Johannisberg Riesling. However, the estate's greatest success has been with a Chardonnay comparable to the greatest white Burgundies.

The Christian Brothers, whose full title is Brothers of the Christian School, are a teaching order whose members also seem to have an innate business sense. They settled in California in 1868 at a place they named Mount La Salle, in memory of their founder, Jean-Baptiste de la Salle, on the Redwood Road at the edge of the Napa Valley. Today, their 500 hectares (1235 acres) of vineyards, and their large Greystone aging cellar in St. Helena, their wineries and distillation plant, constitute the biggest wine business in California. The Christian Brothers are best known for their brandies, vintage wines, liqueur wines and sparkling wines.

Domaine Chandon is a very beautiful 600 hectares (1483 acres) estate established by the French group Moët-Hennessy. Since 1977 it has specialized in the production of sparkling wines (the champagne name ought not be used here) from their Carneros vines planted with Pinot Noir and Pinot Chardonnay. The Mumm estate is the result of an association between Seagrams and the French champagne firm of Mumm. The estate is just beside the Sterling Winery which Seagrams already owned. In 1986, it officially launched its famous "Domaine Mumm Cuvée Napa".

Freemark Abbey Winery, north of St. Helena, produces varietal wines including Pinot Noir, Cabernet, Cabernet-Sauvignon, Johannisberg Riesling and, above all, Pinot Chardonnay. All these wines are aged in oak casks specially imported from Europe.

The Inglenook Napa Valley Vineyards owns a winery at Rutherford and vineyards on Mount St. John. The estate was founded in 1879 by Captain Gustave Niebaum and transferred to a Mr. Inglenook in 1908. The 90 hectares (222 acres) of the estate have been entirely replanted with Cabernet-Sauvignon, Pinot Noir, Sémillon, Pinot Chardonnay, Pinot Blanc and Traminer. Very recently, Gamay, Beaujolais and Merlot du Bordelais have been added. Quality here has always been more than just the rule, it has been a way of life. This has resulted in the fact that the oldest bottles of Cabernet-Sauvignon are now rarely obtainable, and only for a king's ransom (the estate now belongs to Heublein).

The Charles Krug Winery is proud of being the oldest winery in Napa. It was founded in 1861 and still owns its old vinification buildings on Highway 29, the great wine road through the Napa Valley, north of St. Helena. Charles Krug, the founder, is the great legendary figure of the valley. He was a disciple of Colonel Haraszthy,

producing his first wine in 1858, using a cider-press. His name and his wines soon spread throughout the United States and even reached Europe. In 1943, the Charles Krug Winery was bought by Mondavi; in 1962, another 200 hectares (500 acres) were added to it, through the purchase of the famous and historic To Kalon vineyard at Oakville, said to be the best in the whole Valley. Krug made the first California wine from Chenin Blanc grapes. They also planted Chardonnay, Gewürtztraminer, Johannisberg Riesling, Sémillon and Sauvignon Blanc. As for the red varieties, they include Cabernet-Sauvignon, Gamay and Pinot Noir. It is important to note the differences between the wines produced by C. Mondavi and Son. Wines bearing the label Charles Krug are varietal wines of which only 400,000 cases a year are sold; the wines bearing the label C.K. Mondavi are mainly table wines, and a million cases a year are sold. Another famous Napa figure is Robert Mondavi. He learned his trade from Charles Krug before opening his own firm in 1966, and separating from his brother, Pierre.

The Robert Mondavi Winery in Yountville is a major California tourist attraction with its Mission architecture and famous belltower. The life he leads with his sons Michael and Timothy and his daughter Marcia is one of perpetual struggle - the struggle for quality. Today, his 100% pure varietal wines are considered by many experts to be the best in the United States. This is hardly surprising, when you see the 20000 barrels which Robert Mondavi has had manufactured from French oak - although American barrels cost three times less - and from white oaks from the Black Forest for his Johannisberg Riesling. His ambition is to withhold 10% of his annual production for at least five years. It would be worth the trouble. His Chardonnays are comparable to the best White Burgundies and his Pinot Noir would not make a Red Burgundy "blush". However, Robert Mondavi's greatest achievement is an incomparable Fumé Blanc (dry Sauvignon).

Although part of his 400-hectare (988-acre) vineyard has been bought by the Rainer Brewing Company of Seattle, Robert Mondavi is still very much in charge, and is always introducing innovations. For instance, there is his association under the name of Opus One with Baron Philippe de Rothschild, owner of the famous Château Mouton-Rothschild. Together, they have created a wine, the Mondavi-Rothschild, grown on a 60-hectare (148-acre) plot, which promises to have a brilliant future. Robert Mondavi is one of the last great aristocrats of wine, an honour he can perhaps share with Angelo Gaya of Piedmont, the producer of Barbaresco.

He has managed to create an exceptional estate and produce wines which are admired throughout the world since he is obsessed with quality. He has been the bridge between the Old World of Europe and the New World of California, the new wine El Dorado. Nothing happens in Burgundy or Bordeaux without Robert Mondavi being there to learn and to improve. For him, wine is a culture, an art of living associated with painting, music (he holds concerts) and good food. He does his best to share this philosophy of life with his compatriots. Long live Robert Mondavi! The Martini family, who own the Louis M. Martini winery, is one of the great families of the valley. The founder, Louis M. Martini, was born in Italy but emigrated to the United States at the beginning of the century and established his winery at St. Helena just after Prohibition ended.

Today the reputation of his wines and the huge vineyard of 1000 hectares (2471 acres) in the Carneros, Sonoma, St. Helena and Healdsburg districts has spread throughout the United States. Chardonnay and Cabernet are grown in Napa, Cabernet-Sauvignon, Zinfandel, Chenin Blanc and Johannisberg at St. Helena and Merlot, Gamay, Gewürtztraminer and Zinfandel in Sonoma.

Other Napa vineyards worthy of note are the superb terraced vineyards of Mayacamas, whose Zinfandel Rosé is noteworthy and the 50 hectares (123 acres) west of Yountville bought by Moueix and the heirs of John Daniel (Christian Moueix, son of one of the owners of Château Pétrus, has invested everything he has in a Cabernet dubbed "Dominus", which is worth watching out for). Francis Ford Coppola, the movie producer, has invested in the Niebaum Estate and hopes for a great Cabernet-Sauvignon; the owners of the Schramsberg Vineyards have gone into partnership with Rémy-Martin, distillers of the famous French brandy from Cognac to produce 100% American brandy.

Sterling Vineyards is a famous wine-growing centre and tourist attraction with its funicular cablecar ascending to the top of the valley, and the Trefethen Estate produces excellent Chardonnays and Pinot Noirs. Finally, there is the very surprising association between the biggest restaurants in the region and Robert Mondavi to buy the Vichon Winery, thus ensuring the promotion of their Chardonnay and Cabernet-Sauvignon varietal wines and their Cru Chevrignon, a mixture of Sauvignon Blanc and Sémillon, which is worth watching out for.

SONOMA

Sonoma and Napa are two parallel valleys, separated by the famous Mayacamas Mountains. Jack London called it "the valley of the moon" because its Indian name means "the valley of seven moons", since the moon disappears and reappears from behind the seven hills of the Valley. Sonoma has more than 120 wine-growers who own its 12500 hectares (30,887 acres) of vines. The wines produced here are respectable table wines, nothing more, and sparkling wines.

Colonel Agoston Haraszthy's Buena Vista Winery and Vineyards still stands here, a monument to the pioneer of Californian viticulture, a little to the east of Sonoma. Despite the Phylloxera, earthquakes and a succession of ownerships, the winery still prospers and produces excellent wines from Pinot Noir, Cabernet-Sauvignon, Traminer and Riesling.

The Korbel Brothers, who came from Czechoslovakia, made their first champagne in the late 19th century at Guerneville in Sonoma County. F. Korbel & Bros. is still on the banks of the Russian River and 70% of its production is still sparkling wines. There are Korbel Brut, Korbel Extra, Extra Dry, Korbel Rosé, Korbel Sec and a Blanc de Blancs made from Pinot Noir and Chardonnay. This great firm has belonged to the Jack Daniels Distillery since 1966.

The story of the Sebastiani family is a real American success story. Samuele Sebastiani was a little Italian immigrant who fathered a dynasty. He managed to establish his own winery in Sonoma a few years after arriving in the United States. He did so well in the bulk wine trade that he was able to set up a winery in the historic square of Sonoma, in the very place where in 1840 Sonoma was declared the capital of California. The 300 hectares (740 acres) of his vineyards, spread over six sites, produce good wines from Zinfandel, Chardonnay, Cabernet-Sauvignon, as well as Barbera, a reminder of the Italian origin of the family. A grandson of the founder started his own firm in 1986, the San Sebastiani Vineyards.

The successors of Colonel Agoston Haraszthy, who have established vineyards and wineries in the Sonoma Valley, are a very mixed bunch. For instance, there is a banker from Geneva, Switzerland, Jean-Jacques Michel, who founded the Domaine Michel in 1985 in Dry Creek valley and a former U.S. ambassador to Italy, James D. Zellerbach who created the Hanzell Vineyards modelled on Clos Vougeot. This property has been bought by Countess Barbara de Brye. A professional dancer acquired the Rodney Strong Vineyards which is now owned by a New York importer and by Piper-Heidsick, under the name of Piper-Sonoma. A former pilot, Bruce Cutter-Jones, bought 200 hectares (495 acres) of vineyard in the Russian River Valley and at Carneros. The Sonoma-Cutter Vineyards specialize in Chardonnay. The newspaper publisher, Frank H. Bartholomew, owned the prestigious Buena Vista Vineyards which he sold to buy the Hacienda Wine Cellars, a 44 hectares (109 acres) winery in the centre of the Valley. These are just some examples of the very varied backgrounds of those who have devoted themselves to producing wine in the Sonoma Valley.

MENDOCINO

Mendocino lies to the north-west of Sonoma and it was long neglected by wine-growers due to irrigation problems. Today, thanks to the installation of rainwater reservoirs, the acreage of vineyards has increased from 500 hectares (1235 acres) in 1970 to more than 5000 hectares (12355 acres) today. The varieties grown are mainly Gamay Beaujolais, Cabernet-Sauvignon, Zinfandel and Pinot Chardonnay.

The Cresta Blanca Winery is one of major wine firms in California. It was formerly located in the Livermore Valley and is now established north of Ukiah. It was founded in 1882 by Charles Wetmore and in 1900 it won several medals at the Exposition Universelle in Paris. It has now been bought by the Guild Wine Company, and is known for its good varietal wines.

LIVERMORE

This Valley in Alameda County , south-east of San Francisco, grows only 800 hectares (1977 acres) of vines. It has acquired a reputation for its full-bodied, sweet white wines which are similar to Sauternes. Cresta Blanca which was originally established in this valley, planted it in 1882 with cuttings brought from the Bordeaux region, and especially Château d'Yquem. The southern section of Livermore, very near San Francisco Bay, produces as many red wines as whites, as well as sparkling wines, dessert wines and aperitif wines. Weibel Vineyards specialises in champagnes fermented in the bottle, and is the major producer of sparkling wines of the country. Wente Bros name each grape variety on the label (and not the Appellation d'Origine as in Europe). This winery is known for its excellent Graves- and Sauternes-type varietal wines.

SANTA CLARA - SANTA CRUZ

These counties grow thousands of acres of vines south of San Francisco. The best Californian table wines are produced in the Los Gatos and Saratoga districts, at the foot of the Santa Cruz Mountains and on the mountain slopes. The Evergreen Vineyards, one of the best-known, is located to the east of San José on the slopes of Mount Hamilton. San Benito which grows 1800 hectares (4447 acres) of varietal wines, of which a large amount belongs to the Almadén Vineyards). In 1982, it was recognized as a new wine-producing region by the BATF, the Line Kiln Valley. It has an Appellation of Origin, Chalone, covering 3500 hectares (8648 acres) in San Benito County. Almadén Vineyards lies within the San José connurbation and is a "historic" estate. The name comes from the Almadén vineyard planted in 1852 with European varieties by two gentlemen from Bordeaux, Charles le Franc and Etienne Thée, at the foot of the Santa Cruz Mountains. The rocky slopes of Almadén are cooled by the evening mists rising off the Pacific Ocean. They produce good wines, especially Pinot Chardonnay and Cabernet-Sauvignon. Paul Masson Vineyards were founded by a Burgundian who arrived in California in 1878 and founded a winery in Santa Clara county. His wines and champagnes were so successful that he was able to build a true château and a vinification centre in the heart of his vineyards. He was the first to produce a Gamay Beaujolais from French vine-stocks which was, is, and certainly still will be praiseworthy. Today, the Paul Masson Vineyards have been sold to Seagrams and much of the operation has been transferred to the city of Monterey. The firm is now known for its "exclusive" blends made from hybrids such as Rubion and Emerald Dry, developed by the University of

California at Davis. Paul Masson also produces many varietals, fortified wines, champagnes and brandies.

MONTEREY - SACRAMENTO VALLEY - SAN JOAQUIN VALLEY

Monterey, to the south-west of San Francisco and the Sacramento Valley to the north-east, are promising regions. The Monterey district has more than 12000 hectares (30,000 acres) of vineyards in the Salinas Valley, the Soledad Hills and in the Pinnacles National Monument area. A distinction is made between Upper Monterey in the north-west whose cool climate (zones 1 and 2) produces Pinot Noir, Gewürtztraminer and Riesling, and the warmer district to the south-east which is more favourable for Cabernet-Sauvignon, Merlot, Zinfandel and Sauvignon blanc. The wine-growing area of the Sacramento and Joaquin Valleys, north-east of San Francisco Bay, benefits from relatively cool weather. The 1200 hectares (3000 acres) of vines are to be found mainly in San Joaquin and Sacramento counties, south of Sacramento, the capital, near the town of Elk Grove. There are areas which produce table wines, fortified wines of the Port type and dessert wines. The Central Valley and the San Joaquin Valley are home to wine-production on a massive scale, especially in the region of Escalon and Modesto, south of Stockton. Modesto contains the headquarters of the biggest winery in the world, the E. and J. Gallo Winery, which presses 500,000 tonnes of grapes annually. Gallo bottles almost one quarter of the wines drunk in the United States (about 1.5 millon bottles a day). For Americans, Gallo is a generic name for popular, inexpensive wines. This family, originally from Piedmont region of northern Italy, has lived in the San Joaquin Valley since 1933. In the 1950's, it concentrated on dessert wines, but it followed the fashion for table wines and in the 1960's it launched Pop Wines, a marketing ploy to promote fruity wines low in alcohol but very aromatic. Today, the company is also aiming at the top end of the market. Its varietals are marked "Wine Cellars of Ernest and Julio Gallo", it has installed excellent wine-cellars and is aging its wines in French and Yugoslav oak casks. Gallo is a wine empire with 3000 employees and its own laboratories are the most productive in California with departments for chemistry, œnology and microbiology. The Guimarra Vineyards are typical of the Fresno region of the San Joaquin Valley, in the central sector where the climate is almost tropical. This 3200 hectares (7900 acres) vineyard was created in 1906 by "Papa Joe" Guimarra, a Sicilian immigrant. The wines are marketed under the Central Coast brand name and have the merit of being honest. They are made from Johannisberg Riesling, Chenin Blanc, Cabernet, Riesling and Colombard grapes.

THE EAST COAST

Although Maryland is the home state of the Catawba variety - a hybrid of Labrusca and Riparia which reached its peak of popularity in the 19th century - all that is left of vine cultivation here are a few vineyards around Baltimore. Yet the climate is suitable for grape-growing.

Further west, Ohio was the most important wine-growing state in the Union during the 19th century, producing 20 million litres (4,400,000 gallons) a year. It was here, in the famous area nicknamed "the American Rhine" around Cincinnati and Ripley, that the first American champagne was made. It was called Sparkling Catawba.

There is little to say about Michigan. There are a few vineyards in the south of the state at Paw-Paw and Benton Harbor which produce vins ordinaires of mediocre quality from Concord, Catawba and Delaware grapes. The exception is Lake Michigan Shores which might be a brand to watch.

NEW YORK STATE

New York is the second most important wine-producing state after California. It has an output of 1.2 million hectolitres (26,400,000 gallons) from 8000 hectares (19768 acres) of vines. There are 75 viticultural enterprises. Of the 75,000 tonnes of grapes harvested, 50% consist of Labrusca, 40% are hybrids and 10% are vinifera.

In around 1650, when Peter Stuyvesant was governor of the New York, vines grew on Manhattan Island, as well as in Brooklyn and Long Island. They continued to do so until the mid-19th century. Brother-Hood Winery was the first major wine-producing enterprise. It began operations in the Hudson River area in 1839. New York wines still have the reputation of being sweet but "foxy", a property so typical of the Concord variety of Vitis labrusca, which is the commonest New York variety. Foxiness is a musky odour in wine which makes it smell like wet fur.

So the question might be asked, why pursue cultivation of Vitis labrusca ? Might it not be better to grow Vinifera varieties or hybrids? This may be settled in the near future.

Another problem is the New York climate. The autumn tends to be wet, the winters are too harsh, and the thaw comes too early. This makes vine cultivation a risky undertaking. The only way to ensure that wines remain of constant quality is chaptalization. Everyone agrees that the white varieties are best able to overcome these disadvantages (the very passable sparkling wines are proof of this), although attempts have been made to give the reds the qualities of an Italian Lambrusco, freshness, pleasantness and a slight "fizz".

There are 16000 hectares (40,000 acres) of vineyards on the east coast, including Lake Erie and Long Island. The most famous wine-producing region is Finger Lakes, around Hammondsport and Pleasant Valley (between Lake Ontario and Pennsylvania), 300 kilometres (186 miles) northwest of New York. This is a beautiful area of lakes scattered in a network of depressions dug by ancient glaciers. Seen from above, they are long and extended like the fingers of a hand, hence the name. Grape vines seem to like the volcanic soil as much as the climate which is tempered by the presence of the lakes. The lakes have Indian names - Kenko, Canandaigua, Seneca and Cayuga. The wines made here are mainly sparkling and are produced from Catawba, Delaware and Elvira vines blended with more neutral wines from California. It is here that the Pleasant Valley Wine Company makes Great Western New York State, the most famous sparkling wine in the State.

There is another well-known wine producing sector, the Hudson Valley north

THE RED VARIETIES

East of the Rockies, one finds mainly the Concord, a variety of Labrusca which has a very "foxy" taste. Of the 12000 hectares (29652 acres) of Concord grapes which grow in the State of New York, only one-fifth are used for wine-making. The wine is generally sweet, very pale red, and sometimes sparkling. Catawba is a hybrid of Labrusca which is even older than Concord. The other hybrids include Black Baco (about 400 hectares (988 acres), a cross between Folle Blanche and Riparia. The wines it produces are thus fruity. Chancellor, which was very common in France prior to World War II, is still very much grown in the eastern United States. Like Marshall Foch, it is very resistant to cold, ripens early, has a good saccharine content and is used to reinforce the colour and strength of wines made from other varieties.

THE WHITE VARIETIES

The climate and the slate soil seem to suit New York Riesling which is pleasantly aromatic. It is also good for Chardonnay, Gewürtztraminer, Seyvol Blanc and certain other hybrids such as Cayuga (the name of one of the Finger Lakes because it was developed by the experimental station at nearby Geneva). Vidal Blanc, a cross containing Ugni Blanc, produces fruity wines with a good acidity level and a high sugar content.

of New York City between Highland and Newburgh. The 400 hectares (988 acres) produce red wines. At this point the valley is very sheltered, the climate is maritime and the soil consists of a mixture of schist, limestone and slate. This is a rather special region, because vines have been grown here uninterruptedly since 1677.

CANADA

Believe it or not, Canada was once called Vineland[1]. When Leif Erikson, son of Eric the Red, arrived in the 10th century and landed on what is believed to be the north coast of Newfoundland, he discovered such a large quantity of wild vines (which were actually blueberries) that in ancient Scandinavian legends the land remained known as the Island of Vineland.

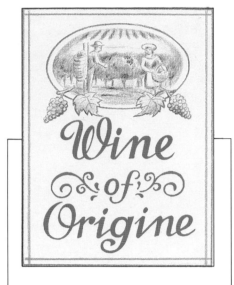

Wine of Origine

REGULATION:

By law, wine can only be marketed by the producers, and, except in Ontario, wine can only be sold through the Alcohol Bureaux (Bureaux de controle des Alcools which has a monopoly on retail sales.
In Ontario, the system is different because the wine-maker can sell his wines either to the Alcohol Bureau which controls a chain of 600 liquor stores, or direct to the consumer through cooperative stores.
There is a sort of appellation, Ontario Superior.
This sort of quality control ought to be extended to other wine-growing areas.

It was not until 1497 that Canada was officially discovered by John Cabot, a Venetian navigator in the service of the king of England.

The first colonization of Canada, then known as New France, began in 1608, under Samuel de Champlain the founder of Quebec city.

It is said that one of his companions, a certain Poutrin court, planted a few vines. They were insignificant in yield when compared to the numerous wild vines which were used by missionaries to make wine for mass.

The true impetus for Canadian viticulture, contrary to what is generally believed, was not due to a Frenchman but to a German,

John Schiller, who settled in Cooksville, near Toronto, in 1811, and who planted vines and made wine there.

Today, Canada has 11000 hectares (27000 acres) of vines and makes about 300,000 hectolitres (6,600,000 gallons) of wine a year. Four-fifths of Canadian vineyards are to be found growing on the rich alluvial soil of the Niagara peninsula, the 54 kilometres (86 miles) strip of land along the U.S.-Canadian border through which the Niagara River flows, connecting Lake Ontario to Lake Erie.

The river is, of course, famous for the Niagara Falls. The best Canadian vineyards are to be found west of the Falls where the lakes create an ideal microclimate for viticulture, making the winters more temperate than in the surrounding area. Winter temperatures average -4°C, rainfall is moderate, the summers are hot and the autumns mild (the famous "Indian summers"). As in the rest of the North American continent east of the Rockies, Vitis labrusca has long dominated the Niagara Peninsula, especially the Concord and Niagara varieties with their musky (or foxy) odours.

However, present demand is for quality and more than 45% of new plantings are of Vitis vinifera varieties such as Riesling, Chardonnay and the Franco-American hybrids Seyval and Marechal Foch. There are about 60 major producers in Canada, of whom the most important, T.G. Bright and Company near Niagara Falls, is the very symbol of the development of Canadian viticulture. T.G. Bright is famous for its sparkling wines made from Pinot-Chardonnay and Pinot Noir grapes. Other producers of note are Chateau-Gai, Jordan Winery (which has an interesting Museum of Wine at Twenty Mile Creek), Chateau de Charmes and Inniskillin, all of which are in southern Ontario.

The other major wine-growing region is the Okanagan Valley in British Columbia, east of Vancouver between the Trepanier Valley and the Monashee Mountains. Lake Okanagan creates a mild climate and provides irrigation water during dry periods. Californian grapes are no longer

THE GRAPES OF CANADA

The Canadian vines are undergoing a drastic change.
The traditional varieties of Vitis labrusca - Concord with its very foxy taste, Niagara and Elvira, white grapes with an equally musky flavour - are losing ground everywhere.
They now constitute no more than 45% of vines. The consumers are tending to prefer more subtle wines made from Vitis vinifera stock of European origin such as Chardonnay, Riesling, Gewurztraminer, Pinot Noir, as well as hybrids which are mostly Franco-American.
These last include the Seyval variety, which is descended from Chardonnay, producing white wines of very good quality.

imported for mixing with the local varieties.

By law, at least 80% of the grapes used must be locally-grown, a de facto recognition of the efforts made by Okanagan growers to improve quality. They have successfully planted vinifera varieties such as Riesling, Chardonnay, Gewürztraminer and white Seyval. The grapes seem to do as well here as they do on the Niagaran Peninsula on the other side of the continent.

Only thirty years ago, almost all Canadian production was vinified into port-type fortified wines.

Today the trend has reversed in favour of table wines which represent 90% of production.

1. "Vineland" is the name given by the Ontario Ministry of Agriculture to the viticultural research station which has experimented with the acclimatization of 300 different grape varieties.

VINTAGE SELECTION

BACO NOIR

A superior, full-bodied, rich red wine, vinted from the distinguished Baco Noir grape.

12% alc./vol.   750 ml

RED WINE   VIN ROUGE

PRODUCT OF CANADA · T.G. BRIGHT & CO. LIMITED, NIAGARA FALLS, CANADA · PRODUIT DU CANADA

SOUTH AMERICA

Vines are grown over one third of this vast continent, mainly south of the Tropic of Capricorn, where the climate is more temperate. Argentina is by far the largest producer of wines (it is the fifth-largest in the world), followed by Chile which provides South America with its finest wines. Vines are also grown in Uruguay and even Brazil, where they are cultivated in the southern part of the country in the province of Rio Grande Do Sul. Peru lies north of the Tropic of Capricorn, so vines are only grown at high altitude.

The story of South American viticulture begins in the 16th century with the arrival of the missionaries and the conquistadors who planted the Pais variety on the Pacific coast. This grape had been brought from Spain, and is believed to be related to a Californian variety called Miniou. It is now tending to decline in importance.

Chile owes the quality of its wines to the Bordeaux grape varieties introduced into the country in the mid-19th century. The Argentinian vineyards show a marked Italian influence, due to the mass influx of immigrants from that country after World War I.

Nowadays, the American varieties which were selected for their resistance to the hot, damp climate are tending to be replaced by European varieties of better quality.

Chile, the Copiaco Valley.

CHILE

The word Chile derives from the Indian word for "land's end". It is a strip of land 2920 miles long, parallel to the Pacific Ocean. To the north lie Peru and Bolivia. The Cordillera of the Andes separates Chile from Argentina the other major South American wine-producing country. Vines grow between the 30th and 40th parallels of the southern latitude. This appears to be just the right spot, because Chilean wines are unquestionably the best in South America.

The vine was introduced in the 16th century before the first Spanish missionaries who arrived just after the conquistadors. They planted Muscat d'Alexandrie and a variety whose name is

REGULATION

not known but is identified merely as "Pais" ("the country"). The vine was long cultivated around the monasteries by the religious orders for ritual use. In 1840, Chile became the main wine-producer in Latin America. However, in 1851, Silvestre Ochagavia caused a revolution in Chilean wine production by bringing over viticulture experts from France who planted the great French varieties - Cabernet, Sauvignon, Pinot Noir, Sauvignon Blanc, Sémillon Blanc and Merlot - in the central valley. This is still the best vineyard in the country. Here, in this region of the Maipo River near Santiago, Bordeaux wines have found ideal soil, climate and exposure.

Chile enjoys such a favourable situation that vines have been planted directly into the soil, without the need for grafting on to hardy root-stocks to avoid the ravages of mildew and phylloxera. Chile is one of the very few countries in the world to have escaped both plagues. When Bordeaux's vineyards were devastated by phylloxera in the late 19th century, the French vines were re-introduced into France from Chile. Two geographical features protect Chilean wines, the Andes and the Atacama Desert which separates Chile from Peru. A few statistics will indicate the importance of the vine in Chile. The wine industry employs 35,000 people - more than the copper-mines. Production stands at 8 million hectolitres (176 million gallons) annually for 130,000 hectares (321,230 acres) of vines. Five per cent of the wine is exported to the United States. Even if consumption per inhabitant is only 40 litres (70 pints) a year, this is because this figure has been arbitrarily fixed by the government in a massive campaign against alcoholism.

In general, there are three types of wines. These are liqueur wines in the north, excellent quality table wines in the centre, and vins ordinaires in the south. There are also three vine-growing areas. The northern region extends from the Atacama Desert to the Choapa River. There is little rainfall and the vine survives thanks to irrigation and a temperate climate caused by the cold ocean current which flows parallel to the coast of Peru. In general, the wines are fortified like Madeira and Port. The central region lies between two rivers, the Aconcagua and the Maule. The influence of claret is predominant in the vine stocks and vinification techniques. Although the soil composition and climate are very similar to those of Bordeaux, there is one major difference - Chilean vineyards are irrigated. The high valley of the Maipo, south-east of Santiago, produces the best

THE GRAPES OF CHILE

The only local vine variety, the "Pais", is the most widely cultivated in Chile, comprising 40% of production. It originates from Spain or the Canaries, though no trace of it has been found there. According to legend, it comes from the grape-pips in the raisins in the sailors' rations. They were planted when the conquistadores landed, and proved to be an amazing success. Pais is a robust vine; although the juice content is low, the grape ripens quickly. It is the main component in the vino piperro, the everyday wine drunk by Chileans. If the vines are irrigated, they can yield as much as 30 tonnes per hectare (2¹/₂ acres). In the less fertile soils of the Cordillera de la Costa and without the help of irrigation, the wine produced is of better quality.

wines in the country, especially Cabernet-Sauvignon and Sauvignon Blanc. The last region is the southern region, between the rivers Maule and Bio-Bio. The vines here produce mainly red wines which are not as good as those from the centre, as well as light, low-alcohol white wines. This is the heartland of the Pais vine which has a high yield and is blended with other wines to produce the most popular Chilean wine. Chilean wines are made from a wide variety of grapes. They have body and flavour, aroma and bouquet. If they retain a slight taste of old wood, that is due to the way the wine is processed, but buying French barrels will eliminate this defect. This wine has no vintages because the climatic conditions are unvarying. There is always the same amount of sunshine and the rains are never excessive. Another major Chilean advantage is that the price of the wine is unbeatably low!

ARGENTINA

In 1516, Diaz de Solís landed at Rio de la Plata; the viticultural history of Argentina began only a few years later. In 1556, the Jesuits planted the country's first vine in the Cuyo region. It was the ancestor of the Criolla Grande and the Cereza varieties. These two native vines now account for 30% and 10% respectively of the very high-yielding Argentian crop.

The annual production from 300,000 hectares (741,300 acres) of vines is 20 millon hectolitres (440 million gallons), putting Argentina in fifth place as a producer after Italy, France, Spain and the USSR. This huge quantity of wine is destined exclusively for internal consumption. There are 30 million

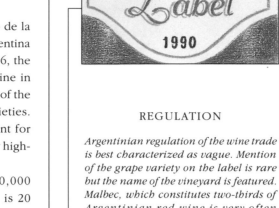

REGULATION

Argentinian regulation of the wine trade is best characterized as vague. Mention of the grape variety on the label is rare but the name of the vineyard is featured. Malbec, which constitutes two-thirds of Argentinian red wine is very often blended with Barbera or Syrah. If you open a bottle of Argentinian Riesling, there's a good chance you'll find yourself drinking a Sylvaner. A Pinot Blanc may actually be a Chenin Blanc and a Cabernet-Sauvignon could be anything from a coarse, vulgar wine to an excellent vintage similar to a Médoc. There are also some rather strange blends, especially the unnatural marriage between Riesling and Chardonnay. It is best to stick to reliable producers and exporters with a good reputation.

Argentinians and they drink 70 litres (122 pints) of wine per capita annually which explains how little of the wine gets exported to North America. Things have greatly changed since the great days immediately after World War II when Argentina was exporting a quarter of its production, especially to Great Britain. Argentinian wine is produced on an industrial scale. The largest producer in Mendoza processes one million hectolitres (22 million gallons) of wine a year, fermenting and aging a total of 10,000 hectolitres (220,000 gallons). It is easy to see how vin ordinaire represents 70% of national production.

The two great wine-growing regions are the provinces of Mendoza and San Juan, in the north-west of the country, where vast vineyards grow at an altitude of 2,500 feet in the Andes foothills. The population of the province originates mainly from Italy and Spain and has applied its native production methods, putting quantity first. Fortunately, things are changing, thanks to the French wine-producers who have been trying to improve the quality of the wines for several years now.

THE MENDOZA AND SAN JUAN REGIONS

The Mendoza region, 1000 kilometres (620 miles) west of Buenos Aires, devotes 40% of its arable land to vine cultivation and produces 70% of Argentine wine. Grape varieties such as the Criollas, Malbec and Pedro Ximénez proliferate, thanks to irrigation by the region's two great rivers, the Tunuyán and the Mendoza. The best Argentinian wine, a Malbec even better than Cabernet-Sauvignon, is a product of north-western Mendoza. Although there are 40,000 vine-growers in the province of Mendoza, served by 1000 bodegas (little

GRAPES OF ARGENTINA

Red wine is made from seven grape varieties which account for 30% of production. These are Malbec, Bonarda, Tempranilli, Cabernet, Sauvignon, Merlot and Barbera. However, two native varieties, Criolla Grande and Cereza, which date back to 1556, account for 30% and 10% respectively of the Argentinian crop. These two varieties of Vitis vinifera are perfectly suited to the climate and to the Mendoza region in which irrigated yield is in the order of 200 hectolitres (4400 gallons) per hectare (2½ acres). They produce coarse wines for everyday drinking. However, they are tending to be replaced by imported vines of better quality. The white wine varieties are Pedro Ximénez, Chenin, Sémillon and Tokay Friulano.

wine-processing plants), there are only a dozen or so large firms, who also own vines and who account for a quarter of the production and marketing of the wines. San Juan lies to the north of Mendoza, and is the other great wine-producing region of Argentina. Since it is closer to the equator, the climate it hotter and consequently the wines are stronger. It produces 20% of Argentine wines in the river valleys of the Zonda, the Ullun and the Tulun. The vines are irrigated, and are used mainly for white wines. The grape varieties are Muscatel, Pedro Ximénez and Ugni Blanc for the whites and Barbera, Nebbiolo, Lambrusco and Malbec for the reds. the Criollas are used to make rosé. To complete the picture, mention should be made of the provinces of Rio Negro and Neuquén in the south of the country and La Rioja further north. These regions have a total of 18000 hectares (44,478 acres) under cultivation.

AUSTRALIA

Australia, what a country and what viticulture! On a historic day in 1788, Captain Phillip, who had just landed at the head of a fleet of 12 ships, planted the first few vine seedlings on the site of what is now the Sydney Botanical Gardens. Everything here is a superlative. Australia is the largest island in the world (7,682,300 square kilometres or 47,735,507 square miles), but it is not really an island, it is a continent.

Originally populated with aboriginal tribes, it was discovered by the Dutch in 1605. However, it was not until Captain Cook landed in 1770 that the country was colonized. This island at the opposite end of the world, almost unexplored, served as a penal colony for Britain until 1840.

It is difficult to indentify the true father of Australian viticulture. John MacArthur (famous for his disputes with Governor Bligh) planted the first vineyard in Camden Park, only 30 miles from Sydney. His two sons, James and William extended it. However, Gregory Blaxland sent the first hundred litres of red wine to London from his estate at Panamatta. Blaxland was a truly extraordinary man, the discoverer, with Lawson and Wentworth, of the vast fertile plains beyond the Blue Mountains.

However, most people would agree that the honour falls to James Busby. Busby disembarked at Sydney one fine day in 1824. This 24-year-old Scotsman had the immense cheek to claim that, on the basis of his few months' experience in the French vineyards, he would transform Australia into the El Dorado of the vine. He wrote his first book on the subject of growing vines and the art of wine-making. His enthusiasm was catching because he was granted about 800 hectares (nearly 2,000 acres) of land in the Hunter Valley, which he named Kirkton. He brought over the best stocks from France and Spain, acclimatised them, and made an arrangement with Blaxland and MacArthur to distribute the available plants to anyone who was willing to grow them.

The Barossa Valley, near Adelaide, is the most fertile wine-growing region in Australia.

AUSTRALIA

Australian wine has long been known only through its Burgundy-type wines such as Harvest and Burgoyne's Tintara, Gilbey's Rubicund, etc. which are sold exclusively in Britain. After World War I, the Bruce-Page government encouraged demobilized soldiers to plant vines. This policy lead to over-production. Two measures were taken to remedy the situation, export premiums were paid and tax was reduced on the brandies used to fortified the wines. Thus, after 1936, Australia became one of the biggest exporters of Sherry-type wines in the world, selling 170,000 hectolitres (3,740,000 gallons) a year, mainly in Great Britain and Canada.

Prior to the 1960s, Australians drank

REGULATION

For two centuries, vine-growing in Australia has been totally unrestricted without any tradition of regulation to bother the growers.

This makes it hard to distinguish between the wines. Wines that roughly correspond to European types are called Claret, Burgundy, Bordeaux, Moselle, Tokay, and so on.

However, the labels are increasingly tending to indicate the grape variety and region of origin.

As for vintages, is it not said in Australia that each year is a good year for wine?

very little table wine, but all that changed in the 1970s, and dry wines suddenly became so popular that Australian wine-growers had difficulty meeting the demand. They discovered cooler locations and began to produce wines that were lighter and subtler.

Today, Australian viticulture is undergoing major changes and is always seeking new land. All the states, even the northern ones, grow vines but southern Australia produces the most wine, since the climate is cooler.

Although the Australian climate is generally too hot, humid or dry for good wine, the 70,000 hectares (172,970 acres) of vines are able to benefit from numerous micro-climates. There are also suitable soils - alluvial, clay, sandy or volcanic. Today, 3.5 million hectolitres (77 million gallons) of wine are produced annually. "Every year is a good year for wine", they say in Australia. There are 33 separate wine regions, though this figure is by no

means definitive, as more are being added every year. At present, the approximately 7,000 vineyards are run by 600 producers. Australians now drink 21 litres (nearly 37 pints) of wine per capita per year, and demand is so great that the best quality Australian wines are rarely exported.

WESTERN AUSTRALIA

WESTERN AUSTRALIA

Western Australia is a huge state bordered by the Indian Ocean in the west and the Timor Sea in the north. The eastern half is desert. Vineyards are confined to a very small area between the capital, Perth, and Albany. The output is 50,000 hectolitres (1,100,000 gallons) a year.

The Swan Valley, just east of Perth, is legendary. It contains several large vineyards owned by the major producers, such as Hardy and Sandalford. Wines produced here are of the Burgundy type, vigorous, full-bodied, and slightly sweet. Their very special aroma makes them similar to the

THE GRAPES OF AUSTRALIA

For a long time, Australia specialized in dessert wines of the Port and Sherry types, a tradition which dates back to the 19th century. In the warmer regions, the Muscat d'Alexandrie (Gordo Blanco) grape is as common as Riesling. However, one also finds Palomino, Pedro Ximénez, Carracazo and Dorodillo from the Jerez region of Spain. A group of Portugese varieties which are very suitable for the Australian climate have also been identified. These are Verdelho, Touriga Bonvedro and Tinta Amarella.

One third of the red wine varieties are made from the grape called Shiraz in Australia (actually a Syrah variety). In Australia, they are considered to be ordinary table wines because the yields are too high and vinification takes place at too high a temperature. As for the whites, Riesling predominates to such an extent that Australians have become the specialists (as in the case of the Rieslings grown in the Barossa Valley).

The present consumption trend is towards lighter, dryer, chilled wines. The opportunities for finding suitable micro-climates and cooler sites for vines are enormous, especially in south-western Australia. It is here, in the Adelaide Hills, Upper Hunter Valley and along the Margaret River, that Chardonnay, Sauvignon Blanc and Sémillon vines have been planted.

wines of Hunter Valley in New South Wales, but the whites are more refined and elegant. There are three other districts which are noteworthy, the Margaret River district south-west of Perth, the Frankland district and the Mount Barker district north of Albany. These are very promising regions because they already produce excellent Pinot Noir, Cabernet, Hermitage and Zinfandel, so their wines are well worth watching.

SOUTH AUSTRALIA

This state, beside the Great Bay of Australia and the Indian Ocean, is alone responsible for 40% of Australian wine production. The climate is of the Mediterranean type, and the land is fairly flat except for the Flinders Range, a mountain range in which the highest peak is only 3000 feet. The mountains lie on a north-south axis and stretch between the Great Artesian Basin, a desert zone, right to the surburbs of Adelaide. The vineyards are run by big cooperatives, such as Angove's, Consolidated Cooperative Wineries Ltd. (in Berri county) and Loxton Cooperative Ltd. Much Australian table wine comes from the irrigated vineyards of the Murray Valley in the south-east, at the boundary with the State of Victoria.

Adelaide is the capital of South Australia and one of the few large cities in the world in which vines grow as far into centre as the business district. It is proud to be the home of Grange Hermitage, the best-known Australian red wine.

The whole of this coastal zone is cool and humid and produces wines resembling Bordeaux and Port-type dessert wines (Vintage or Tawny Port). The wine-growing centre of MacLaren Vale, cooled by sea-breezes from the Gulf of St. Vincent, produces Old Reynella, the best of these fortified wines.

The vineyards in the north extend inland to Clare, 100 kilometres (62 miles) from Adelaide and Coonawarra at the

southeastern extremity of the State, 400 kilometres (248 miles) from the capital. The Barossa Valley, between Clare and Adelaide, is the most scenic tourist spot in Australia, popular for its grape harvests. German colonists settled here in the 19th century, and they even speak their own local dialect, Barossa Valley Deutsch. The region has a very large number of vineyards and thirty major wine-producers, including Yalumba and Seppeltsfield. In addition to the dessert wines, Riesling grown on the slopes of Burings, Orlando and Yalumba is as good as the best German Rieslings, being both delicate and fruity, an exceptional wine. Further south, Coonawarra has had a love affair with Cabernet-Sauvignon for several decades. This wine-growing district is very clearly demarcated, because its soil forms a belt, 15 kilometres (9 miles) long and 800

metres (875 yards) wide of "terra rossa", a rich red soil consisting of a mixture of chalk and very fertile limon, irrigated by a subterranean water course. The newly-planted Chardonnay stocks are so promising that all the big wine-producers - Lindermans, Wynns, Mildara and Penfolds - have acquired land here. Sevenhill Estate, in the north of the Clare Valley-Watervale area, has been cultivated by the Jesuits of Aloysius College since 1840. They produce wines for the Catholic rite throughout the Pacific. This is a warmer but breezier region, producing dry white Rieslings which are very aromatic.

NEW SOUTH WALES

If New South Wales is the birthplace of the Australian wine industry, Hunter Valley is its symbol. This valley is 180 kilometres (112 miles) north of Sydney and is an almost mythical place. The first vines were planted here in 1828. The white wine made here is so golden and rich that it is called "Hunter honey". The Syrah grape (called Shiraz here) does very well as does Sémillon, but Tyrrell's, one of the big growers in the region, has also planted Chardonnay which has done very well. Since the local woods do not make good barrels, these are imported from France and the United States. Today, many œnologists put Hunter Valley Chardonnay and Sémillon in the top world class. The biggest growers, including Lindeman, MacWilliam, Tulloch, Drayton and Wyndham Estate, own land in Hunter Valley. However, the smaller and newer enterprises such as Brokenwood, Peterson's Allandale, Lake's Folly and Hunter Estate are bringing much imagination to bear on the creation of new wines. The Murrumbidgee Irrigation Area (M.I.A.) near Griffith Leeton, accounts for 18% of Australian wine. The wines produced are of the Port, Sherry, Muscat and Vermouth types.

The Mudgee region, a new vine-growing region, is up in the mountains, where the cool air produces such excellent wines as Huntington Estate, Botobolar and Miramar, to name but a few.

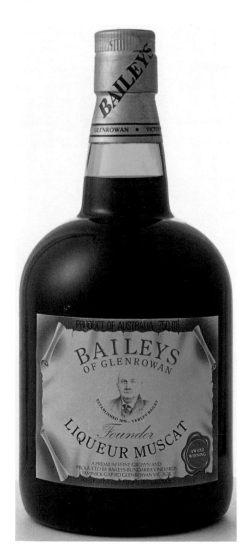

THE STATE OF VICTORIA

Victoria was once famous for its gold mines. The oldest vineyard, at Yering near Lilydale, dates from 1838 and at the turn of the century, it was the biggest wine-producing region of Australia. At the time there were 1200 vineyards growing throughout the state. They were responsible for 70% of Australian wines - until they were hit by phylloxera, which destroyed almost every vine.

Fifty years later, all that was left were the irrigated regions of Mildura and Swan Hill. A few great names survived, such as Château Tahbilk in central Victoria and Great Western, near Ararat, an arid region which produces Great Western champagne, the best Australian sparkling wine, on arid soil. In the north-east, Wangaratta, Milawa and Glenrowan are known for their dessert wines and their strong red wines. The reddish-brown Muscat de Frontignan grapes are grown at Rutherglen, producing the famous Liqueur Muscats wine which, like Tokay, can be left to age for 50 years in barrels.

In the west of the State, the Swiss planted the famous vineyards of the Grampian Mountains in the mid-19th century. They produce light white Rieslings and robust, aromatic red wines. Today, there are about 100 wine-growing companies, grouped into large regions of which the most important is Mildura-Robinvale (10% of Australian production). There are also Murray Valley, Goulburn Valley, Bendigo Central Highlands and the Victorian Pyrenees.

Vine-growing expanded again in the 1960s, using only classic grape varieties, such as Cabernet-Sauvignon, Pinot Noir, Chardonnay, Sauvignon Blanc and Riesling.

NEW ZEALAND

New Zealand is one of the youngest wine-growing countries in the world. Like Australia and Chile, it lies between the 35th and 40th parallel of the southern hemisphere. It is a surprising country in many ways.

New Zealand was discovered by Abel Tasman in 1642. The British did not take possession of it until 1840, under the Treaty of Waitangi which guaranteed that the Maori tribes could retain ownership of their land - although this promise was never kept. New Zealand became a British colony in 1851.

Wine of Origine

Production once consisted entirely of liqueur and sherry-type wines. In 1946, the authorities declared the district too cool and humid for the production of quality dessert wines since the grapes could not accumulate enough sugar. Since then, production has tended to concentrate on table wines, especially whites.
table wines: 47% (6% red and rosé)
sparkling wines: 12%
fortified wines: 30%
bulk wines: 7%.

The birth of the New Zealand vineyards is due to two Australian pioneers - and a French bishop! Samuel Marsden, senior chaplain to the Government of New South Wales and an agronomist in his spare time, and James Busby, the first British resident of New Zealand, settled in the Bay of Islands in the early 19th century. They introduced the first vine cuttings. "I have planted about 100 vine seedlings of various varieties bought in Port Jackson (Sidney). As far as I can judge, the type of soil and climate of New Zealand seems to be promising", noted Marsden on September 15, 1819. In 1835, Monseigneur Pompallier, a French missionary bishop who headed a congregation of Marist Brothers, introduced vines to Hawke's Bay. However, it was Romeo Bragata, an

Italian œnologist, who really built up the New Zealand wine industry. A few years later, when the famous French explorer, Dumont d'Urville, returned to New Zealand, he wrote in his diary that he was offered, "A light, very sparkling white

Objects in Shade by Evelyn Page   Collection: Robert McDougall Art Gallery, Christchurch, N.Z.

Chardonnay
1988

GIESEN WINE ESTATE
Christchurch, New Zealand

The Verandah by Olivia Spencer Bower (Christchurch Polytechnic Collection)
Reproduced by kind permission of The Olivia Spencer-Bower Foundation

Cabernet Sauvignon

1987

Alc.
12.5%
by Vol.

750 ml

GIESEN WINE ESTATE
Christchurch, New Zealand

wine with an exquisite taste". The North and South Islands soon had flourishing vineyards, thanks to French and German colonists who settled in Akaroa and Nelson. However, this expansion was halted by the joint effects of phylloxera and Prohibition. By 1923, only 180 hectares (44,478 acres) of vineyards were left, owned by Yugoslav immigrants and the Marist fathers at Greenmeadows in Hawke's Bay. The revival of New Zealand viticulture dates from World War II when the country had to live on its own resources.

Today, annual production is estimated at 600,000 hectolitres (13,200,000 gallons) from an area of 4000 hectares (9884 acres), 95% of which are planted with Vitis vinifera varieties (especially Chardonnay, Riesling, Sauvignon and Sémillon). The climate is oceanic (temperate). The two main islands, the North Island and the South Island are 1500 kilometres (932 miles) long and lie on a north-south axis in the path of the Westerlies, winds that are strong and humid. The South Island, with the exception of the Marlborough and Nelson areas, is too cold for viticulture.

NORTH ISLAND

The biggest wine-growing district in New Zealand lies between Auckland and Hamilton. It includes the districts of Henderson, Hawke's Bay, Poverty Bay and the east coast around the towns of Napier and Gisborne. Surprisingly, New Zealand has a better climate and more sunshine than either Switzerland or Germany, especially the Blenheim region. Hawke's Bay has been compared to Burgundy, so it is not surprising that the Cabernet-Sauvignon produced there has a distinguished record in international competitions. The best red wines are made from Pinot Noir, Pinot Meunier, Hermitage and Pinotage (a full-bodied South African variety). The wines have been accused of being too acid and astringent and lacking in body, but these defects of youth are tending to disappear. The whites are often the best. They are made from Pinot Chardonnay, Traminer and especially Riesling-Sylvaner. Müller-Thurgau grapes

GRAPES OF NEW ZEALAND

Almost all the hybrids have been uprooted and now account for only 6% of the crop. They have been replaced by vinifera grapes, especially Müller-Thurgau which accounts for half the harvest. However, New Zealanders tend to prefer much drier wines made from Sauvignon Blanc, Gewürtztraminer, Chenin Blanc and Chardonnay grapes. Curiously, Riesling has not been as successful as it has in Australia, although the climate here is closer to that of Germany. It should also be noted that a rather surprising mixture of Merlot and Cabernet exists in the Auckland region.

are made into one of the most popular white wines in New Zealand, sold under the name of Riesling. In fact, after Germany, New Zealand is the biggest producer of wines from the Müller-Thurgau grape.

If annual consumption is 17 litres (30 pints) per inhabitant per year, it is very low compared to the annual beer consumption which stands at 130 litres (227 pints). New Zealanders prefer fortified wine of the Madeira, Port and Sherry type which are obtained by adding cane sugar (up to 30%) to the wine. The climate is best for light white wines and these account for 75% of production.

A good proportion of the vineyards is in the hands of the large Australian producers such as La Montana Wine Limited in Auckland, the Seagram group, McWilliams and Corbans.

SOUTH AFRICA

In 1498, Vasco da Gama rounded the Cape of Good Hope and disembarked at what is now Natal. It was not until 1657 that Jan van Riebeck set up the first colony in South Africa on behalf of the Dutch East Indies Company. His baggage included vine cuttings which had come from the Rhine Valley. They must almost certainly have been Muscatel and Steen varieties, the latter being called Steendruif by the Afrikaners. On February 2, 1659, he noted in his diary: "Today, the Lord be praised, for the first time wine has been made from Cape grapes". This first vine, planted at the foot of Tagelberg Mountain near the Cape, was a foretaste of what was to come, the Union of South Africa, three centuries later, a major wine-producer.

Label 1990

REGULATION

In 1978, the KWV was created, a wine-growing cooperative headquartered in Paarl. The aim was to control prices and absorb any surpluses. Today, it has more than 6000 members and owns five vinification plants. It was at its instigation that in 1982 the South African government adopted a system of control of wines of origin. Thus, 14 producing regions were defined and 14 estates accepted as "wines of estates of origin". The title W.O. (Wine of Origin) on the bottle cap guarantees the place of production, the vine cultivar and the vintage indicated on the label. The best wines of origin are marked W.O.S.

The introduction of these rules has caused a minor revolution in the South African wine industry. In order to attain the quality demanded, more and more Sauvignon Blanc, Riesling, Chardonnay, Pinot Noir and Cabernet Sauvignon vines are being planted.

There are five important dates in South Africa's viticultural history. In 1684, Simon van der Stel, Governor of the Cape, planted the Groot Constantia, the most famous vineyard in the country. It produced Constance wine, a dessert wine which made the Cape famous. Napoleon and Bismarck were both enthusiastic about it. In 1688, French Huguenots who were fleeing persecution after the revocation of the Edict of Nantes, settled in the Franschaek, Paarl, Drakenstein and Stellenbosch regions. They were responsible for the major expansion of vine-growing in South Africa. In 1885, phylloxera hit the vineyards and laid them waste. The vineyards were re-established in 1917 but there was overproduction and

prices collapsed. In 1978, the KWV (Kooperative Wijnbouwern Vereniging) Association was founded, whose aim was to protect the interests of the vine-growers. Today, South Africa devotes 140,000 hectares (345,940 acres) to vine-

growing, producing 8 million hectolitres (176 million gallons) of wine per year. The traditional importer of South African wines is Great Britain, but the KWV tries to

GRAPES OF SOUTH AFRICA

The wines which the South Africans call Riesling - South African Riesling, Cape Riesling, Paarl Riesling and Clare Riesling - are in fact a single variety, Cruchen Blanc whose real identity is a vine from Gascony whose name means "crunchy", and which is also known as vin de sables. It grows in the Paarl-Stellenbosch region and produces a dry, rather aromatic wine. Pedro Luis, another white variety, is used for making Sherry. It is found on the sandy soil of Paarl and Malmesbury. Then there is Chenel, a cross between Chenin and Ugni Blanc, a vigorous and high-yielding plant. Its wines are light and lively.

As for red wines, the Pinotage is an example of the originality of South African wine production. It is a cross between the Hermitage (a Cinsault variety) and Pinot Noir - hence the name. It was created in 1925 by Professor Perold and gained legitimacy when a wine from the Bellevue de Stellenbosch Estate won first prize at the Cape Wine Exhibition in 1959. If it lacks body, it has a good colour and a very special aroma. Pontac is said to come from Medoc and have been introduced by the Huguenots. Today, its poor yield makes it a variety which is on the decline. However, it produces a distinguished, tonic, highly-coloured wine with a good bouquet. Furthermore, it ages well.

export to more than 30 countries.

Wine consumption per inhabitant in South Africa is very low at only 11 litres (19 1/4 bottles) per capita per year. This is compensated for (if that is the right phrase!) by an excessive consumption of alcohol in the form of whisky, brandy and gin. However, this trend is reversing itself in favour of natural and fortified wines of the best quality.

South Africa can be divided into two wine-growing areas, the coastal area which extends back from the coast to the first mountain ranges, and the Little Karoo or Klein Karoo region which ends at Black Mountain or Swartberg.

THE COASTAL REGION

This region extends from the coast to the Drakenstein mountain range and includes the districts of Stellenbosch, Paarl and Wellington. In the west it covers the area from Malmesbury to Tulbagh. In fact, it covers the whole of the Cape peninsula, including the famous Valley of Constantia, home of the beginnings of the South African wine industry (the Constantia vines are now managed by the State as an experimental station).

The south-west of the Cape region lies between the 33rd and 34th south parallel and its Mediterranean climate makes it retain its position as the major wine-producing region of South Africa. There is little to fear from bad years. Harvesting takes place in February or March (because this is the southern hemisphere) and soil, climate and topography are all excellently suited to the making of fine wine.

Vines are usually cultivated on the hillsides. Every type of wine is made - dry wines, red wines, white wines, and particularly fortified wines of the Port and Sherry types. The Paarl valley (Paarl is one of the oldest cities in the Cape) and the districts of Stellenbosch (headquarters of the National Institute that controls the quality of wines) and Durbanville produce the best wines, 80% of them whites. However, they may be a little full-bodied and not dry enough for European tastes. The varieties are Cape Riesling, Gewürztraminer, Colombard and Clairette Blanche. The red wines are mainly of the Burgundy type made from the Hermitage, Shiraz, Pontac and Gamay vines.

Wines of the Somerset-West region are lighter and more closely resemble Bordeaux. In general, the wines of the Cape are good and well vinified. The rosés are new but have made a very promising start. The coastal region has a sandstone soil mixed with organic sediment or clay, and the Little Karoo district has a thick layer of very fertile alluvial soil.

THE LITTLE KAROO DISTRICT

Little Karoo begins just behind the Drakenstein Mountains and stops at the Black Mountain or Swartberg. It covers the regions of Worcester, Robertson, Montagu, Oudtshoorn and Ladismith. These are highlands, whose a harsher climate and lack of humidity are compensated for by irrigation.

The grape varieties which prosper here are the Hermitage, Steendruif, Hanepoot, Muscatel and Sultana. This last produces sweet Muscats on the best soils and Sherry-type wines and brandies on the poorer soils.

JAPAN

In Japan, grape juice has traditionally been prized for its medicinal qualities. Even though wine has been made since the 12th century, the very hesitant expansion of the grape-growing industry dates from the 19th century and the arrival of Europeans and Americans.

REGULATION

Japan imports 200,000 hectolitres (4,400,000 gallons) of wines and spirits annually. Local production stands at 150,000 hectolitres (3,300,000 gallons), 60% of which is in the hands of three big producers, Suntory, Manswine and Mercian, all of whom have acreages in the Fotu Valley.

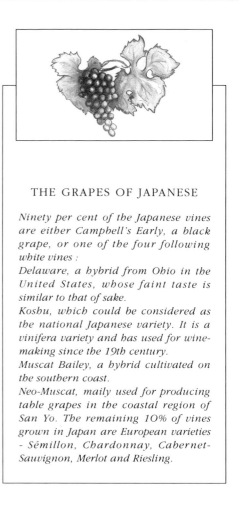

THE GRAPES OF JAPANESE

Ninety per cent of the Japanese vines are either Campbell's Early, a black grape, or one of the four following white vines :
Delaware, a hybrid from Ohio in the United States, whose faint taste is similar to that of sake.
Koshu, which could be considered as the national Japanese variety. It is a vinifera variety and has used for wine-making since the 19th century.
Muscat Bailey, a hybrid cultivated on the southern coast.
Neo-Muscat, maily used for producing table grapes in the coastal region of San Yo. The remaining 10% of vines grown in Japan are European varieties - Sémillon, Chardonnay, Cabernet-Sauvignon, Merlot and Riesling.

Today, the Japanese produce about 150,000 hectolitres (3,300,000 gallons) of wine a year from a total area of 3000 hectares (7,500 acres). The Japanese drink beer, sake, but very little wine, barely 1 litre per inhabitant per year. Vines are grown in small plots on Hondo, the main island, 120 kilometres (75 miles) west of Tokyo, around Yamanashi in the Kofu Valley, around Osaka and to a very smal extent around Yamagata and Nagano. The climate is humid and the soil acid. Grapes need to ripen early, before the torrential September rains. The vines are European - Cabernet, Sauvignon, Merlot and Sémillon - and American - Concord and Delaware. There is a native Japanese variety, Koshu. The best wines are rather dry and light and are reminiscent of the Hunter Valley wines of Australia.

CHINA

Wine was being made in China 2000 years ago. It was called Liu Chang and not Tsiu, as it is today. The vine was brought to China from Persia in about 130 b.c. after the conquests of Alexander the Great. However, it was the Chu dynasty which spread it throughout China in the 11th century A.D.

Marco Polo relates that when he visited China he found vines growing abundantly in the Chan-si province. In the 17th century, Emperor K'anghi brought vines from Turkestan and planted the first great vineyards.

Although vines grow wild in southern China, the Chinese have never been particularly fond of wine. With the exception of a few of the Emperor's courtesans and poets such as Li Po, who wrote verses in praise of wine, most Chinese prefer alcoholic drinks based on rice. Even today, beer or lemonade are drunk with meals. Wine is reserved for very rare occasions.

There are 30,000 hectares (74,130 acres) of vines in China, whether native or of European or American origin. The vine is cultivated in north-western Sinkiang Province, north of the Yangtse River, in central China in the Yantai region, and

THE GRAPES OF CHINESE

China cultivates ten or more white varieties with very imaginative names such as "cow's udder", "dragon's eye" or "rooster's heart". However, the traditional varieties are gradually being replaced by Cabernet-Sauvignon, Merlot, Pinot Noir, Carignan, Sauvignon, Gamay and especially Muscat de Hambourg. This last appears to be particularly successful.

A red hybrid, Beichu, is a cross between the wild vines of the south (vitis amuranis) and the European vitis vinifera. It seems to like a hot, humid climate and is used to make dessert wines or blends. This vine has a very high yield.

beside the Great Wall near the Liao River. The wines produced are red, white or rosés. They may be dry, sweet or sparkling. For instance, the Tsinghao and Shefu grape varieties, grown on the same latitude as Gibraltar, produce wines which resemble Sherry or light Port. Experimental viticultural stations are being established in China. The French firm of Rémy Martin has been working with the Tianfin Commune since 1970 to produce a mellow white wine called "Dynasty". It is a blend of Muscat de Hambourg and a local variety with the reassuring name "Eye of the Dragon". Another wine with quite a good reputation is called "Great Wall".

The favourite wine of the Chinese is made not from grapes but from rice. Shafohsing, also known as "yellow wine", is obtained by fermenting high-gluten rice with fruit wines. The alcohol content is higher than in grape wines - between 15° and 19°. It is drunk mainly in the provinces along the Yangtse River.

WINE CONSUMER

Because wine is alive, it deserves infinite care. Because it is a pleasure, it deserves as much consideration as a friend - whose friendship must above all be kept.

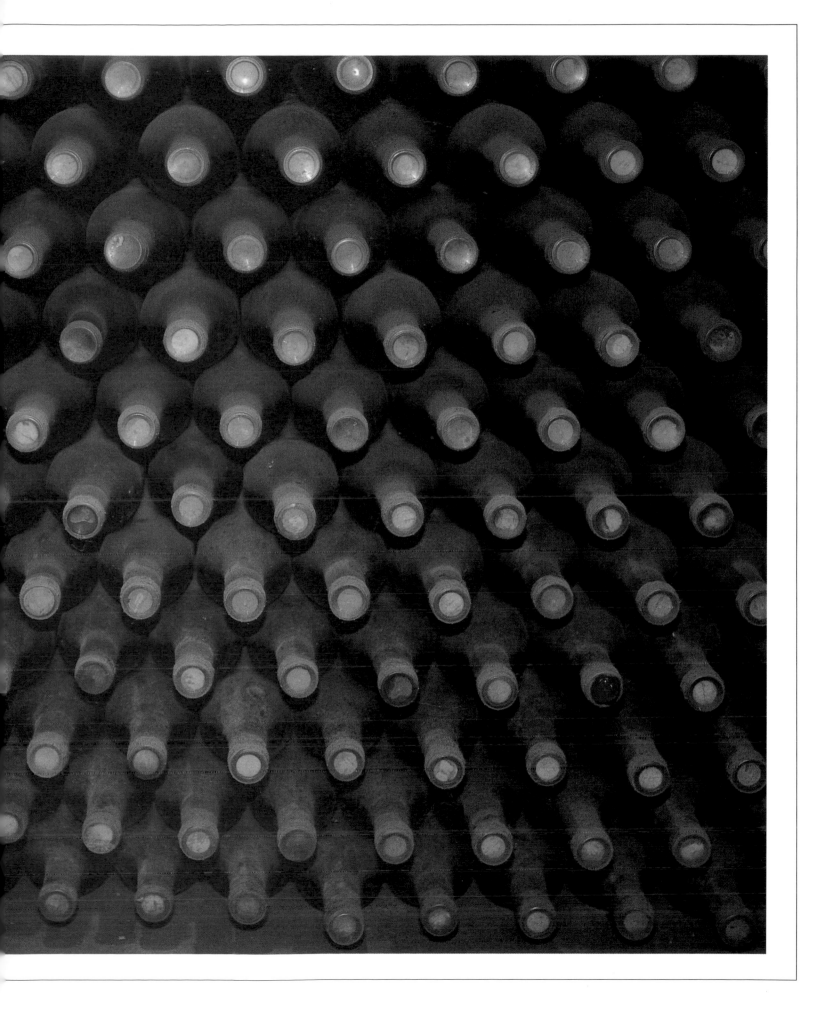

CHOOSING WINE

The selection of wines is largely a matter of taste, finances and lifestyle, and thus a very personal decision. However, this arbitrariness can at least take one aspect into account, the infinite diversity of wine. The variety is such that, in order to avoid appearing sacrilegious, the most modest wine-cellar must contain the minimum range - a few dry whites, a few medium-dry or mellow whites, some light reds, some full-bodied reds, some great sweet wines, and a little Champagne. The reason is that specific wines go well with specific foods. This is not a matter of mere empty convention, but a principle of harmony and reciprocal enhancement.

The experience of centuries shows that visual appearance is a fairly sure guide. Thus, pale-coloured food, such as fish or white meat, calls for white wine or a light rosé, while game, whose meat is almost dark-brown, demands a dark wine. As a general rule, a rich dish goes with a strong wine. Indeed, it is hard to imagine lobster à l'américaine (lobster in a rich sauce) with a simple dry white wine, or venison casserole with a fresh, light red.

For anyone who respects wine, there are even dishes which require it to be omitted altogether. This is true of eggs cooked in most ways, most soups, and of any salad with vinaigrette dressing, because nothing kills a wine more effectively than vinegar. Moreover, most desserts, including with acidic fruit, ice cream or chocolate, go more readily with a simple glass of water, if only a transient one.

On the other hand, certain so-called classic food-and-wine combinations should be treated with caution. Experience clearly shows that a strong cheese will always have the effect of murdering a Grand Cru, even the most full-bodied one. On the other hand, some less familiar combinations work wonders. Goats' cheese goes perfectly with a dry white wine, while a veined cheese such as Roquefort will find no better accompaniment than a syrupy white.

These exceptions however do not invalidate a few simple rules dictated by common sense:
white wine should be taken before red;
dry wine before sweet;

St. Emilion, Bordeaux, Cheval Blanc, first "grand cru."

The "Souper Fin" by Marchetti.

light wine before full-bodied.
Which amounts to the wise dictum: "The bottle being drunk should never make one regret the one that has just been drunk".

TASTING WINE

To learn how to taste wine - to appreciate its flavours and to detect all the subtleties of its aromas - is not only to pay legitimate tribute to it, but also to increase your own pleasure tenfold. This way, you will eventually be able to gauge the true quality of a wine. Becoming an expert wine-taster is a matter of individual aptitude as much as of application and practise. Wine-tasting exercises almost all of the senses. The following come into play:

THE EYES

It is well-known that wine begins by pleasing the eye. It is generally clear, unclouded by suspended particles, and reveals varying degrees of brilliance. Its colour can be pale or strong, varying from a very pale yellow tinted with green to golden-yellow and amber in the whites, and from garnet to brick-red, via ruby, cherry and peony in the reds.

THE NOSE

This presides over the most important moment in wine-tasting. Smell in fact plays a dominant role, and its close connection with taste is too often ignored. A simple experiment proves this convincingly. Even the strongly-perfumed product becomes insipid if you try to taste it while pinching your nostrils.

One of the pleasures of wine-tasting is the detection of the many aromas which the processes of vinification and aging have created in plain grape juice. The aromas of wine fall into an almost natural order. First there are the flower scents, then those of fruit, and then vegetables and sometimes even animal scents.

How can they be detected? It is a good idea to begin by conducting simple experiments. For example, practise by trying to identifying the many apple scents which are characteristic of most white wines. Similarly, the scent of vanilla is easily detectable in red wines which have been kept in wood.

Thus, by making greater demands on one of most atrophied senses, the subtleties of a complex bouquet can be detected. The various types of wine will reveal the scents of:

flowers (acacia, reseda, rose, violet,etc.),
fresh fruit (apple, banana, blackcurrant, cherry, etc.),
dried fruit (prune, glacé cherry, hazelnut, roasted almond, etc.),

Angelo Gaja, one of the biggest vintners in Barolo, Italy.

grasses and foliage (fern, humus, undergrowth, etc.),
smells of roasting (coffee, toast, etc.),
herbs and spices (vanilla, liquorice, pepper, etc.),
animal scents (amber, musk, civet...).

After the first sniff, the taster swirls the liquid in his glass; this is not merely to impress onlookers, as to be better able to detect the nuances of aroma, which are accentuated by this aeration.

THE MOUTH

This also plays its part in the appraisal of odours, by means of the phenomenon of retro-olfaction. The back of the mouth does, in fact, communicate with the olfactory mucous membrane via the nasal sulcus so that the mouth, in turn, detects odours which can even be very volatile.

The expression "to have a palate" is therefore used incorrectly if it is not understood in this sense. In fact, apart from this function, the mouth itself only perceives a very limited register of flavours. These are saltiness, sweetness, acidity and bitterness. These four flavours each determine a particular sensation, and it is important to distinguish them properly in order appreciate the balance of the wine.

Finally, there are also some tactile sensations caused by the temperature of the liquid and the amount of carbon dioxide present. Almost all the senses are thus involved in tasting wine. It is far from a pointless exercise to train and educate them since the aim is to achieve increased pleasure. Without training one merely progresses into drunkenness.

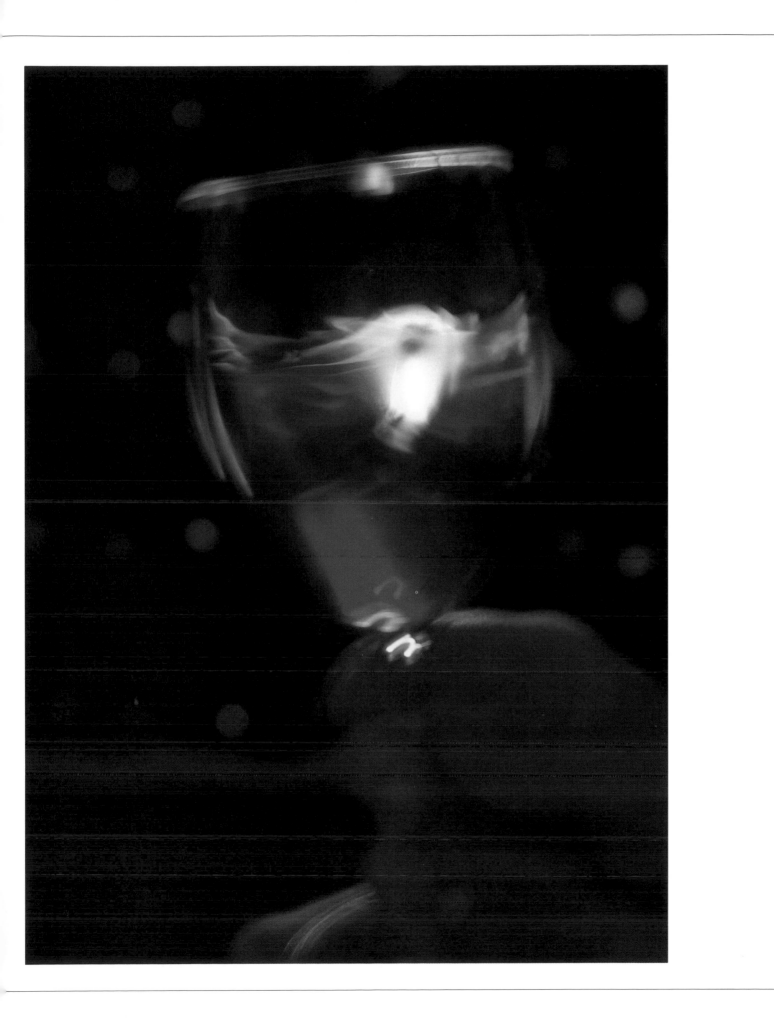

STORING WINE

There is nothing better than a good wine-cellar for storing the bottles, regardless of how long each one is going to remain there. However, what constitutes a "good" cellar?

First of all, it must be dark, because ultraviolet rays can even penetrate thick, dark glass. Darkness is therefore necessary to protect the wine from premature aging.

It must also be moderately humid, with just enough moisture to stop the corks from drying out so that they can continue to prevent the air from penetrating. It is thus best to have an earth floor, because this retains the humidity better than concrete or cement.

It is also important for the place to be sufficiently well-ventilated to avoid an unpleasant musty smell, and the presence of coal or heating oil should obviously be avoided. The place must also be quiet, or at least protected from violent tremors.

Finally, and most importantly, the ambient temperature plays a decisive role. While it should be neither too low nor too high (ideally around 10°C), the first requirement is that it should remain constant, or at least not vary too greatly or too suddenly.

In short, the ideal cellar is something of a rare luxury. However, it is also true that all these principles are relative, and one can make compromises without the wine necessarily suffering as a consequence. Indeed, experience shows that, in the absences of a true cellar, a converted spare room in an apartment can fulfil this role, so long as it is not overheated and the bottles can be placed horizontally in darkness. Only two precautions should always be applied to the bottles. The corks must always be kept clean and the bottles never handled roughly.

Medoc, Bordeaux, special cellar for storing old wines of Chateaux Ausone and Mouton Rothschild.

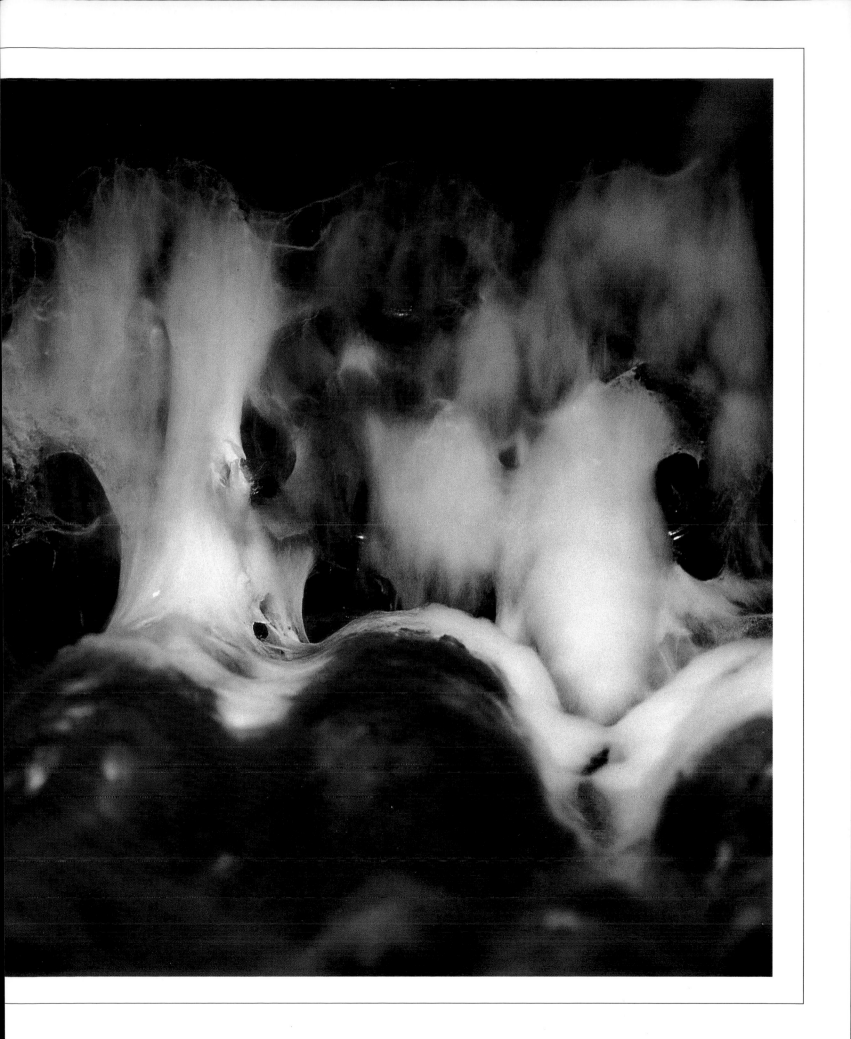

SERVING WINE

Sharing the pleasure of a good bottle is a celebration and, like all celebrations, it must be well-prepared in advance. Such preparations involve:

Bringing the wine to the correct temperature

Most white wines should be served chilled, i.e. at an average of about 8° to 10°C (about 50°F). This causes no problem if the cellar in which the bottles have been kept in is an "ideal" one. If this is not the case, it is better not to give in to the temptation of putting the bottle in the freezer or in crushed ice, which both have the side-effect of "breaking" the wine. It is better to resort to two solutions which are both just as effective, i.e., placing the bottle in the bottom of the refrigerator, or putting it in a bucket containing a mixture of water and ice cubes.

As for red wines, younger and lighter ones should be served at about 12° to 13°C (52° to 55°F), while older ones require 3 or 4 extra degrees of warmth. The latter are said to be required to be served "chambré" (brought up to room temperature), but it should be remembered that this expression dates from a time when central heating was unknown. Today, no wine can be served at ambient temperature and, if it has been warmed too much (it will warm up by 1°C for every ten minutes in a room at 20°C), the best thing to do is to put the bottle into some cold water. If on the other hand, the bottle is too cool, there is only one remedy, a little patience - and no placing it on the radiator!

Uncorking the bottle smoothly

Before removing the cork,the capsule must be sliced off cleanly to just below the collar of the neck. The neck should then be wiped with a clean cloth.

The best corkscrews are those that avoid jolts, making manual traction inadvisable. They should also have a sufficiently long screw, and the spiral should not be too compact or it may damage the cork. Today a very practical model is on the market, a corkscrew with an endless screw, which you turn with a continuous and effortless movement. On the other hand, the leaf corkscrew, which is also excellent, requires experience and skill to manipulate.

TO DECANT OR NOT TO DECANT

Decanting means transferring the wine to a carafe or decanter in order to separate it from its lees. This is an operation which is becoming increasingly unnecessary, since the wines are generally served younger than they used to be, are aged for less time in the wood, and are therefore less tannic. Furthermore, almost all modern wines have been filtered. Therefore, only bottles in which a deposit has formed should be decanted. So if wine has to be decanted, why not do so well in advance? Simply because decanting has the side-effect of violently aerating the wine and because there is a risk that this will cause the older wines to lose some of their bouquet. Therefore, if the operation is necessary, it

is preferable to carry it out at the last moment. To do this, the clean neck should be placed against the rim of the carafe, then the carafe should be tilted so that the wine runs gently along the inside. A candle or some other source of light placed beneath the neck will then help to detect the arrival of the deposit. The bottle must be tilted back upright immediately, to prevent the lees being poured into the decanter.

CHOOSING THE RIGHT GLASSES

Although there appears to be a vast choice among the glasses available on the market, only a few shapes are actually suitable for enjoying wine. Here again, the basic rules owe nothing to pure convention, but arise from carefully considered custom.

Tinted or heavily-decorated glasses should be ruled out because they prevent one from evaluating the colour of the wine and its clarity. A stemmed glass also helps in viewing the wine and prevents it from becoming heated upon contact with the hand. The reason why the rim of the glass should not be too wide is that a slightly narrow opening helps to concentrate the aromas. Finally, the reason why the glass should not be too large and why it should never be filled more than one-third is that the empty space facilitates perception of the aromas.

To sum up, the type of glass described corresponds quite simply to the tulip-shaped glass, the only one which is ideally suited to the sampling of all types of wine. This includes Champagne which should preferably be served in the long, tall glasses called "flutes", but never in the shallow cocktail glasses called champagne glasses.

BIBLIOGRAPHY

Adams, Leon D. The Wines of America, New York, 1985

Ambrosi, Hans. Welt-Atlas des Weines, Bielefeld, 1983

Anderson, Burton. The Pocket Guide to Italian Wines, New York, 1982

Anderson, Burton. Vino: The Wine and Winemakers of Italy, Boston, 1980

Aspler, Tony. Vintage Canada, Scarborough, 1983

Benson, Robert. Great Winemakers of California, Santa Barbara, 1977

Bradley, Robin. The Small Wineries of Australia, Melbourne, 1982

Broadbent, Michael. Pocket Guide to Wine Tasting, London, 1982

Cité de la Villette, La Vigne et le Vin, Paris, 1988

Chaptal. L'Art de faire du vin, Paris, 1981

Club des Gourmets. Guia Practica de los Vinos de España, Madrid, 1983

Crestin-Billet, Fredérique and Paireault, Jean-Paul. Les grands Crus classés du Médoc, Paris, 1988

Crestin-Billet, Fredérique and Paireault, Jean-Paul. Les grands Crus classés du Saint Emilion, Paris, 1989

Crestin-Billet, Fredérique and Paireault, Jean-Paul. Les grands Crus classés des Graves et Sauternes, Paris, 1990

Enjalbert, Henri. Histoire de la vigne et du vin; l'avenement de la qualité, Paris, 1975

Evans, Len. The Complete Book of Australian Wine, Melbourne, 1985

Fletcher, Wyndham. Port: An Introduction to its History and Delights, London, 1978

George, Rosemay. Guia de los vinos y Bodegas de España, Barcelona, 1984

Gold, Alec. Wines and Spirits of the World, Coulsdon, 1972

Gunyon, R.E.H. The Wines of Central and Southeastern Europe, New York, 1971

Halasz, Zoltan. Hungarian Wines Through the Ages, Budapest, 1962

Hallgarten, F.L and S.F. The Wines and Wine Gardens of Austria, London, 1979

Hallyday, James. Wines and Wineries of New South Wales, St Lucia, 1980

Hazan, Victor. Italian Wine, New York, 1982

Heinen, Winifried. Rheinpfalz: Gesamtwerk Deutscher Wein, Essen, 1980

Hutchinson, Ralph E.; Figiel, Richard; Meredith, Ted Jordan. A Dictionary of America Wines, New York, 1985

Hyams, Edward. Dionysos, A Social History of the Wine Vine, London, 1965

Ibar, Leandro. El Libro del Vino, Barcelona, 1982

James, Walter. Wine in Australia, Melbourne, 1963

Jamieson, Ian. Pocket Guide to German Wines, London, 1984

Johnson, Hugh. Hugh Johnson's Modern Encyclopedia of Wine, New York, 1893

Johnson, Hugh. Pocket Wine Book, New York, 1986

Johnson, Hugh. The Atlas of German Wine, London, 1986

Johnson, Hugh. The Wine Companion, London, 1983

Johnson, Hugh. The World Atlas of Wines, New York, 1985

Le Guide del Gambero. Vini d'Italia, Roma, 1989

Lichine, Alexis. Encyclopedia of Wines and Spirits, New York, 1988

Lichine, Alexis. Guide to the Wines and Vineyards of France, New York, 1979

Mayne, Robert. The Great Australian Wine Book, New South Wales, 1985

Moore, Rodrigo Alvarado. Chile, Tierra del Vino, Santiago, 1985

Navarre J.P. Manuel d'Œnologie, Paris, 1979

Penning-Rowsell, Edmund. The Wines of Bordeaux, London, 1985

Peppercorn, David. Pocket Guide to the Wines of Bordeaux, New York, 1986

Peynaud, Emile. Connaissance et travail du vin, Paris, 1981

Peynaud, Emile. Le Goût du vin, Paris, 1983

Piallat R. et Deville P. Œnologie et crus des vins, Paris, 1983

Platter, John. John Platter's South African Wine Guide, Cape, 1989

Ray, Cyril. Robert Mondavi of the Napa Valley, Novato, 1984

Read, Ian. Pocket Guide to Spanish Wines, London, 1983

Read, Ian. The Wines of Portugal, London and Winchester, 1982

Read, Ian. The Wines of Spain, London and Winchester, 1982

Renouil, Yves. Dictionnaire du vin, Bordeaux, 1962

Ribereau-Gayon J., Peynaud, E., Sudraud, P., Ribereau-Gayon, P. Sciences et techniques du vin, Paris, 1975

Robinson, Jancis. The Great Wine Book, London, 1982

Roncarati, Bruno. Viva Vino, D.O.C., Wines of Italy, London, 1976

Saunders, Peter. A Guide to New Zealand Wine, Auckland, 1982

Stabilisierungsfonds für Wein. German Wine Atlas, London, 1977

Sutcliffe, Serena. André Simon's Wines of the World, New York, 1981

Sutcliffe, Serena. The Wine Handbook, New York, 1987

Thompson, Bob. The Pocket Encyclopedia of California Wines, New York, 1980

Torres, Miguel. Los Vinos de España, Barcelona, 1983

INDEX

INDEX OF WINEMAKERS

Austria

DIENSTLGUT LOIBEN
Winzergenossenschaft, 3601 Unter Loiben 51
ELFENHOF (WEINGUT)
J & E Holler Baumgartengasse 11, 7071 Ruller
FISHER ALFRED (WEINGUT)
Haupstrabe 1-3, 7023 Pottelsdorf Stottera
INFUHR KARL KG
Albrechstrabe 127, 3402 Klosterneuburg,
phone: 222371568
KLOSTERKELLER SIEGENDORF
Rathausplatz 12, 7011 Siegendorf,
phone: 26878252
LENZ MOSER GHG
Lenz Moser Strasse 4-6, 3495 Rhorendorf Im
Felde
MANTLERHOF
Hauptstrabe 50, 3494 Gadersdorf Bei Krems,
phone: 27358248
MOORHOF (WEINGUT) ALEXANDER UNGER
Hauptstrasse 106, 7062 St Margarethen,
phone: 26802235
NIEDERMAYER JOHANN VINOTHEK
WEINKELLEREI
Reisernersrafse 1, 1030 Wien
SCHORCK HEIDI (WEINGUT)
Rathauplatz 8A, 7071 Rust
TERRA GALOS
Gols Obere Haupstrasse Neubau, 7122 Gols,
phone: 21732755

France

ALSACE
ALBRECHT LUCIEN (DOMAINE)
9 Grande Rùe, Orschwhir, 68500 Guebwiller,
phone: 89-76-95-18
BEBLENHEIM (CAVE VINICOLE DE)
14 rue De Hoen, 68980 Beblenheim,
phone: 89-47-90-02
BECKER J.
4 route d'Ostheim, Zellenberg,
68340 Riquewhir, phone: 89-47-90-16
BENNWIHR (CAVE VINICOLE DE)
3 rue du Général de Gaulle, 68630 Benwhir-
Mittelwhir, phone: 89-47-90-27
BEYER LEON
2 rue de la Première Armée, 68420 Eguisheim,
phone: 89-41-41-05
COMTES DE LUPFEN (DOMAINE DES)
32 Grande Rue, Kientzheim, 68420
Kaysersberg, phone: 89-78-23-56
DEISS MARCEL (DOMAINE)
15 route du vin, 68750 Bergheim

DOPFF "AU MOULIN"
68340 Riquewhir, phone: 89-47-92-23
DOPFF & IRION (SOCIETE)
1 cours du Château, BP3, 68340 Riquewhir
EGUISHEIM (CAVE VINICOLE D')
Eguisheim, 68420 Herrlisheim,
phone: 89-41-11-06
FERNAND GRESSER (DOMAINE)
12 rue Deharbe, 67140 Andlau,
phone: 88-08-89-83
GAEC BLANCK PAUL & FILS
32 Grande Rue, Kientzheim,
68420 Kaysersberg, phone: 89-78-23-56
GILG ARMAND & FILS
Mittelbergheim, 67140 Barr,
phone: 88-08-92-76
GRESSER ANDRE & REMY (DOMAINE)
2 rue de l'Ecole , 67140 Andlau,
phone: 88-08-95-88
HAULLER LOUIS
92 rue du Maréchal Foch, 67650 Dambach la
Ville, phone: 88-92-41-19
HUGEL & FILS
rue de la Grande Armée, 68340 Riquewhir,
phone: 89-47-92-15
KREYDENWEISS MARC (DOMAINE)
12 rue Deharbe, 67140 Andlau,
phone: 88-08-95-83
KUENTZ-BAS
14 route du Vin, 68420 Husseren les Châteaux,
phone: 89-49-30-24
LAUGEL MICHEL
102 rue du Général de Gaulle,
67520 Marlenheim, phone: 88-87-52-20
LORENTZ GUSTAVE
35 Grande Rue, 68750 Bergheim,
phone: 89-73-63-08
MUHLBACH (CELLIER DU)
55 rue du 3 décembre, 68150 Ribeauville,
phone: 89-73-88-58
NEUMEYER (MAISON)
19 rue du Général de Gaulle, 67120 Molsheim,
phone: 88-38-12-45
REECHT PIERRE
13 Grande Rue, Katzenthal,
68230 Turckheim, phone: 89-27-09-33
ROLLY GASSMANN
1-2 rue de l'Eglise, Rorschwihr,
68150 St Hippolyte, phone: 89-73-63-28
ROLLY PIERRE
Dieffenthal, 67650 Dambach la Ville,
phone: 88-92-40-69
SCHERER A. (VIGNOBLE)
12 route du vin, 68420 Husseren les Châteaux,
phone: 89-49-30-33

SCHLUMBERGER (CAVE COOPERATIVE DE
DAMBACH DOMAINE)
100 rue Théodore Deck, 68500 Guebwiller,
phone: 89-74-27-00
SEILLY JEAN-PAUL
18 rue du Général Gournaud, 67210 Obernai,
phone: 88-95-55-80
SIPP JEAN (DOMAINE)
60 rue de la Fraternité, 68150 Ribeauville
SPARR PIERRE & FILS
2 rue de la Première Armée, BP1,
68240 Sigolsheim, phone: 89-78-24-22
STEIN
60 rue principale, Mittelbergheim, 67140 Barr,
phone: 88-08-19-80
TRIMBACH F.E.
15 route de Bergheim, BP64,
68150 Ribeauville, phone: 89-73-60-30
UNIONS DE PRODUCTEURS CAVE
COOPERATIVE
2 route de Colmar, 68150 Ribeauville,
phone: 89-73-61-80
WANTZ ALBERT & FILS (CAVE)
3 rue des Vosges, Mittelbergheim, 67140 Barr,
phone: 88-08-91-43
WEINFACH (DOMAINE)
25 route du Vin, 68420 Kaysersberg,
phone: 89-47-13-21
WEINGARTEN (DOMAINE)
14A rue de Lorraine, 67730 Chatenois,
phone: 88-82-04-21
ZIND-HUMBRECHT (DOMAINE)
34 rue Joffre, Wintzenheim, 68000 Colmar,
phone: 89-27-02-05

BORDEAUX
ANGLUET (CHATEAU D')
Cantenac, 33460 Margaux, phone: 56-58-41-41
ARCHE PUGNEAU (CRU D')
Preignac, 33720 Langon, phone: 56-63-24-84
ARMAJAN DES ORMES (CHATEAU D')
Preignac, 33720 Langon, phone: 56-63-45-99
ARMAND, CHATEAU LA RAME
Ste Croix du Mont, 33410 Cadillac,
phone: 56-62-01-50
AUSONE (CHATEAU)
33330 St Emilion, phone: 56-24-70-94
BACHY, CHATEAU SUDUIRAUT
Preignac, 33210 Langon, phone: 56-63-27-29
BALY, CHATEAU COUTET
33940 Barsac, phone: 56-27-15-46
BARJENEAU (CHATEAU)
Sauternes, 33720 Langon, phone: 56-63-63-14
BEAU REGARD (CHATEAU)
Pomerol, 33500 Libourne, phone: 56-57-14-09
BERGEY, CHATEAU DE DAMIS

Ste Foy la Longue, 33490 St Macaire,
phone: 56-63-71-42
BERNARD MARYSE, CHATEAU GRAVAS
Barsac, 33720 Podensac, phone: 56-27-15-20
BEYCHEVELLE (CHATEAU)
St Julien Beychevelle, 33250 Pauillac,
phone: 56-59-05-14
BLANCHERIE-PEYRET (CHATEAU LA)
33650 Labrede, phone: 56-20-20-39
BOISSONNEAU P. & C., CHATEAU DE LA
VIEILLE TOUR
St Michel de Lapujade, 33190 La Réole,
phone: 56-61-72-14
BOSSUET J., CHATEAU PEYBONHOMME
Cars, 33390 Blaye, phone: 57-42-11-95
BOURGNEUF-VAYRON (CHATEAU)
Pomerol, 33500 Libourne, phone: 57-51-20-47
BOUYOT (CHATEAU)
Barsac, 33720 Podensac, phone: 56-27-19-46
BRANAIRE (CHATEAU)
St Julien Beychevelle, 33250 Pauillac,
phone: 56-59-08-08
CADET-PIOLA (CHATEAU)
33330 St Emilion, phone: 56-24-70-67
CAMUS F., CHATEAU BONNAT-JEANSOTTE
St Selve, 33650 Labrede, phone: 56-20-25-11
CAPLANE (DOMAINE DE)
Sauternes, 33720 Langon, phone: 56-63-62-11
CARILLE JEAN FRANCOIS
Placc Marcadicu, 33330 St Emilion,
phone: 57-24-74-46
CATUSSEAU, (DOMAINE PRATS)
33500 Libourne, phone: 57-44-11-37
CHASSE SPLEEN (CHATEAU)
Moulis, 33480 Castelnau de Médoc,
phone: 56-58-02-37
CHEVAL BLANC (CHATEAU)
33330 St Emilion, phone: 56-24-70-70
CITRAN (CHATEAU)
Avensan, 33480 Castelnau de Médoc,
phone: 56-58-21-01
CLOS DU ROCHER
Pomerol, 33500 Libourne, phone: 57-51-47-54
CLOS HAUT-PEYRAGUEY
Bommes, 33720 Langon, phone: 56-63-61-53
CLOS LA MAURASSE
33210 Langon, phone: 56-63-39-27
CLOS LARDIT
Barsac, 33720 Podensac, phone: 56-27-17-85
CLOSIOT (CHATEAU)
Barsac, 33720 Podensac, phone: 56-27-05-92
CLOTTE (CHATEAU LA)
33330 St Emilion, phone: 56-24-72-52
COMTE DE BOURNAZEL, CHATEAU DE
MALLE
Preignac, 33210 Langon, phone: 56-63-28-67
COMTESSE DE CHABANNES, CHATEAU DE LA
BREDE
33650 Labrede, phone: 56-21-80-49
COMTESSE DURIEU DE LACARELLE,

CHATEAU FIHOT
33720 Langon, phone: 56-62-61-09
COTE (DOMAINE DE LA)
Le Bourg, Fargues, 33720 Langon,
phone: 56-63-51-05
COUFRAN (CHATEAU)
St Seurin de Cadourne, 33250 Pauillac,
phone: 56-59-31-02
COURRIAN-BLAIGNAN P., CHATEAU LA
TOUR HAUT-CASSAN
33340 Lesparre, phone: 56-09-00-77
COUTREAU-VENSAC H., CHATEAU DAVID
33590 St Vivien de Médoc, phone: 56-09-44-62
CRUSE & FILS FRERES, CHATEAU DE TAILLAN
33320 Le Taillan, phone: 56-35-02-29
D'ARCHE (CHATEAU)
Sauternes, 33720 Langon, phone: 56-63-66-55
DARRICARRERE P., CHATEAU DE MENDOCE
Villeneuve, 33710 Bourg sur Gironde
phone: 57-42-25-95
DAUZAC (CHATEAU)
Labarde, 33460 Margaux, phone: 56-88-32-10
DILLON CLARENCE, CHATEAU HAUT-BRION
33600 Pessac, phone: 56-48-73-24
DUCOS F., CHATEAU MOULIN DE
FERREGRAVE
33590 St Vivien de Médoc, phone: 56-09-42-37
DUCRU-BEAUCAILLOU (CHATEAU)
St Julien Beychevelle, 33250 Pauillac,
phone: 56-59-05-20
DUCS D'EPERNON (CHATEAU DES)
Maison du vin, 33410 Cadillac,
phone: 56-27-11-38
FARGUES (CHATEAU DE)
Fargues, 33720 Langon, phone: 56-44-07-45
FOMBRAUGE (CHATEAU)
St Christophe des Bardes, 33330 St Emilion
phone: 57-24-77-12
GAFFELIERE (CHATEAU LA)
33330 St Emilion, phone: 56-51-72-15
GISCOURS (CHATEAU)
Labarde, 33460 Margaux, phone: 56-58-34-02
GLORIA (CHATEAU)
St Julien Beychevelle, 33250 Pauillac,
phone: 56-59-08-18
GOMBAUDE-GUILLOT (CHATEAU)
Pomerol, 33500 Libourne, phone: 57-51-17-40
GROMAND D'EVRY, CHATEAU DE
LAMARQUE
Lamarque, 33460 Margaux, phone: 56-58-90-03
HAUT CLAVERIE (DOMAINE DU)
Fargues, 33720 Langon, phone: 56-63-12-65
HAUT SARPE (CHATEAU)
33330 St Emilion, phone: 57-24-70-98
HUE G., CHATEAU HAUT-GARIN
Prignac en Médoc, 33340 Lesparre,
phone: 56-09-00-02
ISSAN (CHATEAU D')
Cantenac, 33460 Margaux, phone: 56-58-40-72
JAUBERT, CHATEAU FALFAS

Bayon, 33710 Bourg sur Gironde,
phone: 57-64-84-04
LABUZAN/LANDIRAS P. & P., DOMAINE DU
MOULIN A VENT
33720 Podensac, phone: 56-62-50-66
LAFITE-ROTHSCHILD (CHATEAU)
33250 Pauillac, phone: 56-59-01-04
LAFOSSE D., CLOS BOURGELAT
Cerons, 33720 Podensac, phone: 56-27-01-73
LAGUNE (CHATEAU LA)
Ludon Médoc, 33290 Blanquefort,
phone: 56-30-44-07
LALANDE J., CHATEAU PIADA
Barsac, 33720 Podensac,
phone: 56-27-16-13
LAMOTHE-GUIGNARD (CHATEAU)
Sauternes, 33210 Langon, phone: 56-63-60-28
LANESSAN (CHATEAU)
Cussac Fort Médoc, 33460 Margaux,
phone: 56-58-94-80
LASCOMBES (CHATEAU)
33460 Margaux, phone: 56-58-40-66
LATOUR (CHATEAU)
33250 Pauillac, phone: 56-59-00-51
LAUJAC (CHATEAU)
Begadan, 33340 Lesparre, phone: 56-41-50-12
LAVILLE J.H., CHATEAU DES TUQUETS
St Sulpice de Pommiers, 33540 Sauveterre de
Guyenne, phone: 56-71-53-56
LEGRAND-DUPUY, DOMAINE DE CAILLOUX
Romagne, 33760 Targon, phone: 56-23-60-17
LEOVILLE LAS CASES (CHATEAU)
St Julien Beychevelle, 33250 Pauillac,
phone: 56-59-05-19
LEPPERT B., CHATEAU HILLOT
Illats, 33720 Podensac, phone: 56-62-53-38
LEVEQUE H. & F., CHATEAU DE
CHANTEGRIVE
33720 Podensac, phone: 56-27-17-38
LEYMARIE J.P., CHATEAU LAFARGUE
Martillac, 33650 Labrede, phone: 56-23-73-30
LIONNE (CHATEAU DE)
Illats, 33720 Podensac, phone: 56-27-03-29
LOUDENNE (CHATEAU)
St Yzans de Médoc, 33340 Lesparre
LURTON ANDRE, CHATEAU LA LOUVIERE
33850 Leognan, phone: 56-21-75-87
LYNCH BAGES (CHATEAU)
33250 Pauillac, phone: 56-59-01-84
MAGDELAINE (CHATEAU)
33330 St Emilion
MARGAUX (CHATEAU)
33460 Margaux, phone: 56-88-70-28
MATHEREAU (CHATEAU)
33560 Ste Eulalie, phone: 56-06-05-56
MAYNE-VIEIL (CHATEAU)
33133 Galgon, phone: 57-74-30-06
MENTZELPOULOS M.
33460 Margaux, phone: 56-30-30-28
MERCIER (CHATEAU)

St Trojan, 33710 Bourg sur Gironde,
phone: 57-64-92-34
MIAILHE E., CHATEAU GOUFRAN
St Seurin de Cadourne, 33250 Pauillac,
phone: 56-59-31-02
MISSION HAUT BRION (CHATEAU LA)
67 rue Peybouquey, 33400 Talence,
phone: 56-48-76-54
MOULIN NEUF (DOMAINE DU)
quartier la Garenne, Preignac, 33720 Langon,
phone: 56-63-28-72
MOUTON ROTHSCHILD (CHATEAU)
BP32, 33250 Pauillac, phone: 56-59-01-15
NAVARRE (CRU)
Preignac, 33720 Langon, phone: 56-63-41-41
OFFICE VITICOLE DE BARSAC
place de la Mairie, Barsac, 33720 Podensac,
phone: 56-27-15-44
PALMER (CHATEAU)
Cantenac, 33460 Margaux, phone: 56-58-30-02
PARMENTIER R., CHATEAU LES CHAUMES
Fours, 33390 Blaye, phone: 57-42-18-44
PAVIE (CHATEAU)
33330 St Emilion, phone: 56-24-72-02
PETIT VILLAGE (CHATEAU)
Pomerol, 33500 Libourne, phone: 56-51-21-08
PETRUS (CHATEAU)
Pomerol, 33500 Libourne, phone: 56-51-17-96
RAGON P., CHATEAU LE TUQUET
Beautiran, 33640 Portets, phone: 56-20-21-23
RAYMOND-LAFON (CHATEAU)
Sauternes, 33720 Langon, phone: 56-63-21-02
REMPART (DOMAINE DU)
Pomerol, 33500 Libourne, phone: 57-51-06-97
SANDERS D., CHATEAU HAUT-BAILLY
33850 Leognan, phone: 56-21-75-11
SATURNY PIERRE, CHATEAU TAYAC
33710 Bourg sur Gironde, phone: 57-68-40-60
SAUTERNES (MAISON DU)
Sauternes, 33720 Langon, phone: 56-63-60-37
SIRAN (CHATEAU)
33460 Margaux, phone: 56-58-34-04
SOCIONDO (CHATEAU)
Cars, 33390 Blaye, phone: 57-64-33-61
SOUTARD (CHATEAU)
33330 St Emilion, phone: 56-24-72-23
ST ESTEPHE (MAISON DU VIN DE)
St Estephe, 33250 Pauillac, phone: 56-59-30-59
SUBLETT, CHATEAU DE ROQUES
Puisseguin, 33570 Lussac, phone: 57-74-69-56
TACH B., CHATEAU LUBAT
St Pierre de Mont, 33210 Langon,
phone: 56-63-25-07
TAILLEFER (CHATEAU)
33500 Libourne, phone: 57-51-50-63
TINON J.M., CHATEAU LA GRAVE
Ste Croix du Mont, 33410 Cadillac,
phone: 56-62-01-65
TOUR DE BY (CHATEAU LA)
33340 Lesparre, phone: 56-41-50-03

TOUR DU HAUT MOULIN (CHATEAU LA)
33152 Cussac Fort Médoc, phone: 56-58-91-10
TOUR DU ROY (DOMAINE)
La Gravette, 33500 Libourne,
phone: 57-51-68-80
VICOMTE DE BARITAULT, CHATEAU
ROQUETAILLADE
Mazères, 33210 Langon, phone: 56-63-24-16
VIEUX CHATEAU CERTAN
Pomerol, 33500 Libourne, phone: 56-51-17-33
VISAGE RAYMOND, DOMAINE DE LA FLEUR
Pomerol, 33500 Libourne, phone: 57-51-44-87
VRAY CROIX DE GAY (CHATEAU)
Pomerol, 33500 Libourne, phone: 57-51-64-58
YQUEM, HERITIERS DE LUR-SALUCES
(CHATEAU)
33720 Langon, phone: 56-62-61-02
ZUGER R., CHATEAU MALESCOT ST EXUPERY
33460 Margaux, phone: 56-58-40-68

BURGUNDY
ALOXE CORTON (CHATEAU D')
21420 Savigny les Beaunes,
phone: 80-21-40-10
AMPEAU ROBERT & FILS
6 rue Cromin, 21190 Meursault,
phone: 80-21-20-35
ANJOUX & CIE
Les Bois de Loyse, 71570 La Chapelle de
Guinchay, phone: 85-36-70-92
AUDIFFRED BERNARD
Brouilly, Odenas, 69830 St Etienne des
Ouillères, phone: 74 03 48 17
AURORE (COOPERATIVE VINICOLE DE L')
rue des Charmes, BP6, 71260 Lugny
AUXERROIS-BAILLY (VIGNOBLES)
5 quai de l'Yonne, 89530 St Bris le Vineux,
phone: 86-53-34-00
BARATIN JEAN
Au Signaud, 69830 St Etienne la Varenne,
phone: 74 03 44 58
BEAUNE TEURONS
Au Château, 21200 Beaune,
phone: 80-22-14-41
BELLEVILLE (DOMAINE DE)
rue de la Loppe, Rully, 71150 Chagny,
phone: 85-91-22-19
BENON JEAN
Les Blémonts, 71570 La Chapelle de Guinchay,
phone: 85 36 71 92
BERGER J., DOMAINE DU CHATEAU DE
MERCEY
71150 Chagny, phone: 85-87-17-10
BERNARD GEORGETTE
Le Mont, 69820 Fleurie, phone: 74 04 10 65
BERNARD JEAN (DOMAINE)
Chateau de Leynes, 71570 La Chapelle de
Guinchay
BERTHAULT ALAIN
Cercot Moroge, 71390 Buxy,
phone: 85-47-91-03

BERTHIER J.C.
2 rue Champ du Fort, 89800 Chablis,
phone: 86-42-12-52
BERTRAND & COLLIER
Château de Grand Pré, 69820 Fleurie,
phone: 74 04 13 61
BERTRAND MICHEL
La Verpillière, Charentay, 69220 Belleville,
phone: 74 66 12 23
BICHOT ALBERT (MAISON)
6 bis boulevard J. Coppeau, BP49,
21200 Beaune, phone: 80-22-17-99
BIZE SIMON & FILS (DOMAINE)
rue du Chanoine Donin, 21420 Savigny les
Beaunes, phone: 80-21-50-57
BLONDEAU-DANNE (DOMAINE DU
CHATEAU)
St Aubin, 21190 Meursault, phone: 80-21-31-46
BLOUD
Château du Moulin à Vent, 71570 Romanèche
Thorins, phone: 85 35 50 68
BOCARD J.M., DOMAINE STE CLAIRE
Préhy, 89800 Chablis, phone: 86-41-42-11
BOIS DE LA SALLE, (CHATEAU DU)
69840 Juliénas, phone: 74-04-42-61
BOISSET J.C. (DOMAINE)
rue des Frères Montgolfier, 21700 Nuits St
Georges, phone: 80-61-00-06
BOUCHARD PASCAL (DOMAINE)
17 boulevard Lamarque, 89800 Chablis,
phone: 86-42-18-64
BOUCHARD PERE & FILS
Au Château, 21200 Beaune,
phone: 80-22-14-41
BOULON GEORGES
Le Bourg, 69115 Chiroubles,
phone: 74 04 20 12
BRIDAY JACQUES
Les Chères, 69840 Juliénas, phone: 74 04 42 00
BRINTET (DOMAINE)
Grande Rue, 71640 Mercurey,
phone: 85-45-14-50
BRONDEL PATRICK
Le Signerin, 69640 Denice, phone: 74 67 57 35
BROSSETTE PAUL-ANDRE, DOMAINE DE
CRUIX
Theize, 69620 Le Bois d'Oingt,
phone: 74 71 24 83
BRUCK LIONEL S.A.
6 Quai Dumorey, 21700 Nuits St Georges,
phone: 80-06-07-24
BURGAUD DANIEL
Le Bourg, 69430 Lantignie
CALVET (MAISON)
6 boulevard Perpreuil, 21200 Beaune,
phone: 80-22-06-32
CAUVARD (DOMAINE)
18-34 bis route de Savigny, 21200 Beaune,
phone: 80-22-29-77
CHAFFANJON BERNARD

Les Rochons, St Jean d'Ardières,
69220 Belleville, phone: 74 66 12 18
CHAGNY PAUL
Les Etoux, 69430 Beaujeu, phone: 74 04 87 71
CHAIZE (CHATEAU DE LA)
Odenas, 69380 St Etienne des Ouillères,
phone: 74-03-41-05
CHALMEAU J.
11 place de l'Eglise, Chitry, 89530 St Bris le
Vineux, phone: 86-41-40-74
CHAMPIER BERNARD
Brouilly, Odenas, 69830 St Etienne des
Ouillères, phone: 74 03 42 70
CHAMPIER PASCAL & ELIE
69430 Le Vernay, phone: 74 03 43 74
CHANAISE (DOMAINE DE LA)
69910 Villié Morgon, phone: 74-69-10-20
CHANAY JEAN-LOUIS
Le Trève, 69830 St Etienne des Ouillères,
phone: 74 03 43 65
CHANCELIER (CAVES DU)
1 rue Zeim, 21200 Beaune, phone: 80-22-50-29
CHANRION RAYMOND & NICOLE
Le Bourg, Cercie, 69220 Belleville,
phone: 74 66 37 04
CHANSON PERE & FILS
10-12 rue Paul Chanson, 21200 Beaune,
phone: 80-22-33-00
CHANZY FRERES, DOMAINE DE
L'HERMITAGE
Frère Chanzy, Bouzeron, 71150 Chagny,
phone: 85-87-23-69
CHARRETIER PAUL
Le Bourg, Charentay, 69220 Belleville,
phone: 74 66 11 32
CHARTRON & TREBUCHET
13 Grande Rue, Puligny Montrachet,
21190 Meursault, phone: 80-21-32-85
CHATELET ARMAND
Le Pérou, 69910 Villié Morgon
CHAZOUX (CHATEAU DE)
71780 Hurigny, phone: 85-29-21-22
CHENAS (CAVE DU CHATEAU DE)
Chenas, 69840 Juliénas, phone: 74-04-11-91
CHENEPIERRE (DOMAINE DE)
Les Deschamps, Chenas, 69840 Juliénas,
phone: 85-36-70-74
CLEMENT LOUIS
rue de l'Eglise, Bouzeron, 71150 Chagny,
phone: 85-87-17-72
CLOS DE VOUGEOT (CHATEAU DU)
21640 Vougeot, phone: 80-06-86-09
CLOS DES LAMBRAYS (DOMAINE DU)
rue Basse, Morey St Denis, 21700 Gevrey
Chambertin, phone: 80-51-84-33
CLOS DES TOURNONS, FAMILLE CHEVALIER
BP8, 71850 Charnay les Macon
CLOS DU CHAPITRE (DOMAINE)
St Amour Bellevue, 71570 La Chapelle de
Guinchay, phone: 85-37-41-99

CLOS DU FIEF
Les Gonnards, 69840 Juliénas,
phone: 74-04-41-62
CLOS ST LOUIS
10 rue de l'Abbé Chevalier, Fixin,
21700 Gevrey Chambertin, phone: 80-52-45-51
CLOS VERDY (DOMAINE DU)
69115 Chiroubles, phone: 74-04-20-12
COLINOT PERE & FILS
Irancy, 89290 Champs sur Yonne,
phone: 86-42-20-76
COMBE AUX LOUPS (DOMAINE DE LA)
69115 Chiroubles, phone: 74-04-24-02
COMBES (DOMAINE DES)
Charentay, 69220 Belleville,
phone: 74-66-82-21
COMPAGNIE DES VINS FINS
38 faubourg St Nicolas, 21200 Beaune,
phone: 80-22-00-05
CONDEMINE BERNARD
Saburin, Quincie, 69430 Beaujeu,
phone: 74 04 34 81
CONDEMINE FRANCOIS
Le Château, 69840 Juliénas, phone: 74 04 41 43
CONDEMINE MICHEL
Les Jonnerys, Quincie, 69430 Beaujeu,
phone: 74 04 33 23
CONFURON J.J. (DOMAINE)
Les Vignottes, RN74, Prémeaux Prissey,
21700 Nuits St Georges, phone: 80-62-31-08
CONSEILLERIE DES TONNELIERS
24 bis rue des Tonneliers, 21200 Beaune,
phone: 80-22-45-10
CORPEAU (CAVES DE)
Corpeau, 21190 Meursault, phone: 80-21-32-51
CORTON-ANDRE (CHATEAU DE)
21920 Aloxe-Corton, phone: 80-26-44-25
DE CHABANNES ANDRE
Nervers, Odenas, 69830 St Etienne des
Ouillères, phone: 74 03 40 53
DE FAURE ROGER
Le Bourg, Chenoves, 71940 St Boil,
phone: 85-44-02-49
DE LAUNAY PAUL, DOMAINE DU MEIX
FOULOT
Touches, Mercurey, 71640 Givry,
phone: 85-45-13-92
DE MARCILLY FRERES
22 avenue du 8 Septembre, 21200 Beaune,
phone: 80-22-16-21
DE MARENCOURT (STE)
9 boulevard Clémenceau, 21200 Beaune,
phone: 80-22-28-01
DE VILLAMONT HENRI
16 rue du Seizième Chasseur, 21200 Beaune,
phone: 80-22-20-15
DEFAIX ETIENNE & DANIEL (DOMAINE)
23 rue Champlain, Milly, 89800 Chablis,
phone: 86-42-42-05
DEGOIX RENE

1 rue du Bief Chichée, Chichée, 89800 Chablis,
phone: 86-42-13-45
DELACHANAL (DOMAINE)
Odenas, 69830 St Etienne des Ouillères,
phone: 74 03 42 47
DELAGRANGE & FILS (DOMAINE)
rue du 11 Novembre, 21190 Meursault,
phone: 80-21-22-72
DELORME LUCIEN
Les Marcellins, 69910 Villié Morgon
DELORME MEULIEN (CAVES)
71150 Rully, phone: 85-87-10-12
DENIZOT LUCIEN
Les Moirots, Bissey sous Cruchaud,
71390 Buxy, phone: 85-92-16-93
DEPARDON ROBERT
Les Chaffongeons, 69820 Fleurie,
phone: 74 04 11 20
DERAIN JEAN
Bissey sous Cruchot, 71390 Buxy,
phone: 85-92-10-94
DESMURES ARMAND
Le Bourg, 69115 Chiroubles,
phone: 74 69 10 61
DIOCHON (DOMAINE DE)
Romanèche-Thorins, 71570 La Chapelle de
Guinchay, phone: 85-35-52-42
DOAT
Château de Bois franc, 69640 Denice,
phone: 74 68 20 91
DROIN J.P.
14 bis rue Jean Jaurès, 89800 Chablis,
phone: 86-42-16-78
DROUHIN JOSEPH
7 rue d'Enfer, 21200 Beaune,
phone: 80-22-06-80
DUFOUR JEAN
La Ville, 71570 St Amour Bellevue,
phone: 85 37 14 71
DUMAS MICHEL
Pierreux, Odenas, 69830 St Etienne des
Ouillères, phone: 74 03 40 89
DURIEU ENNEMOND
Briante, Saint Lager, 69220 Belleville
DUSSOULIER (DOMAINE)
Odenas, 69830 St Etienne des Ouillères
DUVERNAY DENIS
Saburin, Quincie, 69430 Beaujeu,
phone: 74 04 33 64
DUVERNAY ROGER
La Poyebade, Odenas, 69380 St Etienne des
Ouillères, phone: 74-03-41-77
EDMUND CHALMEAU (DOMAINE DU)
20 rue Ruisseau, 89530 Chitry,
phone: 86-41-42-09
EGLANTIERE (DOMAINE DE L')
4 Grande Rue, Maligny, 89800 Chablis,
phone: 86-47-44-49
ENGEL RENE (DOMAINE)
place de la Mairie, Vosne Romanée,

21700 Nuits St Georges, phone: 80-61-10-54
FARJAT ROBERT
Combiaty, 69830 St Etienne la Varenne,
phone: 74 03 42 45
FEVRE WILLIAM
14 rue Jules Guesdes, 89800 Chablis,
phone: 86-42-12-51
FLEYS (DOMAINE DU CHATEAU DE)
rue Haute, Fleys, 89800 Chablis,
phone: 86-42-45-19
FOLIE (DOMAINE DE LA)
71150 Chagny, phone: 85-87-18-59
FOURNELLES (DOMAINE DES)
Godefroy, St Lager, 69220 Belleville,
phone: 74-66-12-00
FROMONT-MOINDROT (DOMAINE)
8 rue Guy Dupas, Ligny les Chatel, 89230
Pontigny, phone: 86-47-43-81
GAEC MORIN
Javernand, 69115 Chiroubles,
phone: 74-04-24-32
GAEC NESME
Chavannes, 69430 Quincie, phone: 74 04 31 02
GAGET FRANCIS
Pierreux, Odenas, 69830 St Etienne des
Ouillères, phone: 74 03 41 17
GARLON JEAN
Beauvallon, Theize, 69620 Le Bois d'Oingt,
phone: 74 71 72 52
GAUMONT J.C.
Quenne, 89290 Champ sur Yonne,
phone: 86-52-77-41
GAUTHIER PAUL
Les Granges, 69460 Blace, phone: 74 67 53 55
GELIN PIERRE (DOMAINE)
21710 Fixin, phone: 80-52-45-24
GEOFFRAY CLAUDIUS & FILS
Chavannes, Quincie, 69430 Beaujeu,
phone: 74 04 30 94
GEOFFROY ALAIN (S.A. DOMAINE)
4 rue de l'Equerre, Beine, 89800 Chablis
phone: 86-42-43-76
GERMAIN ALAIN
Les Crières, 69380 Charnay, phone: 78 43 98 60
GEVREY-CHAMBERTIN (CAVE COOPERATIVE
DE)
1 rue de Paris, 21700 Gevrey Chambertin,
phone: 80-34-30-26
GFA DE COMBIATY
Combiaty, 69830 St Etienne la Varenne,
phone: 74 03 42 45
GFA DE LA ROCHE
St Etienne la Varenne, 69830 St Etienne des
Ouillères
GFA DE LA VOUTE DES CROZES
Cercie, 69220 Belleville, phone: 74 66 02 71
GFA DOMAINE DE CHEYSSON
Le Bourg, 69115 Chiroubles,
phone: 74 04 22 02
GFA DOMAINE DESVIGNES

Les Gandelins, 71570 La Chapelle de
Guinchay, phone: 85 36 70 91
GFA GEOFFROY CHARLES
Le Bourg, 69115 Chiroubles,
phone: 74 04 23 57
GFA LANEYRIE EDMOND
Pontanevaux, 71570 La Chapelle de Guinchay,
phone: 85 36 72 54
GILOUX PATRICK
Leynes, 71570 La Chapelle de Guinchay
GIRARD RENE
Rue du Lac, Odenas, 69830 St Etienne des
Ouillères, phone: 74 03 46 32
GOUBARD MICHEL
71390 St Désert, phone: 85-47-91-06
GOY CLEMENT
Saint Joseph, 69910 Villié Morgon
GRACIEUX-CHEVALIER (DOMAINE)
La Ferme Pérignon, 89460 Cravant,
phone: 86-42-20-51
GRANDES CAVES DIJONNNAISE
74 avenue du Drapeau, 21000 Dijon,
phone: 80-74-41-80
GRANDS VINS DE FLEURIE (CAVE
COOPERATIVE DES)
Le Bourg, 69840 Juliénas, phone: 74-04-11-70
GRANDS VINS ROSES (CAVE COOPERATIVE
DES)
27 rue des Vignes, 21160 Marsannay la Côte,
phone: 80-52-15-14
GUERIN GEORGES
Le Bourg, 69840 Chenas, phone: 74 04 12 46
GUYON ANTONIN (DOMAINE)
rue de Chorey, 21420 Savigny les Beaunes,
phone: 80-21-51-49
HASENKLEVER F.
rue du Moulin, 21700 Nuits St Georges,
phone: 80-23-51-61
HAUTES COTES (CAVE COOPERATIVE DES)
route de Pommard, 21200 Beaune,
phone: 80-24-63-12
ILES (DOMAINE DES)
12 rue de Poinchy, 89800 Chablis,
phone: 86-42-40-98
JABOULET-VERCHERRE (STE)
5 rue Colbert, 21200 Beaune,
phone: 80-22-50-61
JADOT LOUIS (DOMAINE)
5 rue Samuel Legay, BP121, 21200 Beaune,
phone: 80-22-10-57
JAMBON-CHANRION (ETS)
Quincie, 69430 Beaujeu, phone: 74-04-33-09
JOLY PERE & FILS
Grande Rue au bourg Bassot, Mercurey,
71640 Givry, phone: 85-45-28-28
JOSEPH DROUHIN (MAISON)
7 rue d'Enfer, 21200 Beaune,
phone: 80-22-06-80
JUILLARD DANIEL
71570 Chanes, phone: 85 36 52 13

JULHIET-MALHERBE (DOMAINE)
Château Thivin, Odenas, 69380 St Etienne des
Ouillères, phone: 74 65 55 08
JULIENAS (CHATEAU DE)
69840 Juliénas, phone: 74-04-41-43
LA CHABLISIENNE (CAVE COOPERATIVE)
8 boulevard Pasteur, 89800 Chablis,
phone: 86-42-11-24
LA P'TIOTE CAVE (DOMAINE)
Chassey le Camp, 71150 Chagny,
phone: 85-87-15-21
LAMARTINE (DOMAINE DE LA CAVE)
vers l'Eglise, St Amour Bellevue, 71570 La
Chapelle de Guinchay, phone: 85-37-12-88
LANGOUREAU AIME (DOMAINE)
Le Gamay, St Aubin, 21190 Meursault,
phone: 80-21-32-63
LAPIERRE GERARD
Les Dechamps, 69840 Chenas,
phone: 85 36 70 74
LAPLANCHE JEAN-LOUIS, CHATEAU DE
POMMARD
21630 Pommard, phone: 80-22-07-99
LAROCHE (DOMAINE)
10 rue Auxerroise, 89800 Chablis,
phone: 86-42-14-30
LAROCHE JEAN
La Prat, 69830 St Etienne la Varenne,
phone: 74 03 26 44
LAUNAY RAYMOND (DOMAINE)
21630 Pommard, phone: 80-22-12-23
LAVIS BERNARD
Les Moriers, 69820 Fleurie, phone: 74 69 81 91
LE CELLIER DE LA VIEILLE EGLISE
69840 Juliénas
LES VIGNES DE LA CROIX
Caves des Vignerons, 71390 Buxy,
phone: 85-92-03-03
LONGIN HENRI
La Chaize, Odenas, 69830 St Etienne des
Ouillères, phone: 74 03 43 88
LORON PIERRE
La Rochelle, 69840 Chenas, phone: 74 69 80 68
LUMP FRERES, GAEC DE L'ORCENE
45 rue de Jambles, Poncey, 71640 Givry,
phone: 85-44-33-09
LUPE CHOLET STE
14 rue du Général de Gaulle, 21700 Nuits St
Georges, phone: 80-61-25-02
MAISON DES VIGNERONS (CAVE
COOPERATIVE LA)
Le Bourg, 69115 Chiroubles,
phone: 74-04-20-47
MAISON DU VIN (LA)
Grande Rue, Mercurey, 71640 Givry,
phone: 85-45-23-62
MALANDRES (DOMAINE DES)
63 rue Auxerroise, 89800 Chablis,
phone: 86-42-41-37
MANIGAND ROGER

Le Pavé, St Lager, 69220 Belleville,
phone: 74 66 35 10
MANOIR MURISALTIEN
Le Clos Mazeray, 21190 Meursault,
phone: 80-21-21-83
MARQUIS DE JOUENNES (DOMAINE DU)
71640 Mercurey, phone: 85-45-22-22
MARTIN JEAN & FILS
Les Gonnards, 69840 Juliénas,
phone: 74 04 41 64
MARTIN RENE (DOMAINE)
Le Bourg, Sampigny les Maranges,
71150 Chagny, phone: 85-91-15-48
MAS DES TINES
St Amour Bellevue, 71570 La Chapelle de
Guinchay, phone: 85-37-41-31
MATHIAS FRERES
Chaintre, 71570 La Chapelle de Guinchay,
phone: 85-35-60-67
MAX LOUIS (ETS)
6 rue de Chaux, 21700 Nuits St Georges,
phone: 80-61-11-23
MENAND PERE & FILS, CHAMEROSE
Mercurey, 71640 Givry, phone: 85-47-14-14
MENETRIER-BELNET (STE)
58 rue de Lorraine, 21200 Beaune,
phone: 80-22-25-68
MERCEY (DOMAINE DU CHATEAU DE)
71150 Cheuilly les Maranges,
phone: 85-91-11-96
MEZIAT BERNARD
Le Verdy, 69115 Chiroubles,
phone: 74 04 24 61
MICHELOT BUISSON (DOMAINE)
rue de la Velle, 21190 Meursault,
phone: 80-21-23-17
MOILLARD (DOMAINE)
Clos de Thorey, BP6, 21700 Nuits St Georges,
phone: 80-61-03-34
MOMMESSIN
La Grange St Pierre, 71000 Macon,
phone: 85-38-05-00
MONASSIER A., DOMAINE DU PRIEURE
71150 Rully, phone: 85-87-13-57
MONGENIE ELIE
Aux Berthaux, 71570 St Amour Bellevue,
phone: 85 37 14 70
MOREAU & FILS
route d'Auxerre, 89800 Chablis,
phone: 86-42-40-70
MORETAUX JEAN & SONS
Nantoux, Chassey le Camp, 71150 Chagny,
phone: 85-87-19-10
MORGON (CAVEAU DE)
69910 Villié Morgon, phone: 74-04-20-99
MORIN PERE & FILS
Quai Fleury, 21700 Nuits St Georges,
phone: 80-06-05-11
MOULIN A VENT (CHATEAU DU)
Romanèche, 71570 La Chapelle de Guinchay

MOULIN JEAN
Les Bruyères, Chanes, 71570 St Amour
Bellevue, phone: 85 37 12 91
NAUDIN VARRAULT (STE)
13 rue des Vignobles, 21200 Beaune,
phone: 80-22-16-65
NINOT P.M. (DOMAINE)
Rully, 71150 Chagny, phone: 85-87-07-79
OLIVIER GEORGES
Les Levrières, Graves, 69480 Anse,
phone: 74 67 02 91
PARDON JEAN-PAUL
La Chevrière, 69460 Blace, phone: 74 67 55 45
PATRIARCHE PERE & FILS
Ancien couvent des Visitandines, 5-7 rue du
Collège, 21200 Beaune, phone: 80-22-23-20
PEPIN CLEMENT
Gorge de Loup, St Lager, 69220 Belleville,
phone: 74 66 02 85
PERE BENOIT (DOMAINE DU)
Bergiron, St Lager, 69220 Belleville,
phone: 74 66 08 43
PERNOT PERE & FILS (DOMAINE)
place du Monument, Puligny Montrachet,
21190 Meursault, phone: 80-21-32-35
PERRIER RAYMOND
Le Saule, 69430 Lantignie
PETITE CAVE DE POMMARD
1 route de Beaune, 21630 Pommard,
phone: 80-24-69-51
PILLETS (DOMAINE DES)
69910 Villié Morgon, phone: 74-04-21-60
PIRON DOMINIQUE
69910 Villié Morgon
PONT, LE CELLIER VOLNAYSIEN
Volnay, 21190 Meursault, phone: 80-21-61-04
POPE CLAUDE
69840 Juliénas, phone: 85-36-74-31
PRIEU-BRUNET (DOMAINE)
rue Narosse, Rémigny, 71150 Chagny,
phone: 80-20-60-56
PRIEURE (DOMAINE DU)
rue de Bourgogne, 21420 Savigny les Beaunes,
phone: 80-21-54-27
PROTHEAU-KOLHER M.
69910 Villié Morgon
PY DE BULLIAT (DOMAINE DU)
Régnie Durette, 69430 Beaujeu,
phone: 74-04-20-17
RAGOT JEAN-PIERRE & JEAN-PAUL
71640 Givry, phone: 85-44-35-67
REINE PEIDAUQUE (CAVES EXPOSITION DE
LA)
21420 Aloxe-Corton, phone: 80-26-40-00
REMORIQUET HENRI & GILLES
25 rue de Charmois, 21700 Nuits St Georges,
phone: 80-61-08-17
REMPARTS (DOMAINE DES)
1 route des Champs, 89530 St Bris le Vineux,
phone: 86-53-80-77

ROBIN EMILE
Chenas, 69840 Juliénas, phone: 74 04 15 19
ROCHE ANDRE
Brouilly, Odenas, 69830 St Etienne des
Ouillères, phone: 74 03 40 85
RODET ANTONIN
Mercurey, 71640 Givry, phone: 85-45-22-22
ROLLAND (DOMAINE)
Les Signauds, Odenas, 69830 St Etienne des
Ouillères, phone: 74 03 42 23
ROUX (DOMAINE)
St Aubin, 21190 Meursault, phone: 80-21-32-92
SABURIN (DOMAINE)
Les Vayvolets, Quincie, 69430 Beaujeu,
phone: 74-04-34-35
SAINT ETIENNE (CAVE COOPERATIVE DES)
69640 Denice
SANDRIN HENRI
La Fouillouse, Rivolet, 69640 Denice,
phone: 74 67 37 56
SAUZET E. (DOMAINE)
Puligny Montrachet, 21190 Meursault,
phone: 80-21-32-10
SENARD DANIEL (DOMAINE)
21420 Aloxe-Corton, phone: 80-21-41-65
SERMET PERE & FILS
19 rue Fagon, 21700 Nuits St Georges,
phone: 80-61-19-96
SERVIN (DOMAINE)
20 avenue d'Oberwesel, 89800 Chablis,
phone: 86-42-12-94
SORIN LUC (DOMAINE)
13 bis rue de Paris, 89530 St Bris le Vineux,
phone: 86-53-36-87
SORNET BENOIT
Challier, Pommiers, 69400 Villefranche,
phone: 74 68 18 23
SPAY PAUL
Le Bourg, 71570 St Amour Bellevue,
phone: 85 37 12 88
ST JULIEN DE PEYROL (CAVE COOPERATIVE
DE)
4 route de Joigny, 89210 Brienon sur
Armançon, phone: 86-56-12-63
STE MARIE LA BLANCHE (CAVE
COOPERATIVE DE)
Sainte Marie la Blanche, 21200 Beaune,
phone: 80-26-60-60
TACHON JEAN MARIE
Sottizon, 69830 Vaux en Beaujolais,
phone: 74 03 22 80
TANNERIES (CAVEAU DES)
1 rue des Tanneries, 21200 Beaune,
phone: 80-22-48-35
TERRIER HENRI (DOMAINE)
Les Bruyères, 71570 La Chapelle de Guinchay,
phone: 85-37-40-05
TERRIER JEAN
La Piat, 71570 St Amour Bellevue,
phone: 85 37 10 64

TETE RAYMOND & FILS
Les Gonnards, 69840 Juliénas,
phone: 74 04 41 62
THEVENET ANDRE
Le Bourg, 69820 Fleurie, phone: 74 04 10 63
THEVENET JEAN
Les Gandelins, 71570 La Chapelle de
Guinchay, phone: 85 36 72 68
TOMATIS ANTOINE
Crozet, 69115 Chiroubles, phone: 74 04 23 68
TOUR (DOMAINE DU CHATEAU DE LA)
Clos Vougeot, 21460 Vougeot,
phone: 80-62-86-13
TOUR BAJOLE (DOMAINE DE LA)
71490 St Maurice les Couches,
phone: 85-49-67-60
TOURS (DOMAINE DES)
Combillaty, 69830 St Etienne la Varenne,
phone: 74-03-42-45
TRICHARD BERNARD
Les Nazins, St Lager, 69220 Belleville,
phone: 74 66 15 85
TRICONT OLIVIER
8 rue Berthelot, 89800 Chablis,
phone: 86-42-10-37
UNION DES PRODUCTEURS
Grande Rue, Mercurey, 71640 Givry,
phone: 85-45-22-96
VERGER (DOMAINE LE)
4 rue de l'Equerre, Beine, 89800 Chablis,
phone: 86-42-43-76
VERPOIX F., CLOS DE LA CHAPELLE DES
BOIS
69820 Fleurie, phone: 74-04-10-95
VIEILLE GRANGE (CELLIER DE LA)
27 boulevard G. Clémenceau, 21200 Beaune,
phone: 80-22-40-06
VIGNERON (CAVE DU)
2 bis place Carnot, 21200 Beaune,
phone: 80-24-10-59
VIGNERONS DE MERCUREY (CAVEAU LES)
Pont Latin, Mercurey, 71640 Givry,
phone: 85-45-20-01
VINCENT-SOURICE
Pierreclos, 71960 Fuissé, phone: 85-83-61-44
VINS D'AUTREFOIS (COMPAGNIE DES)
9 rue Celer, 21200 Beaune, phone: 80-22-21-31
VINS DE FRANCE (CAVE DES)
rue des Courtives, 89600 St Florentin,
phone: 86-35-32-02
VIOLAND LOUIS (DOMAINE)
125 faubourg St Nicolas, 21200 Beaune,
phone: 80-22-21-19
VIORNERY VICTOR
Brouilly, Odenas, 69380 St Etienne des
Ouillères, phone: 74-03-41-86
VIRE (CAVE DE)
71260 Viré
VOCORET & FILS (DOMAINE)
25 rue Emile Zola, 89800 Chablis,

phone: 86-42-12-53
VOIRET (DOMAINE)
48 faubourg St Martin, 21200 Beaune,
phone: 80-22-24-05

CHAMPAGNE
ABELE HENRI (CHAMPAGNE)
50 rue de Sillery, 51100 Reims,
phone: 26-85-23-86
BARON ALBERT (CHAMPAGNE)
Porteron, 02310 Charly sur Marne,
phone: 23-82-02-65
BARON DE SIGOGNAC
33 cours Xavier Arnozan, 33000 Bordeaux,
phone: 56-44-19-75
BARTON & GUESTIER PERRIER-JOUET
53 rue du Dehez, BP30, 33292 Blanquefort
Cedex, phone: 56-35-84-41
BAUGET-JOUETTE (CHAMPAGNE)
60 rue Claude Ruelle, 51200 Epernay,
phone: 26-54-44-05
BEAUFORT HERBERT (CHAMPAGNE)
28-32 rue de Tours, Bouzy, 51150 Tours sur
Marne, phone: 26-57-01-34
BEAUMEY (CHAMPAGNE)
3 rue Malakoff, BP247, 51207 Epernay Cedex,
phone: 26-54-53-34
BERAT (CHATEAU)
rue St Roch, Boursault, 51200 Epernay,
phone: 26-58-42-45
BERNARD (CHATEAU)
21 rue du Corbier, 51160 Ay,
phone: 26-50-60-36
BESSERAT DE BELLEFON (CHAMPAGNE)
allée du Vignoble, BP301, 51100 Reims Cedex,
phone: 26-36-09-18
BILLECART-SALMON (S.A. CHAMPAGNE)
40 rue Carnot, Mareuil sur Ay, 51160 Ay,
phone: 26-50-60-22
BLIN (CHAMPAGNE)
5 rue de Verdun, Vincelles, 51700 Dormans,
phone: 26-58-20-04
BOIZEL (CHAMPAGNE)
14-16 rue de Bernon, 51200 Epernay,
phone: 26-55-21-51
BOLLINGER J. (CHAMPAGNE)
BP4, 51160 Ay, phone: 26-50-12-34
BONNET F. PERE & FILS
route du Mesnil, Oger, 51190 Avize,
phone: 26-57-52-43
BOUCHE PERE & FILS (CHAMPAGNE)
10 rue du Général de Gaulle, 51200 Epernay,
phone: 26-54-12-44
BRETON FILS (INGE BRETON)
12 rue courte-Pilate, Congy, 51270 Montfort,
phone: 26-59-31-03
BRICOUT & CIE
29 Rempart du Midi, 51190 Avize,
phone: 26-57-26-57
CANARD DUCHENE (CHAMPAGNE)
89 rue de la Faisanderie, 75116 Paris,

phone: 45-03-21-31
CATTIER (CHAMPAGNE)
6-11 rue Dom Pérignon, Rilly la Montagne,
51500 Chigny les Roses, phone: 26-03-42-11
CAVEAU BUGISTE (LE)
Vongnes, 01350 Culoz, phone: 79-87-92-37
CHARBAUT & FILS (CHAMPAGNE)
17 avenue de Champagne, BP150, 51250
Epernay Cedex, phone: 26-54-37-55
CHARLIER (CHATEAU)
4 rue des Pervenches, Montigny sur Chatillon,
51200 Epernay, phone: 26-58-35-18
CHARPENTIER (CHATEAU)
rue de Rueil, Villiers sur Chatillon,
51200 Epernay, phone: 26-58-05-78
CHEURLIN & FILS
13 rue de la Gare, 10250 Gye sur Seine,
phone: 25-38-20-27
COLLERY (CHATEAU)
2 place de la Libération, 51160 Ay
DE CAZANOVE CHARLES (CHAMPAGNE)
1 rue des Cotelles, 51200 Epernay,
phone: 26-54-23-46
DESMOULINS A. (CHAMPAGNE)
44 avenue Foch, BP10, 51200 Epernay,
phone: 26-54-24-24
DEVAUX A. (CHAMPAGNE)
Domaine de Villeneuve, BP117, 10110 Bar sur
Seine, phone: 25-29-85-57
FEUILLATTE NICOLAS (CHAMPAGNE)
BP 210, Chouilly, 51200 Epernay,
phone: 26-54-50-60
FREZIER (CHATEAU)
8 rue Poittevin, Monthelon, 51200 Epernay,
phone: 26-59-70-16
GAILLOT (CHATEAU)
12 rue de la Liberté, 51200 Epernay,
phone: 26-55-31-42
GONET SULCOVA
13 rue Henri Martin, 51200 Epernay,
phone: 26-54-37-63
GOSSET
69 rue Jules Blondeau, BP7, 51160 Ay,
phone: 26-55-14-18
HEIDSIECK & CO MONOPOLE
83 rue Coquebert, 51100 Reims,
phone: 26-07-39-34
HEIDSIECK CHARLES S.A. (CHAMPAGNE)
46 rue de la Justice, 51100 Reims,
phone: 26-40-16-13
HOSTOMME (CHATEAU)
5 rue de l'Allée, Chouilly, 51200 Epernay,
phone: 26-55-40-79
HUSSON J.P.
2 rue Jules Lobet, 51160 Ay,
phone: 26-55-43-05
JACQUART (CHATEAU)
6 avenue de la République, Le Mesnil sur Oger,
51190 Avize, phone: 26-57-94-06
KRUG, VINS FINS DE CHAMPAGNE

5 rue Coquebert, 51100 Reims,
phone: 26-88-24-24
LAUNOIS (CHATEAU)
3 avenue de la république, Le Mesnil sur Oger,
51190 Avize, phone: 26-57-50-15
LE BRUN (CHATEAU)
17 route d'Epernay, Cuis, 51200 Epernay,
phone: 26-55-12-35
LECLERC-BRIANT (CHAMPAGNE)
Cumières, 51200 Epernay, phone: 26-54-45-33
LENOBLE A.R. (CHAMPAGNE)
35 rue Paul Douce, 51480 Damery,
phone: 26-58-42-60
LOPEZ MARTIN
Les côtes de l'Hery, Hautvilliers, 51160 Ay,
phone: 26-59-42-17
MAILLY CHAMPAGNE, SOCIETES DE
PRODUCTEURS
51500 Mailly Champagne, phone: 26-49-41-10
MAIZIERES GEORGES
1 rue du stade, Trépail, 51150 Tours sur Marne,
phone: 26-57-05-04
MARTEL
4 rue Paul Bert, 51318 Epernay,
phone: 26-51-06-33
MARTIN BRICE, CHAMPAGNE BARANCOURT
place Tritant, BP3, Bouzy, 51150 Tours sur
Marne, phone: 26-57-00-67
MARTIN PAUL LOUIS (CHAMPAGNE)
3 rue d'Ambonnay, 51150 Bouzy
MERCIER (CHAMPAGNE)
73 avenue du Champagne, 51200 Epernay,
phone: 26-51-74-74
MIGNON PIERRE
5 rue des Grappes d'Or, Le Breuil,
51210 Montmirail, phone: 26-59-22-03
MOET & CHANDON (CHAMPAGNE)
18 avenue de Champagne, 51200 Epernay,
phone: 26-54-71-11
MOREAU (CHATEAU)
rue du Moulin, Vandières, 51700 Dormans,
phone: 26-58-01-64
MUMM G.H. & CIE
34 rue du Champs de Mars, 51100 Reims,
phone: 26-40-22-73
NOWACK (CHATEAU)
15 rue Bailly, Vandières, 51700 Dormans,
phone: 26-58-02-69
PAILLARD BRUNO (CHAMPAGNE)
rue Jacques Maritain, 51100 Reims,
phone: 26-36-20-22
PERRIER LAURENT (CHAMPAGNE)
avenue de Champagne, 51150 Tours sur
Marne, phone: 26-50-67-22
POMMELET MICHEL
5 rue des Longs Champs, Fleury la Rivière,
51200 Epernay, phone: 26-58-41-04
RENAUDIN R. (CHAMPAGNE)
Moussy, 51200 Epernay, phone: 26-54-03-41
ROCOURT (CHATEAU)

1 rue des Zalieux, Le Mesnil sur Oger,
51190 Avize, phone: 26-57-94-99
ROEDERER LOUIS
21 boulevard Lundy, BP66, 51100 Reims,
phone: 26-47-59-81
ROGER POL & CIE
1 rue Henri Lelarge, 51200 Epernay,
phone: 26-55-41-95
ROGUE (CHATEAU)
15 rue du Général Leclerc, 51150 Vertus,
phone: 26-52-15-68
RUINART PERE & FILS (CHAMPAGNE)
4 rue de Crayères, 51100 Reims,
phone: 26-40-26-60
SENEZ C. (CHAMPAGNE)
10360 Fontette
THIENOT ALAIN (CHAMPAGNE)
14 rue des Moissons, 51100 Reims,
phone: 26-47-41-25
TISSERAND G. (CHAMPAGNE JEANMAIRE)
12 rue Roger-Godart, BP256, 51207 Epernay
Cedex, phone: 26-54-60-32
VERGER (CHATEAU DU)
15 rue de Champagne, Moussy, 51200 Epernay,
phone: 26-54-03-54
VESSELLE GEORGES
16 rue des Postes, 51150 Bouzy,
phone: 26-57-00-15
VEUVE CLICQUOT-PONSARDIN
(CHAMPAGNE)
1 place des Droits de l'Homme, 51100 Reims,
phone: 26-47-33-60

COTES DU RHONE
ASSEMAT J.C., DOMAINE DES GUARRIGUES
30150 Roquemaure, phone: 66-82-65-52
BARGE PIERRE
route de Boucharet, 69420 Ampuis,
phone: 74-56-10-80
BAROUX G., CHATEAU DE BOURDINES
84700 Sorgues, phone: 90-39-36-77
BRUGUIER-DUCROS
chemin des Bracoules, 30210 Vers Pont du
Gard, phone: 66-22-85-79
CARTIER J.P., DOMAINE LES GOUBERT
84190 Gigondas, phone: 90-65-86-38
CHAMP ROBERT, DOMAINE DE CHANABAS
84420 Piolenc, phone: 90-37-63-59
COMBE P., DOMAINE DE TENON
84150 Violes, phone: 90-70-93-29
COMBE R. & FILS, DOMAINE LA FOURMONE
route de Bollène, 84190 Vacqueyras,
phone: 90-65-86-05
COTE-ROTIE DE VALLOUIT
24 avenue Désiré Valette, 26240 St Vallier,
phone: 75-23-10-11
COTEAUX DE FOURNES (CAVE
COOPERATIVE LES)
30210 Fournes, phone: 66-37-02-36
D'OLLINE P.
84330 Le Barroux, phone: 90-62-33-09

DARONA & FILS, LES FAURES
07130 St Peray, phone: 75-40-34-11
DEGOUL R. & FILS, CHATEAU DE
BOUCHASSY
30150 Roquemaure, phone: 66-50-12-49
ENTREFAUX (DOMAINE DES)
quartier de la Beaume-Chanos-Curson,
26600 Tain l'Hermitage, phone: 75-07-33-38
FESCHET & FILS, DOMAINE DU PETIT
BARBARAS
26790 Bouchet, phone: 75-04-80-02
FUMAT ANDRE
rue des Bouviers, 07130 Cornas,
phone: 75-40-42-84
GAEC DE LA SYRAH
Quartier de la Beaume, Chanos-Curson,
26600 Tain l'Hermitage
GARAGNON & FILS, DOMAINE DU GROS
PATA
84110 Vaison la Romaine, phone: 90-36-23-75
GARDINE (CHATEAU DE LA)
84230 Château Neuf du Pape,
phone: 90-23-73-20
GONON PIERRE
rue des Launays, 07300 Mauves,
phone: 75-08-07-95
GRANGEON P. & D., DOMAINE LE
PARANDOU
route d'Avignon, 84110 Sablet,
phone: 90-46-90-52
KLEIN F., DOMAINE DE REMEJEANNE
30200 Cadignac, phone: 66-89-69-95
LA FAGOTIERE, DOMAINE PALESTOR
84100 Orange, phone: 90-34-51-81
LATOUR E., DOMAINE DE L'ESPIGOUETTE
84150 Violes, phone: 90-70-92-55
LEYDIER & FILS, DOMAINE DE DURBAN
84190 Beaumes de Venise, phone: 90-62-94-26
MARTIN F & H, DOMAINE DE
GRANGENEUVE
84150 Jonquières, phone: 90-70-62-62
MAUBERT B., DOMAINE LA VERRIERE
84220 Goult, phone: 90-72-20-88
MONT-REDON (DOMAINE DE)
84230 Château Neuf du Pape,
phone: 90-83-72-75
MONTMIRAIL (CHATEAU DE)
cours St Assart, BP12, 84190 Vacqueyras
NERTHE (CHATEAU DE LA)
route de Sorgues, 84230 Château Neuf du
Pape, phone: 90-83-70-11
PAYAN A., DOMAINE DES MOULINS
30650 Saze, phone: 90-31-70-43
PERE ANSELME (J.P. BROTTE)
BP1, 84230 Château Neuf du Pape,
phone: 90-83-70-07
REMEZIERES (DOMAINE DES)
route de Romans, 26600 Mercurol,
phone: 75-07-44-28
RIQUE P., DOMAINE DE ROQUEBRUNE

30130 St Alexandre, phone: 66-39-27-41

ROUDIL F., DOMAINE DU VIEUX RELAIS
rue Frédéric Mistral, 30126 Tavel,
phone: 66-50-36-52

ROUSSIN LEO, DOMAINE DE FUZIERE
84600 Valréas, phone: 90-35-05-15

SABON AIME, DOMAINE DE LA JANASSE
chemin du Moulin, 84350 Courthezon,
phone: 90-70-86-29

SAHUC A., DOMAINE DE LA GRAND'RIBE
route de Bollène, 84290 St Cécile les Vignes,
phone: 90-30-83-75

TAIN L'HERMITAGE (CAVE COOPERATIVE DE
VINS FINS DE)
22 route de Larnage, BP3, 26600 Tain
l'Hermitage, phone: 75-08-20-87

TERRASSE YVES, DOMAINE DU ROURE
07700 St Marcel d'Ardèche, phone: 75-04-67-67

THOMPSON N., DOMAINE DE L'AMEILLAUD
84290 Cairanne, phone: 90-30-82-02

VERNAY GORGES
1 route Nationale, 69420 Condrieu,
phone: 74-59-52-22

VIGNERONS ARDECHOIS
07120 Ruoms, phone: 75-93-50-55

VIGNERONS DE TAVEL (CAVE DES)
30126 Tavel, phone: 66-50-03-57

VINSON D., DOMAINE DU MOULIN
26110 Vinsobres

LANGUEDOC AND ROUSSILLON

ABELANET JEAN
11510 Fitou, phone: 68-45-71-93

AZAIS S., CHATEAU CABEZAC
Bize-Minervois, 11120 Ginestas,
phone: 68-27-02-57

BACOU J., CHATEAU DU ROC
11700 Montbrun Corbières, phone: 68-43-94-48

BERGES-GRULET, REVERDY
11200 Boutenac, phone: 68 27 07 86

BERTRAND GEORGES
11200 St André de Roquelongue,
phone: 68 45 10 43

BIGORRE MICHEL
11100 Narbonne, phone: 68 41 28 16

BOURDEL H., DOMAINE DU COMBAREL
34360 Assignan, phone: 67-38-04-43

C.A.T. CHATEAU LASTOURS
11490 Portel les Corbières, phone: 68 48 29 17

CAVE PILOTE
11360 Villeneuve les Corbières,
phone: 68-45-91-59

CELLA VINARIA
La Livinière, 34210 Olonzac,
phone: 68-43-42-67

COLOMER PAUL & LOUIS
11350 Tuchan, phone: 68-45-46-34

COMTE HENRI DE COLBERT, CHATEAU
FLAUGERGUES
1744 route de Maugio, 34000 Montpellier,
phone: 67-65-51-72

CONDAMINE BERTRAND (CHATEAU LA)
34320 Paulhan, phone: 67-24-46-01

COSTOS ROUSSOS
11160 Trausse Minervois, phone: 68-78-31-15

COTEAUX DU HAUT MINERVOIS
34210 La Livinière, phone: 68-91-42-67

DAURAT-FORT R., CHATEAU DE NOUVELLES
11350 Tuchan, phone: 68-45-40-03

DE CIBIENS J., SC DOMAINE DE CABRIAC
11700 Douzens, phone: 68 77 16 12

DE THELIN JEAN, CHATEAU DE BLOMAC
11700 Douzens, phone: 68-79-01-54

DE VOLONTAT LES PALAIS
11220 St Laurent de la Cabrerisse,
phone: 68 44 01 63

ENGARRAN (CHATEAU DE L')
34880 Laverune, phone: 67-27-60-89

ETANG DES COLOMBES (CHATEAU)
11200 Lezignan Corbières, phone: 68-27-00-03

FABRE L., DOMAINE LAUBRE-FARENT
11120 Ginestas, phone: 68-46-26-93

FABRE LOUIS, CHATEAU FABRE-GASPARETS
11200 Boutenac, phone: 68 27 07 87

FAIVRE LIONEL, CHATEAU DE CARAGUILHES
11220 St Laurent de la Cabrerisse,
phone: 68 43 62 05

FITOU (CAVES DE PRODUCTEURS DE)
Les Cabanes de Fitou, 11510 Fitou,
phone: 68-45-71-41

FOUNTGRAVES (CHATEAU DE)
34270 Fontanes, phone: 67-55-28-94

G.A.E.C. DU REVEREND
11350 Cucugnan, phone: 68 45 98 45

GAU MARIE-HELENE
11800 Trèbes, phone: 68 79 00 69

GAUTHIER-TREILLES JEAN
11510 Fitou, phone: 68-45-71-52

GILLES PAUL, DOMAINE DE MAS COMBET
34130 Maugio, phone: 67-29-32-70

GREZAN (CHATEAU DE)
34480 Laurens, phone: 67-90-28-23

GUY F. & PEYRE S., CHATEAU COUJAN
34490 Murviel les Béziers, phone: 67-37-80-00

JONQUERES D'ORIOLA, CHATEAU DE
CORNEILLA
66200 Corneilla Del Vercol, phone: 68-22-12-56

LABOUCARIE YVES
Boutenac, 11200 Lezignan-Corbières,
phone: 68 27 03 63

LEMARIE FRANCOIS
11200 Thézan des Corbières,
phone: 68 43 32 71

MAITRES VIGNERONS
66720 Tautavel, phone: 68-29-12-03

MANDOURELLE (DOMAINE DE)
Villeseque les Corbières, 11360 Durban,
phone: 68-45-90-92

MESURBEZY-CARTIER, CHATEAU LES
OLLIEUX
Montseret, 11200 Lezignan Corbières,

phone: 68-43-32-61

MOUJAN (CHATEAU)
11100 Narbonne, phone: 68-32-01-25

MOUREAU MARCEAU, CHATEAU DE
VILLERAMBERT
11160 Caunes Minervois, phone: 68-26-40-26

MULLER-ANDRADA, DOMAINE DU TEMPLE
Cabrières, 34800 Clermont l'Herault,
phone: 67-96-07-98

ORMIERES JEAN-PIERRE, CHATEAU DE FABAS
11800 Laure Minervois, phone: 68-78-17-82

PALAIS (CHATEAU LES)
St Laurent de la Carbrerisse, 11200 Lagrasse,
phone: 68-44-01-63

PANIS-MIAHLE, CHATEAU DU DONJON
Bagnoles, 11600 Conques Orbiel,
phone: 68-77-18-33

RAMI NANCLARES
Ciceron, 11200 Ribaute, phone: 68 43 13 10

REMAURY MARC, DOMAINE DU PECH-
D'ANDRE
34210 Azillanet, phone: 68-91-22-66

ST AURIOL (CHATEAU)
11220 Lagrasse, phone: 68 43 13 31

ST LAURENT (CAVE COOPERATIVE DE)
11200 Lagrasse, phone: 68 44 02 73

STE COOPERATIVE AGRICOLE DE
VINIFICATION
Embres & Castelmaure, 11360 Durban,
phone: 68 45 91 83

SURBEZY-CARTIER
Montseret, 11200 Lezignan-Corbières,
phone: 68 43 32 61

UNION DES CAVES DES CORBIERES
11490 Portel les Corbières, phone: 68 48 28 05

VITICULTEURS REUNIS (LES)
Escales, 11200 Lezignan-Corbières,
phone: 68 27 31 44

VOULTE-GASPARETS (DOMAINE DE LA)
11200 Boutenac, phone: 68-27-07-86

PROVENCE

ARCOISE (CAVE COOPERATIVE DE L')
83460 Les Arcs sur Argens, phone: 94-73-30-29

BAGNIS J. & FILS, CHATEAU DE CREMAT
442 chemin de Crémat, 06200 Nice,
phone: 93-37-80-30

BOISSEAUX COLETTE, CHATEAU VANNIERES
83740 La Cadière d'Azur, phone: 94-29-31-19

BONTOUX-BODIN J.J., MAS DE
FONTBLANCHE
route de Carnoux, 13260 Cassis,
phone: 42-01-01-62

BRONZO L. & M., LA BASTIDE BLANCHE
Ste Anne du Castelet, 83330 Le Bausset,
phone: 94-90-63-20

BRUN F., DOMAINE DE BRIGUE
2 place Pasteur, 83340 Le Luc en Provence,
phone: 94-60-74-38

BRUNET G., CHATEAU VIGNELAURE
route de Jouques, 83560 Rians,

phone: 94-80-31-93
BUNAN PIERRE & PAUL, MOULIN DES
COSTES & MAS DE LA ROUVIERE
83740 La Cadière d'Azur, phone: 94-98-72-76
CHATIN J., MAS DE LA DAME
Les Baux de Provence, 13520 Maussane,
phone: 90-54-32-24
COMTE DEYDIER DE PIERREFEU, CHATEAU
DE GAIROIRD
83390 Cuers, phone: 94-48-50-60
CROISY, CHATEAU ROBERNIER
83570 Montfort, phone: 94-64-49-11
DE LOUVENCOURT MICHEL, DOMAINE DE
LA NAVARRE
83260 La Crau, phone: 94-66-73-10
DOMAINE DE RASQUE DE LAVAL, CHATEAU
STE ROSELINE
83460 Les Arcs sur Argens, phone: 94-73-32-57
DUFFORT G., DOMAINE DE L'HERMITAGE
Le Rouve, 83330 Le Bausset,
phone: 94-98-71-31
DUTHEILDE LA ROCHERE F., CHATEAU STE
ANNE
Ste Anne d'Evenos, 83330 Le Bausset,
phone: 94-90-35-40
DYENS-GIRAUD, CHATEAU DE ROUX
Cannet des Maures, 83340 Le Luc en Provence,
phone: 94-60-73-10
ESTIENNE J., DOMAINE LA LAIDIERE
Ste Anne d'Evenos, 83330 Le Bausset,
phone: 94-90-37-07
FERRARI S., DOMAINE DE LA MALHERBE
83230 Bormes les Mimosas,
phone: 94-64-80-11
GARRASSAN A., DOMAINE DE LA VERNEDE
83170 Puget sur Argens, phone: 94-51-22-55
GRUEY N., CHATEAU GREAND'BOISE
BP2, 13530 Trets, phone: 42-29-22-95
GUERARD, CHATEAU MONTAGNE
83390 Pierrefeu, phone: 94-28-68-58
GUINAND, DOMAINE DE LA GARNAUDE
83590 Gonfaron, phone: 94-78-20-42
IMBERT CHRISTIAN, DOMAINE DE
TORRIACIA
20137 Leci de Porto Vecchio,
phone: 95-71-43-50
LAFRAN VEYROLLES (DOMAINE)
route de l'Argile, 83740 La Cadière d'Azur,
phone: 94-90-13-37
LEMAITRE PIERRE, DOMAINE DE
PEISSONNEL
83550 Vidauban, phone: 94-73-02-96
LORQUES R., DOMAINE DU JAS D'ESCLANS
route de Callas, 83920 La Motte,
phone: 94-70-27-86
MARGAN J.P., CHATEAU DE LA CANORGUE
84480 Bonnieux, phone: 90-75-91-01
MEULNART G., DOMAINE DE LA BERNARDE
83340 Le Luc en Provence, phone: 94-73-51-31
NEGREL G., MAS DE CADENET

Mas de Cadenet, 13530 Trets,
phone: 42-29-21-59
OTT (DOMAINE)
22 boulevard d'Aiguillon, 06600 Antibes,
phone: 93-34-38-91
PAGANELLI A.M., DOMAINE DE
CRESSONNIERE
RN97, 83790 Pignans, phone: 94-48-85-80
PARET F., LA FERME BLANCHE
BP57, 13260 Cassis, phone: 42-01-00-74
PINATEL CONRAD, CHATEAU DE MILLE
84400 Apt, phone: 90-74-11-94
PLAUCHUT E., DOMAINE DE GRANDPRE
83750 Puget Ville, phone: 94-48-32-16
PORTALIS, CHATEAU PRADEAUX
83270 St Cyr sur Mer, phone: 94-29-10-74
REILLANNE (DOMAINE DE)
route de St Tropez, 83340 Cannet les Maures,
phone: 94-60-73-31
RIGORD Y. & F., COMMANDERIE DE
PEYRASSOL
Flassans, 83340 Le Luc en Provence,
phone: 94-69-71-02
ROUGIER R., CHATEAU SIMONE
Meyreul, 13590 Palette, phone: 42-28-92-58
SALLIER F., CHATEAU DE VAUCLAIRE
13650 Meyrargues d'Aix en Provence,
phone: 42-57-51-44
ST ANDRE DE FIGUIERE (DOMAINE)
83250 La Londe, phone: 94-66-92-10
SUMEIRE REGINE, CHATEAU BARBEYROLLES
83580 Gassin, phone: 94-56-33-58
TERRES BLANCHES
RN99 , 13210 St Rémy de Provence,
phone: 90-95-91-66
VALLONGUE (DOMAINE DE LA)
BP4, 13810 Eycalières, phone: 90-95-91-70
JURA AND SAVOY
BRUGUIER DUCROS, DOMAINE DE
VALSENIERE
chemin des Bracoules, 30210 Vers Pont du
Gard, phone: 66-22-85-79
BULABOIS G., CAVEAU DU VIEUX PRESSOIR
Pupillin, 39600 Arbois, phone: 84-66-02-61
CHAMPAGA (DOMAINE)
84330 Le Barroux, phone: 90-62-43-09
COTEAUX DE FOPURNES (CAVE
COOPERATIVE LES)
30210 Fournes, phone: 66-37-02-36
DEGOUL ROBERT & FILS, CHATEAU DE
BOUCHASSY
30150 Roquemaure, phone: 66-50-12-49
DUPASQUIER
Aimavigne, 73170 Jongieux,
phone: 79-44-02-23
GRAND FRERES
Passenans, 39230 Sellières, phone: 84-85-28-88
KLEIN F., DOMAINE DE LA REMEJEANNE
30200 Cadignac, phone: 66-89-69-95
LAC ST ANDRE (CAVEAU DU)

St André les Marches, 73800 Montmelian,
phone: 79-28-13-32
LATOUR EDMOND, DOMAINE DE
L'ESPIGOUETTE
84150 Violes, phone: 90-70-92-55
MAUBERT B., DOMAINE LA VERRIERE
84220 Goult, phone: 90-72-20-88
PAYAN ANDRE, DOMAINE DES MOULINS
30650 Saze, phone: 90-31-70-43
RIQUE PIERRE, DOMAINE DE ROQUEBRUNE
30130 St Alexandre, phone: 66-39-27-41
ROUDIL F., DOMAINE DU VIEUX RELAIS
rue Frédéric Mistral, 30126 Tavel,
phone: 66-50-36-52
VIGNERON SAVOYARD (LE)
Apremont, 73190 Challes les Eaux,
phone: 79-28-33-23
THE LOIRE VALLEY
AGUILAS PIERRE, LES SAULES
49290 Chaudefonds, phone: 41-78-10-68
ALLIAS DANIEL, CLOS DU PETIT-MONT
37210 Vouvray les Vins, phone: 47-52-74-95
AULANIER, CHATEAU DE L'OISELINIERE
44190 Georges, phone: 40 06 91 59
BAHUAUD DONATIEN & CIE
Les Loges, BP1, La Chapelle Heulin,
44330 Vallet, phone: 40-06-70-05
BALLAND CHAPUIS JOSEPH (DOMAINE)
La Croix St Laurent, BP24, Bue,
18300 Sancerre, phone: 48-54-06-67
BARRE BERNARD, DOMAINE DE LA
GACHETIERE
49320 Brissac, phone: 41-91-25-43
BAUD (S.A.)
Le Port, 44690 La Haya Fouassière,
phone: 40 33 98 42
BELIN DANIEL, LES TOUCHES COUTURES
49320 Coutures, phone: 41-54-22-26
BIDET A., LES ERABLES
66 Grande Rue, 49190 Rablay sur Layon,
phone: 41-78-32-68
BLANLOEIL & FILS
La Huperie, 44690 Monnières,
phone: 40 54 60 57
BOIS BRULEY (DOMAINE DU)
44115 Basse Goulaine, phone: 40-34-52-91
BONHOMME AUGUSTE
1 rue de la Roche, 44190 Georges,
phone: 40 06 91 61
BONNARD B. (DOMAINE)
Les Chailloux, route de Chavignol,
18300 Sancerre, phone: 48-54-17-47
BONNET PIERRE, DOMAINE DE LA
BRONIERE
44330 Vallet, phone: 40 36 35 22
BOSSIS LAURENT
11 rue Beauregard, 44690 St Fiacre sur Maine,
phone: 40 36 94 94
BOURGEOIS H. (DOMAINE)
Chavignol, 18300 Sancerre, phone: 48-54-21-67

BROSSEAU ROBERT, DOMAINE DES MORTIERS GOBAIN
44690 La Haya Fouassière, phone: 40 54 80 66

CAILLEAU FRANCIS & PASCAL, VIGNOBLE DU SAUVEROY
49190 St Lambert du Lattay,
phone: 41-78-30-59

CHENOUARD PIERRE
1 route de Clisson, 44330 Vallet,
phone: 40 33 92 80

CHEREAU-CARRE, CHATEAU DE CHASSELOIR
44690 St Fiacre, phone: 40-54-81-15

CHON GILBERT & FILS, CHATEAU DE LA JOUSSELINIERE
44450 St Julien de Concelles,
phone: 40 54 11 08

CLOS LA CHATELLENIE
18 rue St Martin, BP13, 18300 Sancerre,
phone: 48-54-21-50

CLOS LA PERRIERE (CAVE DU)
Verdigny, BP47, 18300 Sancerre,
phone: 48-54-16-93

COCHARD & FILS, DOMAINE DE MICHOUDY
49121 Aubigne Briand, phone: 41-59-46-52

COMTE BERNARD DE COLBERT, CHATEAU DE BREZE
49260 Breze, phone: 41-51-62-06

COMTE DE MALESTROIT, CHATEAU LA NOE
44330 Vallet, phone: 40 33 92 72

COULY RENE (DOMAINE)
12 rue Diderot, 37500 Chinon,
phone: 47-93-05-84

DABIN JEAN & FILS, DOMAINE DE GRAS MOUTON-LE BOURG
44690 St Fiacre sur Maine, phone: 40 54 81 01

DE THUY M., CHATEAU DE MONTREUIL
49260 Montreuil Bellay, phone: 41-52-33-06

DEHEUILLER C., DOMAINE DES VARINELLES
28 rue du Ruau, 49400 Varrains,
phone: 41-52-90-94

DENERICHE ALAIN, DOMAINE DE LA PETITE CROIX
49380 Thouarce, phone: 41-91-45-00

DOMAINE DE LA LOUVETERIE
Les Brandières, 44690 La Haya Fouassière,
phone: 40 54 83 27

DUMONT A. (DOMAINE DU MORILLY)
Cravant les Coteaux, 37500 Chinon,
phone: 47-93-06-86

EPIRE (CHATEAU D')
Epire, 49170 St Georges sur Loir,
phone: 41-77-16-23

FONTAINE AUDON (DOMAINE LA)
Bannay, 18300 Sancerre, phone: 48-72-40-97

FRESCHE (DOMAINE DU)
Le Fresche, 49620 La Pommeraye,
phone: 41-77-74-63

GAEC AUDOUIN FRERES, DOMAINE DE LA MOMENIERE
44430 Le Landreau, phone: 40 06 43 04

GAEC DES CHAUSSELIERES
12 rue des Vignes, 44330 Le Pallet,
phone: 40 8040 12

GAMBIER J., DOMAINE DES GALUCHES
37140 Bourgueil, phone: 47-97-72-45

GITTON PERE & FILS
Chemin de Lavaud, 18300 Menetreol sous Sancerre, phone: 48-54-38-84

GOIZIL VINCENT, LE PETIT VAL
49380 Chavagnes les Eaux, phone: 41-54-31-14

GUINDON JACQUES
La Couleuverdière, 44150 St Gereon,
phone: 40 83 18 96

HALLEREAU JOSEPH
Les Chaboissières, 44330 Vallet,
phone: 40 33 94 44

HUCHET YVES
La Chauvinière, 44960 Chateau Thebaud,
phone: 40 06 51 90

HUET
Le Haut Lieu, 37210 Vouvray,
phone: 47-52-78-87

JOUSSET & FILS, LOGIS DU PRIEURE
49700 Concourson sur Layon,
phone: 41-59-11-22

LAFFOURCADE M., CHATEAU DE L'ECHARDERIE
49190 Beaulieu sur Layon, phone: 41-78-42-14

LEMORE (DOMAINE)
Le Bourg-Houssay, 41800 Montoire,
phone: 54-85-06-28

LUNEAU PIERRE & REMY, DOMAINE DE LA GRANGE
44430 Le Landreau, phone: 40 06 43 90

MARQUIS DE GOULAINE, CHATEAU DE GOULAINE
Haute-Goulaine, 44115 Basse-Goulaine,
phone: 40-54-91-42

MARTIN MARCEL
La Sablette, 44330 Mouzillon,
phone: 40 33 94 84

MORON F., DOMAINE DES MAURIERES
8 rue de Perinelle, 49190 St Lambert du Lattay,
phone: 41-78-30-21

MOULINS A VENT (CAVES LES)
39 avenue de la Thuilerie, 58150 Pouilly sur Loire, phone: 86-39-10-99

MOUSSIERE (DOMAINE LA)
3 rue Porte César, BP18, 18300 Sancerre,
phone: 48-54-07-41

NOGUE LOUIS, CHATEAU DES GUILLIERES
44690 La Haya Fouassière, phone: 40 34 02 57

NOZET (CHATEAU DU)
Domaine de la Doucette, 58150 Pouilly sur Loire, phone: 86-39-10-16

OCTAVIE (DOMAINE)
Marcé Oisly, 41700 Contres,
phone: 54-79-54-57

OGEREAU FILS, DOMAINE DE LA PIERRE BLANCHE

44 rue de la Belle Angevine, 49190 St Lambert du Lattay, phone: 41-78-30-53

PAPIN CHRISTIAN, DOMAINE DES HAUTES PERCHES
49320 Ste Melaine sur Aubance,
phone: 41-91-15-20

PAULAT A., COTEAUX DU GIENNOIS
Villemoison, 58200, phone: 86-28-22-39

PELTIER JACQUES, DOMAINE DE BREILLANT
49560 Passavant sur Layon, phone: 41-59-51-32

PETIT THOUARS (CHATEAU DU)
Le Petit Thouars, St Germain sur Vienne,
37500 Chinon, phone: 47-95-96-40

PIERRIS (CAVES DES)
Champtin, Crezancy en Sancerre,
18300 Sancerre, phone: 48-79-02-84

PINARD & FILS
Le Bourg, Bue, 18300 Sancerre,
phone: 48-54-33-89

REBEILLEAU J.P. & A., DOMAINE DES RAYNIERES
33 rue du Ruau, 49400 Varrains,
phone: 41-52-95-17

REMPARTS (CAVEAU DES)
Remparts des Abreuvoirs, 18300 Sancerre,
phone: 48-54-03-08

ROCHE AUX MOINES (DOMAINE DE LA)
La Roche aux Moines, 49170 Savennières,
phone: 41-72-21-33

ROLANDEAU, CAVE DE LA FREMONDERIE
49230 Tillières, phone: 41 70 45 93

RONCEE (DOMAINE DU)
Panzoult, 37220 L'Ile Bouchard,
phone: 47-58-53-01

ROULEAU EMILE, DOMAINE DE L'ARCHE
49700 Concourson sur Layon,
phone: 41-59-11-61

SANCERRE (CHATEAU DE)
Marnier Lapostolle, 18300 Sancerre,
phone: 48-54-07-15

SANZAY-LEGRAND P., DOMAINE DES SANZAY
93 Grande Rue, 49400 Varrains,
phone: 41-52-91-30

SAUTEJEAU MARCEL, DOMAINE DE L'HYVERNIERE
44330 Le Pallet, phone: 40 06 73 83

SAUVION & FILS, CHATEAU DU CLERAY
BP3, 44330 Vallet, phone: 40 36 22 55

SCEA DU DOMAINE DES COSSARDIERES
Les Cossardières, 44430 Le Landreau,
phone: 40 06 43 22

SCHAEFFER J. N., DOMAINE DE LA HAUTE-MAISON
44860 St Agnan de Grand, phone: 40-31-01-83

THEBAUD GABRIEL
La Hautière, 44690 St Fiacre sur Maine,
phone: 40 54 81 13

TIJOU PIERRE-YVES, DOMAINE DE LA SOUCHERIE

49190 Beaulieu sur Layon, phone: 41-78-31-18
VIGNERONS (CAVES DES)
Route du Saumoussay, St Cyr en Bourg,
49260 Montreuil Bellay, phone: 41-51-61-09
VIGNERONS DE LA NOELLE
BP102 , 44157 Ancenis cedex,
phone: 40 98 92 72
VIGNERONS DE SAUMUR (CAVE DES)
49260 St Cyr en Bourg, phone: 41-51-61-09
VINET D.G., LA QUILLA LA CROIX-
MORICEAU
44690 La Haya Fouassière, phone: 40 54 88 96
VINS DE POITOU (CAVE COOPERATIVE DES)
32 rue Alphonse Plault, 86170 Neuville de
Poitou, phone: 49-51-21-65
VINS DE SANCERRE (CAVE COOPERATIVE
LES)
Avenue de Verdun, 18300 Sancerre,
phone: 48-54-19-24

THE SOUTH-WEST

AILLOUD JEAN-LOUIS, DOMAINE DE
PIALENTOU
81600 Gaillac, phone: 63-57-17-99
ALARD
24240 Monbazillac, phone: 53-57-30-43
ALDHUY BERNARD, FANTOU
46220 Prayssac, phone: 65-30-61-85
ALMON JEAN, CHATEAU DE FRAUSSEILLES
Frausseilles, 81170 Cordes, phone: 63-56-06-28
ALQUIER FRANCIS, MAS DE GROUZE
81800 Rabastens, phone: 63-33-80-70
ARMAGNAT CHRISTIAN, LAMARIE
46140 Luzech, phone: 65-30-74-24
BALDES & FILS, TRIGUEDINA
46700 Puy l'Evèque, phone: 65-21-30-81
BANIZETTE
24230 Nastringues, phone: 53-24-77-72
BELON ALAIN , BEGOUX
46000 Cahors, phone: 65-35-57-46
BERGERAC (CAVE DE)
Boulevard de l'Entrepot, 24100 Bergerac,
phone: 53-58-32-82
BESSET CLAIRE, LAGERIE
46700 Puy l'Evèque, phone: 65-21-33-94
BEZIOS J.M., LA CROIX DES MARCHANDS
Le Rivet, Montans, 81600 Gaillac,
phone: 63-57-19-71
BOULOUMIE A., LES CAMBOUS
46220 Prayssac, phone: 65-30-61-69
BOURDINE (CHATEAU DE)
Route d'Entraigues, 84700 Sorgues,
phone: 90-83-36-77
BOUYSSET R., LES CARIS
46220 Prayssac, phone: 65-30-61-74
BURC R. & FILS, DOMAINE DE LA PINERAIE
Leygues, 46700 Puy l'Evèque, phone:
65-30-82-07
CANDIA F., BALAGES
Lagrave, 81150 Marssac sur Tarn,
phone: 63-57-74-48

CAVE COOPERATIVE
24240 Monbazillac, phone: 53-57-06-38
CAZOTTES J., LES TERRISSES
St Laurent, 81600 Gaillac, phone: 63-57-09-15
CLOS DE GAMOT
46220 Prayssac, phone: 65-22-40-26
COURSIERES E., DOMAINE DE GRADD
Campagnac, 81140 Castelnau de Montmiral,
phone: 63-33-12-61
COURT LES MUTS (CHATEAU)
Razac de Saussignac, 24240 Sigoules,
phone: 53-27-92-17
CUNNAC H. & FILS, DOMAINE DE
BERTRAND
Donnazac, 81170 Cordes, phone: 63-56-06-52
DAVID J. & FILS, DOMAINE CLEMENT TERMES
Les Fortis, 81310 Lisle sur Tarn,
phone: 63-57-23-19
DE MESLON J., PLANQUE
24100 Bergerac, phone: 53-58-30-18
DECAS R. & FILS (DOMAINE)
Trespoux Rassiels, 46000 Cahors,
phone: 65-35-37-74
DELPECH R., DOMAINE DE LAVAUR
Soturac, 46700 Puy l'Evèque,
phone: 65-36-56-30
FEYTOUT YVES, DOMAINE DE LA TRUFFIERE
24240 Monbazillac, phone: 53-58-30-23
GALBERT (DOMAINE)
Ingancls, 46700 Puy l'Evèque,
phone: 65-21-32-64
GILIS & FILS, DOMAINE DU PEYRIE
Soturac, 46700 Puy l'Evèque,
phone: 65-36-57-15
HAUT PECHARMANT (DOMAINE DU)
24100 Bergerac, phone: 53-57-29-50
JOUVES J., COYRNOU
St Vincent Rive d'Olt, 46140 Luzech,
phone: 65-20-14-09
LABASTIDE DE LEVIS (CAVE DE
VINIFICATION DE)
RN88, 81600 Gaillac, phone: 63-57-01-30
LAMOUROUX (DOMAINE DE)
La Chapelle Rouss, 64110 Jurançon,
phone: 59-21-74-41
LAMOUROUX J.L., LA POULINE
46700 Puy l'Evèque, phone: 65-21-30-68
LASBOUYGUES R , LES SALLES
Villeseque, 46000 Cahors, phone: 65-36-94-32
LATRILLE PIERRE-YVES, CHATEAU JOLYS
64290 Gan, phone: 59-21-72-79
LECOMTE THIERRY, MATENS
81600 Gaillac, phone: 63-57-43-96
LEY J.R., DOMAINE DES TEMPLIERS
24240 St Michel de Montaigne,
phone: 53-58-63-29
LIBARDE (DOMAINE DE)
Nastringues, 24230 Velines, phone: 53-24-77-72
MARTRENCHARD & FILS, VIGNOBLES DU
MAYNE

24240 Sigoules, phone: 53-58-40-01
MAUREL Y., DOMAINE DES BOUSCAILLOUS
Montels, 81140 Castelnau de Montmiral,
phone: 63-33-18-85
MONBOUCHE MARCEL, LE MARSALET
24100 St Laurent des Vignes,
phone: 53-57-07-07
MONESTIE A., DOMAINE DE MOUSSENS
Cestayrols, 81150 Marssac sur Tarn,
phone: 63-56-81-66
MONTELS C., DOMAINE DES ISSARDS
Amarens, 81170 Cordes, phone: 63-56-08-03
PLAGEOLES ROBERT, DOMAINE DES TRES
CANTOUS
81140 Cahuzac sur Vere, phone: 63-33-90-40
PRODUCTEURS DE JURANCON (CAVES DES)
53 avenue Henri IV, 64290 Gan,
phone: 59-21-57-03
RAYNAL J.P., DOMAINE DE SOULEILLOU
Douelle, 46140 Luzech, phone: 65-20-01-88
RAZ (CHATEAU LE)
24610 St Méard de Gurçon, phone: 53-82-48-41
ROTIER & FILS, DOMAINE DU PETIT NAREYE
Cadalen, 81600 Gaillac, phone: 63-41-75-14
SALVADOR RENE, MATUFLE
46220 Prayssac, phone: 65-22-43-10
SAVARINES (DOMAINE DES)
46090 Trespoux, phone: 65-35-50-55
TECOU (CAVE DE)
Técou, 81600 Gaillac, phone: 63-33-00-80
TIREGANG (CHATEAU DE)
Creysse, 24100 Bergerac, phone: 53-23-21-08
TROIS CLOCHERS (LES)
St Salvyn de Coufens, 81310 Lisle sur Tarn,
phone: 63-57-34-04
UNIDOR
24100 St Laurent des Vignes,
phone: 53-57-40-44
VALIERE J.C., BOVILA
Fargues, 46800 Montcuq, phone: 65-36-91-30
VIDAL (CHATEAU LA BORDERIE)
Monbazillac, 24240 Sigoules,
phone: 53-57-00-36
VINCENS, FOUSSAL
46140 Luzech, phone: 65-30-74-78

Greece

A.V.E.P.A.S.A.
Ag Vassilis, 26500 Patras, phone: (061)993183
ACHAIA CLAUSS WINE CO S.A.
PO Box 51176, 14510 Kifissia Athens,
phone: (01)8075312
ARCHANES WINE-OLIVE OIL AND CREDIT
COOPERATIVE
70100 Archanes Iraklion-Crete,
phone: (081)751814
ARGO WINE APOSTOLAKIS BROS
2nd km Larisis Str, 38000 Volos,
phone: (0421)63579

BABAZIM A. BABAZIM INC.
17 Arkadioupoleos Str, 54632 Thessaloniki,
phone: (031)519705
BIOHYM CITRUS JUICES AND WINE
PRODUCING CO, S.A.
1 Therissou Str, 73100 Chania Crete,
phone: (0821)23861
BOTRYS S.A.
20 Amalias Ave, 10557 Athens,
phone: (01)323331
BOUTARI J. AND SON S.A.
19Th km Athens-Rafina road, Pikermi,
19009 Rafina, phone: (01)6677456
CABEROS HELLENIC TRADING CO.
30-34 Atthidon Str, 17671 Kallithea Athens,
phone: (01)9592039
CAIR S.A.
59A Kapodistriou, Str PO Box 81,
85100 Rhodes, phone: (0241)22385
CALLIGAS J. & G. S.A. "INOEXAGOGIKI"
11 Androutsou Str, 17455 Kalamaki Athens,
phone: (01)9834226
CAMBAS ANDREW P. CAMBAS S.A.
PO Box 3885, 10210 Athens Kantza Attica,
phone: (01)6659779
CAVINO S.A.
44 Alkiviadou Str, 10440 Athens,
phone: (01)8211448
CENTRAL UNION OF CHANIA
N. Plastira Apokoronou, 73100 Chania,
phone: (0821)23034
COOPERATIVE WINERY OF NEMEA
9 N. Ikonomou, 20500 Nemea,
phone: (0746)22896
COOPERATIVES' ASSOCIATION OF THEBES'
VINEGROWERS LTD
PO Box 2, 32200 Thebes, phone: (0262)29096
CRETA OLYMPIAS S.A.
10 Kouskoura Str, 54622 Thessaloniki,
phone: (031)260785
DISTILLERY ZORBALA EV. G. STRAVROU
14 Arethousis, 34100 Chalkis,
phone: (0221)22488
EMERY S.A.
132 Sygrou Ave, 11741 Athens,
phone: (01)9218885
FOTIOS EMM. STRONGILIS GMBH
73 Ionidon, 18537 Piraeus, phone: (01)4511204
FOTOPOULOS NIC. WINES AND SPIRITS
PRODUCING CO
109 G. Pigis, 25100 Egio, phone: (0691)22249
G.E.A.S.A.
6 Platia Kyprou, 71000 Iraklion,
phone: (081)289814
GENKA S.A.
2 Galaxia Str, 11745 Athens,
phone: (01)9232612
KARELAS G. S.A. "OINIKI"
75 Navarinou Str, 26222 Patras,
phone: (061)321000

KISSAMOS G. KOUTSOURELIS S.A.
56 Polykratous Str, 10442 Athens,
phone: (01)5226024
KOURTAKI D. S.A.WINE PRODUCING AND
BOTTLING CO
19003 Markopoulo Attika, phone: (0299)22231
MANZAVINO S.A. KOMITOPOULOS BROS.
WINERY
219 Imittou Ave, 11632 Athens,
phone: (01)7510205
MARKO
19003 Markopoulos Messogia Attikis,
phone: (0299)25210
MINOS CRETAN WINE EXPORT CO
MILIARAKIS BROS
Peza Pediados, 71306 Iraklion,
phone: (081)741213
NICOLAOU D. SONS S.A.
40-42 Paparigopoulou Str Peristeri,
12132 Athens, phone: (01)5719719
PAPAIONNOU A. & G. VINEYARDS-WINERY
20500 Ancient Nemea Corinthias,
phone: (0746)23138
PEZA GROWERS COOPERATIVES
ASSOCIATION
Kalloni, 71000 Iraklion, phone: (081)741202
PORTO CARRAS TOURISTIKI-GEORGIKI-
EXAGOGIKI S.A.
9 Frangini Str, 54624 Thessaloniki,
phone: (031)268626
PRODUCTIVE COOPERATIVE OF NEA
ANCHIALOS "DEMETRA"
37400 N. Anchialos-Volos, phone: (0241)76210
SEMELI AGRICULTURAL AND
TECHNICAL S.A.
16 Pindarou Str, 10673 Athens,
phone: (01)3643581
SPILIOPOULOS B.G. S.A.
7 El Venizelou Av, 17671 Kallithea Athens,
phone: (01)9568455
STRATOS KONIORDOS CO
14 Archelaou Str, 11635 Athens,
phone: (01)7224692
TSANTALIS E. S.A.
PO Box 10600, 54110 Thessaloniki,
phone: (031)239475
UNION DES COOPERATIVES VINICOLES DE
SAMOS
83100 Samos, phone: (0273)27375
UNION OF AGRICULTURAL COOPERATIVES
"TAOL" OF LEFCADE
30 Akarnania Str, 31100 Lefcade,
phone: (0645)22319
UNION OF AGRICULTURAL COOPERATIVES
OF AMYNDEON
2 Sofokleous Str, 53200 Amyndeon,
phone: (0386)22176
UNION OF AGRICULTURAL COOPERATIVES
OF ATTIKI
58 Ippokratous Str, 10680 Athens,

phone: (01)3621740
UNION OF AGRICULTURAL COOPERATIVES
OF IOANNINA
38 Charilaou Trikoupi, 45332 Ioannina,
phone: (0651)26570
UNION OF AGRICULTURAL COOPERATIVES
OF KARDITSA
13 Ag. Titou Str, 712 01 Iraklion,
phone: (081)284325
UNION OF AGRICULTURAL COOPERATIVES
OF PAROS
84400 Paros, phone: (0284)21258
UNION OF AGRICULTURAL COOPERATIVES
OF PATRAS
3 Andrew Str, Pantanassis, 26221 Patras,
phone: (061)277571
UNION OF AGRICULTURAL COOPERATIVES
OF PRODUCTS FROM SANTORINI
84700 Santorini island, phone: (0286)22233
UNION OF AGRICULTURAL COOPERATIVES
OF ZAKYNTHOS
56 Lombardou Str, 29100 Zakynthos,
phone: (0659)22005
UNION OF WINE PRODUCING AND
AGRICULTURAL COOPERATIVES OF SITIA
74 Missonos Str, 72300 Sitia,
phone: (0843)22211
VARVITSIOTIS G. SONS S.A. WINES AND
SPIRITS FACTORY
28 Ioulinaou Str, 10434 Athens,
phone: (01)8229173
WINE COOPERATIVE OF TIRNAVOS
1St km Tirvanos-Larissa road, 40100 Tirvanos,
phone: (0492)22230

Germany

ADMINISTRATION PRINZ FRIEDRICH VON
PREUSSEN
Schloss Reihartshausen, 6228 Eltville Erbach
Rheingau, phone: 6123040009
ANHEUSER PAUL WEINGUT
Stromberger Strasse 15-19, 6550 Bad
Kreuznach, phone: 67128748
ASBACH & CO BRANDY DISTILLERY
Am Rottland 2-10, 6220 Rudesheim Am Rhein,
phone: 6722120
BADISCHER WINZERKELLER
Zum Kaiserstuhl 6, 7814 Breisach,
phone: 7722522
BASSERMANN JORDAN'SCHES WEINGUT
Postfach 120, 6705 Deidesheim,
phone: 63266006
BAYERISCHE
Residenzplatz 3, Postfach 296, 8700 Wurzburg,
phone: 93150701
BLACK TOWER WEIN VERTRIEBSGESE
Mainzerstrasse 57-59, Postfach 1444,
6530 Bingen/Rhein, phone: 67217010
BONNET ALFRED (WEINGUT)

Weinstrasse, 6701 Friedelheim,
phone: 632202162
BROMSERBURG RHEINGAU-UND WEIN
MUSEUM
Rheinstrasse 2, 6720 Rudensheim Am Rhein,
phone: 67222348
BUHL (REISCHSRAT VON)
Weinstrasse 16-24, PO Box 260,
6705 Deidesheim, phone: 63261851
BURGERMEISTER ANTON BALBACH ERBEN
WEINGUT
Mainzerstrasse 64, 6505 Nierstein,
phone: 61335585
BURGERSPITAL ZUM HEILIGEN GEIST
Theaterstrasse 19, 8700 Wurzburg,
phone: 931503634
BURKLIN-WOLF WEINGUT
Weinstrasse 65, 6706 Wachenheim,
phone: 63228955
C.A. KUPFERBERG & CIE.
Kupferberg Terrasse, 6500 Mainz Am Rhein,
phone: 61311051
CASTELL'SCHES FURSTLICH DOMANEMAMT
Schlossplatz 5, 8711 Castell, phone: 932560170
CHARTA-WEINGUTER (WEREINIGUNG DER)
Postfach 1169, 6720 Rudensheim Am Rhein,
phone: 67221027
DATBERG'SCHES WEINGUT PRINZ ZU SALM
Schloss Wallhausen, 6551Wallhausen,
phone: 6706769
DEINHARD & CO
Deinhardplatz 3, 5400 Koblenz,
phone: 2611040
DEMMER JAKOB KG
Rathenaustrasse 16, 6555 Sprendlingen,
phone: 67011825
DEUTSCH EMIL
Amalienstrasse 7-11, 6730 Neustadt,
phone: 63212344
DEUTSCHES WEININSTITUT GMBH
Gutenbergplatz 3-5, 6500 Mainz 1,
phone: 613128290
DEUTSCHES WEINTOR
GEBIETSWINZERGENOSSENSCHAFT
6741 Ilbesheim, phone: 634138150
DOMDECHANT WERNER'SCHES WEINGUT
Rathausstrasse 30, 6203 Hochheim,
phone: 614602008
DR. V. BASSERMANN-JORDAN'SCHES
WEIGUT
Postfach 20, Deidesheim, 6705 Rheinpfalz,
phone: 6326206
DR. ZENZEN WEINHANDEL UND EXPORT
Moselstrasse 61, 5591 Valwig, phone: 2671228
DRATHEN EWALD THEOD.
Auf der Hill, 5584 Alf/Mosel, phone: 65428010
EARATH KLAUS
Bahnhofstrasse 29, 6735 Maikammer,
phone: 63215556
FABER SAAR SEKT KELLEREI

Niedrekircherstrasse 27, 5500 Trier/Mosel,
phone: 6518140
FRANKEN-GEBIETS
WINZERGENOSSENSCHAFT
Postfach 505, 8710 Kitzingen 2,
phone: 932170050
FREIHERR KNYPHAUSEN (WEINGUT)
Klosterhof Drais, 6228 Eltville/Rheingau,
phone: 612362177
GEBIETSWINZERGENOSSENSCHAFT
FRANKEN EG
8710 Kitzingen Repperndorf, phone: 32170050
GEBRUDER WEBER GMBH
Olewiger Strasse 133, 5500 Trier,
phone: 65133058
GEORG BREUER
6720 Rudensheim Am Rhein, phone: 67221027
GESSERT GUSTAV, WEINGUT
Worrstadterstrasse 84, 6505 Nierstein,
phone: 613305642
GROTH U. CONSORTEN
Friendensalle 35, 2000 Hamburg 50,
phone: 40391755
GUNTRUM LOUIS WEINTRADITION 1648
Rheinallee 62, PO 1142, 6505 Nierstein,
phone: 61335101
HAAG FRITZ WEINGUT
Dusemonderhof, 5551 Braunberg/Mosel
HEGER (DR WEINGUT)
Bachenstrasse, 7817 Ihringen 1,
phone: 7766805405
HUESGEN ADOLPH WINES
Am Bahnhof 52-54, 5580 Traben Trabach,
phone: 65419281
ISC INTERNATIONAL SERVICE CENTER
KOELNMESSE
Messeplatz 1, Postfach 210760, 5000 Koeln 21,
phone: 221082112066
JOHANNES KARST & SOHNE
Weingut und Weinkellerei, 6702 Bad
Durkheim, phone: 63222103
JOHANNISHOF (WEINGUT)
Im Grund 63, 6222 Geisenheim Johannisberg,
phone: 67228216
JULIUSSPITAL WEINGUT
Klinikstrasse 5, PO Box 5848, 8700 Wurzburg
1, phone: 9313084147
KAYSER
Am Getraidespeicher 30, 6500 Mainz 1,
phone: 61316190
KENDERMANN HERMANN
Mainzerstrasse 57/59, Postfach 1444,
6530 Bingen/Rhein, phone: 67217010
KOLL J. MOSELWEINKELLERIE
Postfach 1305, 5590 Cochem/Mosel,
phone: 267107066
LANG HANS WEINGUT
Rheinallee 6 , 6228 Eltville Hattenheim,
phone: 67232475
LANGENBACH & CO GMBH

Alzeyerstrasse 31, Postfach 840,
6520 Worms/Rhein, phone: 624150020
LANGGUT ERBEN GMBH & CO
Postfach 120D, 5580 Traben Trabach,
phone: 6541170
LOEWENSTEIN (FURST)
6227 Oestrich Winkel, phone: 672305056
LORCH HEINRICH WEINGUT-WEINKELLEREI
Kurfurstendstrasse 11, PO Box 60, 6748 Bad
Bergzabern, phone: 6343205
MORHENA WINE EXPORT ASS.
Rissbacherstrasse 1 , 5580 Traben Trabach,
phone: 65419041
MOSELLAND EG ZENTRAKELLEREI MOSEL
SAAR RUWER
Bornweise 6, 5550 Bernkastel Kues,
phone: 65316063
MUELLER SCHARZOF WEINGUT
5511 Wiltingen
MULLER EGON WEINGUT
Scharzhof, 5511 Wiltingen, phone: 65012432
NAHE WINZER KELLEREIEN EINGETRAGENE
GENOSSENSCHAFT
Winzenheimerstrasse 30, 6551 Bretzenheim
Nahe, phone: 6712232
NELL CHRISTOPH (WEINGUT)
5501 Kasel im Ruwertal, phone: 65105180
NIKOLAIHOF WEINGUT
3512 Mautern Wachau, phone: 273282901
PAULY DR. BERGWEILER (WEINGUT)
Gestade 15, 5550 Bernkastel Kues,
phone: 130022063
PETER MERTES KG
In der Bornwiese 4, Postfach 1360,
5550 Bernkastel Kues, phone: 6531550
PIEDMONT (WEINGUT OKONOMIERAT)
5503 Konz Filzen
PLODIMEX AUSSENHANDELSGESELISCHAFT
Hans Henny Jahnn Weg 19, 2000 Hamburg 76,
phone: 402271150
PRUM ERBEN, SA PRUM
Ufeallee 25/26, 5550 Bernkastel Kues,
phone: 65313110
RAPPENHOF-WEINGUT DR REINHARD MUTH
6526 Alsheim, phone: 62494015
RAUTENSTRAUCH'SCHE
WEINGUTVERWALTUNG
Warthaenserhof, 5500 Trier-Eitelsnbach,
phone: 6515121
REH CARL WEINKELLEREI
Am Bahnhof , 5501 Leiwen Mosel,
phone: 65074010
REH FRANZ & SHON GMBH & CO
Romerstrasse 27, 5559 Leiwen Mosel,
phone: 65074090
REICHSGRAFF VON KESSELSTATT
(WEINGUT)
Liebfrauenstrasse 9, 5500 Trier/Mosel,
phone: 65175101
RESS BALTHASAR WEINGUTSBESITZER

Rheinallee 7, 6228 Eltville Hattenheim,
phone: 67233011
RESS STEFAN B. KG. WEINKELLEREI
6220 Rudesheim Am Rhein, phone: 672247341
RICHTER MAX FERD. (WEINGUT)
Haupstrasse 37/85, Postfach 27, 5556 Mulheim
Mosel, phone: 6534704
RICHTERSHOF
PO Box 25, 5556 Mulheim Mosel,
phone: 65340702
RUDESHEIMER WEINKELLEREI
Albertistrasse, 6720 Rudensheim Am Rhein,
phone: 672203055
RUDOLF MULLER WEIN UND SETKELLEREI
Postfach 20, 5586 Reil/Mosel, phone: 6532610
SCHAFER MICHAEL (WEINGUT)
Hauptstrasse 15 , 6531 Burg Layen,
phone: 672143097
SCHLINK GUNTHER WEINGUTER U.
WEINKELLEREIEN
Planigerstrasse 154, 6550 Bad Kreuznach,
phone: 6716605153
SCHLOB GROENESTEYN WEINGUT INH.
FREIHERR VON RITTER ZU GR
Suttonstrasse 22, 6229 Kiedrich,
phone: 612302492
SCHLOB SCHOENBORN DOMANEN
WEINGUT
Hauptstrasse 53, 6228 Eltville Hattenheim,
phone: 6723020007
SCHLOSS JOHANNISBERG FURERST VON
METTENICH WINNEBURG
Schloss Johannisberg, 6222 Geisenheim
Johannisberg, phone: 6722080027
SCHLOSS VOLLRADS
6227 Oestrich Winkel, phone: 672305056
SCHMIDT-KUNZ WEINGUT
Bahnhofstrasse 19, 6531Windesheim,
phone: 0006707242
SCHMITT SOHNE
Weinstrasse 8, 5559 Longuich/Mosel,
phone: 65024090
SCHOLL & HILLEBRAND GMBH
Geisenheimerstrasse 9, Postfach 1169,
6720 Rudensheim Am Rhein, phone: 67221028
SELBACH OSTER
Uferallee, 5553 Zeltingen Mosel,
phone: 653202081
SICHEL H. SOHNE GMBH
Werner von Siemens Strasse 14/18,
Postfach 1505, 6508 Alzey, phone: 67314060
ST. URSULA WIENKEILLEREI GMBH
Mainzerstrasse 186, 6530 Bingen/Rhein,
phone: 672170225
TOBIAS (WEINGUT)
5561 Osann-Monzel
VEREINIGTE HOSPITIEN
Guterverwaltung, Krahnenufer 19,
5500 Trier/Mosel, phone: 65176051
VERLAG MEININGER GMBH

Maximilianstrasse 7-17, Postfach 100762,
6730 Neustadt, phone: 632189080
VERWALTUNG DER BISCHFLICHE,
WEINGUTER
Gervasiusstrasse 1, 5500 Trier/Mosel,
phone: 65172352
VERWALTUNG DER STAATLICHEN
WEINDOMANEN
Deworastrasse 1, 5500 Trier/Mosel,
phone: 65148068
VERWALTUNG DER STAATSWEINGUTER
Schwalbacherstrasse 56-62, 6228 Eltville Am
Rhein, phone: 612341556
VOLLMER HEINRICH WEINGUT
Gohnheimerstrasse 52, 6701 Ellerstadt,
phone: 62376611
VON HOEVEL (WEINGUT)
5503 Konz Oberemmel, phone: 650115384
WEINGUTER APPOLLINAR JOSEPH KOCH
Scharzhof, 5511 Wiltingen
ZIMMERMANN GRAEFF GMBH
Marientaletau 23, 5583 Zell/Mosel,
phone: 65424190

Italy

ADANTI (AZ. AGR. F. LLI)
Loc. Arquata 37, 06031 Bevagna (PG),
phone: 0742/360295
AGRICOLTORI ASSOCIATI DI PANTELLERIA
91017 Pantelleria (TP), phone: 0923/911253
ANGELO (CASA VINICOLA D')
Via Provinciale 8, 85028 Rionero in Vulture
(PZ), phone: 0972/721517
ANSELMI ROBERTO (AZ. AGR.)
Via San Carlo 46, 37032 Monteforte (VR),
phone: 045/7611448
ANTICA CASA VINICOLA SCARPA
Via Montegrappa 6, 14049 Nizza Monferrato
(AT), phone: 0141/721331
ARVEDI D'EMILEI (AZ. AGR.)
Via Palazzo Emilei 5, 37010 Cavalcaselle (VR),
phone: 045/7553662
BELLAVISTA (AZ. AGR.)
Via Case Sparse 17, 25030 Erbusco (BS),
phone: 030/7267474
BOLLA FRATELLI S.P.A.
Piazza Cittadella 3, 37122Verona,
phone: 045/594055
BOSCAINO PAOLO E FIGLI SPA
37020 Valgatara
BRUNORI MARIO E GORGIO (AZ. VIN.)
Viale della Vittoria 103, 60035 Jesi (AN),
phone: 0731/701920
BUCCI (AZ. AGR. F. LLI.)
Via Cona 30, 60010 Ostra Vetere (AN),
phone: 071/96179
CÀ DEL BOSCO (AZ. AGR.)
Via Case Sparse 11, 25030 Erbusco (BS),
phone: 030/7267196

CALBANE DI CESARE RAGGI (LE)
Via Passaduro 9, 47010 Rico Meldola (FO),
phone: 0543/494486
CANTINA GIANNI MASCIARELLI
Via Gamberate 1, 66010 S. Martino Sulla
Marrucina (CH), phone: 0871/85241
CANTINA SOCIALE
Via Paules, 09020 Samugheo (OR),
phone: 0783/64013
CANTINA SOCIALE DELLA RIFORMA
AGRAVIA DI ALGHERO
07040 Santa Maria la Palma (SS),
phone: 079/999008
CANTINA SOCIALE DI TERLANO
Via Colline d'Argento 1, 39018 Terlano (BZ),
phone: 0471/57135
CANTINA SOCIALE DI VALDOBBIADENE
Via S. Giovanni 65, 31030 Bigolino (TV)
CANTINA SOCIALE MONTELLIANA E DEI
COLLIASOLNI
31030 Biadene
CANTINA TOLLO SOC. COOP.
Viale Garibaldi, 66010 Tollio (CH),
phone: 0871/959726
CANTINA VINI GREGOLETTO LUIGI
Via S. Marino 1, 31050 Premaur di Miane (TV)
CANTINE LAMEZIA LENTO, SOCIETA
COOPERATIVA
Via del Progresso 1, 88046 Lamezia Terme,
phone: 0968/28028
CANTINE LUNGAROTTI
Via Mario Angeloni 16, 06089 Torgiano (PG),
phone: 075/982348
CANTINE SOCIALE MARMILLA
Bivio Villasanta, 09025 Sanluri (CA),
phone: 070/9307608
CARPENE MALVOLTI S.P.A.
Via Carpene 1, 31015 Conegliano
CASCINA FEIPU (AZ. AGR.), DI BICE E PIPPO
PARODI
Loc. Massaretti 8, 17030 Bastia d'Albenga (SV),
phone: 0182/20131
CASCINA LA PERTICA
25080 Picedo di Polpenazze (BS),
phone: 0365/651471
CASTELLO DELLA SALA (AZ. AGR.)
Fraz. Sala, 05016 Ficulle (TR),
phone: 0763/86051
CASTELLO DI RONCADE (AZ. AGR.)
Via Roma 141, 31056 Roncade (TV),
phone: 0422/708736
CASTELLO DI SAN POLO IN ROSSO
53013 Giaole in Chianti, phone: 0577/746045
CASTELLUCCIO (AZ. AGR.)
Parrocchia Casale 34, 47015 Modigliana (FO),
phone: 0546/92486
CAVALLERI (AZ. AGR.)
Via Provinciale 74, 25030 Erbusco (BS),
phone: 030/7267060
CENTRO ESTERO DELLE CAMERE DI

COMMERCIO DEL VENETO
Via G. Pepe 104, 30172 Ve Mestre
CENTRO REGIONALE COMMERCIO ESTERO
PUGLIA
Corso Cavour 2, 70100 Bari
CERETTO (AZ. VIT.)
Corso Langhe 3, 12051 Alba (CN),
phone: 0173/42484
CHERCHI GIOVANNI (VITICOLTORE)
Via Ossi 12, 07049 Usini (SS),
phone: 079/48273
CLERICO DOMENICO (AZ. AGR.)
Loc. Manzoni-Cucchi 67, 12065 Monforte
d'Alba (CN), phone: 0173/78171
COLLAVINI E. (CASA VINICOLA)
Corno di Rosazzo, 33040 Udine
COLLI DI TUSCOLO VINI DI FRACA STI
Passolombardo 137, 00133 Roma,
phone: 06/7970211
COLOMBIERA (AZ. AGR. LA)
Loc. Montecchio, 19030 Castelnuovo Magra
(SP), phone: 0187/674265
CONSORZIO SIENA EXPORT
Piazza Matteotti 30, 53100 Siena
CONTE DI SEREGO ALIGHIERI
37020 Gargagnado di Valpolicella (VR),
phone: 045/7701696
CONTE OTTO BARATTIERI (AZ. AGR.)
Fraz. Albarola di Vigolzone, 29010 Vigolzone
(PC), phone: 0523/87111
CONTINI ATTILIO (AZ. VIN.)
Via Genova 48-50, 09072 Cabras (OR),
phone: 0783/290806
COOP. AGR. CANTINA SOCIALE VINI DEL
POLLINO
C. da Ferrocinto, CASTROVILLARI (CS),
phone: 0981/33085
CORA S.P.A
14055 Costigliole d'Asti, phone: 0141/968491
CORIA GUISEPPE (AZ. AG.)
Via Principe Umberto 70, 97019 Vittoria (RG),
phone: 0932/985611
CORNALETO (AZ. AGR.), DI LUIGI LANCINI
Via Cornaleto 2, 25030 Adro (BS),
phone: 030/7356256
CROTTA DE VEGNERONS (LA)
Piazza Roncas 2, 11023 Chambave (AO),
phone: 0166/46670
CURRADO ALFREDO & C, CANTINA VIETTI
Piazza Vittorio Veneto 5, 12060 Castiglione
Falleto (CN), phone: 0173/62825
D'AMBRA VINI D'ISCHIA
Panza d'Ischia, 80075 Forio (NA),
phone: 081/907246
DISTILLERIE RIUNITE LIQUORI SO LARO
GALLIANO INTER
CP10735, 20100 Milano
DUCA D'ASTI
S.S. Nizza Canelli, 1402 Calamandrana,
phone: 0141/75231

DUCA DI SALAPARUTA (CASA VINICOLA)
Via Nazionale SS 113, 90014 Casteldaccia (PA),
phone: 091/953988
ENOTECA BISSON
C. So Gianelli 28R, 16043 Chiavari,
phone: 0185/314462
ENOTRIA (AZ. VIT.), PRODUTORI AGRICOLI
ASSOCIATI
S.S. Loc. San Gennaro , 88072 Ciro Marina
(CZ), phone: 0962/31098
EQUIPE TRENTINA SPUMANTI
38017 Mezzolombardo (TN),
phone: 0461/601512
FABRINI ATTILO (AZ. AGR.)
Via G. Leopardi 12, 62020 Serrapetrona (MC),
phone: 0733/908121
FATTORIA DI AMA
53013 Ama di Gaiole in Chianti (SI),
phone: 0577/746031
FATTORIA DI MONTE FERTINE
53017 Radda in Chianti (SI),
phone: 0577/738009
FATTORIA DI MONTESECCO
61045 Montesecco di Pergola (PS),
phone: 0721/778277
FATTORIA MONTE OLIVETO SPA
Localita Palagio, 53030 Castels Giminiano,
phone: 0577/953004
FATTORIA PARADISO DI MARIO PEZZI
Via Palmeggiana 285, 47032 Bertinoro (FO),
phone: 0543/445044
FIORINA FRANCO (CASA VINICOLA)
Via della Liberazione 3, 12051 Alba (CN),
phone: 0173/42248
FONTANAFREDDA TENIMENTI
12050 Serralunga d'Alba (CN),
phone: 0173/53161
FONTODI (TENUTA AGRICOLA)
50020 Panzano in Chianti (FI),
phone: 055/852005
FRANCO NINO
Via Garibaldi 167, 31049 Valdobbiadene (TV),
phone: 0423/972051
FRATELLI AVERNA
Via M. Gioia 168, 20125 Milano
FUGAZZA M. E G. (AZ. AGR.)
Castello Di Luzzano, 27040 Rovescala (PV),
phone: 0523/863277
GAROFOLI GIOACCHINO (CASA VINICOLA)
Via Alighieri 25, 60025 Loreto (AN),
phone: 071/977658
GRAI GIORGIO
Piazza Walter 8, 39100 Bolzano,
phone: 0471/973676
GRIFONI COCCI (AZ. AGR.)
Contrada Messieri 39, 63030 S. Savino di
Ripatransone (AP), phone: 0735/90143
GROSJEAN DELFINO (AZ. AGR.)
Regione Ollignan, 11020 Quart (AO),
phone: 0165/765283

GUERRIERI E. RIZAARDI
Piazza Principe Amedeo, 37011 Bardolino
HAUNER CARLO (AZ. AGR.)
Loc. Lingua, 98055 S. Marina di Salina (ME),
phone: 090/9843141
HOFSTÄTTER J. (CANTINA)
Piazzia Municipio 5, 39040 Termeno (BZ),
phone: 0471/860161
IPPOLITO VINCENZO (AZ. VIN.)
Via Tirone 118, 98072 Ciro Marina (CZ),
phone: 0962/31106
LA MARCA CONSORZIO CANTIE SOC ITALI
DELLA MARCA TREVIGIANA
Via Baite 14, 31046 Oderzo
LA MUIRAGHINA (AZ. AGR.)
Fraz. Molinazzo 2, 27040 Montu Beccaria (PV),
phone: 0385/61303
LAGEDER ALOIS (AZ. VIT.)
Via Druso 235, 39100 Bolzano,
phone: 0471/920164
LAMBERTI S.A.
37010 Pastrengo (VR)
LE RAGOSE (AZ. AGR.) DI MARIA
MARTA GALLI
Loc. Le Ragose, 37020 Arbizzano di Negrae
(VR), phone: 045/7513241
LUPI (AZ. VIN.)
Via Mazzini 9, 18026 Pieve di Teco (IM),
phone: 0183/36161
MACULAN (AZ. AGR.)
Via Castelletto 3, 36042 Breganze (VI),
phone: 0445/873124
MALGA DI MARISA DAYNE
Fraz. Champagnolle, 11018 Villeneuve (AO),
phone: 0165/95286
MARCHESI DE FRESCOBALDI
Via S. Spirito 11, 50125 Firenze,
phone: 055/218751
MARCHESI L. E P. ANTINORI
Piazza Antinori 3, 50123 Firenze,
phone: 055/282202
MASCARELLO E FIGLIO GUISEPPE
(AZ. AGR.)
Via Borgonuova 108, 12060 Monchiero (CN),
phone: 0173/792126
MASI AGRICOLA
37020 Gargagnado di Valpolicella (VR),
phone: 045/7701696
MASTROBERARDINO MICHELE (AZ. VIN.)
Via Manfredi 89, 83042 Atripalda (AV),
phone: 0825/626123
MERLOT DI SPELLO (AZ. AGR.) DI RUGGERO
VENERI
Limiti di Spello, 06038 Spello (PG),
phone: 0742/651274
MONTORI CAMILLO (AZ. AGR.)
Piane Tronto 23, 64010 Controguerra (TE),
phone: 0861/89043
MUSTILLI (AZ. AGR.)
Via dei Fiori 20, 82019 Santa Agata dei Goti

(BN), phone: 0823/953036
ODOARDI GIOVAN BATTISTA (AZ. AGR.)
88047 Nocera Ternese, phone: 0984/29961
PASQUA F.LLI SPA
Via Belviglieri 30, 37131 Verona
PIEROPAN LEONILDO (AZ. AGR.)
Via Giulio Camuzzoni 3, 37038 Soave (VR),
phone: 045/7680044
PIGHIN
Viale Grado, 33050 Risano Udine
PIO CESARE
Via Balbo 6, 12051 Alba (CN),
phone: 0173/42407
PODERI ALDO CONTERNO
Localita Bussia 48, 12065 Monforte d'Alba
(CN), phone: 0173/78150
PREMIOVINI SPA
Via Corsica 12, 25100 Brescia
PRUNOTTO ALFREDO (CASA VINICOLA)
Regione S. Cassiano 49, 12051 Alba (CN),
phone: 0173/280017
PUDDU JOSTO (AZ. VIN.)
Via S. Lussorio 1, 09070 S. Vero Milis (OR),
phone: 0783/53329
QUINTARELLI GUISEPPE
37024 Negrar (VR), phone: 045/7500016
REGIONE PIEMONTE (PROMARK SPA)
Corso Traiano 84, 10135 Torino
REGIONE TOSCANA GUITA REGIONALE
Via di Novoli 26, 50127 Firenze
RENATO RATTI, ANTICHE CANTINE ABBAZIA
DELL'ANNUNZIATA
Fraz. Annunziata, 12064 La Morra (CN),
phone: 0173/50185
ROCCA DELLE MACIE
Localita le Macie, 53011 Macie,
phone: 0577/743067
RUFFINO (CHIANTI)
Via Corsica 12, CP407, 25100 Brescia
SARTORI (CASA VINICOLA), CAV. PIETRO
37024 S. Maria di Negrar
SASSO FRANCESCO (CASA VINICOLA)
Via Roma 211, 85028 Rionero in Vulture (PZ),
phone: 0972/721022
SAVI FLORIO & INGHAM WALKER
Via Buozzi 6, 10121 Torino
SCHENK SPA
Via Perathoner 31, BP408, 39100 Bolzano
SEBASTE (CANTINE)
Loc. S. Pietro Delle Viole, 12060 Barolo (CN),
phone: 0173/56266
SELLA & MOSCA (TENUTE)
Loc. I Piani, 07041 Alghero (SS),
phone: 079/951281
SERENELLI (AZ. VIN.)
Via Bartolini 2, 60125 Ancona,
phone: 071/35505
SPUMANTE FERRARI DEI F.LLI LUNELLI
Via del Ponte di Ravina 15, 38100 Trento,
phone: 0461/922500

TENUTE CISA ASINARI DI MARCHESI
DE GRESY
Via Rabaja 43, 12050 Barbaresco (CN),
phone: 0173/63522
TRE MONTI (AZ. AGR.)
Via Lola 3, 40026 Imola (BO),
phone: 0542/657122
TURCO INNOCENZO (AZ. AGR.)
Via Bertone 7-1, 17040 Quiliano (SV),
phone: 019/887153
UNIONE CONSORZI VINI VENETI
DO C U.VI.VE.
Corso Porta Nuova 96, 37100 Verona
VAL DI SUGA (AZIENDA AGRICOLA SPA)
Via Firenzi, 20060 Trezzano Rosa (MI)
VALENTINI (AZ. AGR.)
Via del Baio 2, 65014 Loreto Aprutino (PE),
phone: 085/826138
VECCHIO SAMPERI (AZ. AGR.) DI MARCO
DE BARTOLI
Contrada samperi 292, 91025 Marsalta (TP),
phone: 0923/962093
VEVEY ALBERTO
Strada Villa 57, 11017 Morgex (AO),
phone: 0165/809835
VIGNE DI S. PIETRO DI NEROZ ZI SERGIO
37066 Sommacampagna
VIGNE DI SAN PIETRO (AZ. AGR. LE)
Via San Pietro 23, 37066 Sommacampagna
(VR), phone: 045/510016
VIGNETO DELLE TERRE ROSSE
Via Predossa 83, 40069 Zola Predosa (BO),
phone: 051/755845
VILLA BANFI
Loc. S. Angelo Scalo, 53020 Montalcino (SI),
phone: 0577/864111
VILLA GIRARDI (TENUTA)
La Villa Girardi, 37029 S. Pietro in Cariano (VE)
VINITALY
Ente Fiere di Verona, BP525, Vial del Lavoro,
37100 Verona, phone: 045/588288
ZACCAGNINI CICCIO (AZ. AGR.)
Contrada Pozzo, 65020 Bolognano (PE),
phone: 085/8880195
ZENI ROBERTO (AZ. AGR.)
Via Marconi 31, Frazione Grumo, 38010 S.
Michele All'Adige (TN), phone: 0461/650456

Portugal

BARROS (GRUPO)
rua D. Leonor de Freitas 182, apartado 39,
4401 Vila Nova de Gaia Cedex, phone: 302320
BURMESTER J.W. & CIA LDA
rua Belomonte 39-1, 4000 Porto,
phone: 2321274
CARVAHLO RIBIERO & FERREIRA LDA
avenida da Republica 19-1, 1900 Lisboa,
phone: 562427
CASA DO DOURO

rua dos Camilos, 5050 Peso da Regua,
phone: 5423811
CAVE SOLAR SAS FRANCESAS S.A.
avenida Infante D. Enrique 153, 1900 Lisboa,
phone: 382007
DELAFORCE SON & CA VINHOS LDA
rua dos Corados 72, apartado 6, 4401 Vila Nova
de Gaia, phone: 302212
DOM SILVANO (VINHOS) LDA
rua da Chavinha, 335 Vilar do Paraiso,
4405 Valaderes, phone: 718505
DOM TEODOSIO (CAVES)
rua Dr Francisco Barbosa 17, 1040 Rio Major,
phone: 92005
FORRESTIER & CIA LDA
rua do Choupelo 260, apartado 61,
4401 Vila Nova de Gaia Cedex, phone: 304111
HENRIQUES LDA, CAVES DA MONTANHA
3781 Anadia, phone: 52260
I.C.E.P. (INSTITUTO DO COMMERCIO
EXTERNO DE PORTUGAL)
avenida 5 Outubro 101, 1016 Lisboa Cedex,
phone: 730103
INSTITUTO DO VINHO DA MADEIRA
rua 5 de Outobro 78, 9000 Funchal Ile de
Madère, phone: 20581
INSTITUTO DO VINHO DO PORTO
rua Ferreira Borges, 4000 Porto, phone: 26522
MESSIAS SARL (SOCIEDADE AGRICOLA &
COMMERCIAL DOS VINHOS)
apartado 1, 3050 Mealhada, phone: 22027
PIRES JOAO E FILHOS LDA
rua Infantc Dom Henrique 59, 2955 Pinhal
Novo, phone: 2360032
PORTO POCAS
rua Visconde das Davasas 186, PO Box 56,
4401 Vila Nova de Gaia, phone: 57300212
QUINTA DO NOVAL VINHOS SARL
rua Candido dos Reis 575, apartado 57, 4401
Vila Nova de Gaia, phone: 2302020
SANGALHOS SARL (CAVES ALIANCIA-
VINICOLA DE)
apartado 6, Sangalhos, 3781 Anadia Cedex,
phone: 742260
SOGRAPE (VINHOS DE PORTUGAL SARL)
avenida da Boavista 1163, 4000 Porto,
phone: 690061
TAYLOR FLADGATE & YEATMAN
VINHOS DOS
BP24, 4401 Vila Nova de Gaia Cedex,
phone: 57304545
VERCOOPE (UNIAO DAS ADEGES
COOPERATIVAS DA REGIAO VINHOS VERDE)
Granda Agrela, 4780 Santo Tirso,
phone: 209671512

Spain

AGE, BODEGAS UNIDAS, S.A.
barrio de la Estacion, Fuenmayor, La Rioja,

phone: 41450200
ALVAREZ DIEZ, S.A.
16 Nava del Rey, Valladolid, phone: 83850136
ALVINO VEGAS (BODEGAS)
Santiuste de S. Juan Baustitsa, Segovia,
phone: 11596002
AMPURDAN (CAVAS DEL)
Conde de Zabella S/N, Perelada, Gerona,
phone: 72502762
ANDRADE (BODEGAS)
avenida de la Coronacion 35, Bollullos par des
Condado, Huelva, phone: 55410106
ANTONITA (BODEGA LA)
Huertas 45, Valencia de Alcantara, Caceres,
phone: 27580238
ASENSIO CARCELEN, N.C.R.
Baron del Solar 1, Jumilla, Murcia,
phone: 68780418
BANDEIRA ANTONIO, S.A.
apartado 68, Vigo, Pontevedra,
phone: 86330962
BARBADILLO ANTONIO, S.A.
11 Sanlucar de Barrameda, Cadiz,
phone: 56360894
BENITO RICARDO (BODEGAS)
Charcones S/N, Navalcarnero, Madrid,
phone: 18110812
BERBERANA (BODEGAS)
carretera Elciego, Cenicero, La Rioja,
phone: 41454100
BERONIA (BODEGAS)
carretera Ollauri-Najera km1, Ollauri, La Rioja,
phone: 41338000
BLASQUEZ BENITO (BODEGAS)
carretera Venta del Obisquo S/N, Cebreros,
Avila, phone: 18630025
BODEGA COMARCAL COOPERATIVA VINOS
DEL BIERZO
avenida Jose Antonio 106, Cacabelos, Leon,
phone: 87546150
BORJA (SOCIEDAD COOPERATIVA
AGRICOLA DE)
carretera Gallur-Agreda S/N, Borja, Zaragoza,
phone: 76867116
CALVO J. (BODEGAS)
2 Bollulos par des Condado, Huelva,
phone: 55410034
CAMPO VIEJO (BODEGAS)
Gustavo Adolfo Becquer 3, Logrono, La Rioja,
phone: 41238100
CANALS Y MUNNE
Pza Pau Casals 6, San Sadurni de Noya,
Barcelona, phone: 38910318
CANTO LOPEZ ANGEL (BODEGAS
ROSENDO)
Albacete, phone: 37300121
CAPEL (BODEGAS)
Molino Alfatego S/N, Espinardo, Murcia,
phone: 68830700
CARRION (BODEGAS)

Paseo de la Constitucion 34, Alpera, Albacete,
phone: 67330067
CARTHAGO (DESTILLERIAS)
avenida Estacion 44, 30700 Pacheco,
phone: 68577500
CASTILLO DE MONTEALEGRE (BODEGAS)
Camino Carcabas S/N, Poblado de Hortaleza,
Madrid, phone: 17632200
CAVA MERCHAN JOSE
carretera Andalucia 15, Manzanares, Ciudad
Real, phone: 26612919
CHERUBINO VALSANGIACOMO, S.A.
Vicente Brull 4 apartado 6092, Grao,
46080 Valencia, phone: 3672350
CIVINASA
carretera Santa Cruz 1, Tarancon, Cuenca,
phone: 66110200
CLEMENTE CUESTA
avenida Antonio Huertas 131, Tomelloso,
Ciudad Real, phone: 26511333
CLUB DES GOURMETS
Bajo, Madrid 35, phone: 12091042
CODORNUIU S.A. GRUPO DE EMPRESAS
Gran Via 644, 08007 Barcelona,
phone: 33014600
COLOMA (BODEGAS)
Finca el Colmera, Alvarado, Badajoz,
phone: 24440028
COMARCAL VINICOLA DEL
NORDESTE,S.A.(COVINASA)
Espolla 9, Mollet de Perelada, Gerona,
phone: 72563150
COMPANIA VINICOLA DEL NORTE DE
ESPANA
avenida Costa del Vino 21, Haro, La Rioja,
phone: 41310650
CORDONU, S.A.
Afueras S/N, San Sadurni de Noya, Barcelona,
phone: 38910125
CORELLANAS (BODEGAS)
Santa Barbara 29, Corella, Navarra,
phone: 48780029
COSECHEROS ALAVESES S. COOP
Mayor 48, Laguardia, Alava, phone: 41100119
CRIADO JUAN (BODEGAS)
carretera Nacional 2 km30, Alcala de Henares,
Madrid, phone: 18880720
CRISMONA (BODEGAS)
Buena 25, Dona Mencia, Cordoba,
phone: 56676000
DAIMIELEÑA
(COOPERATIVA DEL CAMPO LA)
P. del Carmen S/N, Daimiel, Ciudad Real,
phone: 26852100
DE TERRY FERNANDO (S.A)
apartado de correos 30, Puerto de Santa Maria,
phone: 56871786
DIEZ MERITO
Cervantes 3, Jerez de la Frontera, Cadiz,
phone: 56330700

DOMECQ (BODEGAS)
carretera Villabueno S/N, Elciego, Alava,
phone: 41106001
DOMECQ PEDRO
San Ildefonso 3, Jerez de la Frontera, Cadiz,
phone: 56331800
EGLI AUGUSTO C.
calle Maderas 21, 46022 Valencia,
phone: 63230950
ELVIRA NICOLAS (VINOS)
La Vega de Arriba S/N, Guernica, Vizcaya,
phone: 46851512
ESPARZA PABLO (HIJOS DE)
Havda Serapio Huici 1-3, Villava, Navarra,
phone: 48111900
ESPUMOSOS DEL CAVA, CAVAS BLANCHER
Plaza Pont Roma 5, San Sadurni de Noya,
Barcelona, phone: 38910786
EVARISTO MATEOS, S.A.
Generalisimo 56, Noblejas, Toledo,
phone: 25140082
FELANITX (BODEGA DE), SOCIEDAD
COOPERATIVA
Guillermo Timoner S/N, Felanitx, Mallorca,
phone: 71580110
FERRER FRANJA ROJA JOSE L. (BODEGAS)
carretera Palma-Alcudia km22, Binisalem,
Mallorca, phone: 71511050
FERRER MATEU JOSE
avenida Penedes 27, Santa Margarita y
Monjous, Barcelona, phone: 38980105
FLORES HERMANOS
avenida de los Guindos 20, Malaga
GALLERO GONGORA JOSE
59, Villanueva del Ariscal, Seville,
phone: 54113700
GANDIA PLA VICENTE, S.A.
calle de la Maderas 13, Valencia 2,
phone: 63670258
GARCIA (BODEGAS Y DESTILERIAS)
avenida Maria Auxiliadora, Zaragoza,
phone: 76600644
GARCIA (BODEGAS)
Fernandez de los Rios S/N, Los Yebenes,
Toledo, phone: 25320140
GARCIA AVILA (BODEGAS)
carretera Circunvalacion S/N, Villanueva de la
Serena, Badajoz, phone: 24840582
GARCIA CARRION J.
carretera de Murcia, Jumilla, 30520 Jumilla
Murcia, phone: 68780612
GARCIA HERMANOS, S.A.
avenida Marques Vega de Armijo 4, Montilla,
Cordoba, phone: 57650162
GASCA UBIDE LUIS
carretera Zaragoza-Valencia km37, Longares,
Zaragoza, phone: 76377242
GERUNDA (DESTILLERIAS)
San Joan Bosco 59, 17007 Gerona,
phone: 72215800

GRANERO (CUEVA DEL)
Los Hinojosos, Cuenca, phone: 25180262
GRATALLOPS (COOPERATIVA AGRICOLA)
Gratallops, Tarragona
GRIFO (BODEGAS EL)
carretera de Masdache, San Bartolome de
Lanzarote, Las Palmas, phone: 28812500
GURPEGUI (BODEGAS)
31570 San Adrian, phone: 48670050
HEREDAD MONTSARRA
Finca Montsarra, Torroelles de Foix, Barcelona,
phone: 38991329
HERNANDEZ MENOR MARTIN
Pintor Juan Gris 31, Villena, Alicante,
phone: 65801486
HILL (CAVAS)
Bonavista 1, Moja, Barcelona, phone: 38900588
I.N.D.O. (SUBDIRECCION GENERAL)
C/Dulcinea 4, 28020 Madrid
I.N.F.E. (INSTITUTO DE FOMENTO DE LA
EXPORTACION)
Paseo de la Castellana 14, 28020 Madrid,
phone: 4311240
IBAÑEZ (BODEGAS)
San Francisco 48, Teruel, Zaragoza,
phone: 74601533
IBERWINES S.A.
Bruch 42-44 5 B, 08100 Barcelona,
phone: 33187033
IGLESIAS (BODEGAS)
2 Bollullos par del Condado, Huelva,
phone: 55410439
INDUSTRIAS VINICOLAS DEL OESTE
(INVIOSA)
avenida de la Paz 23, Almendralejo, Badajoz,
phone: 24660977
INFANTES ORLEANS (BODEGAS DE LOS)
Banos 1, Sanlucar de Barrameda, Cadiz,
phone: 56360352
INSTITUT CATALA DE LA VINA I EL VI
(INCAVI)
Conseil des Cent 333 8e, 08007 Barcelona
INVENCIBLE (SOCIEDAD COOPERATIVA
LIMITADA LA)
Raimundo Caro Paton 102, Valepenas, Ciudad
Real, phone: 26321777
JAUBERT (MARIEN) SAT DOMINIO DE LA
TORRES
Yecla, Murcia
JESUS NAZARENO (BODEGA COOPERATIVA)
avenida 18 de Julio 62, El Barco de Valdeorras,
Orense, phone: 88320262
JOSE BUSTAMANTE, S.L.
San Francisco Javier 3, Jerez de la Frontera,
Cadiz, phone: 56341494
LALANNE
Torre de San Marcos, Barbastro, Huesca,
phone: 74310689
LANGA HERMANOS (BODEGAS)
carretera Nacional 2 km241, Calatayud,

Zaragoza, phone: 76881818
LARDON Y CIA (HERMANOS)
carrtera Albunol S/N, Albondon, Granada
LEON (VINOS DE)
La Vega S/N, Armunia, Leon, phone: 87209712
LITTORAL (BODEGAS DEL)
Industria S/N, Hospitalet, Barcelona,
phone: 33327800
LOPEZ HERMANOS
C/Canada 10, 29006 Malaga, phone: 52330300
LOPEZ PELAYO (BODEGAS)
Cerro Bodega S/N, Almonacid de la Sierra,
Zaragoza, phone: 76627015
MAGANA (BODEGAS)
calle San Miguel 4, Barilla, Navarra
MARQUES DE MONISTROL (VINOS Y CAVAS)
Monistrol S/N, San Sadurni de Noya,
Barcelona, phone: 38910276
MARQUES GRIGNON (BODEGAS)
Vinexo SA Serrano 213, 28016 Madrid
MARTINEZ GUTIERREZ JESUS (BODEGAS)
Bodegas Atlas S/N, Almonacid de la Sierra,
Zaragoza, phone: 76334458
MASACHS (CAVAS)
08720 Villafranca del Penedes,
phone: 38900593
MASIA BARRIL
Bellmut del Priorato, Tarragona,
phone: 77830192
MATEOS LUIS (BODEGAS)
Eras de Santa Catalina S/N, Toro, Zamora,
phone: 88690898
MEDINA GROUP
Banda de la Plaza 46-5, Sanlucar de
Barrameda, Cadiz, phone: 56361456
MEGIA LUIS (BODEGAS)
13300 Valdepenas, phone: 263220604
MESTRE SAGUES ANTONIO
Plaza Ayuntamiento 8, San Sadurni de Noya,
Barcelona, phone: 38910043
MONT MARCAL (BODEGAS MANUEL
SANCHO Y HIJOS)
Finca Manieu Castellvi de la Marca, Penedes,
phone: 8918281
MONTEALEGRE (BODEGAS)
Sebastian Eslava 29, Malaga, phone: 52270031
MUERZA (BODEGAS)
Plaza de Vera Magallon 1, san Adrian, Navarra,
phone: 48670054
MUGA (BODEGAS)
barrio de la Estacion, apartado de correos 28,
Haro Logrono, phone: 41310498
NUESTRA SEÑORA (BODEGA COOPERATIVA)
33, Torreperogil, Jaen, phone: 53776162
OCHOA PALAO ENRIQUE S.L.
Paraji los Quinones S/N, 30150 Yecla Murcia,
phone: 6879264
OLIVER (VINOS)
Font 26, Petra, Balearics, phone: 71561117
ONDARRE (BODEGAS)

carretera Aras S/N, 31230 Viana Navarra,
phone: 48645034
OR (VINS D')
Gremio Albaniles 8, Palma de Mallorca,
Mallorca, phone: 71291612
ORUSCO OLMEDA JUAN B.
Alcala 24, Valdilecha, Madrid, phone: 18737506
OSBORNE Y CIA S.A.
C/Fernan Caballero 3, 11500 Puerto de Santa
Maria Cadiz, phone: 56855211
PALACIO (BODEGAS)
San Lazaro 1, Laguardia, 01300 Rioja Alavesa,
phone: 41100148
PALACIO DE ARGANZA, S.A.
avenida Diaz Ovelar 17, Villafranca del Bierzo,
Leon, phone: 87540023
PALACIO REYMONDO (BODEGAS)
Poligono de Cantabria 26, Logrono, 26006 La
Rioja, phone: 941237177
PALIMINO Y VERGARA
Box 1, Jerez de la Frontera, phone: 56330950
PANIAGUA (HIJO DE)
carretera Provincial 170, Vigo, Pontevedra,
phone: 86418646
PENALBA LOPEZ (BODEGAS)
Paseo Primo de Rivera 4-5, 09400 Aranda de
Duero, phone: 27501381
PEÑASCAL (BODEGAS)
Tudela de Duero, Valladolid, phone: 14015258
PEREZ BARQUERO, S.A.
avenida Andalucia 31, Montilla, Cordoba,
phone: 57650500
PEREZ ESTEVE VICENTE, S.L.
Gandia 16, Castellon, phone: 64210897
PEREZ LAHERA (BODEGAS)
Vaquero Jacoste 4, Tudela, Navarra,
phone: 48821263
PINORD (BODEGAS)
Pasteur 6, Villafranca del Penedes, Barcelona,
phone: 938900793
POZO (BODEGAS)
Reloj 3, Cordoba, phone: 57473257
PRIMICIA (BODEGAS)
Laguardia, Rioja Alavesa, phone: 45224336
PROSEMA (ALIMENTARIA)
Ronda Universidad 144A, 08007 Barcelona,
phone: 343017286
RAIMAT, S.A.
Raimat, Lerida, phone: 73724000
RAPOSO (BODEGAS)
35-37 Bollulos par del Condado, Huelva,
phone: 55410565
REQUENENSE (COOPERATIVA AGRICOLA)
General Pereira 5, Requena, Valencia,
phone: 62300350
RIBEIRO (COOPERATIVA VITIVINICOLA DEL)
Valdepereira, Ribadavia, Orense,
phone: 88470175
RIOJA SANTIAGO (BODEGAS)
avenida de Brasil 17, Planta 13, 28020 Madrid,

phone: 4552526
RIOJANAS (BODEGAS)
Estacion 1, Cenicero, La Rioja,
phone: 41454050
RIVE
Baeza 6 Edificio Apartex, Madrid 2,
phone: 14159072
RIVERO ULECIA FAUSTINO
carretera Garay km73, Arendo, La Rioja,
phone: 41380057
RODRIGUEZ CABRERA CESAR
Macher 17, Tias, Lanzarote, Las Palmas
RODRIGUEZ ESCOBAR ADELAIDO
Calvo Sotelo S/N, Noblejas, Toledo,
phone: 25140222
SAN ISIDRO (BODEGA COOPERATIVA)
carretera Murcia S/N, Jumilla, Murcia,
phone: 68781142
SAN VALERO (BODEGAS)
carretera Zaragoza-Valencia, km46, Carina,
Zaragoza, phone: 761620400
SANCHEZ ROMATE HERMANOS, S.A.
Lealas 26, Jerez de la Frontera, Cadiz,
phone: 56332204
SANTA EULALIA (COOPERATIVA)
La Horra, Burgos, phone: 47540368
SARRIA (BODEGA DE)
Senorio de Sarria, Puente la Reina, Navarra,
phone: 48267562
SAVIN, S.A.
Paseo del Urumea S/N apartado 504, San
Sebastian, 20014 Guipuzcoa, phone: 43429350
SENORIO DE ARANA, S.A.
carretera San Vicente a Labastida, Labastida,
Alava, phone: 41331150
SHERRY (EXPORTADORES DE)
avenida Alcade Alvaro Domecq 2, Jerez de la
Frontera, Cadiz, phone: 56341046
SICAM INTERNACIONAL, S.A.
San Cesareo 34, Poligono Villaverde Alto,
28021 Madrid, phone: 7977387
SOCIEDAD COOPERATIVA CHESTE VINICOLA
la Estacion S/N, Cheste, Valencia,
phone: 62510311
SOLIS FELIX (BOGEDAS)
carretera Madrid-Cadiz km199,
13300 Valdepenas, phone: 26322400
SOMONTANO (BODEGAS COOPERATIVA)
carretera Barbastro-Naval km3, Hesca,
phone: 74311289
SORIA MARQUET JOAQUIM
Ribo Izquierdo 11, Carienena, Zaragoza,
phone: 76620069
SUCESORES DE ALFONSO ABELLAN, S.A.
Rambla de la Mancha 54, Almansa, Albacete
TARRACO VINICOLA (LA)
P. Estacion 3, Salomo, Tarragona,
phone: 77629036
TORRES FILOSO (BODEGAS)
Nueva 9, Villarrobledo, Albacete,

phone: 67140090
TORRES MIGUEL
Comercio 22, 08720 Villafranca del Penedes,
phone: 38900100
TREVIN, S.A.
Gremio Carpinteros 13, Poligono Son Castello,
phone: 71255843
UNION AGRARIA (COOPERATIVA DEL
CAMPO)
Afueras S/N, Ainzon, Zaragoza,
phone: 76868096
UNION AGRARIA COOPERATIVA
Arrabal San Pere 5-7, Reus, Tarragona,
phone: 77304847
UNION VITIVINICOLA DE INFANTES, S.A.
carretera Fuentellana S/N, Villanueva de los
Infantes, Ciudad Real, phone: 26360158
VALDEOBISPO, S.L.
Yedra 10, Villafranca des Bierzo, Leon,
phone: 87540197
VELAZQUEZ (BODEGAS)
C/Azcarrago 27-29, 26350 Cenicero La Rioja,
phone: 41454037
VILLAFRANQUINA (COOPERATIVA VINICOLA
COMARCAL)
carretera Madrid-La Coruna S/N, Leon,
phone: 87540237
VILLARAN A., S.A.
25 Bollullos par del Condado, Huelva,
phone: 55410377
VINA (COOPERATIVA VINICOLA LA)
Portal de Valencia 52, Fuente la Higuera,
Valencia, phone: 62290052
VINICOLA DE CASTILLA, S.A.
Poligono Industrial S/N, Manzanares, Ciudad
Real, phone: 26610450
VINICOLA NAVARRA, S.A.
avenida Roncesvales 2, 31002 Pamplona
Navarra, phone: 48360151
VINICOLA TENEGUIA, S.L.
Los Canarios, Fuencaliente, La Palma, Santa
Cruz de Tenerife, phone: 22444078
VINICOLA TINERFENA, S.A.
Laderas de San Lazaro Los Rodeos, la Laguna,
Tenerife, phone: 22257640
VINIVAL (EXPORTADORA VINICOLA
VALENCIANA S.A.)
avenida Blasco Ibanez 44, 46120 Alboraya
Valencia, phone: 63710111
VINOCA, S.A.
carretera Cabanas S/N, Ocana, Toledo,
phone: 25130764
VINOS DE RIOJA (GRUPO EXPORTADORES)
Gran Via, 26002 Logrona La Rioja,
phone: 41257555
VIRGEN DE LA POVEDA (BODEGA)
Extramuros S/N, Villa del Prado, Madrid,
phone: 18620068
ZAYMAR (BODEGAS)
Teniente Verdu 14, Los Santos de Maimona,

Badajoz, phone: 24544137

Switzerland

BON PERE-BERMANIER BALAVAUD
1963 Vetroz Valais, phone: 4102700361216
DETTLING ARNOLD DISTILLERIE
INH. F.X., 6440 Brunnen, phone: 43312424
EBNETER EMIL (LIKORFABRIK)
9050 Appenzell, phone: 71871717
FEDERATION SUISSE DU COMMERCE DES
SPIRITUEUX
Engestrasse 3 Case Postale, 3000 Berne 26,
phone: 31232126
GRAPILLON S.A. (JUS DE RAISINS)
1181 Mont sur Rolle, phone: 21751757
SCHENK S.A. (JUS DE RAISINS)
place de la Gare, 1180 Rolle, phone: 21751714
TRANSPORT FERT & CIE
2 rue Fendt, 1211 Genève, phone: 22348800

United States

ACACIA WINERY
2750 Las Amigas road, 94558 Napa,
phone: 707.226.9991
ADAIR VINEYARDS
75 Allhusen road, 12561 New Paltz,
phone: 914.255.1377
ADELSHEIM VINEYARD
97132 Newberg
ALDERBROOK VINEYARDS
2306 Magniola Drive, 95448 Healdsburg,
phone: 707.433.9154
ALEXANDER VALLEY VINEYARDS
8644 Highway 128, 95448 Healdsburg,
phone: 707.433.7209
ALMADEN VINEYARDS
1530 Blossom Hill road, 95118 San Jose,
phone: 408.269.1312
ALPINE VINEYARDS
97330 Corvalis
AMBERLEAF VINEYARDS
Riverroad North, 12590 Wappingers Falls,
phone: 914.831.4362
AMITY VINEYARDS
97101 Amity
ANDERSON S. VINEYARD
1473 Yourtville Crossroad, 94558 Napa,
phone: 707.944.8642
ARBOR HILL GRAPERY
6459 Route 64, 14512 Naples,
phone: 716.374.2406
ARTERBERRY
97128 Mcminnville
BACCALA WILLIAM WINERY
95482 Ukiah
BARRINGTON CHAMPAGNE COMPANY
2081 Route 230, 14837 Dundee,
phone: 607.243.8844

BATAVIA WINE CELLARS
School street & Hewitt place, 14020 Batavia,
phone: 716.344.1111
BEAULIEU VINEYARD
94573 Rutherford, phone: 707.963.2411
BEDELL CELLARS
Route 25, Main road, 11930 Cutchogue,
phone: 516.734.7537
BELLEROSE VINEYARD
435 West Dry Creek road, 95448 Healdsburg,
phone: 707.433.1637
BELVEDERE WINE COMPANY
4035 Westside road, 95448 Healdsburg,
phone: 707.433.8236
BENMARL WINE COMPANY
Highland avenue, 12542 Marlboro,
phone: 914.236.4265
BERINGER VINEYARDS
2000 Main street, 94574 Santa Helena,
phone: 707.963.7115
BIDWELL VINEYARDS
Route 48, 11935 Cutchogue,
phone: 516.734.5200
BILTMORE ESTATE WINERY
28801 Asheville
BOISSET JEAN CLAUDE VINEYARDS
94574 Santa Helena
BOUCHAINE VINEYARDS
1075 Buchli Station road, 94558 Napa
BRIMSTONE HILL VINEYARD
Brimstone Hill road, Box 142, 12566 Pine
Bush, phone: 914.744.2231
BROTHERHOOD AMERICA'S OLDEST
WINERY LTD
35 North street, 10992 Washingtonville,
phone: 914.496.3661
BRUCE DAVID WINERY
21439 Bear Creek road, 95030 Los Gatos,
phone: 408.395.9548
BUEHLER VINEYARDS
820 Greenfield road, 94574 Santa Helena,
phone: 707.963.2155
BUENA VISTA WINERY AND VINEYARDS
18000 Old Winery road, 95476 Sonoma,
phone: 707.938.1266
BURGESS CELLARS
1108 Deer Park road, 94574 Santa Helena,
phone: 707.963.4766
BYNUM DAVIS WINERY
8075 Westside road, 95448 Healdsburg,
phone: 707.433.5852
CAIN CELLARS
3800 Langtry road, 94574 Santa Helena,
phone: 707.963.1616
CAKEBREAD CELLARS
8300 Santa Helena Highway, 94573 Rutherford,
phone: 707.963.5221
CAMBIASO WINERY AND VINEYARDS
95448 Healdsburg
CANANDAIGUA WINE COMPANY

Sonnenberg Gardens, 151 Charlotte street,
14424 Canandaigua, phone: 716.394.7680
CARMENET VINEYARD
1700 Moon Mountain Drive, 95476 Sonoma,
phone: 707.996.5870
CARNEROS CREEK WINERY
1285 Daily Lane, 94558 Napa,
phone: 707.253.9463
CASA LARGA VINEYARDS
27 Emerald Hill Circle, 14450 Fairport,
phone: 716.223.4210
CASSAYRE-FORNI CELLARS
1271 Manley Lane, 94573 Rutherford,
phone: 707.255.0909
CAYMUS VINEYARDS
8700 Conn Creek road, 94573 Rutherford,
phone: 707.963.4204
CHALET DEBONNE VINEYARDS
95 653 Madison
CHAMISAL VINEYARDS
7525 Orcutt road, 93401 San Luis Obispo,
phone: 805.544.3576
CHAPPELLET VINEYARD
Pritchard Hill, 94574 Santa Helena,
phone: 707.963.7136
CHARLES KRUG WINERY
2800 Santa Helena Highway, 94574 Santa
Helena, phone: 707.963.5057
CHATEAU BENOIT WINERY
Minera Springs road, Route 1, Box 29B1,
97111 Carlton, phone: 503.864.2991
CHATEAU DE LEU WINERY
1635 W. Mason road, 94585 Suisun,
phone: 707.864.1517
CHATEAU DU LAC
95453 Lakeport
CHATEAU GEORGES, WINES OF RIVENDELL
714 Albany Post road, 12561 New Paltz,
phone: 914.255.0892
CHATEAU JULIEN
8940 Carmel Valley road, 93291 Carmel,
phone: 408.624.2600
CHATEAU MONTELENA
1429 Tubbs Lane, 94515 Calistoga,
phone: 707.942.5105
CHATEAU POTELLE
3875 Mount Veeder road, 94558 Napa,
phone: 415.322.1771
CHATEAU ST JEAN
8555 Sonoma Highway, PO Box 293, 95452
Kenwood, phone: 707.833.4134
CHRISTIAN BROTHERS-GREYSTONE
2555 Main street, 94574 Santa Helena,
phone: 707.967.3112
CLINTON VINEYARDS
Schultzille road, 12514 Clinton Corners,
phone: 914.266.5372
CLOS DU BOIS
5 Fich street, 95448 Healdsburg
CLOS DU VAL

5330 Silverado Trail, 94558 Napa,
phone: 707.252.6711
CONCANNON VINEYARDS
4590 Tesla road, 94550 Livermore,
phone: 415.447.3760
CONN CREEK WINERY
8711 Silverado Trail, 94574 Santa Helena,
phone: 707.963.9100
CORBETT CANYON VINEYARDS
2195 Corbett Canyon road, 93401 San Luis
Obispo, phone: 805.544.5800
CORDTZ BROTHERS CELLARS
95417 Cloverdale
COTES DES COLOMBES VINEYARD
97106 Banks
COTTURRI H. & SONS
PO Box 396, 95442 Glen Ellen,
phone: 707.996.6247
CRAISTAL VALLEY CELLARS
95355 Modesto
CRESTA BLANCA WINERY
95482 Ukiah
CRIBARI VINEYARDS
93722 Fresno
CULBERTSON WINERY
32575 Rancho California road,
92390 Temecula, phone: 714.699.4403
D'AGOSTINI WINERY
95669 Plymouth
DE LOACH VINEYARD
1791 Olivet road, 95402 Santa Rosa,
phone: 707.526.9111
DEHLINGER WINERY
6300 Guerneville road, 95472 Sebastopol,
phone: 707.823.2378
DIAMOND OAKS VINEYARD
26900 Dutcher Creek road, 95425 Cloverdale,
phone: 707.894.3191
DOMAINE CHANDON
California drive, 94599 Yountville,
phone: 707.944.2280
DOMAINE LAURIER
8075 Martinelli road, 95436 Forestville,
phone: 707.887.9791
DONATONI WINERY
10604 S. La Cienega Blud, 90304 Inglewood,
phone: 213.645.5445
DONNA MARIA VINEYARDS
95448 Healdsburg
DR FRANK VINIFERA WINE CELLARS
Middle road, 14840 Hammondsport,
phone: 607.868.4884
DRY CREEK VINEYARD
3770 Lambert Bridge road, 95448 Healdsburg,
phone: 707.433.1000
DUBOEUF GEORGES & SONS WINERY
95448 Healdsburg
DUCKHORN VINEYARD
3027 Silverado Trail, 94574 Santa Helena,
phone: 707.963.7108

DURNEY VINEYARD
Nason road, 93922 Carmel,
phone: 408.625.5433
EATON VINEYARDS
Rural Route 1, Box 370, 12567 Pine Plains,
phone: 914.373.9021
EBERLE WINERY
Highway 46 East, 93446 Paso Robles,
phone: 805.238.9607
EDMEADES VINEYARDS
95466 Philo
EDNA VALLEY VINEYARD
2585 Biddle Ranch road, 93401 San Luis
Obispo, phone: 805.544.9594
EHLERS LANE WINERY
3222 Ehlers Lane, 94574 Santa Helena,
phone: 707.963.0144
ELK COVE VINEYARDS
Olson road, Route 3, Box 23, 97119 Gaston,
phone: 503.985.7760
ELLENDALE VINEYARDS
97338 Dallas
ESTRELLA RIVER WINERY
Highway 46 East, PO Box 96, 93446 Paso
Robles, phone: 805.238.6300
EYRIE VINEYARDS
97115 Dundee
FACELLI LOUIS WINERY
83676 Wilder
FAR NIENTE WINERY
Accacia Drive, 94562 Oakville,
phone: 707.944.2861
FELTON EMPIRE VINEYARDS
95018 Felton
FENESTRA WINERY
83 E. Vallecitos road, 94586 Sond,
phone: 415.862.2377
FETZER VINEYARDS
13500 South Highway 101, 95449 Hopland,
phone: 707.744.1737
FIELD STONE WINERY
10075 Highway 128, 95448 Healdsburg,
phone: 707.433.7266
FIRESTONE VINEYARD
Zaca Station road, PO Box 244, 93441 Los
Olivos, phone: 805.688.3940
FRANCISCAN VINEYARDS
1178 Galleron road, Highway 29, 94574 Santa
Helena, phone: 707.963.7111
FREEMARK ABBEY WINERY
3022 St Helena Highway North, 94574 Santa
Helena, phone: 707.963.9694
FREY VINEYARDS
14000 Tomki road, 95470 Redwood Valley,
phone: 707.485.5177
FRICK WINERY
23072 Walling road, 95441 Geyserville,
phone: 415.362.1911
FROG'S LEAP WINERY
3358 Santa Helena Highway, 94574 Santa

Helena, phone: 707.963.4704
GALLO E. & J. WINERY
3387 Dry Creek road, 95448 Healdsburg,
phone: 209.579.3111
GEMELLO WINERY
2003 El Camino Real, 94040 Mountain view,
phone: 415.726.9463
GEYSER PEAK WINERY
22281 Chianti avenue, 95441 Geyserville,
phone: 707.433.6585
GIRARD WINERY
7717 N. Silverado Trail, 94562 Oakville,
phone: 707.944.8577
GIRARDET WINE CELLARS
97470 Roseburg
GLEN CREEK WINERY
97305 Salem
GLEN ELLEN WINERY
1883 London Ranch road, 95442 Glen Ellen,
phone: 707.996.1066
GLENORA WINE CELLARS
5435 Route14, 14837 Dundee,
phone: 607.243.5511
GRAND CRU VINEYARDS
1 Vintage Lane, 95442 Glen Ellen,
phone: 707.996.8100
GRGICH HILLS CELLARS
1829 Santa Helena Highway, 94573 Rutherford,
phone: 707.963.2784
HACIENDA WINE CELLARS
1000 Vineyard Lane, PO Box 416,
95476 Sonoma, phone: 707.938.3220
HAFNER
95448 Healdsburg
HANZELL VINEYARDS
18596 Lomita avenue, 95476 Sonoma,
phone: 707.996.3680
HAYWOOD WINERY
18701 Gehricke road, 95476 Sonoma,
phone: 707.996.4298
HEITZ WINE CELLARS
436 Santa Helena highway South, 94574 Santa
Helena, phone: 707.963.3542
HENRY WINERY
97470 Roseburg
HIDDEN SPRINGS WINERY
97101 Amity
HILLCREST VINEYARD
240 Vineyard Lane, 97470 Roseburg,
phone: 503.673.3709
HINMAN VINEYARDS
97412 Eugene
HOOD RIVER VINEYARDS
97031 River
HOP KILN WINERY
6050 Westside road, 95448 Healdsburg,
phone: 707.433.6491
HOSMER
6999 Route 89, 14521 Ovid,
phone: 607.869.5585

HUNT COUNTRY VINEYARDS
4021 Italy Hill road, 14418 Branchport,
phone: 315.595.2812
HUNTER ROBERT
94574 Santa Helena
HUSCH VINEYARD
4900 Star Route, 95466 Philo,
phone: 707.895.3216
INGLENOOK VINEYARDS
1961 Santa Helena Highway South,
94573 Rutherford, phone: 707.967.3363
IRON HORSE VINEYARDS
9786 Ross Station road, 95472 Sebastopol,
phone: 707.887.1507
JAEGER INGLEWOOD WINERY
94574 Santa Helena
JIMARK WINERY
602 Limerick Lane, 95448 Healdsburg,
phone: 707.433.3118
JOHNSON TURNBULL VINEYARD
8210 Santa Helena Highway, 94562 Oakville,
phone: 707.963.5839
JORDAN VINEYARD AND WINERY
1474 Alexander Valley road, 95448 Healdsburg,
phone: 707.433.6955
KALIN CELLARS
61 Galli Drive, 94947 Novato,
phone: 415.883.3543
KARLY WINES
11076 Bell road, 95669 Plymouth,
phone: 209.245.3922
KENNEDY KATHRYN WINERY
13180 Pierce road, 95070 Saratoga,
phone: 408.867.4170
KENWOOD VINEYARDS
9592 Sonoma Highway, 95452 Kenwood,
phone: 707.833.5891
KEUKA SPRING VINEYARDS
50 Sugar Maple Drive, 14615 Rochester,
phone: 716.621.4850
KISTLER VINEYARDS
Nelligan road, 95442 Glen Ellen,
phone: 707.996.5117
KNAPP VINEYARDS
2770 Couty road 128, 14541 Romulus,
phone: 607.869.9271
KNUDSEN ERATH WINERY
Worden Hill road, Route 1, Box 368,
97115 Dundee, phone: 503.538.3318
KONOCTI WINERY
Highway 29 at Thomas Drive, 95451
Kelseyville, phone: 707.279.8861
KORBEL CHAMPAGNE CELLARS
13250 River road, 95446 Guerneville,
phone: 707.887.2294
LA CREMA VINERA
971 Transport Way, 94953 Petaluma,
phone: 707.762.0393
LAKESHORE WINERY
5132 Route 89, 14541 Romulus,

phone: 315.549.8461
LAKEWOOD VINEYARDS
4024 Route 14, 14891 Watkins Glen,
phone: 607.535.9252
LANDMARK VINEYARDS
9150 Los Amigos road, 95492 Windsor,
phone: 707.838.9466
LATAH CREEK WINE CELLARS
99213 Spokane
LAUREL GLEN VINEYARD
PO Box 548, 95442 Glen Ellen,
phone: 707.526.3914
LENZ WINERY
Route 25, Box 28, 11958 Peconic,
phone: 516.734.6010
LIVERMORE VALLEY CELLARS
1508 Wetmore road, 94550 Livermore,
phone: 415.447.1751
LLORDS & ELWOOD WINERY
PO Box 2500, 94599 Yountville,
phone: 707.944.8863
LOHR J. WINERY
1000 Lenzen avenue, 95126 San Jose,
phone: 408.288.5057
LONG VINEYARDS
PO Box 50, 94574 Santa Helena,
phone: 707.963.2496
LOWER LAKE WINERY
95457 Lower Lake, San Francisco
LUCAS VINEYARDS
Country road 150, 14847 Unterlaken,
phone: 607.532.4825
LYETH VINEYARDS & WINERY
24625 Chianti road, 95441 Geyserville,
phone: 707.857.3562
LYTTON SPRINGS WINERY
650 Lytton Springs road, 95448 Healdsburg,
phone: 707.433.7721
MAGNANINI WINERY
501 Strawridge road, 12589 Wallkill,
phone: 914.895.2767
MARK WEST VINEYARDS
7000 Trenton-Healdsburg road,
95436 Forestville, phone: 707.544.4813
MARTINI LOUIS M. WINERY
254 Santa Helena Highway, 94574 Santa
Helena, phone: 707.963.5292
MASSON PAUL VINEYARDS
700 Carnnery Row, 93940 Monterey,
phone: 408.646.5446
MATANZAS CREEK WINERY
6097 Bennett Valey road, 95402 Santa Rosa,
phone: 707.528.6464
MATTITUCK HILLS WINERY
4250 Bergon avenue, 11952 Mattituck,
phone: 516.364.3633
MAYACAMAS VINEYARDS
1155 Lokoya road, 94558 Napa,
phone: 707.224.4030
MC DOWELL VALLEY VINEYARDS

3811 Highway 175, PO Box 449, 95449
Hopland, phone: 707.744.1053
MC GREGOR VINEYARD WINERY
5503 Dutch street, 14837 Dundee,
phone: 607.292.3999
MEREDYTH VINEYARDS
22117 Middleburg
MERRY VINTNERS
3339 Hartman road, 95402 Santa Rosa,
phone: 707.526.4441
MESSINA HOF WINE CELLAZRS
77803 Bryan
MILANO VINEYARDS AND WINERY
14594 S. Highway 101, 95449 Hopland,
phone: 707.744.1396
MILLBROOK VINEYARDS
Wing & Shunpike roads, Box 167D,
12545 Millbrook, phone: 914.677.8383
MIRASSOU VINEYARDS
300 Abron road, 95135 San Jose,
phone: 408.274.4000
MONT ELISE VINEYARDS
98605 Bingen
MONTALI R. WINERY
94706 Berkeley
MORRIS J.W. WINERY AND VINEYARD
101 Grant avenue, 95448 Healdsburg,
phone: 707.431.7015
MOUNT EDEN VINEYARD
22020 Mt Eden road, 95070 Saratoga,
phone: 408.867.5832
MOUNT VEEDER WINERY
1999 Mt Veeder road, 94558 Napa,
phone: 707.224.4039
MT. PLEASANT VINEYARDS
63332 Augusta
MULHAUSEN VINEYARDS
97132 Newberg
NAPA CELLARS
94562 Oakville
NAPA CREEK WINERY
1001 Silverado Trail, 94574 Santa Helena,
phone: 707.963.9456
NEWTON VINEYARD
2555 Madrona avenue, 94574 Santa Helena,
phone: 707.963.9000
NIEBAUM-COPPOLA ESTATE
1460 Niebaum Lane, 94573 Rutherford,
phone: 707.963.9435
NORTH SALEM VINEYARD
Hardscrabble road, 10560 North Salem,
phone: 914.669.5518
NOVITIATE WINES
300 College avenue, PO Box 128, 95030 Los
Gatos, phone: 408.354.6471
OAK KNOLL WINERY
Burkhalter road, Route 6, Box 184,
97123 Hillsboro, phone: 503.648.8198
PALMER VINEYARDS
108 Sound avenue, 11901 Riverhead,

phone: 516.722.4080
PARDUCCI WINE CELLARS
501 Parducci road, 95482 Ukiah,
phone: 707.462.3828
PARSONS CREEK WINERY
3001 S. State 48, 95482 Ukiah,
phone: 707.462.8900
PAULSEN PAT VINEYARDS
Asti Store road, 95413 Cloverdale,
phone: 707.894.3197
PECONIC BAY VINEYARDS
Box 709, Main road, 11935 Cutchogue,
phone: 516.734.7361
PEDRIZZETTI VINEYARDS
1645 San Pedro avenue, 95037 Morgan Hill,
phone: 408.779.7389
PHELPS JOSEPH VINEYARDS
200 Taplin road, 94574 Santa Helena,
phone: 707.963.2745
PINDAR VINEYARDS
Route 25, 11958 Peconic, phone: 516.734.6200
PLANE'S CAYUGA VINEYARD
6800 Route 89, 14521 Ovid,
phone: 607.869.5158
PREJEAN WINERY
2634 Route 14, 14527 Penn Yan,
phone: 315.536.7524
PRESTON VINEYARDS AND WINERY
9282 West Dry Creek road, 95448 Healdsburg,
phone: 707.433.3372
PUCCI FAMILI VINEYARDS
83809 Sandppoint
PUGLIESE VINEYARDS
2705 Bridge Lane, 11935 Cutchogue,
phone: 516.734.5983
QUAIL RIDGE WINERY
1055 Atlas Peak road, 94558 Napa,
phone: 707.944.8128
RAVENSWOOD WINERY
21415 Broadway, 95476 Sonoma,
phone: 707.938.1960
RIDGE VINEYARDS AND WINERY
17100 Monte Bello road, 94014 Cupertino,
phone: 408.867.3233
ROBERIAN VINEYARDS
2614 King road, 14062 Forestville,
phone: 716.679.1620
ROLLING VINEYARDS FARM WINERY
Route 414 , 14541 Romulus,
phone: 315.549.8326
ROSENBLUM CELLARS
2900 Main street, 94501 Alameda,
phone: 415.865.7007
ROUDON SMITH VINEYARDS
807 Cannery Row, 93940 Monterey,
phone: 408.438.1244
ROUND HILL VINEYARDS
1097 Lodi Lane, 94574 Santa Helena,
phone: 707.963.5251
ROYAL WINE COMPANY

Dock road, 12547 Milton, phone: 914.795.2240
RUTHERFORD HILL WINERY
200 Rutherford Hill road, 94573 Rutherford,
phone: 707.963.9694
RUTHERFORD VINTNERS
1673 Santa Helena Highway, 94573 Rutherford,
phone: 707.963.4117
SAINTBURY
1500 Los Carneros avenue, 94558 Napa,
phone: 707.252.0592
SAN MARTIN VALLEY
12900 Monterey road, 95046 San Martin,
phone: 408.683.2672
SANTA CRUZ MOUNTAIN VINEYARD
2300 Jarvis road, 95065 Santa Cruz,
phone: 408.426.6209
SARAH'S VINEYARD
4005 Hecker Pass Highway, 95020 Gilroy,
phone: 408.842.4278
SAUSAL WINERY
7370 Highway 128, 95448 Healdsburg,
phone: 707.433.2285
SCHARFFENBERGER CELLARS
7000 Highway 128, 95466 Philo,
phone: 707.895.2065
SCHRAMSBERG VINEYARDS
1400 Schramsberg road, 94515 Calistoga,
phone: 707.942.4558
SCHUG CELLARS
6204 Santa Helena Highway, 94558 Napa,
phone: 707.963.3169
SEA RIDGE WINERY
PO Box 287, 95421 Cazadero,
phone: 707.847.3469
SEBASTIANI VINEYARDS
389 Fourth street East, PO Box AA, 95476
Sonoma, phone: 707.938.5532
SHAFER VINEYARDS
6154 Silverado Trail, 94558 Napa,
phone: 707.944.2877
SHOWN AND SONS VINEYARDS
8514 Santa Helena Highway, 94573 Rutherford,
phone: 707.963.9004
SILVER MOUNTAIN VINEYARDS
95030 Los Gatos, phone: 408.353.2278
SILVER OAK CELLARS
915 Oakville Crossroad, 94562 Oakville,
phone: 707.944.8808
SILVERADO VINEYARDS
6121 Silverado Trail, 94558 Napa,
phone: 707.257.1770
SIMI WINERY
16275 Healdsburg avenue, 95448 Healdsburg,
phone: 707.433.6981
SIX MILE CREEK VINEYARD
1553 Slaterville road, 14858 Ithaca,
phone: 607.273.6219
SONOMA HILLS WINERY
4850 Peracca road, 95402 Santa Rosa,
phone: 707.253.3415

SONOMA-CUTRER VINEYARD
4401 Slusser road, 95492 Windsor,
phone: 707.528.1181
SOTOYOME WINERY
641 Limerick Lane, 95448 Healdsburg,
phone: 707.433.2001
SOUNDVIEW VINEYARDS
124 Spilt Oak Drive, 11732 East Norwich,
phone: 516.537.3155
SOUVERAIN CELLARS
Independance Lane, PO Box 528,
95441 Geyserville, phone: 707.433.8281
SQUAM POINT WINERY
Poplar Point road, 14837 Dundee,
phone: 607.243.8602
ST CLEMENT VINEYARDS
2867 Santa Helena Highway North,
94574 Santa Helena, phone: 707.963.7221
ST FRANCIS VINEYARD AND WINERY
8450 Sonoma Highway, 95452 Kenwood,
phone: 707.833.4666
STAG'S LEAP WINE CELLARS
5766 Silverado Trail, 94558 Napa,
phone: 707.944.2020
STELTZNER VINEYARDS
94558 Napa
STEMMLER ROBERT WINERY
3805 Lambert Bridge road, 95448 Healdsburg,
phone: 707.433.6334
STERLING VINEYARDS
1111 Dunaweal Lane, PO Box 365,
94515 Calistoga, phone: 707.942.5151
STONEGATE WINERY
1183 Dunaweal Lane, 94515 Calistoga,
phone: 707.942.6500
STONY HILL VINEYARD
PO Box 308, 94574 Santa Helena,
phone: 707.963.2636
STORYBOOK MOUNTAIN CELLARS
3835 Highway 128, 94515 Calistoga,
phone: 707.942.5310
STRONG RODNEY VINEYARDS
11455 Old Redwood Highway,
95448 Healdsburg, phone: 707.433.6511
SUTTER HOME WINERY
277 Santa Helena Highway South, 94574 Santa
Helena, phone: 707.963.3104
SWAN JOSEPH VINEYARDS
2916 Laguna road, 95436 Forestville,
phone: 707.546.7711
SYCAMORE CREEK VINEYARDS
12775 Uvas road, 94037 Morgan Hill,
phone: 408.779.4738
TAYLOR-GREAT WESTERN GOLD SEAL
WINERY
Country road 88, 14840 Hammondsport,
phone: 607.569.2111
TEPUSQUET VINEYARDS
95046 San Martin
TIJSSELING VINEYARDS

2150 Mc Nab Ranch road, 95482 Ukiah,
phone: 707.462.1810
TOYON WINERY AND VINEYARDS
9643 Highway 128, 95448 Healdsburg,
phone: 707.433.6847
TREFETHEN VINEYARDS
1160 Oak Knoll avenue, 94558 Napa,
phone: 707.255.7700
TRENTADUE WINERY
19170 Redwood Highway, 95441 Geyserville,
phone: 707.433.3104
TULOCAY WINERY
1426 Coombsville road, 94558 Napa,
phone: 707.255.4064
VALLEY OF THE MOON WINERY
777 Madrone road, 95442 Glen Ellen,
phone: 707.996.6941
VICHON WINERY
1595 Oakville Grade, 94562 Oakville,
phone: 707.944.2811
VILLA BANFI
21 Banfi Plaza, 11735 Farmingdale,
phone: 516.293.3500
VILLA MT EDEN WINERY
620 Oakville Crossroad, 94562 Oakville,
phone: 707.944.2414
VILLA ZAPU
3090 Mount Veeder road, 94558 Napa,
phone: 707.226.2501
VOSE VINEYARDS
4035 Mt Veeder road, 94562 Oakville,
phone: 707.944.2254
WALKER VALLEY VINEYARDS
Staete Route 52, Box 24, 12588 Walker Valley,
phone: 914.744.3449
WEIBEL CHAMPAGNE CELLARS
1250 Stanford avenue, PO Box 3398,
94539 Mission San Jose, phone: 415.656.2340
WENTE BROS
5565 Tesla road, 94550 Livermore,
phone: 415.447.3603
WEST PARK WINE CELLARS
Route 9W, 12493 West Park,
phone: 914.384.6709
WHITEHALL LANE WINERY
1563 Santa Helena Highway, 94574 Santa
Helena, phone: 707.963.9454
WIDMER'S WINE CELLARS MANISCHEWITZ
1 Lake Niagara Lane, 14512 Naples,
phone: 716.374.6311
WOODBURY VINEYARDS
South Roberts road, 14048 Dunkirk,
phone: 415.459.4040
WOODSTOCK WINERY
62B Brodhead road, 12494 West Shokan,
phone: 914.657.2018
ZAKON JOSEPH WINERY CROWN REGAL
WINE CELLARS
657 Montgomery street, 11225 Brooklyn,
phone: 718.604.7065

Acknowledgements:

The authors wish to thank the following for their assistance:
Benoit Calvet (Bordeaux, France), Giovanni Cancelarra (Italia import, France), Boubaker Harouni
(Olivins-Tunisie, France), M. Jarousse (Paris, France), M. Laridan (Fauchon, Paris, France), Les Caves Nicolas
(Paris, France) and Professor Thomasson (Treize-Vents, France)